A Trinitarian Theology of Religions

A Trinitarian Theology of Religions

An Evangelical Proposal

GERALD R. MCDERMOTT

HAROLD A. NETLAND

OXFORD
UNIVERSITY PRESS

OXFORD
UNIVERSITY PRESS

Oxford University Press is a department of the University of
Oxford. It furthers the University's objective of excellence in research,
scholarship, and education by publishing worldwide.

Oxford   New York
Auckland   Cape Town   Dar es Salaam   Hong Kong   Karachi
Kuala Lumpur   Madrid   Melbourne   Mexico City   Nairobi
New Delhi   Shanghai   Taipei   Toronto

With offices in
Argentina   Austria   Brazil   Chile   Czech Republic   France   Greece
Guatemala   Hungary   Italy   Japan   Poland   Portugal   Singapore
South Korea   Switzerland   Thailand   Turkey   Ukraine   Vietnam

Oxford is a registered trademark of Oxford University Press
in the UK and certain other countries.

Published in the United States of America by
Oxford University Press
198 Madison Avenue, New York, NY 10016

© Gerald R. McDermott and Harold A. Netland 2014

A copy of this book's Cataloging-in-Publication Data is on file with the Library of Congress.

ISBN 978–0–19–975183–9 (Hbk.)
ISBN 978–0–19–975182–2 (Pbk.)

1 3 5 7 9 8 6 4 2
Printed in the United States of America
on acid-free paper

For Ross David McDermott, who cultivates friendships with religious others all over the world,

and for Scott and Sara (Netland) McKinney, who for many years have been faithful and winsome witnesses to Jesus Christ within a very different and challenging religious culture.

Contents

Preface and Acknowledgments

RELIGION IS VERY much alive, if not always healthy, in the early twenty-first century. Although the number of those claiming to be nonreligious is also increasing, there has been significant growth in the percentage of the world's population who identify themselves as Christians, Hindus, and Muslims. The authors of one study of religion and global politics state that "the portion of the world population adhering to Catholic Christianity, Protestant Christianity, Islam, and Hinduism jumped from 50 percent in 1900 to 64 percent in 2000. Globally speaking, most people—79 percent—believe in God (a slight increase from the late 1980s and early 1990s, which was 73 percent)."[1] While Christians have always been aware to some extent of those who are religiously other, the changes brought about by globalization, massive migrations of peoples in all directions, and telecommunications revolutions have deepened awareness of religious diversity and prompted urgent questions about how Christians should think about and respond to religious others. During the past hundred years or so, Christian theologians and missiologists have given the subject of "other religions" increasing attention, resulting in an enormous literature on the subject. Evangelicals have become part of this conversation since the 1980s and '90s.

This book is an attempt to take stock of the current discussion and to provide an evangelical Christian framework for thinking about other religions and religious others. It does so by considering some of the central issues in the current debate through the core Christian teaching of God as Trinity: Father, Son, and Holy Spirit. It is written by evangelicals and is primarily intended for evangelicals worldwide, although it is our hope that many others will also read it.

The first chapter provides an introductory overview of the development of theology of religions and, in particular, of evangelical participation in the

---

1. Monica Duffy Toft, Daniel Pilpott, and Timothy Samuel Shah, *God's Century: Resurgent Religion and Global Politics* (New York: W. W. Norton, 2011), 2.

discussion. Chapter 2 uses the doctrine of the Trinity as a focal point for assessing several recent theologies of religions that, in our judgment, distort the Trinitarian nature of Christian theology. Chapters 3 and 4 look at two important Christian doctrines—divine revelation and salvation—in light of issues prompted by other religions. A theology of religions is not simply about having a correct understanding of the religions; it also involves questions about how we should live as followers of Jesus Christ among religious others. Chapter 5 explores some issues relating to Christian life and conduct in light of religious diversity. Since a theology of religions is an attempt to understand and respond appropriately to religious phenomena, chapter 6 examines what we mean by the term *religion* and its relation to culture. Finally, chapter 7 picks up again on the matter of how we should live as Christians in a world of religious diversity. Particular attention is given to issues of Christian witness in such contexts.

We have invited four distinguished Christian scholars from different parts of the Christian community and different sections of the globe to offer brief responses to what we have written. Lamin Sanneh, Veli-Matti Kärkkäinen, Vinoth Ramachandra, and Christine Schirrmacher have graciously agreed to do so, and their brief essays are included. We conclude with a short response to what these scholars have written.

This book was Terry Muck's brainchild. He initially called the two of us together, planted the seed for the book in our minds, and helped nurture the project along. He has offered helpful advice and criticism along the way. We are deeply indebted to his vision and wisdom, and we hope he is pleased with this product.

Cynthia Read has been a most helpful editor. She showed interest from the very beginning, advised at points along the way, and has shown extraordinary patience as obstacles have forced repeated resetting of deadlines.

Like all scholars, we stand on the shoulders of many others. We want to thank especially Gordon Nickel, Robert Benne, Paul Hinlicky, Ned Wisnefske, James Peterson, Amos Yong, and Tom McCall for reading various chapters and giving us constructive feedback. They are in no way responsible for deficiencies that remain. Gerald's assistant, Judi Pinckney, was a great help at many points along the way.

Our wives, Jean and Ruth, have gotten used to busy husbands who spend so many hours with their book projects, this one no less than the rest. But we have been blessed with wives who are also sharp readers and thinkers, who despite their many other commitments have made their own valuable intellectual contributions along the way. But most important, we thank them for their love and patience.

Contributors

Veli-Matti Kärkkäinen is Professor of Systematic Theology at Fuller Theological Seminary in Pasadena, California and Docent of Ecumenics at the University of Helsinki in Finland.

Gerald R. McDermott is Jordan-Trexler Professor of Religion at Roanoke College, Distinguished Senior Fellow at the Baylor Institute for Studies of Religion, and Research Associate at the Jonathan Edwards Centre Africa at the University of the Free State in South Africa.

Harold A. Netland is Professor of Philosophy of Religion and Intercultural Studies at Trinity Evangelical Divinity School in Deerfield, Illinois.

Vinoth Ramachandra, who is based in Sri Lanka, serves as the international Secretary for Dialogue and Social Engagement of the International Fellowship of Evangelical Students.

Lamin Sanneh is the D. W. Willis James Professor of World Christianity at Yale Divinity School and Professor of History at Yale College.

Christine Schirrmacher is Professor of Islamic Studies at the Evangelical-Theological Faculty in Leuven, Belgium, and at the University of Bonn in Germany. She is head of the Islam Institute of the German, Austrian, and Swiss Evangelical Alliance and a speaker and adviser on Islam for the World Evangelical Alliance.

PART ONE

Central Issues

I

Theology of Religions and Evangelicals

THIS IS A book by evangelical theologians about the theology of religions, that is, how Christians should think about world religions[1] and live among adherents of other religious paths. We do not presume that every reader will be an evangelical; indeed, it is our hope that Christians of all sorts, and also those who do not identify as Christians, will read and profit from this book. While we have learned immensely from nonevangelicals about the theology of religions, we think that evangelical theology has something to contribute to the growing conversations about Jesus and the religions. But before exploring the contours of an evangelical theology of religions, we should explain briefly what we mean by *evangelical theology*. After clarifying this, we will review the history of Christian reflections about other religious traditions, concluding this chapter with consideration of some recent evangelical contributions to the subject.

Evangelical Theology?

The word *evangelical* is derived from the Greek noun *euangelion*, which means "glad tidings," "good news," or "gospel," the last of which goes back to an Old English word for "God story." Three times the New Testament says that someone who proclaims the gospel of Christ dying for our sins is an *euangelistes*, or evangelist (Acts 21:8; Eph. 4:11; 2 Tim. 4:5).

---

1. Although we will address more fully in chapter 6 what we mean by *world religions*, we should note at the outset that in this book, we do not include Judaism among the world religions. Judaism has a special relation to Christianity, for in an important sense, the Christian faith is itself a variety of Judaism. It represents what Christians believe is the fulfillment of Judaism: Jesus and the apostles were Jews, they believed their devotion was to the Jewish messiah, and they considered their worship and life to be the full flowering of what Torah and the prophets promised. Most Jews will not agree with this designation, and that is understandable after nearly two millennia of suffering from Christian persecution of Jews. Yet that sad history, we believe, should not obscure our recognition that we have shared scriptures, common hopes, and—in part—one faith. As John Howard Yoder used to say, Judaism is the only non-non-Christian religion. See John H. Yoder, "Judaism as a Non-non-Christian Religion," in *The Jewish-Christian Schism Revisited*, edited by Michael G. Cartwright and Peter Ochs (Grand Rapids, MI: Eerdmans, 2003), 147–159.

Evangelical*ism* as an identifiable movement has always proclaimed this salvation that comes from Christ's death with a special intensity. Thus, Richard Pierard and Walter Elwell speak of evangelicalism as "[t]he movement in modern Christianity, transcending denominational and confessional boundaries, that emphasizes conformity to the basic tenets of the faith and a missionary outreach of compassion and urgency."[2] Mark Noll has shown the origins of the movement in Pietism, the eighteenth-century awakenings, and the Enlightenment.[3] David Bebbington's fourfold definition of evangelicalism as a movement marked by conversionism, biblicism, activism, and crucicentrism is widely accepted.[4] Noll elaborates on these four markers as follows:

- conversion: evangelicals are people who stress the need for a definite turning away from self and sin in order to find God in Jesus Christ;
- the Bible: evangelicals may respect church traditions in varying degrees and may use schooling, reason, and science to assist in explaining Christianity, but the ultimate authority for all matters of faith and religious practice is the Christian Scriptures;
- activism: evangelicals have historically been moved to action—to works of charity, sometimes to works of social reform, but above all to the work of spreading the message of salvation in Christ—because of their own experience of God;
- the cross: evangelicals also have consistently stressed as the heart of Christian faith the death of Christ on the cross and then the resurrection of Christ as a triumphant seal for what was accomplished in that death (evangelicals have regularly emphasized the substitutionary character of this atonement between God and sinful humans whereby Christ receives the punishment due to human sins and God gives spiritual life to those who stand "in Christ").[5]

Whereas evangelicalism has its roots in European Protestant Christianity and until the mid-twentieth century was found primarily in the West, a massive

---

2. Richard V. Pierard and Walter A. Elwell, "Evangelicalism," in *Evangelical Dictionary of Theology*, 2nd ed., edited by Walter A. Elwell (Grand Rapids, MI: Baker, 2001), 405.

3. Mark Noll, "What Is 'Evangelical'?" in *The Oxford Handbook of Evangelical Theology*, edited by Gerald R. McDermott (New York: Oxford University Press, 2010), 19–32.

4. David Bebbington, *Evangelicalism in Modern Britain: A History from the 1730s to the 1980s* (London: Unwin Hyman, 1989), 2–17.

5. Noll, "What Is 'Evangelical'?" 21–22.

demographic shift has taken place so that by the early twenty-first century, the majority of Christians were found in Asia, Latin America, and Africa.[6] Although their social and historical contexts are different from those in Europe and North America, most Protestant Christians outside the West are basically evangelical in theological commitments.[7] Worldwide evangelicals have been unified by their common acceptance of the Lausanne Covenant, written by John Stott for the 1974 International Congress on World Evangelization in Lausanne, Switzerland, and the World Evangelical Alliance.[8]

    While Karl Barth was not an evangelical in the sense in which the word is used in Great Britain or the United States today, his definition would be endorsed by most evangelicals: "*Evangelical* means informed by the gospel of Jesus Christ, as heard afresh in the 16th-century Reformation by a direct return to Holy Scripture."[9] It is true that some important evangelical thinkers, such as N. T. Wright and Thomas Oden, are now questioning the primacy of the Reformation.[10] But all evangelicals would agree with the following six evangelical "fundamental convictions," first proposed by Alister McGrath:[11]

1. The supreme authority of Scripture as a source of knowledge of God and guide to Christian living.
2. The majesty of Jesus Christ, both as incarnate God and Lord and as the Savior of sinful humanity.
3. The lordship of the Holy Spirit.
4. The need for personal conversion.

---

6. See Lamin Sanneh, *Whose Religion Is Christianity? The Gospel beyond the West* (Grand Rapids, MI: Eerdmans, 2003); Douglas Jacobsen, *The World's Christians: Who They Are, Where They Are, and How They Got There* (Oxford: Wiley-Blackwell, 2011).

7. Philip Jenkins, *The New Faces of Christianity: Believing the Bible in the Global South* (New York: Oxford University Press, 2006).

8. The Lausanne Covenant is available at www.lausanne.org/en/documents/lausanne-covenant.html. For a helpful compendium of evangelical perspectives on basic theological issues based on major evangelical statements, including those from the Lausanne Movement and the World Evangelical Alliance, see J. I. Packer and Thomas C. Oden, *One Faith: The Evangelical Consensus* (Downers Grove, IL: InterVarsity, 2004).

9. Karl Barth, *The Humanity of God* (Louisville, KY: Westminster John Knox, 1960), 11.

10. See N. T. Wright, *What Saint Paul Really Said* (Grand Rapids, MI: Eerdmans, 1997); Thomas Oden, *The Rebirth of Orthodoxy* (San Francisco: HarperOne, 2002).

11. See Alister McGrath, *Evangelicalism and the Future of Christianity* (Downers Grove, IL: InterVarsity, 1995), 55–56.

5. The priority of evangelism for both individual Christians and the church as a whole.
6. The importance of the Christian community for spiritual nourishment, fellowship and growth.

To be sure, these six convictions are shared by most other Christians. What makes this list distinctively evangelical, however, is the degree of emphasis that evangelical theology places on the six marks and the forms they take. For example, all Christians say that evangelism is important at one level or another, but not all regard it with the urgency that evangelicals often show. Some regard social service as evangelism, and others do not consider conversion to faith in Christ to be necessary. When Billy Graham conducted his first crusade in New York City, some Protestant mainline leaders ridiculed his efforts, not only because he did not emphasize structural social reform but also because theologians such as Reinhold Niebuhr regarded personal evangelism as theologically wrongheaded. Some of those same churches today speak of personal evangelism as essential to the growth of the church in the world, but they send out fewer missionaries and do less to train their members for the task of evangelism than their evangelical counterparts typically do. While all Christians speak of the need to turn from the world to Christ, evangelicals have placed more emphasis on conversion because of the Puritan and Pietist legacies from which Jonathan Edwards, George Whitefield, and John Wesley learned.

Evangelical theology is often regarded, both by the media and by much of the academy, as little more than fundamentalism put into writing. But there are significant differences between fundamentalists and evangelicals, and most evangelical theologians would distinguish their outlook from fundamentalist perspectives in the following ways.

1. *Interpretation of Scripture.* Although both affirm the truth and full authority of the Bible, fundamentalists tend to read Scripture more literalistically, while evangelical theologians look more carefully at genre and literary and historical context. Another way of saying this is that fundamentalists tend to assume that the meaning of Scripture is obvious from a single reading, while evangelicals are more sensitive to issues relevant to the interpretation of texts. For example, many fundamentalists will understand the first three chapters of Genesis to contain, among other things, scientific statements about beginnings, while evangelicals will focus more on issues of genre and the theological significance of the narratives.

2. *Culture.* Fundamentalists sometimes question the value of human culture that is not created by Christians or related to the Bible, whereas evangelicals more readily see God's common grace working in and through all human cultures. For evangelicals, Mozart may not have been an orthodox Christian and quite possibly was a moral failure as a human being, but his music is a priceless gift from God. Culture is tainted by sin, as are all other human productions, but it nevertheless can reflect God's glory.

3. *Social action.* There was a time when fundamentalists considered efforts to help the poor to be a sign of liberal theology, because proponents of the social gospel during the modernist controversy of the 1920s were theological liberals. Until recently, some fundamentalists limited their view of Christian social action to struggles for religious freedom and against abortion. While not agreeing on all issues, evangelicals have been more vocal in their declarations that the gospel also calls us to fight injustice wherever it appears, including racism, sexism, and poverty.

4. *Separatism.* For much of the twentieth century, fundamentalists preached that Christians should separate themselves from "liberal" Christians (which sometimes meant evangelicals) and even from conservatives who fellowshipped with liberals. This is why, for example, some fundamentalists refused to support Billy Graham in his evangelistic crusades, since Graham cooperated with mainline Protestant and Catholic churches and sent converts from his crusades back to these churches for further nurture. Evangelical theology puts more emphasis on engagement with culture while aiming to transform it and on working with other Christians toward common religious and social goals.

5. *Dialogue with liberals.* Fundamentalists have tended in the past to believe that theologically liberal Christians (e.g., those who reject Jesus's bodily resurrection, the essential sinfulness of humanity, and the importance of blood atonement) were Christian in name only, that there was nothing to learn from them, and that there was no point trying to dialogue with them about theological differences. The evangelical approach, by contrast, has been to talk with those of more liberal persuasion in an effort to learn from them and to persuade them to reconsider orthodox perspectives.

6. *Fissiparousness.* Many evangelical groups have fractured—and then broken again—over what seem to later generations to have been minor issues. But the tendency seems worse among fundamentalists, for whom differences of doctrine, often over minor issues, are considered important enough to warrant starting a new congregation or even denomination. Because evangelical theology makes more of the distinction between essentials and nonessentials,

evangelicals are more willing to remain in mainline Protestant churches and in evangelical churches whose members disagree on nonessentials.

7. *Support for Israel.* Fundamentalists tend to see the modern state of Israel as a direct fulfillment of biblical prophecies and maintain that God's blessing of the United States is contingent on its support for Israel. Evangelicals generally see the creation of Israel in 1948 as at least an indirect fulfillment of prophecy, lacking the complete fulfillment because they don't see the spiritual renewal that the prophets predicted (many Israelis say renewal is taking place, but in ways not obvious to outsiders). Evangelicals run the gamut in support for and opposition to Israeli policies. But while many other Christians see Israel as just another nation-state, fundamentalists and evangelicals typically think today's Israel has continuing theological significance.

If evangelical and fundamentalist ways of thinking differ in both content and practice, evangelical theology differs from classical Protestant orthodoxy more in terms of method. Evangelicalism tends to use the principle of *sola scriptura* more radically than the Protestant traditions out of which it grew. That is, when evangelicals subscribe to the doctrines of the great creeds of the church, most do so not because of any special authority inherent in the creeds but because they believe the doctrines have biblical support. Evangelical theologians are not always averse to reading the great fathers and mothers of the church (such as Macrina, Catherine of Siena, Teresa of Ávila, and now Mother Teresa) or to learn from the historic confessions, but they typically insist that they do so with critical care. They reserve the right to use Scripture as an authoritative criterion over tradition when they see conflict between the two. At the same time, some evangelical theologians are beginning to see the Holy Spirit's providential guidance of the early church's formulation of the creeds as a way to protect orthodox interpretation of Scripture.

Evangelical theologians reject what they see as liberalism's faith in human experience as a final norm for truth and morality. Against the homogenizing tendency of liberal theology, which would postulate an underlying religiosity common to all faiths, evangelical theology emphasizes the particularity of Christian revelation and the uniqueness of Christian spirituality. While liberals place a premium on personal autonomy and appeal to internal norms (conscience and religious experience), evangelicals have usually stressed human responsibility to God, who has given us external norms in Jesus Christ and Scripture.

Evangelicals are sometimes accused of being excessively Christocentric, departing from a robust Trinitarian theology in favor of a more narrow focus on Jesus Christ. There is some truth to this criticism, but there are encouraging signs that evangelicals have greater appreciation for the richness of Trinitarian theology. It is a central contention in this book that a genuinely Christian theology of religions must be thoroughly Trinitarian and that our understanding of Trinitarian theology of religions must be faithful to the clear witness of Scripture and the orthodox heritage of the church.

Theology of Religions

It was only in the late twentieth century that theologians and missiologists began to speak of the theology of religions as a specialized field of study. While there continue to be debates over its proper subject matter and methodology, something of a consensus concerning the new discipline has emerged. Accordingly, Veli-Matti Kärkkäinen has helpfully defined the theology of religions as "that discipline of theological studies which attempts to account theologically for the meaning and value of other religions. Christian theology of religions attempts to think theologically about what it means for Christians to live with people of other faiths and about the relationship of Christianity to other religions."[12] Interest in the theology of religions continues to grow, with most leading Roman Catholic and Protestant theologians now addressing the subject. Since the 1990s, evangelicals have also joined the discussion.[13]

But although the theology of religions is new as an academic discipline, questions about the relation of the Christian faith to other religious and intellectual traditions are as old as the church itself. For better or worse, Christians have been thinking theologically about religious others since the time of the early church fathers. Although our concern here is primarily with evangelical perspectives, we cannot assess evangelical contributions adequately unless we place them within the broader context of twenty centuries of Christian engagement with religious others. In what follows, we give a brief overview of some ways in which Christians in the past have understood other religions, thereby setting the context for more recent evangelical discussions.

---

12. Veli-Matti Kärkkäinen, *An Introduction to the Theology of Religions* (Downers Grove, IL: InterVarsity, 2003), 20.

13. There were, of course, evangelical thinkers such as J. N. D. Anderson and Stephen Neill who were addressing questions about other religions earlier in the century, but it was not until the 1990s that the subject attracted the attention of large numbers of evangelicals. See J. N. D. Anderson, *Christianity and Comparative Religion* (Downers Grove, IL: InterVarsity, 1970); Sir Norman Anderson, *Christianity and World Religions: The Challenge of Pluralism* (Downers Grove, IL: InterVarsity, 1984); and Stephen Neill, *Christian Faith and Other Faiths: The Christian Dialogue with Other Religions* (London: Oxford University Press, 1961).

The Bible and Religious Others

Although the Bible nowhere sets out a comprehensive theology of religions as such, the Scriptures provide ample material for developing a theological framework for understanding and responding to other religious traditions. Both the Old and New Testaments contain repeated references to the religious beliefs and practices of surrounding peoples. Much of the biblical teaching on such religious practices is clear. But there are also more ambiguous—and sometimes surprising—elements. An acceptable theology of religions should be informed by a comprehensive treatment of the biblical testimonies, including not only the many clear texts and themes that affirm the exclusivity of the one God and the obligation to proper worship of God alone but also passages and stories that are more opaque.

The basic themes in Scripture concerning other religious beliefs and practices are clear.[14] For Scripture affirms unambiguously the utter uniqueness and exclusivity of the biblical God, for he alone is God, and there is no other (Isa. 45:22; Exod. 8:10; Exod. 15:11; Deut. 6:4; Isa. 44:6; 1 Cor. 8:5–6). All humans are to worship only the one true God (Exod. 20:2–3; Deut. 5:7; Deut. 6:5, 13; Matt. 4:10; Acts 14:15). Specific practices from surrounding religious communities are condemned (Exod. 20:4–5; Exod. 34:17; Lev. 19:4; Deut. 5:8–9; Deut. 7:1–5, 16, 25; Deut. 13:1–14:2; Jer. 10:8–9; Jer. 11:9–10; Jer. 44:1–30; Hosea 1–3; Hosea 9:10; Acts 19:17–20; Rom. 1:18–32; 1 Cor. 10:14–20; Gal. 5:19–20). Idolatry is typically identified with the religious practices of surrounding peoples. Salvation is restricted to the gracious activity of the biblical God, manifest in the person and work of Jesus Christ, the only Savior for all humankind (Isa. 43:11; Isa. 45:21–22; Isa. 49:6; John 3:16–18, 36; John 14:6; Acts 4:12; Acts 16:30–31; Rom. 3:21–26; Rom. 5:8, 10; Eph. 2:4–10, 16; 1 Tim. 2:5–6; Heb. 9:26; 1 Pet. 3:18). Thus, all persons are called to repent and turn to God alone for salvation (Ps. 67; Ps. 96; Isa. 45:22; Isa. 55:7; Matt. 28:19–20; John 20:21; Acts 1:7–8; 2 Pet. 3:9). Evangelicals have generally been careful to emphasize these themes and passages when thinking about religious others.

But there are also some rather ambiguous elements in the biblical narratives, suggesting partial acceptance of aspects of surrounding religious traditions, which should be taken into account in a biblical theology of religions.

---

14. See Ida Glaser, *The Bible and Other Faiths: Christian Responsibility in a World of Religions* (Downers Grove, IL: InterVarsity, 2005); Christopher J. H. Wright, "The Christian and Other Religions: The Biblical Evidence," *Themelios* 9, no. 2 (1984): 4–15; Wright, "The Uniqueness of Christ: An Old Testament Perspective," in *A.D. 2000 and Beyond: A Mission Agenda*, edited by Vinay Samuel and Chris Sugden (Oxford: Regnum, 1991), 112–124.

For example, the term *El*, used for the one true God worshiped by the patri-archs, the deity acknowledged by Melchizedek and Abilemech (Gen. 14:18–20, 20:1–17, 21:22–24), was also commonly used for the superior deity in Canaanite religion. In Genesis 14:18–20, Melchizedek, king of Salem, "priest of the Most High God" (El Elyon), blesses Abram in the name of "El Elyon, creator of heaven and earth." Abram responds by speaking of "Yahweh, El Elyon, creator of heaven and earth" (Gen. 15:22). Old Testament scholars Christopher Wright and John Goldingay note, "The implication seems to be that Abram and Genesis itself recognize that Malkisedeq [sic] (and presumably other people in Canaan who worship El under one manifestation or another) does serve the true God but does not know all there is to know about that God."[15] Or we could consider the parallels between the Wisdom literature in the Old Testament and some of the literature from ancient Mesopotamia and Egypt.[16] There is also the fascinating but enigmatic narrative about Joseph tak-ing Asenath, daughter of Potiphera, priest of On, a high dignitary of Egyptian religion, as his wife. Through her are born two sons, Ephraim and Manasseh, from whom come two of the twelve tribes of Israel (Gen. 41:45, 50–52; 46:20). Interestingly, the text makes no judgment, positive or negative, on this.

In the New Testament, of course, we have Paul in Acts 17:28 quoting from pagan writers. "In him we live and move and have our being" could well be from the Cretan poet Epimenides and is found also in Callimachus's *Hymn to Zeus*. "We are his offspring" is from the Cilician poet Aratus's *Phainomena*, which begins with an invocation of the Stoic supreme reality, Zeus.[17] We should also note the fascinating narrative of the Magi in Matthew 2:1–12.[18] The identity of the Magi is uncertain, but in all probability, they were astrolo-gers or wise men, possibly from Persia, who were skilled in interpreting the stars and dreams. If so, they might well have been part of the priestly caste associated with Zoroastrian practice or later traditions descended from earlier

15. C. Wright and J. Goldingay, "Yahweh Our God Yahweh One," in *One God, One Lord*, 2nd ed., edited by Andrew Clarke and Bruce Winter (Grand Rapids, MI: Baker, 1992), 48.

16. Ibid., 44–45. See also Michael Pocock, "Selected Perspectives on World Religions from Wisdom Literature," in *Christianity and the Religions*, edited by Edward Rommen and Harold Netland, Evangelical Missiological Society Series No. 2 (Pasadena, CA: William Carey Library, 1995), 45–55.

17. See F. F. Bruce, *Commentary on the Book of the Acts* (Grand Rapids, MI: Eerdmans, 1980), 357–358.

18. See Ben Witherington III, "Birth of Jesus," in *Dictionary of Jesus and the Gospels*, edited by Joel B. Green, Scot McKnight, and I. Howard Marshall (Downers Grove, IL: InterVarsity, 1992), 72–73.

Zoroastrianism. None of these factors in any way undermines the dominant, clear themes noted earlier of the exclusivity of the one God and the call to proper worship of him alone. Nor, of course, should such passages be given undue weight. But neither should they be ignored in a comprehensive biblical theology of religions.[19]

Exclusivism, Inclusivism, and Pluralism

In the 1980s, it became customary to use three general categories to describe Christian perspectives on other religions: exclusivism, inclusivism, and pluralism. It is easy to assume that the terms have a long history in Christian discourse and that they refer to three clearly distinguishable views. But this is not the case. The terms themselves were first introduced by Alan Race in 1983, although John Hick had earlier distinguished three broad approaches to other religions without using these terms to describe them.[20] But the terms have been widely adopted in subsequent literature.

Although there is no uniformly accepted definition of the terms, *exclusivism* is typically understood as the position that maintains that religious truth and salvation are restricted to the Christian faith.[21] Exclusivism is typically depicted in the literature in unflattering terms as embracing highly negative views of religious others. Thus, speaking of exclusivism, Race states, "Undoubtedly, the predominant attitude of the church through Christian history has been to regard the outsider as in error or darkness, beyond the realms of truth and light."[22] Evangelicals are generally categorized—both by themselves and by others—as exclusivists.

Inclusivism, by contrast, refers to a broad spectrum of views that hold the following principles in creative tension: (1) There is a sense in which Jesus Christ is unique and superior to other religious figures, and in some sense, it is through Christ that salvation is made available. (2) God's grace and salvation,

---

19. For further discussion of the ontological status and roles of "the gods," which are referred to repeatedly throughout the Old Testament, see Gerald McDermott, *God's Rivals: Why Has God Allowed Different Religions?* (Downers Grove, IL: InterVarsity, 2007).

20. See Alan Race, *Christians and Religious Pluralism* (London: SCM, 1983); John Hick, *God Has Many Names* (Philadelphia: Westminster, 1980), 29–39.

21. With respect to other religions, there is an important distinction between exclusivism concerning truth and exclusivism concerning salvation; one might be exclusive in one respect but not in the other. See Paul J. Griffiths, *Problems of Religious Diversity* (Oxford: Blackwell, 2001), 21–65, 138–169; Robert McKim, *On Religious Diversity* (New York: Oxford University Press, 2012), 14–100.

22. Alan Race, *Christians and Religious Pluralism*, 10.

which are somehow based on Jesus Christ, are also available and efficacious to sincere followers of other religions. (3) Thus, other religions should be regarded positively as part of God's purposes for humankind. Obviously, there can be enormous diversity among inclusivists on just how these principles are to be understood. But most Roman Catholic theologians after Vatican II and mainline Protestant theologians fall into this broad paradigm.

Religious *pluralism* breaks with both exclusivism and inclusivism by claiming that the major religions should be regarded as more or less equally effective and legitimate alternative ways of responding to the one divine reality. *Religious pluralism* is sometimes used simply as a descriptive term, referring to the obvious religious diversity in our world. But as used here, it goes beyond mere acknowledgment of diversity to include a claim about parity among the religions when it comes to issues of religious truth and soteriological effectiveness. Salvation, liberation, and enlightenment are said to be available in all religions. No single religion can legitimately claim to be superior to others, for all religions are in their own ways complex, historically and culturally conditioned human responses to the one divine reality. Pluralism, in this sense, is widespread in popular culture today and is deeply embedded in religious studies programs at secular universities.

Although use of the three categories can be helpful in sorting out the many views on other religions, the taxonomy is misleading and simplistic.[23] For example, there is little consistency in the meanings of the terms in the literature, so use of the categories can be confusing. Furthermore, although the categories are generally defined in terms of the question of the extent of salvation, the theology of religions is concerned with a wide variety of other issues apart from soteriology. Is there truth or goodness in other religious traditions? To what extent is there continuity between the beliefs, practices, and institutions of other religions and those of Christianity? To what extent, if any, can one adopt and build on other religious terms or practices in the contextualization of the Christian gospel? How should followers of Jesus Christ live in the midst of religious diversity and disagreement? And so on. Not all of the issues lend themselves to simple yes/no answers, and one might be quite

---

23. See Terry C. Muck, "Instrumentality, Complexity, and Reason: A Christian Approach to Religious Diversity," *Buddhist Christian Studies* 22 (2002): 115–121; Harold Netland, "Religious Exclusivism," in *Philosophy of Religion: Classic and Contemporary Issues*, edited by Paul Copan and Chad Meister (Oxford: Blackwell, 2008), 67–80. Significantly, the two most helpful introductions to theology of religions do not use the categories of exclusivism, inclusivism, and pluralism to organize their treatments of the various perspectives. See Kärkkäinen, *An Introduction*; Paul F. Knitter, *Introducing Theologies of Religion* (Maryknoll, NY: Orbis, 2002).

open to other religions on a particular issue but not on others. When the variety of issues demanding attention is taken into account, it becomes clear that the many different, often highly nuanced, perspectives on these questions cannot be forced into three neat, consistent categories.

Finally, it is significant that the three categories have been in use only since the 1980s. Earlier Christians' discussions of other religions were not constrained by this taxonomy, and therefore, the issues were often framed in other ways. Thus, while the standard taxonomy can be helpful, the three positions should not be understood as clearly defined, mutually exclusive categories so much as distinct points on a continuum of perspectives, with particular thinkers falling into one or another category depending on the particular issue under consideration.

Earlier Christian Perspectives on Other Religions

While a comprehensive history of Christian perspectives on religious others is impossible here, it is helpful to remind ourselves of some earlier thinkers and perspectives. In the second and third centuries, for example, some theologians developed sophisticated theological perspectives on earlier Greek religious and philosophical thought. While they were critical of popular religious practices, they thought highly of more developed Hellenistic culture and were concerned with explaining what seemed to them truth and goodness in some of the teaching of earlier thinkers. Justin Martyr (d. ca. 165), for example, appealed to John 1 (especially verse 9) in developing the idea that everyone possesses a seed (*sperma*) of the divine Logos. Even pagan thinkers such as Plato and Socrates had a seminal element of the Logos (*logos spermatikos*), and it was because of this that they were able to discern the truths they taught so effectively.

> Beyond doubt, therefore, our teachings are more noble than all human teaching, because Christ, who appeared on earth for our sakes, became the whole Logos, namely Logos and body and soul. Everything that the philosophers and legislators discovered and expressed well, they accomplished through their discovery and contemplation of some part of the Logos.... The truths which men in all lands have rightly spoken belong to us Christians.... Indeed, all writers, by means of the engrafted seed of the Word which was implanted in them had a dim glimpse of the truth.[24]

---

24. Justin Martyr, "The Second Apology," 10 and 13, in *The Fathers of the Church: A New Translation*, vol. 6, translated by Thomas B. Falls (Washington, DC: Catholic University of America Press, 1948), 129, 133–34.

In language that has provoked much debate over the years, Justin goes beyond simply affirming that non-Christian religious thinkers said things that were true, and he seems to identify, in some way, such thinkers with Christians.

> Those who lived by reason [*logos*] are Christians, even though they have been considered atheists: such as, among the Greeks, Socrates, Heraclitus, and others like them; and among the foreigners, Abraham, Elias, Ananias, Azarias, Misrael, and many others whose deeds or names we now forbear to enumerate, for we think it would be too long. So, also, they who lived before Christ and did not live by reason were useless men, enemies of Christ, and murderers of those who did not live by reason. But those who have lived reasonably, and still do, are Christians.[25]

According to Justin, then, all poets and philosophers who teach truth are, in some sense, followers of Christ insofar as they follow those truths. But he maintained that they do not have full knowledge of God because they do not have personal knowledge of Jesus Christ.[26]

Irenaeus (ca. 145–202), the great missionary bishop of Lyons and father of salvation history, taught that God has always been at work in all the world, working by the Word. Just as God revealed himself and his plan only in stages, as he progressively trained his people through history, so, too, the Logos was speaking through the creation to prepare the nations to receive the fullness of the gospel. The gospel was "heralded" in various ways before the incarnation, when it was finally revealed in Christ. If even a pagan like Job heard this heralding from afar, that did not necessarily mean for Irenaeus that God's salvation was available through other religions. Righteous pagans were saved only by responding to gospel preaching—in Hades on Holy Saturday, in history by hearing the apostles and their successors, and in the millennium. One might, however, infer from Irenaean principles that just as God preached the truth of his Son in various ways conditioned by historical circumstances, so, too, God might use the religions in ways conditioned by their historical particularities.[27]

---

25. Justin Martyr, "The First Apology," 46, in *The Fathers of the Church: A New Translation*, vol. 6, translated by Thomas B. Falls (Washington, DC: Catholic University of America Press, 1948), 83–84.

26. Justin also taught that demons were responsible for those aspects of religious thought and practice that were incompatible with God's truth. For more on Justin, see McDermott, *God's Rivals*, 85–98.

27. Irenaeus, *Adversus Haereses* IV, 34. See McDermott, *God's Rivals*, 99–116.

Clement of Alexandria (ca. 150–ca. 215) agreed with Irenaeus that God was in charge of all of history and that the religions were part of his plan to sum up all things in Christ. He proposed that God even gave some religions as "covenants" to the Gentiles, comparable to the covenant of the Law that he gave to the Jews. All these covenants were meant to lead people to Christ, the fulfillment of all the promises in the covenants. Clement boldly stated that some Gentile religious teachers were "prophets" given by God (but fundamentally different from biblical prophets) and that some defective religious traditions were permitted by God in order to keep their devotees from destruction. They were permitted as secondary way stations on the way to fullness of faith in Christ.[28]

Origen (185–253) warned that exploration of the religions is dangerous, potentially destructive for young believers. He particularly highlighted the spiritual nature of other religions, cautioning that malevolent spirits were behind Christianity's rivals. While the religions must be learned by Christian teachers, especially those helping seekers find the truth, they were live coals that could do permanent damage if not handled rightly.[29]

During the first millennium, most Christians were convinced that *extra ecclesiam nulla salus* (outside the church there is no salvation). As Cyprian (d. 258) put it, "You cannot have God for your Father if you don't have the Church for your mother."[30] Cyprian could say this because he shared the prevailing presumption that the gospel had been promulgated everywhere and that everyone had the opportunity to accept it. Even Augustine (354–430), who knew that some African tribes had not yet heard, generally restricted salvation to the church: he believed that God had foreseen that those Africans who did not hear of the gospel would not accept Christ if, in fact, he were offered to them.[31]

In the second millennium, attitudes began to change. Abelard (1079–1142) spoke of pagan saints such as Job, Noah, and Enoch. Pope Gregory VII (d. 1085) conceded that Muslims who obeyed the Qur'an might find salvation in the bosom of Abraham, and Saint Francis (1181–1226) referred to Muslims as "brothers." Thomas Aquinas (1225–1274) introduced "implicit faith" and the

---

28. McDermott, *God's Rivals*, 117–132.

29. Ibid., 133–156.

30. Cyprian, *Epistles* 73.21; 4.4.

31. Augustine, *Letter* 199.12, 46; translated in Francis A. Sullivan, *Salvation Outside the Church?* (New York: Paulist, 1992), 36.

"baptism of desire" for those who had not heard but would have embraced the gospel had they been given the opportunity.[32] Dante's *Divina Commedia* (ca. 1314) places Muslim theologians Avicenna (Ibn Sina), Averroes (Ibn Rushd), and the Muslim ruler Saladin in limbo, along with Greek and Roman sages and heroes from antiquity.[33] Some Anabaptists in the sixteenth century actually posited an interfaith church of spiritual Semites with three covenants: Jewish, Christian, and Muslim.

The year 1492 was a watershed in many respects, not least in the ways in which European Christians came to understand other religious traditions. The voyages of exploration that followed Columbus's venture to what came to be called America showed Europeans just how vast and varied the world really was. The sheer numbers and enormous diversity among the peoples of the New World called into question long-held assumptions about Europeans, Christianity, and the world. Among the questions raised were those concerning the status of the native peoples in America, Africa, and the Pacific islands.

Were these creatures of the new worlds humans? Did they have souls that needed to be saved? Could they be enslaved or killed? These raised profound questions not only of geography but also of sociology, economics, politics, and theology. In 1537, Pope Paul III proclaimed in *Sublimis Deus*, "[T]he Indians are true men." If so, how should Christians relate to them? The answer was that they were pagans and heathens. They were not Christian heretics, nor were they Muslim infidels who rejected Christian truth. They were people who never had the opportunity to hear the gospel.[34]

Before 1492, it was widely accepted that most of the world had already been exposed to the teachings of the church, and thus, those who remained outside the church—heretics, Jews, Muslims—did so willfully and were culpable for their unbelief. But it was now evident that large numbers of people had not yet even heard of the church. What was their status? Jacques Dupuis states that Columbus's discovery of the New World "called on theologians to reconsider the entire case of the requisites for salvation. No longer would it be possible to hold, without qualification, that faith in Jesus Christ and belonging to the Church were absolutely required for salvation."[35]

---

32. Thomas Aquinas, *Summa theologiae* II, Q.2.A.7; III, Q.68.A.2.

33. Dante, *Inferno*, Canto IV.

34. Paul Hiebert, "Critical Issues in the Social Sciences and Their Implications for Mission Studies," *Missiology* 24, no. 1 (1996): 67.

35. Jacques Dupuis, *Toward a Christian Theology of Religious Pluralism* (Maryknoll, NY: Orbis, 1997), 110–111.

Reports from explorers, merchants, and missionaries fed a growing interest in the cultural and religious practices of peoples around the world. One
of the more remarkable works was *Cérémonies et coutumes religieuses de tous
les peuples du monde* ("Religious ceremonies and customs of the peoples of
the world") by Bernard Picart and Jean Frederick Bernard, published in seven
folio volumes of more than three thousand pages between 1723 and 1737.
A sweeping survey of the religions known to Europeans in the early 1700s, the
book "marked a major turning point in European attitudes toward religious
belief." For it "sowed the radical idea that religions could be compared on
equal terms, and therefore that all religions were equally worthy of respect—
and criticism."[36]

A number of leading Christian voices of the seventeenth and eighteenth
centuries addressed questions about religious others in their writings. The
Dutch jurist and theologian Hugo Grotius (1583–1645), for example, wrote *On
the Truth of the Christian Religion* (1627), intended in part as a training manual
in evidences for the truth of Christianity for those ministering among Muslims
and other non-Christians. The growing exposure to other cultures and religions was a contributing factor to widespread skepticism in the sixteenth and
seventeenth centuries.[37] Awareness of religious diversity and disagreement
had the effect of undermining confidence in the unique truth of the Christian
religion. Some, such as Lord Herbert of Cherbury (1583–1648), who was
deeply troubled by the religious conflicts plaguing post-Reformation Europe,
sought clear criteria for religious truth, since "the wretched terror-stricken
mass have no refuge, unless some immovable foundations of truth resting on
universal consent are established, to which they can turn amid the doubts of
theology and philosophy."[38] Herbert claimed that the following five common
notions in the religions can be established by universal consent: (1) that there
is a supreme God, (2) that this sovereign deity ought to be worshipped, (3) that
the connection between virtue and piety is the most important part of religious practice, (4) that wickedness and vice must be expiated by repentance,

---

36. Lynn Hunt, Margaret C. Jacob, and Wijnand Mijnhardt, *The Book That Changed
Europe: Picart and Bernard's "Religious Ceremonies of the World"* (Cambridge, MA: Harvard
University Press, 2010), 1.

37. See Richard Popkin, *The History of Skepticism from Erasmus to Spinoza* (Berkeley,
CA: University of California Press, 1979); Franklin L. Baumer, *Religion and the Rise of
Skepticism* (New York: Harcourt Brace, 1960), 96–111; *Atheism from the Reformation to the
Enlightenment*, edited by Michael Hunter and David Wooten (Oxford: Clarendon Press, 1992).

38. Lord Herbert of Cherbury, *On Truth in Distinction from Revelation, Probability, Possibility,
and Error*, 3rd ed., translated by Meyrick H. Carre (Bristol, UK: University of Bristol Press,
1937), 117–118.

and (5) that there is reward or punishment in the afterlife.[39] One can see in Herbert's common notions an early anticipation of a broadly theistic pluralism, which sees all (morally acceptable) religions as alternative approaches to the same ultimate deity.

Others were more concerned with defending the unique truth of the Christian religion against the skeptical challenge arising from religious diversity. If Christianity is uniquely true, why are there so many different religious traditions? Is it reasonable to maintain the truth of orthodox Christian faith in light of widespread religious disagreement? One Christian who thought carefully about these issues was the great chemist and philosopher Robert Boyle (1627–1691). Boyle gives eloquent expression to the challenge posed by religious diversity:

> In other words, if we observe how many nations there are in the world, with so many millions of men in them divided into the four great sects, namely Christians, Jews, Mohammedans and pagans, each of which is subdivided into several different systems of belief, and if we further consider with what assurance each one puts faith in its own religion and cause—if, says [the critic], we bear these things in mind, then no man of prudence or moderation will imagine that, surrounded by such a variety of opinions and warring sects, each with learned men amongst its followers, he is at all likely to embrace the one and only true religion, especially when everyone maintains that his religion is true, and all acknowledge that there is only one true one while some suspect that none is wholly true.[40]

In a perceptive essay not published during his lifetime, Boyle responds to this criticism by arguing that there are indeed principles by which we can assess religious claims and that Christians can have confidence that the Christian faith is true despite awareness of rival claims. Boyle proposes a combination of the ethical teachings of Christianity ("the holiness of the doctrine itself") and the evidence of biblical miracles as demonstrating the superiority of Christianity to other religions. Boyle's discussion is remarkably sophisticated and addresses issues that are still hotly debated three centuries later, such as

---

39. Ibid., 58–60.

40. Robert Boyle, "*De diversitate Religionum* (On the Diversity of Religions)," in *The Works of Robert Boyle*, edited by Michael Hunter and Edward B. Davis (London: Pickering and Chatto, 2000), vol. 14: 237-38.

whether awareness of religious disagreement removes epistemic justification for holding that one's own religion is distinctively true.

The eighteenth century's most thoughtful theologian of the religions might have been Jonathan Edwards (1703–1758). Seventeenth-century geographers had estimated that only one-sixth of the planet had heard the gospel, so, according to some Calvinists of the day, at least five-sixths of the world's population was doomed to hell. Beginning with Lord Herbert, the deists suggested that the orthodox Christian God responsible for this scenario was a monster. These deists succeeded in popularizing the disjunction between the heathens who were damned but morally good and the Christians who were saved but morally bad.[41]

Disturbed by deist use of Jesuit reports of noble "heathens" in East Asia to attack the Christian God's goodness and justice, Edwards worked hard to learn about these heathens' religions. He sought out and read travelogues, dictionaries, and encyclopedias of religion available in his time. The books cited in his "Catalogue" include George Sale's translation of the Qur'an, Jesuit reports on China, an analysis of the Kabbalah, comparative mythology, and a wide range of reference works—from skeptic Peter Bayle's *Historical and Critical Dictionary* to Daniel Defoe's *Dictionary of All Religions Ancient and Modern*.

Edwards developed three strategies to defend Christian orthodoxy against deist charges. First, he used the *prisca theologia* (ancient theology) to try to prove that vestiges of true religion were taught by the Greeks and other non-Christian traditions. Therefore, he concluded, five-sixths of the world had *not* been deprived of the basic truths of the gospel. Second, he developed an elaborate typological system to show that God is constantly communicating divine truths wherever the eye can see and the ear can hear—in nature, history, and even the history of religions. Finally, Edwards taught that an inner "disposition" is better evidence of regeneration than precision in belief.

Edwards used these developments primarily to argue for a greater knowledge of religious *truth* among the heathen than his favorite Reformed predecessors—Francis Turretin (1623–1687) and Petrus van Mastrict (1630–1706)—had allowed.[42] Not only in his private notebooks but also in his public

---

41. Gerald McDermott, *Jonathan Edwards Confronts the Gods: Christian Theology, Enlightenment Religion, and Non-Christian Faiths* (New York: Oxford University Press, 2000); Michael McClymond and Gerald McDermott, *The Theology of Jonathan Edwards* (New York: Oxford University Press, 2012), 580–598.

42. Francis Turretin, *Institutio Theologiae Elencticae* (orig. ed. 1679–1685), handwritten translation by George Musgrave Giger at Princeton Theological Seminary, 1:9–16; Petrus van Mastricht, *Theoretica-practica theologia*, 2nd ed. (Utrecht, 1724), I.i.xxii–xxv. Of course,

sermons, he spoke of degrees of inspiration from the Spirit. In his second sermon in *Charity and Its Fruits*, he told his Northampton church that the Holy Spirit spoke through wicked men such as Balaam, King Saul, and Judas. In his *Miscellanies*, he wrote that heathen philosophers such as Socrates and Plato had "some degree of inspiration."[43] Thus, Edwards clearly recognized religious truth given by God to non-Christians, even wicked non-Christians. He did not, however, believe that wicked non-Christians were saved. But on the question of salvation of pagans more generally, he raised the *possibility* that they could be saved by the merits of Christ. Yet he never spoke in the expansively hopeful terms of others such as Richard Baxter or John Wesley.[44]

Modern Missions and Other Religions

Yet a different response to religious diversity was found in the modern missionary movement, which is generally said to have begun with William Carey's (1761–1834) publication in 1792 of *An Enquiry into the Obligation of Christians to Use Means for the Conversion of the Heathens*. Carey left for India in 1793 and had forty years of productive missionary service there. Inspired by Carey's example, numerous missions agencies were formed in the early nineteenth century, as large numbers of European and American Protestant missionaries spread throughout Asia and Africa with the message of salvation through faith in Jesus Christ. The conviction that those in the New World were lost in sin and needed to respond to the gospel of Jesus Christ for salvation was widely shared by these missionaries.[45] As Christians in Europe and North America

---

the *prisca theologia* could cut both ways. While the orthodox used it all the way into the twentieth century to support their tradition, deists and their disciples in the same centuries used it to interpret the Jesus story as one version of an ancient Near Eastern fertility myth. See Michael J. McClymond, *Familiar Stranger: An Introduction to Jesus of Nazareth* (Grand Rapids, MI: Eerdmans, 2004), 23–24, 162-163 nn. 66–68.

43. Jonathan Edwards, *Ethical Writings*, vol. 8 of *The Works of Jonathan Edwards* (New Haven, CT: Yale University Press, 1989), 157, 159–160, 162; Edwards, *The "Miscellanies" 1153–1360*, vol. 23 of *The Works of Jonathan Edwards*, 84–85.

44. Richard Baxter forthrightly granted salvation to those (outside the "Jewish church") who did not have "knowledge of Christ *incarnate*": *The Reasons of the Christian Religion* (London, 1667), 201–202. And John Wesley said that pagans just needed to live up to the light they were given: Sermon LXVIII, "The General Spread of the Gospel," in *The Works of the Rev. John Wesley, A.M.*, 14 vols. (London, 1837), 9:234. See David Pailin, *Attitudes to Other Religions: Comparative Religion in Seventeenth- and Eighteenth-Century Britain* (Manchester, UK: Manchester University Press, 1984), 48.

45. Some of the very missionaries who were preaching the exclusivity of the Christian faith were also involved in producing translations of Indian and Chinese sacred texts; scholarly

became increasingly aware of the large numbers of people who had never heard the gospel, thousands committed their lives to the foreign-mission fields. Undoubtedly, the motives of many were mixed, as missionaries then—just as Christians today—were very much products of their time. But David Bosch appropriately remarks that "a primary motive of most missionaries was a genuine feeling of concern for others; they knew that the love of God had been shed abroad in their hearts and they were willing to sacrifice themselves for the sake of him who died for them."[46]

There was something of a consensus among many nineteenth-century Protestant missionaries on basic theological issues until the fundamentalist–modernist controversies of the 1920s and 1930s.[47] James Patterson observes that, before the controversies, most Protestant missionaries would have accepted the statement by the Board of Foreign Missions of the Presbyterian Church in the USA in 1920 that "the supreme and controlling aim of foreign missions is to make Jesus Christ known to all men as their Divine Savior and Lord and to persuade them to become His disciples."[48] Most missionaries adopted largely negative views of non-Christian religious beliefs and practices. Salvation was available only through faith in Jesus Christ and not through non-Christian religious traditions. Whatever utility they might have on other grounds, non-Christian religions were regarded as the social and cultural matrices within which "heathen" souls were enslaved and from which they needed to be rescued. While not all were comfortable with his style, the evangelist D. L. Moody (1839–1899) expressed a common understanding of

---

analyses of Hinduism, Buddhism, Islam and Chinese religions; and lexical aids and dictionaries for the study of the languages of these religions. See Eric Sharpe, *Comparative Religion: A History* (LaSalle, IL: Open Court, 1986), 44–45. There is considerable irony in the fact that pluralists and other critics of orthodox Christian faith were initially dependent on the work of traditional missionaries in providing the resources for understanding these other traditions.

46. David Bosch, *Transforming Mission: Paradigm Shifts in Theology of Mission* (Maryknoll, NY: Orbis, 1991), 287.

47. During the late nineteenth and early twentieth centuries, theological disputes over issues such as the divine inspiration of the Bible, the virgin birth, biological evolution, the social gospel, and the deity of Jesus Christ split Christian denominations and seminaries into traditionalists and liberals. Conservative defenders of orthodoxy published *The Fundamentals* (1909–1915) in an attempt to respond to the drift of theological liberalism. The often acrimonious conflicts between these groups in churches, denominations, and seminaries became known as the "fundamentalist–modernist" controversies.

48. As quoted in James Alan Patterson, "The Loss of a Protestant Missionary Consensus: Foreign Missions and the Fundamentalist–Modernist Conflict," in *Earthen Vessels: American Evangelicals and Foreign Missions, 1880–1980*, edited by Joel A. Carpenter and Wilbert R. Shenk (Grand Rapids, MI: Eerdmans, 1990), 74.

Christian mission when he said, "I look on this world as a wrecked vessel. God has given me a lifeboat, and said to me, 'Moody, save all you can.'"[49]

Not only was Jesus Christ regarded as the one Lord and Savior for all peoples in all cultures, but Christianity was also assumed to be the one true religion for all humankind. The attitudes toward other religions of many nineteenth-century Protestant missionaries are reflected in the 1896 statement by Judson Smith, a member of the American Board of Commissioners for Foreign Missions: "There is no faith which Christianity is not worthy to replace, which it is not destined to replace. It is not to share the world *with* Islam, or *with* Buddhism, or *with* any other religious system. It is the one true religion for man as man in the Orient and in the Occident, in the first century and in the twentieth century and as long as time shall last."[50] And for many, there was little distinction to be made between empirical Christianity— European or American—and the gospel of Jesus Christ.

By the beginning of the twentieth century, however, influential Protestant missionaries and missions professors were increasingly preoccupied with troubling questions about other religions, with some advocating more positive views of other religious traditions.[51] To some extent, this was a byproduct of broader theological changes taking place in Europe and America. The growing influence of higher critical approaches to Scripture and theological liberalism undermined confidence in the unique inspiration of the Bible and orthodox perspectives on Jesus Christ. There was also greater openness to soteriological universalism, the idea that all people, regardless of religious affiliation, will be saved. But greater openness to other religions also was prompted by a more nuanced understanding of other cultures and a growing appreciation of the impressive cultural achievements of India, China, and Japan. Many theologically orthodox missionaries became convinced that firm commitment to Jesus Christ as Lord and Savior did not necessarily mean total rejection of other religions as nothing but "domains of darkness" but could be compatible with appreciation of truth, goodness, and beauty in other traditions.

---

49. D. L. Moody, "The Second Coming of Christ," in *The Best of D. L. Moody: Sixteen Sermons by the Great Evangelist*, edited by Wilbur M. Smith (Chicago: Moody, 1971), 194.

50. Judson Smith, "Foreign Missions in Light of Fact," *North American Review* (January 1896): 25, as quoted in Robert E. Speer, *The Finality of Jesus Christ* (New York: Revell, 1933), 161–162.

51. See especially Kenneth Cracknell, *Justice, Courtesy, and Love: Theologians and Missionaries Encountering World Religions, 1846–1914* (London: Epworth, 1995); Timothy Yates, *Christian Mission in the Twentieth Century* (New York: Cambridge University Press, 1994).

The more positive perspective on other religions can be illustrated through the work of one of the more remarkable—and controversial—missionaries of the time, John Nicol Farquhar (1861–1929). Born in Aberdeen and educated at Oxford, Farquhar went to India in 1891 as a missionary with the London Missionary Society. He was involved in a variety of ministries, including teaching in a college in Calcutta, evangelism, writing, and lecturing under the auspices of the Indian YMCA. Ill health forced him to leave India in 1923, and during the last years of his life, he served as professor of comparative religion at the University of Manchester.

Farquhar is best remembered for *The Crown of Hinduism* (1913), which called for a more positive appraisal of Hinduism.[52] Farquhar was well aware of what in the late twentieth century would be called globalization—the increasing interconnectedness of peoples around the world. "We have entered upon a new era," he wrote. "All parts of the world have at last been brought into communication with one another. We read news of every land at our breakfast tables."[53] Farquhar argued that Christian missionaries should cultivate a more positive appreciation of Indian culture and religion and should present the Christian gospel as something that does not radically displace Hindu traditions but rather fulfills or brings to completion that which is already anticipated, however imperfectly, within them.[54] Jesus Christ is to be understood as the fulfillment of the best aspirations of other religions. "Every true motive which in Hinduism has found expression in unclean, debasing, or unworthy practices finds in Him [Christ] fullest exercise in work for the downtrodden, the ignorant, the sick, and the sinful. In Him is focused every ray of light that shines in Hinduism. He is the Crown of the faith of India."[55] Farquhar was influenced by the prevailing view of his time, which saw the religions evolving from more "primitive" animistic religions to the "higher" monotheistic religions, culminating (naturally) in Christianity. Thus, he did not regard Hinduism a false religion so much as an incomplete or underdeveloped religion, which finds its fulfillment in Christianity.

Nevertheless, despite his appreciation for Hindu ways, Farquhar was not a pluralist, as the term is used today. He did not think of Hinduism and

---

52. J. N. Farquhar, *The Crown of Hinduism* (1913; reprint New Delhi: Oriental Books Reprint Corp., 1971).

53. Ibid., 11.

54. See Eric J. Sharpe, *Not to Destroy but to Fulfill: The Contribution of J. N. Farquhar to Protestant Missionary Thought in India before 1914* (Uppsala, Sweden: Gleerup, 1965), 330.

55. Farquhar, *The Crown of Hinduism*, 458.

Christianity as equally acceptable or true religions. He believed that it was in Jesus Christ that God has revealed himself in a definitive manner and that it is only in Christ that human beings, regardless of culture or religion, can find true fulfillment and salvation. Therefore, evangelism is essential for the missionary. In a presentation to the Calcutta Missionary Conference in May 1905, Farquhar stated, "Our task is to preach the Gospel of Christ and to woo souls to Him; and to that great end every element of our work should be made strictly subordinate and subservient."[56] Furthermore, he held that there is much in Hindu belief and practice that is false or evil and thus ought to be rejected. So regarding Christ as the fulfillment of Hinduism should not be taken to mean that all Hindu beliefs and practices should be accepted just as they are. Christianity fulfills Hinduism in the sense that it provides the complete answers both to questions arising from within Hinduism itself and to those that Hinduism fails to raise. For it is only in the gospel of Jesus Christ that India will find the resources to address the many problems it confronts in its struggle to find its place in the modern world.

Although Farquhar's views were controversial, the fulfillment motif, in varying forms, was to become a dominant theme in twentieth-century theology of religions. Questions about Christian faith and other religions became increasingly prominent during the first three world missionary conferences, at Edinburgh (1910), Jerusalem (1928), and Tambaram, India (1938). The fulfillment theme was already influential by 1910, as increasing numbers of missionaries acknowledged some continuity between the Christian gospel and other traditions.[57] At Edinburgh in 1910, there was a general acceptance of the need for evangelism, but what was different was the call for greater sensitivity in the ways in which the gospel is shared with religious others and a greater openness to finding continuities between the gospel and other traditions.

By the time of the Jerusalem conference in 1928, however, there were open divisions between those who still thought of Christian mission in terms of evangelism and the call to conversion and those who rejected such traditional understandings. Shifting perspectives on the nature of mission grew out of deeper theological transformations brought about by the growing influence of theological liberalism. More conservative mission leaders became alarmed by what they perceived as theological compromise. Timothy Yates

---

56. J. N. Farquhar, "Missionary Study of Hinduism," as quoted in Eric Sharpe, "J. N. Farquhar," in *Mission Legacies: Biographical Studies of Leaders of the Modern Missionary Movement*, edited by Gerald H. Anderson et al. (Maryknoll, NY: Orbis, 1994), 293.

57. See Cracknell, *Justice, Courtesy, and Love*, 221.

observes: "Great anxiety was being expressed that in the handling of the issue
of the Christian message and its relation to other faiths, there was a discernible shift into syncretism and that the missionary movement was in danger
of moving towards the 'social gospel' position, then widely adopted in North
America."[58]

The decade following the Jerusalem conference was a time of increased
missiological focus on questions of other religions. It was during this time
that the Laymen's Foreign Missions Inquiry submitted its controversial
seven-volume report on the status of Christian missions in Asia. Funded by
Baptist layman John D. Rockefeller, sponsored by eight mission boards in
North America, and led by William Ernest Hocking, professor of philosophy
at Harvard and a Congregationalist layman, the fifteen-member commission
conducted "fact-finding" visits to mission stations in Burma, India, Japan, and
China. A one-volume summary of their findings was published in 1932 as
Re-thinking Missions: A Laymen's Inquiry After One Hundred Years.[59]

Although it contained much valuable information about the status of
Christian missions in Asia and identified problems with some of the ways in
which missions were then being conducted, *Re-thinking Missions* was enormously controversial because of its reinterpretation of both the nature and
the basis of Christian mission. Traditional theological underpinnings of mission were questioned. The report stated that in light of the current theological
climate, "there is little disposition to believe that sincere and aspiring seekers
after God in other religions are to be damned; it has become less concerned
in any land to save men from eternal punishment than from the danger of
losing the supreme good."[60] Changing theological convictions, the emerging
challenges of secularism and nationalism, and the many physical and social
needs in less developed nations were said to demand a fresh understanding
of Christian mission. Evangelism should no longer be understood in terms of
sharing the gospel of Jesus Christ with the intention of conversion from other

---

58. Yates, *Christian Mission*, 65. The social gospel movement, to which Yates refers, was a
way of thinking about the application of biblical ethical principles to the emerging urban
and industrial problems of America in the late nineteenth and early twentieth centuries.
Although evangelicals were active in social reform during the time, the term *social gospel* was
generally associated with the more theologically liberal stream of Christianity, which tended
to reduce the Christian faith to moral principles and social reform.

59. William E. Hocking, ed., *Re-thinking Missions: A Laymen's Inquiry after One Hundred Years*
(New York: Harper, 1932). On the Laymen's Inquiry, see William R. Hutchison, *Errand to the
World: American Protestant Thought and Foreign Missions* (Chicago: University of Chicago
Press, 1987), 158–175; Yates, *Christian Mission*, 70–93.

60. Hocking, *Re-thinking Missions*, 19.

religions to Christian faith. Rather, "ministry to the secular needs of men in the spirit of Christ *is evangelism*."[61] The report called for a new kind of missionary, who would "regard himself as a co-worker with the forces which are making for righteousness within every religious system." The missionary "will look forward, not to the destruction of these [non-Christian] religions, but to their continued co-existence with Christianity, each stimulating the other in growth toward the ultimate goal, unity in the completest religious truth."[62]

Although the report was embraced enthusiastically in liberal circles, it was vigorously attacked by mainstream missions leaders for its relativizing tendencies and theological drift. John Mackay, the Scottish missionary and president of Princeton Theological Seminary, dismissed the report for reflecting a perspective that, far from being cutting edge, was already out of date—"the sunset glow of nineteenth century romanticism."[63] Robert Speer, the Presbyterian missionary statesman and ecumenical leader, recognized that *Re-thinking Missions* signaled more than just a different way of thinking about missions; it advocated an alternative Christology that regarded Jesus as little more than, in the words of Timothy Yates, a "supreme religious teacher and exemplar of a life lived in union with God."[64] The same year that *Re-thinking Missions* was published, Speer delivered the Stone Lectures at Princeton Theological Seminary on "The Finality of Jesus Christ." Eventually published under the same title, the lectures were a direct response to the more pluralistic views of the time and constitute an informed and nuanced defense of the orthodox perspective on Jesus Christ and the importance of evangelism among adherents of other religions.[65]

The issues raised by the popularity of the fulfillment theme and *Re-thinking Missions* formed the backdrop to the consequential International Missionary Conference held at Tambaram, India, in 1938. Is God's revelation, as expressed in Jesus Christ, continuous or discontinuous with the beliefs and practices of other religions? To what extent can we discern God's presence and activity within other religious traditions? Is proclamation of the gospel of Jesus Christ, with the intent of conversion, a legitimate component of Christian

---

61. Ibid., 68; emphasis in original.

62. Ibid., 40, 44.

63. As quoted in Gerald H. Anderson, "American Protestants in Pursuit of Mission: 1886–1986," *International Bulletin of Missionary Research* 12 (July 1988): 107.

64. Yates, *Christian Mission*, 91.

65. Robert E. Speer, *The Finality of Jesus Christ* (New York: Fleming H. Revell, 1933).

mission, or should we think of mission primarily in terms of addressing the
very real physical and social needs of people today?

Hendrik Kraemer (1888–1965), the Dutch scholar and former missionary
to Java, was asked to prepare a special volume for the conference that would
respond to the growing uncertainty about Christian mission amid other religions. In a mere seven weeks, Kraemer produced *The Christian Message in a
Non-Christian World*, a massive four-hundred-fifty-page work defending the
uniqueness of Jesus Christ and the gospel. Against the relativizing currents of
the day, Kraemer affirmed that "missionary...manifestations can only legitimately be called Christian and missionary when they issue directly from the
apostolic urgency of gladly witnessing to God and his saving and redeeming
Power through Christ."[66] For Kraemer, Christianity is uniquely "the religion of
revelation," and he called for a radical discontinuity between the "biblical realism" of God's revelation and salvation in Christ and non-Christian religions.[67]

Although Kraemer later developed a more nuanced understanding of other
religions,[68] his concern at Tambaram was to counter the growing influence
of the fulfillment motif and the tendency to emphasize continuity between
God's saving action in Jesus Christ and other religions. Kraemer stressed the
basic discontinuity between God's action in Christ and all other religious traditions. While highly influential at Tambaram, Kraemer was nevertheless controversial, and his position was vigorously contested by critics such as C. F.
Andrews, A. G. Hogg, William Paton, T. C. Chao, and others who advocated
more positive views of God's presence in other religions.

Vatican II and Religious Others

By the early 1960s, Christian theologians, in addition to missionaries, were
taking seriously the implications of religious diversity for theology. In 1961,
for example, Wilfred Cantwell Smith, the distinguished historian and scholar
of Islam, put the following question to a group of theologians and biblical
scholars:

> How does one account, theologically, for the fact of man's religious
> diversity? This is really as big an issue, almost, as the question of how

---

66. Hendrik Kraemer, *The Christian Message in a Non-Christian World* (New York: Harper,
1938), vi–vii.

67. Ibid., 61–141.

68. See, for example, Hendrik Kraemer, *Religion and the Christian Faith* (London: Lutterworth,
1956); Kraemer, *World Cultures and World Religions* (London: Lutterworth, 1960).

one accounts theologically for evil—but Christian theologians have been much more conscious of the fact of evil than that of religious pluralism.... I would simply like to suggest that from now on any serious intellectual statement of the Christian faith must include, if it is to serve its purpose among men, some sort of doctrine of other religions. We explain the fact that the Milky Way is there by the doctrine of creation, but how do we explain the fact that the Bhagavad Gita is there?[69]

Smith was challenging Christian theologians to develop a theology of religions, and he offered his own answer in an influential version of religious pluralism.[70]

Similarly, toward the end of his life, the Protestant theologian Paul Tillich also acknowledged the significance of other religions for theology. His interest in the subject grew out of a trip to Japan in 1960.[71] Tillich's 1961–62 Bampton Lectures at Columbia University were published as *Christianity and the Encounter of the World Religions*, and his final public lecture was a call for Christian theology to adopt a fresh approach to the study of other religions.[72] By the 1970s and '80s, a growing number of Protestant and Roman Catholic theologians were doing just that.

Some of the most influential thinkers in this area have been Roman Catholics, and the most significant event shaping Catholic approaches to the subject was Vatican II (1962–1965).[73] We will give special attention to Vatican II here, but we should note that by the late twentieth century, the general

---

69. Wilfred Cantwell Smith, "The Christian in a Religiously Plural World," in *Religious Diversity: Essays by Wilfred Cantwell Smith*, edited by Willard G. Oxtoby (New York: Harper & Row, 1976), 15–16.

70. See Wilfred Cantwell Smith, *The Meaning and End of Religion* (New York: Macmillan, 1963); Smith, *The Faith of Other Men* (New York: New American Library, 1965); Smith, *Faith and Belief* (Princeton, NJ: Princeton University Press, 1979); Smith, *Towards a World Theology* (Maryknoll, NY: Orbis, 1981). John Hick's later views on religious pluralism and religious truth were influenced by Smith's writings; see Hick's Foreword to the 1978 edition of Smith, *The Meaning and End of Religion*, ix–xvii.

71. See "Tillich Encounters Japan," edited by Robert W. Wood, *Japanese Religions* 2 (May 1961): 48–71.

72. Paul Tillich, *Christianity and the Encounter of the World Religions* (New York: Columbia University Press, 1963); Tillich, "The Significance of the History of Religions for Systematic Theology," in *The Future of Religions*, edited by Jerald C. Brauer (Chicago: University of Chicago Press, 1966), 80–94.

73. For the most complete statement of post–Vatican II Roman Catholic perspectives on the theology of religions, see *Catholic Engagement with World Religions: A Comprehensive Study*, edited by Karl J. Becker and Ilara Morali (Maryknoll, NY: Orbis, 2010).

approach to other religions set out by the Second Vatican Council was, with appropriate modifications, adopted by many Protestant denominations and theologians.[74] Pope John XXIII convened the Second Vatican Council as an *aggiornamento* (updating) of the Catholic Church in light of the new realities of the twentieth century. It is difficult to exaggerate the impact of Vatican II on the church, and nowhere is this more evident than in its attitude toward other religions. Before the Council, there were some voices within the church calling for more accommodating approaches to followers of other religious paths, but by and large, Roman Catholic perspectives were characterized by the early church formula *extra ecclesiam nulla salus* (outside the church no salvation), which had become official Church doctrine at the 1442 Council of Florence.

Yet by the mid-twentieth century, some leading Catholic thinkers were exploring much more positive perspectives on religious others. The Jesuit theologian Karl Rahner (1904–1984), a major influence at Vatican II, introduced the concept of "anonymous Christian" to designate, as Jacques Dupuis puts it, "the hidden, unknown operative presence of the mystery of Christ in other religions."[75] Rahner argued that under certain conditions, sincere adherents of other religions might experience and respond appropriately to God's grace right where they are, within their own religious matrix, and thus could be regarded as anonymous Christians even though they have had no direct contact with the Christian gospel or the visible church.[76] Rahner's general approach is reflected in several of the documents of Vatican II that address directly the issue of salvation and other religions.[77]

The two most significant documents from Vatican II for the question of other religions are *Nostra Aetate* (Declaration on the Relation of the Church to Non-Christian Religions) and *Ad Gentes* (Decree on the Church's Missionary Activity). Two other documents, *Gaudium et Spes* (Pastoral Constitution on the

---

74. See Kärkkäinen, *An Introduction*, 190–255.

75. Dupuis, *Toward a Christian Theology*, 143.

76. See Karl Rahner, "Christianity and Non-Christian Religions" and "Anonymous Christian," in *Theological Investigations* (Baltimore: Helicon, 1966), 5:115–134, 6:390–398; Rahner, "Anonymous Christianity and the Missionary Task of the Church," in *Theological Investigations* (New York: Seabury, 1974), 12:161–178. For a helpful exposition and defense of Rahner's position, see Gavin D'Costa, *Theology and Religious Pluralism: The Challenge of Other Religions* (Oxford, UK: Blackwell, 1986).

77. There have been different interpretations of the implications of statements from Vatican II on other religions. For different views on the subject, see Paul F. Knitter, *Jesus and the Other Names* (Maryknoll, NY: Orbis, 1996), 125–164; Thomas F. Stransky, "The Church and Other Religions," *International Bulletin of Missionary Research* 9 (October 1985): 154–158; Mikka Ruokanen, *The Catholic Doctrine on Non-Christian Religions according to the Second Vatican Council* (Leiden: Brill, 1992); and Dupuis, *Toward a Christian Theology*, 130–179.

Church in the Modern World) and *Lumen Gentium* (Dogmatic Constitution
of the Church), are also important. Vatican II is unequivocal in affirming
the unique person and work of Jesus Christ, the eternal Word incarnate, the
one Lord and Savior for all humankind. In the words of *Nostra Aetate*, "It
is in [Christ], in whom God reconciled all things to himself (2 Cor. 5:18–19),
[that] men find the fullness of their religious life."[78] Moreover, there is still
some sense in which the Church is held to be necessary for salvation. *Lumen
Gentium* states, "Basing itself upon scripture and tradition, [this holy Council]
teaches that the Church, a pilgrim now on earth, is necessary for salvation: the
one Christ is the mediator and the way of salvation; he is present to us in
his body which is the Church."[79] Since Jesus Christ is the one Savior for all
humankind and the Church is necessary, in some sense, for salvation, it is
hardly surprising that Vatican II also affirms the responsibility of the Church
to proclaim the gospel of Jesus Christ to all peoples. Thus, *Ad Gentes* strongly
affirms the missionary imperative: "Hence the Church has an obligation to
proclaim the faith and salvation which comes from Christ.... Everyone, therefore, ought to be converted to Christ, who is known through the preaching
of the Church, and ought, by baptism, to become incorporated into him, and
into the Church which is his body."[80]

At the same time, however, Vatican II calls for a much more positive perspective on adherents of other religions and acknowledges the possibility of
their salvation. *Lumen Gentium* claims that "those who have not yet received
the Gospel are related to the Church in various ways." Those who have not
had explicit contact with the Church or the gospel of Jesus Christ can nevertheless be saved.

> Those who, through no fault of their own, do not know the Gospel
> of Christ or his Church, but who nevertheless seek God with a sin-
> cere heart, and, moved by grace, try in their actions to do his will as
> they know it through the dictates of their conscience—those too may
> achieve eternal salvation. Nor shall divine providence deny the assis-
> tance necessary for salvation to those who, without any fault of theirs,
> have not yet arrived at an explicit knowledge of God, and who, not with-
> out grace, strive to lead a good life. Whatever good or truth is found

78. *Documents of Vatican II*, edited by A. P. Flannery (Grand Rapids, MI: Eerdmans, 1975), 739.

79. Ibid., 365–366.

80. Ibid., 817, 821.

amongst them is considered by the Church to be a preparation for
the Gospel and given by him who enlightens all men that they may at
length have life.[81]

Dupuis observes that although the possibility of salvation outside of the
church had been recognized earlier, there is a new optimism about this with
Vatican II: "What in previous Church documents was affirmed—firmly but
cautiously—as a *possibility* based on God's infinite mercy and in any event
to be left to his counsel is being taught by the council with unprecedented
assurance: in ways known to him, God can lead those who, through no fault
of their own, are ignorant of the Gospel to that faith without which it is impossible to please him."[82] Two questions must be distinguished here: Can followers of other religions be saved without explicitly responding to the gospel
and becoming joined to the church? Is God's saving grace available through
other religions as such, that is, through the institutions, beliefs, and practices of non-Christian religions? Most observers agree that the Second Vatican
Council documents clearly answer the first question affirmatively, but there is
disagreement over their implications for the second question.[83] It is notewor-
thy that the Council documents stop short—according to some, purposely—
of stating that salvation could ever come through non-Christian religions
themselves.

Nostra Aetate adopts a positive stance toward certain elements of other religions and calls for Christians to engage in dialogue with followers of other
religions: "The Catholic Church rejects nothing of what is true and holy in
these religions.... The Church urges her sons to enter with prudence and
charity into discussions and collaboration with members of other religions."[84]
And yet Vatican II also makes it clear that the Christian faith is superior to
other religions, for Jesus Christ is unlike any other religious leader. "Indeed,
[the Church] proclaims and must ever proclaim Christ 'the way, the truth, and
the life' (John 14:6), in whom men find the fullness of religious life, and in
whom God has reconciled all things to Himself."[85]

---

81. Ibid., 367–368.

82. Dupuis, *Toward a Christian Theology*, 161.

83. See, for example, Kärkkäinen, *An Introduction*, 114–118; Dupuis, *Toward a Christian Theology*, 180–201; Paul F. Knitter, *No Other Name? A Critical Survey of Christian Attitudes toward the World Religions* (Maryknoll, NY: Orbis, 1985), 120–130.

84. *Documents of Vatican II*, 739.

85. Ibid.

During the decades following Vatican II, many Roman Catholic theologians took advantage of the fresh approach charted by the Second Vatican Council, becoming heavily involved in interreligious dialogue and developing theologies of religions. While some theological models clearly remained within the parameters set by the Council, others pushed the boundaries. Church officials became alarmed by the more pluralistic views being proposed by some and the perception that interreligious dialogue was replacing traditional views of mission and evangelization. In 1975, Pope Paul VI issued the apostolic exhortation *Evangelii Nuntiandi* (On Evangelization in the Modern World), a major statement on the nature and importance of evangelization, which, according to Stephen Bevans and Roger Schroeder, "marked the beginning of the rebirth of the Catholic missionary movement."[86] In 1990, on the twenty-fifth anniversary of Vatican II's *Ad Gentes*, Pope John Paul II issued the encyclical *Redemptoris Missio*. This called for an understanding of mission centered on proclamation of the gospel of Jesus Christ to those who have not yet heard it—many of whom are adherents of other religions—and establishing the Church where it does not yet exist. "Such a Christocentric, ecclesiological emphasis was intended to counter current movements that were deemphasizing, the pope thought, the central place of Christ and the church in salvation history and the importance of mission *ad gentes*."[87]

But the Vatican also affirmed that although proclamation has a central place in mission, it should not be construed as incompatible with interreligious dialogue. The Pontifical Council for Interreligious Dialogue and the Congregation for the Evangelization of Peoples jointly published *Dialogue and Proclamation* in 1991. The document declares that proclamation and dialogue are "both viewed, each in its own place, as component elements and authentic forms of the one evangelizing mission of the Church. They are both oriented towards the communication of salvific truth."[88] In 2000, the Roman Catholic Congregation for the Doctrine of the Faith issued *Dominus Iesus*, a document prompted by the concern that the "Church's constant missionary proclamation is endangered today by relativistic theories which seek to justify religious

---

86. Stephen B. Bevans and Roger P. Schroeder, *Constants in Context: A Theology of Mission for Today* (Maryknoll, NY: Orbis, 2004), 253.

87. Ibid., 254.

88. "Dialogue and Proclamation," in *New Directions in Mission and Evangelization 1: Basic Statements 1974–1991*, edited by James A. Scherer and Stephen B. Bevans (Maryknoll, NY: Orbis, 1992), 178.

pluralism."[89] Signed by Cardinal Joseph Ratzinger, who later became Pope Benedict XVI, the document insisted on "the definitive and complete character of the revelation of Jesus Christ" as a "remedy for this relativistic mentality." It asserted that belief in other religions "is still religious experience in search of the absolute truth and still lacking assent to God who reveals himself." Furthermore, it maintained, the only religious texts inspired by the Holy Spirit are the Old and New Testaments, and non-Christian religions serve "as a preparation for the gospel and can only be understood in reference to Christ the Word who took flesh by the power of the Spirit." The followers of other religions "can receive divine grace," but "*objectively speaking* they are in a gravely deficient situation in comparison with those who, in the Church, have the fullness of the means of salvation."[90]

This strong assertion of the insufficiency of other religions was prompted by post–Vatican II Catholic theologies of religions that had struggled to keep in proper tension the dual themes of the uniqueness and normativity of God's revelation and salvation through Jesus Christ along with acknowledgment of God's presence and saving grace among religious others. This tension has also characterized mainline Protestant theologians' approaches to the subject, and both Roman Catholic and Protestant thinkers have looked to the doctrine of the Trinity as a way to develop this dual emphasis. Some of the issues in Trinitarian theologies of religions will be explored below in chapter 2.

The Shift to Pluralism

By the late 1970s, a growing number of Christian theologians were dissatisfied with the assumption that there is something unique or distinctively normative about Jesus Christ and the Christian gospel. Influential theologians argued

---

89. As quoted in Gavin D'Costa, "Christian Orthodoxy and Religious Pluralism: A Response to Terrence W. Tilley," *Modern Theology* 23, no. 3 (July 2007): 435. For an interesting debate over the implications of *Dominus Iesus* for religious pluralism, see Terrence W. Tilley, "Christian Orthodoxy and Religious Pluralism," *Modern Theology* 20, no. 1 (January 2006): 51–63; D'Costa, "Christian Orthodoxy and Religious Pluralism," 435–446; Tilley, "'Christian Orthodoxy and Religious Pluralism': A Rejoinder to Gavin D'Costa," *Modern Theology* 23, no. 3 (July 2007): 447–454; D'Costa, "'Christian Orthodoxy and Religious Pluralism': A Further Rejoinder to Terrence Tilley," *Modern Theology* 23, no. 3 (July 2007): 455–462; D'Costa and Tilley, "Concluding Our *Quaestio Disputata* on Theologies of Religious Diversity," *Modern Theology* 23, no. 3 (July 2007): 463–468.

90. *Dominus Iesus*, pars. 4, 7, 12, 22; http://www.vatican.va/roman_curia/congregations/cfaith/documents/rc_con_cfaith_doc_20000806_dominus-iesus_en.html; emphasis in original.

that we should openly acknowledge parity among the religions with respect to truth and salvation. No single religion can legitimately claim to be distinctively true or normative for all people; all religions (or at least the morally respectable ones) should be regarded as complex historically and culturally conditioned ways in which various peoples can respond to the divine reality. Thus, although Christians can hold that Jesus is unique and normative *for them*, they should not maintain that he is normative in an objective sense for all people in all cultures. Jesus may be the savior for Christians, but he is not the one Savior for all people. This perspective, generally referred to as religious pluralism, has been summarized by Peter Byrne, a leading contemporary pluralist, as follows: "Pluralism as a theoretical response to religious diversity can now be summarily defined by three propositions. (1) All major forms of religion are equal in respect of making common reference to a single, transcendent sacred reality. (2) All major forms of religion are likewise equal in respect of offering some means or other to human salvation. (3) All religious traditions are to be seen as containing revisable, limited accounts of the nature of the sacred: none is certain enough in its particular dogmatic formulations to provide the norm for interpreting the others."[91]

This view was not unknown in earlier times. The idea that there are many paths to the divine and that each people and culture has its own way was commonplace in the ancient Mediterranean world. Robert Wilken states, "The oldest and most enduring criticism of Christianity is an appeal to religious pluralism....All the ancient critics of Christianity were united in affirming that there is no one way to the divine."[92] One can also find expressions of pluralism among early-modern thinkers, and it becomes a recurring theme among intellectuals in the nineteenth century. One of the first Christian theologians to embrace pluralism explicitly was the German theologian Ernst Troeltsch (d. 1923).[93] But it was not until the late twentieth century that there were significant numbers of Christian theologians and philosophers who advocated religious pluralism.

91. Peter Byrne, "It Is Not Reasonable to Believe That Only One Religion Is True," in *Contemporary Debates in Philosophy of Religion*, edited by Michael L. Peterson and Raymond J. VanArragon (Oxford, UK: Blackwell, 2004), 204. See also Byrne, *Prolegomena to Religious Pluralism: Reference and Realism in Religion* (New York: St. Martin's, 1995), 12.

92. Robert Wilken, *Remembering the Christian Past* (Grand Rapids, MI: Eerdmans, 1995), 27, 42.

93. See Troeltsch's "The Place of Christianity among the World Religions," written for delivery before the University of Oxford in 1923. Troeltsch died before he was able to deliver the lecture. The essay is reprinted in *Christianity and Plurality: Classic and Contemporary Readings*, edited by Richard J. Plantinga (Oxford, UK: Blackwell, 1999), 209–222.

The most influential defense of religious pluralism has come from theologian and philosopher John Hick (1922–2012). Although he had been a respected defender of traditional Christian theism, in 1973 Hick published *God and the Universe of Faiths*, a work that called for a "Copernican revolution" in theology, involving "a shift from the dogma that Christianity is at the centre to the realization that it is *God* who is at the centre, and that all religions of mankind, including our own, serve and revolve around him."[94] During the next decade, Hick continued refining his views, moving away from the theism implicit in the above statement to a model of religious pluralism that (supposedly) does not privilege either theistic or nontheistic perspectives on the religious ultimate. Hick's proposal is set out most completely in *An Interpretation of Religion*, which is based on his 1986–87 Gifford Lectures.[95] Hick contends that the religions are to be regarded as culturally and historically conditioned human responses to an ultimate ineffable Reality, which is the source and ground of everything and which is such that insofar as the religious traditions are in soteriological alignment with it, they are contexts of salvation/ liberation. These traditions involve different human conceptions of the Real (the religious ultimate), with correspondingly different forms of experience of the Real and correspondingly different forms of life in response to the Real.[96]

In 1987, Hick and Paul Knitter coedited *The Myth of Christian Uniqueness*, a volume intended by the contributors to serve as a "crossing of a theological Rubicon" or a public embrace of a genuinely pluralistic view of the major religions: "Through this collection of essays we hope to show that such a pluralist turn is taking shape, that it is being proposed by a variety of reputable Christian thinkers, and that therefore it represents a viable, though still inchoate and controversial, option for Christian believers."[97] Contributors to the volume include some of the most influential theologians of the late twentieth century. Paul Knitter, who has developed his views on pluralism out of a concern for social justice and in dialogue with Buddhism, now identifies himself

---

94. John Hick, *God and the Universe of Faiths* (New York: St. Martin's, 1973), 131; emphasis in original.

95. John Hick, *An Interpretation of Religion* (New Haven, CT: Yale University Press, 1989). A second edition of the book was published in 2004. Other works in which Hick develops his thesis include *Disputed Questions in Theology and the Philosophy of Religion* (New Haven, CT: Yale University Press, 1993), *A Christian Theology of Religions: The Rainbow of Faiths* (Louisville, KY: Westminster John Knox, 1995), and *The Fifth Dimension: An Exploration of the Spiritual Realm* (Oxford, UK: Oneworld, 1999).

96. Hick, *A Christian Theology of Religions* (Louisville, KY: Westminster John Knox, 1995), 27.

97. Paul F. Knitter, Preface to *The Myth of Christian Uniqueness*, edited by John H. Hick and Paul F. Knitter (Maryknoll, NY: Orbis, 1987), viii.

as both a Christian and a Buddhist.[98] Other influential pluralists include Wilfred Cantwell Smith, Keith Ward, Gordon Kaufmann, Joseph Runzo, and Philip Quinn.[99] While explicit pluralism remains a minority perspective among Christian theologians, it is adopted by some of the most influential theologians today. It is also widespread in the academy and is increasingly influential in popular culture.

Evangelicals Join the Debate

By the early 1990s, evangelicals were also giving attention to issues in the theology of religions.[100] It is helpful to frame the discussion of evangelical developments in relation to two significant markers of international evangelical identity that emerged in the twentieth century: the Lausanne Movement and the World Evangelical Fellowship, now the World Evangelical Alliance (WEA). The Lausanne Movement, guided by the Lausanne Committee for World Evangelization, convened three influential International Congresses on World Evangelization at Lausanne (1974), Manila (1989), and Cape Town (2010). The Lausanne Covenant, produced at Lausanne I, has become a symbol of evangelical identity worldwide. The WEA, which, according to its official website, is a network of churches in 129 nations representing more than 600 million evangelical Christians, has also sponsored consultations addressing other religions.[101]

Initially, evangelical discussions of other religions were limited to concerns directly relating to evangelism and missions. Evangelical statements

---

98. See Knitter, *No Other Name?*; Knitter, *Jesus and the Other Names*; Knitter, *One Earth Many Religions: Multifaith Dialogue and Global Responsibility* (Maryknoll, NY: Orbis, 1995); *The Uniqueness of Jesus: A Dialogue with Paul Knitter*, edited by Leonard Swidler and Paul Mojzes (Maryknoll, NY: Orbis, 1997); and Knitter, *Without Buddha I Could Not Be a Christian* (Oxford, UK: Oneworld, 2009).

99. See Smith, *Towards a World Theology*; Keith Ward, "Truth and the Diversity of Religions," *Religious Studies* 26, no. 1 (March 1990): 1–18; Gordon Kaufman, *God, Mystery, Diversity: Christian Theology in a Pluralistic World* (Minneapolis: Fortress, 1996); Joseph Runzo, "Pluralism and Relativism," in *The Oxford Handbook of Religious Diversity*, edited by Chad Meister (New York: Oxford University Press, 2011), 61–76; Runzo, *Reason, Relativism, and God* (London: Macmillan, 1986); Philip L. Quinn, "Toward Thinner Theologies," *International Journal for Philosophy of Religion* 38 (December 1995), 145–164.

100. See Harold Netland, "Christian Mission among Other Faiths: The Evangelical Tradition," in *Witnessing to Christ in a Pluralistic World: Christian Mission among Other Faiths*, Regnum Edinburgh 2010 Series, edited by Lalsangkima Pachuau and Knud Jørgensen (Oxford, UK: Regnum, 2011), 45–56.

101. See http://www.worldea.org/whoweare/introduction (accessed November 10, 2013).

from the Berlin Congress on Evangelism (1966), the Wheaton Congress on the Church's Worldwide Mission (1966), the Frankfurt Declaration (1970), and even the Lausanne Covenant (1974) are unambiguous on Jesus Christ as the one Lord and Savior for all humankind and the rejection of soteriological universalism. But they have almost nothing to say about non-Christian religions themselves. The Lausanne Covenant, for example, has only two sentences mentioning non-Christian religions and then only in the context of rejecting syncretism and the idea that Christ's salvation might be available through other religions: "We also reject as derogatory to Christ and the gospel every kind of syncretism and dialogue which implies that Christ speaks equally through all religions and ideologies.... To proclaim Jesus as 'the Saviour of the world' (John 4:42) is not to affirm that all people are either automatically or ultimately saved, still less to affirm that all religions offer salvation in Christ."[102]

Lausanne II in Manila produced the Manila Manifesto, a document that, echoing the Lausanne Covenant, states: "We affirm that other religions and ideologies are not alternative paths to God, and that human spirituality, if unredeemed by Christ, leads not to God but to judgment, for Christ is the only way."[103] But the world had changed considerably in the fifteen years since the Lausanne Congress, and evangelical leaders, especially in Asia, were insisting that theologians and missiologists give greater attention to questions prompted by the resurgence of other religions. Thus, the Manila Manifesto speaks directly about the religiously pluralistic world in which Christians are to make disciples, and it introduces a fresh theme: a call for humility in our witness among religious others: "In the past we have sometimes been guilty of adopting towards adherents of other faiths attitudes of ignorance, arrogance, disrespect and even hostility. We repent of this. We nevertheless are determined to bear a positive and uncompromising witness to the uniqueness of our Lord, in his life, death and resurrection, in all aspects of our evangelistic work including inter-faith dialogue."[104]

But in 1992, two books were published that placed the question of other religions squarely on the agenda of evangelical theologians in the West. The first was Clark Pinnock's *A Wideness in God's Mercy*, which challenged evangelicals to move beyond "restrictivist thinking" that maintains that only those

---

102. *New Direction in Mission and Evangelization 1: Basic Statements 1974–1991*, edited by James A. Scherer and Stephen B. Bevans (Maryknoll, NY: Orbis, 1992), 254–255.

103. Ibid., 293.

104. Ibid., 297.

who hear the gospel and then explicitly respond in faith to the name of Jesus Christ in this life can be saved.[105] Rejecting this as contrary to the biblical understanding of God, Pinnock argued for an "optimism of salvation," which anticipates that God will save many who have never heard the gospel of Jesus Christ. John Sanders's *No Other Name* provided a historical and theological defense of essentially the same position as Pinnock's.[106] Both Pinnock and Sanders claimed that although Jesus Christ is the unique incarnation of God and the only Lord and Savior for all people, we can affirm, based on the biblical witness, that God's saving grace, rooted in the atoning work of Christ on the cross, extends to many who have not heard explicitly about Jesus Christ.

Pinnock's and Sanders's books provoked a vigorous response from conservative evangelicals who were convinced that Scripture clearly teaches that only those who hear and respond to the gospel of Jesus Christ in this life can be saved.[107] We should note, however, that Pinnock and Sanders were not the first evangelicals to put forward what is sometimes called the "wider hope" perspective. J. N. D. Anderson, a highly respected British evangelical and expert on Islam, had earlier advocated essentially the same view. For two decades, Anderson's *Christianity and Comparative Religion* (1970) and *Christianity and World Religions* (1984) constituted the major evangelical treatment of the relation between Christian faith and other religions. Yet Anderson's writings were not particularly controversial, and he was regularly invited by evangelical leaders to speak and write on the subject, expressing a kind of unofficial evangelical perspective on other religions.[108]

---

105. Clark Pinnock, *A Wideness in God's Mercy: The Finality of Jesus Christ in a World of Religions* (Grand Rapids, MI: Zondervan, 1992). See also Pinnock, "The Finality of Jesus Christ in a World of Religions," in *Christian Faith and Practice in the Modern World*, edited by Mark Noll and David F. Wells (Grand Rapids, MI: Eerdmans, 1988), 152–168; Pinnock, "An Inclusivist View," in *Four Views on Salvation in a Pluralistic World*, edited by Dennis L. Okholm and Timothy R. Phillips (Grand Rapids, MI: Zondervan, 1995), 93–148; Pinnock, *Flame of Love: A Theology of the Holy Spirit* (Downers Grove, IL: InterVarsity, 1996).

106. John Sanders, *No Other Name: An Investigation into the Destiny of the Unevangelized* (Grand Rapids, MI: Eerdmans, 1992).

107. See, for example, Ramesh Richard, *The Population of Heaven: A Biblical Response to the Inclusivist Position on Who Will Be Saved* (Chicago: Moody, 1994); John Piper, *Let the Nations Be Glad!* (Grand Rapids, MI: Baker, 1993), chap. 4; Ronald Nash, *Is Jesus the Only Savior?* (Grand Rapids, MI: Zondervan, 1994); R. Douglas Geivett and W. Gary Phillips, "A Particularist View," in *Four Views on Salvation in a Pluralistic World*, edited by Dennis L. Okholm and Timothy R. Phillips (Grand Rapids, MI: Zondervan, 1995), 211–245.

108. See Sir Norman Anderson, "The Gospel: A Story to Tell to the Nations," in *Evangelical Roots*, edited by Kenneth Kantzer (Nashville, TN: Thomas Nelson, 1978), 173–183; Anderson, "Christianity and the World's Religions," in *The Expositor's Bible Commentary*, vol. 1, edited by Frank Gabelein (Grand Rapids, MI: Zondervan, 1979), 143–157; Anderson, "A Christian

Despite ongoing polemical debates over the question of the unevangelized, there were indications already in the early 1990s that some evangelicals were taking a more nuanced approach to the issues. In 1992, eighty-five
evangelical theologians from twenty-eight countries came together in Manila
under the auspices of the World Evangelical Fellowship for a conference on
"The Unique Christ in Our Pluralistic World." The resulting WEF Manila
Declaration combines a strong commitment to the authority of Scripture and
to Jesus Christ as the one Lord and Savior for all peoples with a concern to
take seriously the religious realities of our world. The Declaration acknowledges: "We evangelicals need a more adequate theology of religions."[109] A year
later, veteran evangelical missiologist Ralph Covell observed:

> [Evangelicals] are clear on the uniqueness of Christ and on God's will to
> save all humanity, but they face the dilemma that most of the people of
> the world are comfortable in the religion in which they are born. Christ
> is the unique, but apparently not the universal, savior. When crucial
> target dates appear—1900 and 2000, for example—they mount new
> crusades to spread Christ's message universally, but without giving any
> new, creative thought to the relationship of these efforts to the nag-
> ging questions posed by world religions. For the most part, evangelical
> scholars from the time of the Wheaton Congress on Evangelism (1966)
> to the Lausanne II International Congress on World Evangelization
> (Manila 1989) have been satisfied with predictably repeating their basic
> proof texts on the finality of Christ. Disturbing biblical texts which
> might nuance their attitudes to other religious expressions are glossed
> over, put in footnotes, subsumed under traditional views, or placed in
> the last paragraph of an article.[110]

Approach to Comparative Religion," in *The World's Religions*, edited by Sir Norman Anderson
(Leicester, UK: InterVarsity, 1975), 228–237. Stephen Williams of Union Theological College
in Belfast recalls a conversation with Anderson: "During a visit to the home of Sir Norman
Anderson, in the last years of his life, he told me that he had shown to Martin Lloyd-Jones
the section on the destiny of the unevangelized in *Christianity and World Religions* prior to its
publication. [Anderson] then said something to this effect: 'Martin Lloyd-Jones returned it
to me, slapped it on the desk and said, "I buy every word of it; I am a Calvinist and God can
save whomever he will!" ' " Personal communication from Stephen Williams, November 5,
2009; used with permission.

109. "The WEF Manila Declaration," in *The Unique Christ in Our Pluralist World*, edited by
Bruce J. Nicholls (Grand Rapids, MI: Baker, 1994), 15.

110. Ralph Covell, "Jesus Christ and World Religions: Current Evangelical Viewpoints," in
The Good News of the Kingdom: Mission Theology for the Third Millennium, edited by Charles
Van Engen, Dean S. Gilliland, and Paul Pierson (Maryknoll, NY: Orbis, 1993), 162–163.

More recently, a growing number of evangelical theologians and missiologists have been developing evangelical perspectives on a range of issues relating to other religions. Evangelicals have offered sharp critiques of pluralistic theologies of religions, especially the models of John Hick and Paul Knitter.[111] But evangelicals have also gone beyond simply a critique of pluralism to explore, somewhat tentatively, broader themes and issues in an evangelical theology of religions. A broad range of perspectives were offered at the 2002 Annual Meeting of the Evangelical Theological Society, which was devoted to the subject "Evangelical Christianity and Other Religions."[112]

The Third Lausanne Congress on World Evangelization drew more than four thousand participants from 198 countries to Cape Town, South Africa, in October 2010. Whereas Lausanne 1974 and Manila 1989 issued consensus documents identified as a covenant and a manifesto, respectively, Cape Town adopted a different tone, producing the Cape Town Commitment. The former documents were heavy on affirmations, especially doctrinal beliefs that distinguish evangelicals from other groups. The Cape Town Commitment is a much more extensive document than its predecessors and consists of two parts: a confession of faith, which builds on the previous Lausanne statements, and a commitment to action. Throughout there is a concern for bringing together belief and action, doctrine and praxis. The theme of God's love is dominant throughout the Cape Town Commitment. Robert Schreiter observes: "The confession of faith includes a narrative of God's action in the world, but it is all consciously framed by two theological concepts: love and reconciliation.... The theme of God's love for the world and our response in love frames the entire confession of faith."[113]

---

111. See, for example, Harold Netland, *Encountering Religious Pluralism: The Challenge to Christian Faith and Mission* (Downers Grove, IL: InterVarsity, 2001); Paul Rhodes Eddy, *John Hick's Pluralist Philosophy of World Religions* (Burlington, VT: Ashgate, 2002); Clark Pinnock, "An Evangelical Response to Knitter's Five Theses," in *The Uniqueness of Jesus: A Dialogue with Paul F. Knitter*, edited by Leonard Swidler and Paul Mojzes (Maryknoll, NY: Orbis, 1997), 116–120; John Sanders, "Idolater Indeed!" in *The Uniqueness of Jesus: A Dialogue with Paul F. Knitter*, edited by Leonard Swidler and Paul Mojzes (Maryknoll, NY: Orbis, 1997), 121–125; Daniel Strange, "Perilous Exchange, Precious Good News: A Reformed 'Subversive Fulfillment' Interpretation of Other Religions," in Gavin D'Costa, Paul Knitter, and Daniel Strange, *Only One Way? Three Christian Responses on the Uniqueness of Christ in a Religiously Plural World* (London: SCM, 2011); *Can Only One Religion Be True? Paul Knitter and Harold Netland in Dialogue*, edited by Robert Stewart (Minneapolis: Fortress, 2013).

112. See *Biblical Faith and Other Religions: An Evangelical Assessment*, edited by David W. Baker (Grand Rapids, MI: Kregel, 2004).

113. Robert J. Schreiter, "From the Lausanne Covenant to the Cape Town Commitment: A Theological Assessment," *International Bulletin of Missionary Research* 35, no. 2 (April 2011): 89.

The challenges posed by religious diversity form the backdrop to much of the Cape Town Commitment. Part One acknowledges, for example, "We are tempted to compromise our belief in the uniqueness of Christ under the pressures of religious pluralism."[114] Other religions are not regarded as equally legitimate alternatives to the Christian faith: "The one true God is replaced or distorted in the practice of world religions."[115] Jesus Christ alone is "Saviour, Lord and God.... Just as God called Israel to love him in covenantal faith, obedience and servant witness, we affirm our love for Jesus Christ by trusting in him, obeying him, and making him known."[116] While acknowledging that religious diversity is a fact and that Christians in Asia in particular have had to struggle with the implications of pluralism for centuries, the Commitment states that "postmodern, relativist pluralism is different. Its ideology allows for no absolute or universal truth. While tolerating truth claims, it views them as no more than cultural constructs."[117] In light of this, the Commitment calls for something seldom heard in missiological circles: "greater commitment to the hard work of robust apologetics.... We need to identify, equip, and pray for those who can engage at the highest intellectual and public level in arguing for and defending biblical truth in the public arena."[118]

Section 2.C of Part Two is devoted to issues concerning Christian witness to Jesus Christ among people of other faiths. The amount of space devoted to the subject, the variety of issues addressed, and the carefully nuanced wording all speak to the growing recognition of the importance and development of evangelical thinking about the questions. The key points in this section are framed in terms of Christians living out the love of Christ in interactions with people of other faiths. Schreiter states that in this section, "love is seen as the entry point for dealing with people of other faiths."[119] Here the emphasis is on the importance of living out God's love for religious others in our witness. There is a humble spirit throughout, with candid acknowledgment of past failures in Christian witness: "In the name of the God of love, we repent of our failure to seek friendships with people of Muslim, Hindu, Buddhist and other religious backgrounds. In the spirit of Jesus we will take initiatives to show love, goodwill

---

114. *The Cape Town Commitment: A Confession of Faith and a Call to Action* (Peabody, MA: Hendrickson Publishers and the Lausanne Movement, 2011), I.2.a, 11.

115. Ibid., I.2.b, 11.

116. Ibid., I.4, 13.

117. Ibid., II.A.2, 34.

118. Ibid.

119. Schreiter, "From the Lausanne Covenant to the Cape Town Commitment," 90.

and hospitality to them."[120] The Commitment denounces false depictions or caricatures of other faiths, prejudice, and the incitement of fear of religious others. It calls for "the proper place of dialogue with people of other faiths," a dialogue that "combines confidence in the uniqueness of Christ and in the truth of the gospel with respectful listening to others."[121]

By the time Lausanne III was convened in 2010, evangelicals from around the world were devoting much more thought to the issues of Christian faith and other religions than was the case in the 1970s. The contours of an evangelical theology of religions were beginning to emerge. Timothy Tennent, Winfried Corduan, Harold Netland, Christopher Wright, Stanley Grenz, D. A. Carson, Ida Glaser, Terry Muck, and Gerald R. McDermott, among others, have all developed biblical and theological themes relevant to an evangelical framework for understanding the religions.[122] Some, such as Veli-Matti Kärkkäinen and Keith Johnson, are exploring the implications of the doctrine of the Trinity for an

---

120. *The Cape Town Commitment*, II.C.1.b, 48.

121. Ibid., II.C.1.c and e, 48.

122. See Timothy Tennent, *Christianity at the Religious Roundtable: Evangelicalism in Conversation with Hinduism, Buddhism, and Islam* (Grand Rapids, MI: Baker, 2002); Tennent, *Theology in the Context of World Christianity* (Grand Rapids, MI: Zondervan, 2007); Tennent, "Christian Encounter with Other Religions: Toward an Evangelical Theology of Religions," in Craig Ott and Stephen Strauss, *Encountering Theology of Mission* (Grand Rapids, MI: Baker, 2010), 292–316; Gerald R. McDermott, *Can Evangelicals Learn from World Religions? Jesus, Revelation and Religious Traditions* (Downers Grove, IL: InterVarsity, 2000); McDermott, *God's Rivals* (Downers Grove: InterVarsity, 2007); Winfried Corduan, *A Tapestry of Faiths: The Common Threads between Christianity and World Religions* (Downers Grove, IL: InterVarsity, 2002); Christopher J. H. Wright, "The Christian and Other Religions: The Biblical Evidence," *Themelios* 9, no. 2 (1984): 4–15; Wright, *Thinking Clearly about the Uniqueness of Jesus* (Crowborough, UK: Monarch, 1997); S. J. Grenz, "Toward an Evangelical Theology of Religions," *Journal of Ecumenical Studies* 31 (1994): 49–65; Terry C. Muck, "Is There Common Ground among the Religions?" *Journal of the Evangelical Theological Society* 40, no. 1 (1997): 99–112; D. A. Carson, *The Gagging of God: Christianity Confronts Pluralism* (Grand Rapids, MI: Zondervan, 1996); Ida Glaser, *The Bible and Other Faiths: Christian Responsibility in a World of Religions* (Downers Grove, IL: InterVarsity, 2005); Netland, *Encountering Religious Pluralism*; Harold Netland, "Theology of Religions, Missiology, and Evangelicals," *Missiology: An International Review* 33, no. 2 (April 2005): 142–158; Charles Van Engen, "The Uniqueness of Christ in Mission Theology," in *Landmark Essays in Mission and World Christianity*, edited by Robert L. Gallagher and Paul Hertig (Maryknoll, NY: Orbis, 2009), 160–175. Other significant evangelical works include *One God, One Lord: Christianity in a World of Religious Pluralism*, 2nd ed., edited by Andrew D. Clarke and Bruce W. Winter (Grand Rapids, MI: Baker, 1992); *No Other Gods before Me? Evangelicals and the Challenge of World Religions*, edited by John G. Stackhouse, Jr. (Grand Rapids, MI: Baker, 2001); *The Trinity in a Pluralistic Age: Theological Essays on Culture and Religion*, edited by Kevin J. Vanhoozer (Grand Rapids, MI: Eerdmans, 1997); *Christianity and the Religions: A Biblical Theology of World Religions*, Evangelical Missiological Society Series No. 2, edited by Edward Rommen and Harold Netland (Pasadena, CA: William Carey Library, 1995).

evangelical understanding of other religions.[123] Although his proposal is controversial, Amos Yong has developed a creative pneumatological approach to the theology of religions, moving beyond approaches that rely on Christological criteria without what he regards as proper attention to the role of the Holy Spirit in the religions.[124] Yong's views will be examined more fully below in chapter 2.

Evangelicals are also calling for a different approach in our witness among adherents of other religions. Evangelicals generally remain unwavering in their conviction of the need for evangelism and mission among all peoples, including sincere followers of other religions. But there is a growing recognition that the realities of the early twenty-first century demand fresh thinking about how we should go about making disciples of Jesus Christ. Ours is a postcolonial, globalizing world in which religion is a powerful force often closely associated with ethnic, national, and cultural identities. While religion can be an instrument for much good, it also is a volatile force that provokes tensions and can erupt in violence. This has implications for Christian mission. Ajith Fernando, for example, who has extensive experience in Christian witness among Buddhists and Hindus in Sri Lanka, is uncompromising in his commitment to the uniqueness of Jesus Christ and the gospel, and yet he calls for a much more winsome and sensitive witness that reflects Christ's love.[125] In 2009, Terry Muck and Frances Adeney produced a groundbreaking work, *Christianity Encountering World Religions*, which combines history with theology and missiology in a creative approach—that of "giftive mission"—to understanding and responding to religious others.[126] A final indication of greater sensitivity among evangelicals on these issues is the publication of the document "Christian Witness in a Multi-Religious World: Recommendations for Conduct," produced jointly by the World Council of Churches, the

---

123. Veli-Matti Kärkkäinen, *Trinity and Religious Pluralism: The Doctrine of the Trinity in Christian Theology of Religions* (Burlington, VT: Ashgate, 2004); Keith E. Johnson, *Rethinking the Trinity and Religious Pluralism: An Augustinian Assessment* (Downers Grove, IL: InterVarsity, 2011).

124. Amos Yong, *Discerning the Spirit(s): A Pentecostal-Charismatic Contribution to Christian Theology of Religions* (Sheffield, UK: Sheffield Academic, 2000); Yong, *Beyond the Impasse: Toward a Pneumatological Theology of Religions* (Grand Rapids, MI: Baker, 2003); Yong, "The Holy Spirit and the World Religions: On the Christian Discernment of Spirit(s) 'after' Buddhism," *Buddhist-Christian Studies* 24 (2004): 191–207; Yong, *The Spirit Poured Out on All Flesh: Pentecostalism and the Possibility of Global Theology* (Grand Rapids, MI: Baker, 2005).

125. Ajith Fernando, *Sharing the Truth in Love: How to Relate to People of Other Faiths* (Grand Rapids, MI: Discovery House, 2001).

126. Terry Muck and Frances S. Adeney, *Christianity Encountering World Religions: The Practice of Mission in the Twenty-First Century* (Grand Rapids, MI: Baker, 2009).

Pontifical Council for Interreligious Dialogue of the Roman Catholic Church, and the World Evangelical Alliance. While acknowledging the need for witness among followers of other religious ways, the document suggests some helpful principles for responsible witness in a multireligious world. In chapter 7 below, we will consider further some of these principles that should guide Christians in their witness concerning the gospel of Jesus Christ in our religiously diverse world.

2

The Triune God

HISTORICALLY, EVANGELICALS HAVE paid relatively little attention to the doctrine of the Trinity. In part because of their investment in Enlightenment presuppositions, they have paid greater attention to discrete theological doctrines related to the human agent, such as conversion, holiness, and (even some versions of) world mission.[1] While Jonathan Edwards—perhaps evangelicalism's greatest theologian—made the Trinity central to his theology, "the ultimate focus [of evangelicalism generally] was the individual, in contrast to the unity-in-diversity of the Trinity."[2] Evangelicals have largely ignored the churchly context of the giving of Scripture and the historical process of the church's interpretation of Scripture. Many evangelicals have tended to place their own interpretations of the Bible above those of the historic tradition, which has privileged the Trinity.[3] But in the wake of the twentieth-century renaissance of Trinitarianism launched by Karl Barth and Karl Rahner, evangelicals are now starting to reclaim the Trinity for their theologies of religions.[4]

---

1. There have been notable exceptions, such as the hymns by the Wesleys and the work of B. B. Warfield.

2. Robert Letham, "The Triune God," in *The Oxford Handbook of Evangelical Theology*, edited by Gerald R. McDermott (New York: Oxford University Press, 2010), 109. On Edwards and the Trinity, see Michael J. McClymond and Gerald R. McDermott, *The Theology of Jonathan Edwards* (New York: Oxford University Press, 2011), 193–206.

3. This is despite the fact that the favorite theologians of many evangelicals—Luther, Calvin, and Owen—placed the Trinity at or near the center of their theological vision.

4. Clark Pinnock made unsystematic but incisive explorations: *A Wideness in God's Mercy: The Finality of Jesus Christ in a World of Religions* (Grand Rapids, MI: Zondervan, 1992); *Flame of Love: A Theology of the Holy Spirit* (Downers Grove, IL: InterVarsity, 1996). Timothy Tennent dipped briefly into Indian Christian reflections: *Christianity at the Religious Roundtable: Evangelicalism in Conversation with Hinduism, Buddhism, and Islam* (Grand Rapids, MI: Baker, 2002), 211–230. Amos Yong sketched a Trinitarian outline while emphasizing the Spirit's work: *Discerning the Spirit(s): A Pentecostal-Charismatic Contribution to Christian Theology of Religions* (Sheffield, UK: Sheffield Academic, 2000); *Beyond the Impasse: Toward a Pneumatological Theology of Religions* (Grand Rapids, MI: Baker, 2003). Veli-Matti Kärkkäinen has helpfully surveyed recent Trinitarian theologies of religions and pointed a way forward: *Trinity and Religious Pluralism: The Doctrine of the Trinity in Christian Theology of Religions* (Aldershot, UK: Ashgate, 2004). George R. Sumner has argued for the "final primacy" of Christ within a Trinitarian framework: *The First and the Last: The Claims*

The Significance of the Trinity for Theology of Religions

It is our contention that this renewed interest in the Trinity must become normative for future reflection on the religions. It is the Trinity that most sharply distinguishes Christian theology from all other views of reality, and it has been misunderstanding and misuse of the Trinity that have produced significant problems in theologies of religions. The Trinity emerged historically from the early church's realization that while God remained God as Father, Jesus came to reveal God as his only Son, and that God remained among believers as the Holy Spirit to show them both the Son and the Father. In other words, it was rooted in the church's recognition that only God knows and reveals God and that the Trinity was the name for this self-revealing God in three persons who work inseparably together.[5] Christian theologies of religions run into problems, as we shall see below, when they marginalize the Trinity or misconstrue the inseparability of the three persons.

The uniqueness of the Christian doctrine of the Trinity becomes clear when it is contrasted with two popular pluralistic perspectives on the religions. On a popular, unsophisticated level, it is not unusual to hear someone declare that once we get beyond the surface differences among the religions, it becomes evident that all religions are really just different ways of worshiping the same God. In the West, this perspective uses "God" as a marker for a generic deity that is understood in different ways in the religions. Something like this has also been widely accepted in Asian cultures but with a less theistic understanding of the ultimate object of religious devotion. In Japan, for example, this sentiment is expressed in a popular saying: "Although the paths up the mountain may vary, from the summit we all see the same moon." In other words, there is a fundamental unity to religions, and the only differences concern nonessential matters.

of Jesus Christ and the Claims of Other Religious Traditions (Grand Rapids, MI: Eerdmans, 2004). Keith E. Johnson has evaluated several theologians of the religions by using Augustine's Trinitarianism: ; *Rethinking the Trinity and Religious Pluralism* (Downers Grove, IL: InterVarsity, 2011). It should be noted that Tennent has produced a missiology shaped explicitly by a Trinitarian model: *Invitation to World Missions: A Trinitarian Missiology for the Twenty-First Century* (Grand Rapids, MI: Kregel, 2010).

5. J. N. D. Kelly, *Early Christian Doctrines* (San Francisco: HarperSanFrancisco, 1978), especially chaps. 4, 5, 10; Larry Hurtado, *Lord Jesus Christ: Devotion to Jesus in Earliest Christianity* (Grand Rapids, MI: Eerdmans, 2003), 349–426.

But in spite of its enormous appeal today, taken literally, this view is obviously untenable. Commenting on this perspective in the West, religious studies scholar Stephen Prothero states:

> This is a lovely sentiment but it is dangerous, disrespectful, and untrue. For more than a generation we have followed scholars and sages down the rabbit hole into a fantasy world in which all gods are one. This wishful thinking is motivated in part by an understandable rejection of the exclusivist missionary view that only you and your kind will make it to heaven or paradise.... But the idea of religious unity is wishful thinking nonetheless, and it has not made the world a safer place. In fact, this naive theological groupthink—call it Godthink—has made the world more dangerous by blinding us to the clashes of religion that threaten us worldwide. It is time we climbed out of the rabbit hole and back to reality.[6]

The religions do not all agree on what is religiously ultimate. Jews, Muslims, and Christians believe in an eternal creator God. Jains and Buddhists deny that there is such a God. Christians believe that God is a Holy Trinity—Father, Son, and Spirit. Muslims deny this. And so on.

But there are more sophisticated versions of pluralism that acknowledge the very real differences among the religions while also maintaining that despite these undeniable differences, the various religions can be regarded as roughly equally true and effective ways of responding to the same religious ultimate. The most influential proposal along these lines is that developed by the British philosopher and theologian John Hick.

Although identifying himself as a Christian, Hick argues that no single religion, including Christianity, is distinctively true or salvific. The religions are all to be regarded as culturally and historically conditioned human responses to "an ultimate ineffable Reality which is the source and ground of everything, and which is such that in so far as the religious traditions are in soteriological alignment with it they are contexts of salvation/liberation." The religions, in other words, "involve different human conceptions of the Real [the religious ultimate], with correspondingly different forms of experience of the Real, and correspondingly different forms of life in response to the Real."[7]

---

6. Stephen Prothero, *God Is Not One: The Eight Rival Religions That Run the World—and Why Their Differences Matter* (New York: HarperCollins, 2010), 2–3.

7. John Hick, *A Christian Theology of Religions: The Rainbow of Faiths* (Louisville, KY: Westminster John Knox, 1995), 27. Hick's model is developed most fully in *An Interpretation of Religion*, 2nd ed. (New Haven, CT: Yale University Press, 2004).

"The Real" is Hick's term for what is postulated as the ultimate reality, the ultimate referent behind particular conceptions of the ultimate in the religions. For Muslims, the ontological ultimate is Allah; for Christians, it is God the Holy Trinity; Hindus speak of Brahman; Buddhists refer to Emptiness or Nirvana; and so on. But in each case, according to Hick, these terms do not denote what is actually the religious ultimate. Rather, these are penultimate symbols or conceptual constructs through which various religious communities understand and thus respond to what is, in fact, religiously ultimate—the Real: "our various religious languages—Buddhist, Christian, Muslim, Hindu...—each refer to a divine phenomenon or configuration of divine phenomena. When we speak of a personal God, with moral attributes and purposes, or when we speak of the non-personal Absolute, Brahman, or of the Dharmakaya, we are speaking of the Real as humanly experienced: that is, as phenomena."[8] In other words, contrary to what Christians claim, God the Holy Trinity is *not* the ontological ultimate; the Trinity is simply a conceptual symbol through which Christians can respond to what is truly ultimate, the Real.

There is a large literature addressing Hick's model, and we cannot pursue it further here.[9] The important point for our purposes, however, is that this is *not* how Christians have traditionally understood the doctrine of the Trinity or how devout followers of other religions understand their respective teachings on the ultimate. Indeed, Hick's proposal is flatly incompatible with orthodox Christian teaching on God. When Christians speak of God as Trinity—Father, Son, and Spirit—they mean that the triune God is the ontological ultimate (that is, ultimate in being), not simply a symbol or concept through which we approach the ineffable Real.

Apostolic Testimony

Before we look at the implications of the Trinity for theology of religions per se, let us scan the apostolic testimony. John suggests repeatedly that Jesus was no independent agent but an emissary sent by his Father: "My food is to do the

---

8. Hick, *An Interpretation of Religion*, 246.

9. See *Problems in the Philosophy of Religion: Critical Studies of the Work of John Hick*, edited by Harold Hewett (London: Macmillan, 1991); Paul Rhodes Eddy, *John Hick's Pluralist Philosophy of World Religions* (Burlington, VT: Ashgate, 2002); *The Philosophical Challenge of Religious Diversity*, edited by Philip L. Quinn and Kevin Meeker (New York: Oxford University Press, 2000); Harold Netland, *Encountering Religious Pluralism* (Downers Grove, IL: InterVarsity, 2001), chap. 7.

will of him who sent me" (4:34); "My teaching is not mine, but his who sent
me" (7:16); "He who sent me is reliable" (8:26); "The one who sent me is with
me" (8:29); "Now I am going to him who sent me" (16:5) (see also 5:24, 6:38,
7:33, 9:4, 12:44–45, 13:20, 15:21). Mark and Matthew show that the Son was sent
as a plenipotentiary with authority that Jews knew was rightfully only God's,
the authority to forgive sins (Mark 2:10) and the authority to be the judge at the
end of the world (Matt. 25:31-46). But not only did the Father send the Son, he
was also *in* the Son and is revealed by the Son: "The Father is in me and I am
in the Father" (John 10:38); "I and the Father are one" (John 10:30); "Whoever
has seen me has seen the Father" (John 14:9). Both Matthew and John assert
that the Father is made known only by the Son because only the Son knows
the Father: "No one knows the Father except the Son and anyone to whom the
Son chooses to reveal him" (Matt. 11:27); "No one has ever seen God; the only
God, who is at the Father's side, he has made him known" (John 1:18). For the
gospel authors, there is no knowledge of God without participation in the
Son's knowledge of the Father.

If the Son reveals the Father, it is knowledge of the Son that enables us to
determine if the Father is present. We shall see below that this has implications for theologies of religions that claim the identity of other gods with the
Triune God. Not only does it suggest the necessity of Christological criteria for
identifying the presence of the Triune God in religious phenomena outside
the church, but it also mandates the absolute centrality for Christian faith
of the life and teachings of the God-man Jesus Christ. It is the story of this
God-man that interprets all other supposed stories of God. And it is this *person* of the God-man—not an idea about him or a notion of deity or a concept
of incarnation—that is the criterion by which we evaluate all other claims to
divine presence. It is the *event* of this person's life, death, and resurrection—
not a Christic principle or transformative experience—that is determinative
in theology of religions. Jesus Christ is not a symbol of something else—not
even God—but the second person of the God whose name is Father, Son, and
Spirit. As Bonhoeffer wrote, only the "facts" of the life and death of Jesus of
Nazareth can tell us who God is. We know of no abstract divinity or human
nature as such; the meaning of humanity and divinity both are found only in
knowing Jesus Christ.[10]

The Son's knowledge is exhaustive knowledge. Because the Father sent the
Son and is in the Son, and Jesus of Nazareth *is* the Son, Jesus contains, as it

---

10. Dietrich Bonhoeffer, *Christ the Center*, translated by Edwin H. Robertson (San
Francisco: HarperOne, 1978), 102–106.

were, all the deity of the Father. "In him *all* the fullness of God was pleased to dwell" (Col. 1:19); "In him the *whole* fullness of deity dwells bodily" (Col. 2:9). The word "bodily" (*somatikōs*) indicates that for the author of Colossians, the incarnate Word contained all of the eternal Word. Not only did Jesus know all of the Father, but in him *was* all of the Father. Furthermore, John intimates that the eternal Word is the crucified Word. When Jesus declares at the Feast of Booths that he will give living water to those who thirst, John adds that "this he said about the Spirit," but at this point, "the Spirit had not been given, because Jesus was not yet glorified" (John 7:39). Readers of John's gospel have known for millennia that in that account, Jesus was glorified on the cross (John 12:23, 13:31–32, 17:5). For John, then, Jesus is the source of the Spirit—but only as the crucified Jesus who is glorified in and through his passion. There is no eternal Word who can be known apart from the crucified Son.[11]

When this crucified Son was resurrected and then ascended to the right hand of the Father (Acts 1:8, 2:33), he sent the Spirit upon the church and especially to its apostles, who he said would be guided by the Spirit "into *all* the truth" (John 16:13). There will never be a time when this truth will be fully understood, but these words claim that the apostolic testimony has no need to be supplemented when it comes to knowledge of God. All the truth about God was entrusted to their testimony; implicitly, there is no truth about God that is not contained in the church's Spirit-led progressive understanding of that testimony. That understanding will no doubt continue to progress, but it will never include assertions that contradict apostolic testimony.[12]

This is another way of saying that the Spirit's teaching will never be untethered from the Son's. For Paul says the Spirit is the "Spirit of Christ" (Rom. 8:9). According to John's gospel, the Spirit was sent by the Son (16:7), the Spirit convicts human beings of their unbelief in the Son (16:9), and the Spirit does not speak on his own authority but only what he hears from the Son

---

11. By this, we do not mean that the crucified Son had flesh before the Incarnation but that we cannot and should not speculate about the eternal Word apart from the only clear manifestation we have been given, when "the Word became flesh and dwelt among us" (John 1:14). Evangelical philosopher Paul Helm, however, goes so far as to say that the eternal Word is and was, in a sense unimaginable to us, *always* incarnate: "Divine Timeless Eternity," in *God and Time*, edited by Gregory E. Ganssle (Downers Grove, IL: InterVarsity, 2000), 28–60.

12. We take *humas* ("you" plural) in John 16:13 to refer *first* to the apostolic community, which seems to mean in this context that the New Testament that this community would produce would contain "all the truth" about God, when read as commentary on the Old Testament. We say "first" because we would affirm the historic church's judgment that the Spirit continued to guide the whole church in its understanding of biblical revelation, so that more and more of "all the truth" would be apprehended.

(16:13).[13] The Spirit does this by taking what is of the Son and declaring it (16:14)—bearing witness about the Son (15:26). The Spirit does not speak for himself because he is not from himself: "But when the Helper comes, whom I will send to you from the Father, the Spirit of truth, who proceeds from the Father, he will bear witness about me" (15:26). Still other aspects of the Spirit's work tie the Spirit to the Son: he conforms believers to the image of the Son (Rom. 8:29) and by virtue of being the Spirit who "raised Jesus from the dead," will also give life to the mortal bodies of believers (Rom. 8:11). Even when working outside the economy of the incarnate Son—namely, among the Old Testament prophets—it was still the "Spirit of Christ" (1 Pet. 1:4).

But it is not only the Spirit and the Son who are inseparable. All three persons mutually indwell one another, so that when any one acts, the other two are also acting in him. John 16:15 epitomizes this coinherence of the Three: "All that the Father has is mine; therefore I said that he [the Spirit] will take what is mine and declare it to you." The Father gives all of himself to the Son; the Spirit takes that "all" and gives it to believers. If the Spirit brings anyone to God, it is only by his taking from the Son what the Father has given to the Son. Paul suggests this happens even when Christ is not known by name; he tells of "our fathers" who were under the cloud and passed through the sea in the wilderness wanderings. They did not know that it was the Messiah, but "they drank from the spiritual Rock that followed them, and the Rock was Christ" (1 Cor. 10:1, 4). As John would have it, they might have thought only of Yahweh leading them, but it was really Christ sent by the Father in and by the Spirit. Therefore, while theologians speak of the economy of the Word and the economy of the Spirit, there is really only one economy for the apostolic authors, especially John's gospel—the Father does all things through the Word by the Holy Spirit.

---

13. We use the masculine pronoun for the Spirit not because it is unproblematic but because there are more problems with the alternatives. While most of the New Testament authors use the Greek neuter pronoun because *pneuma* is neuter, the English translation "it" suggests an impersonality that undermines the biblical emphasis on God's personal nature and risks confusion with, for example, the impersonal *nirguna* Brahman of Hinduism. The female pronoun would follow the grammatical feminine of the Old Testament Hebrew *ruach* and the occasional feminine imagery for God in the Bible (Num. 11:12; Ps. 22:9–10, 71:6, 139:13; Isa. 49:15, 66:9, 13; Matt. 23:37). But it might also pit the femininity of the Spirit against the supposed masculinity of the Father and the Son; it could suggest a female God akin to the goddesses of the ancient Near East, which Israel fiercely resisted; and it could conjure up the specter of a female spirit restraining male aggression, which is alien to the gospels' insistence on triune unity. So we side with John, who in his gospel uses the masculine pronoun for the Spirit.

The Indivisibility of the Trinity

This principle of the inseparability of the divine persons in all divine acts was developed most notably by Saint Augustine in his battles against Arian tendencies in the churches. He was building on the work of earlier pro-Nicene theologians such as Ambrose and Hilary, who stressed common nature, common power, and common operations among the divine persons. Anti-Nicenes (those opposed to the Nicene formula) focused on the distinct activities of each of the divine persons so as to represent the three persons as three different beings, with the Father as a superior being. This obviously undermined the Council of Nicaea's affirmation of the Son as being *homoousios* (same essence or being) with the Father. Augustine agreed with the pro-Nicene theologians that all three persons are involved in the works of creation, providence, and redemption: "Just as Father and Son and Holy Spirit are inseparable, so do they work inseparably."[14] Hence Augustine's rule, *opera Trinitatis ad extra indivisa sunt*: the works of the triune God in the economy of redemptive history are not divided. Even when the Son seemed to be alone in being born to the flesh of Mary, suffering on the cross, and being raised from the dead, the Father was active in all those actions. "The Son indeed, and not the Father, was born of the Virgin Mary; but this birth of the Son, not the Father, from the Virgin Mary was the work of both Father and Son. It was not indeed the Father, but the Son who suffered; yet the suffering of the Son was the work of both Father and Son. It wasn't the Father who rose again, but the Son; yet the resurrection of the Son was the work of both Father and Son."[15] When Jesus said the Father and Son would come to the one who loves him and "make our home with him" (John 14:23), Jesus did not mean that the Spirit would be left out: the Spirit "will not therefore withdraw when the Father and the Son arrive, but will be with them in the same abode for ever; for as matter of fact, neither does he come without them nor they without him....[For] this same three is also one, and there is one substance and godhead of Father, Son and Holy Spirit."[16]

Augustine has been criticized for so emphasizing the common substance of the three that he risked modalism, the notion that there is only one person in God who assumes different modes at different times. Some of these same

---

14. Augustine, *The Trinity*, translated by Edmund Hill (Brooklyn, NY: New City, 1991), 70–71.

15. Augustine, *The Works of Saint Augustine: A Translation for the 21st Century*, Vol. 3.3, *Sermons III (51–94)*, Sermon 52.8, 53–54; cited in Keith E. Johnson, *Rethinking the Trinity*, 117–118.

16. Augustine, *The Trinity*, 83.

critics have noted that the only real distinctions he saw among the three were their relations—namely, that the Father is not the Son but the Father of the Son, the Son is not the Father but the Son of the Father, and the Spirit is the One who proceeds from both Father and Son. But even if Augustine was less than adequate in distinguishing the three persons one from another, his principle of the unity of the divine essence has stood the test of time. As we have shown above, it is exegetically sound. It is also theologically coherent: if "the Lord our God, the Lord is one" (Mark 12:29), it stands to reason that any one of the three persons in that oneness would also involve the presence and activity of the other two in the same oneness. To divide the Trinity by separating the work of one person from the work of the other two is to violate the Trinitarian logic of the gospels, that since each of the persons coinheres in the other two, it is impossible for one person to be separated from the other two.

Dividing the Spirit and the Son

Yet this is what has been happening in some theologies of religions. A number of theologians have pressed to divide the work of the Spirit from that of the Son. The Catholic theologian Raimundo Panikkar, whose mother was a Spanish Roman Catholic and whose father was an Indian Hindu, envisioned "the Spirit pushing the Christian forward beyond what we call 'Christianity,' beyond, I am tempted to add, even the institutional and visible Church." It would be necessary, Panikkar suggested, because Christians tie the Spirit too closely to the historical Jesus: "If we remain attached exclusively to the 'Savior,' to his humanity and his historicity, we block, in a manner of speaking, the coming of the Spirit and thus revert to a stage of exclusive iconolatry."[17] Jacques Dupuis, perhaps the most distinguished Catholic theologian of religions at the end of the twentieth century, asked why, if the Spirit before the Incarnation was at work, the work of the Spirit after the Incarnation would have to be "limited" to the Incarnation. When the Trinitarian Christology model is considered alongside the "enlivening by the Spirit," it is possible to see truth and grace that were "not brought out with the same vigor and clarity in God's revelation and manifestation in Jesus Christ" but that now "represent additional and *autonomous* benefits."[18] In other words, the Spirit

---

17. Raimundo Panikkar, *The Trinity and the Religious Experience of Man* (New York: Orbis, 1973), 57, 58.

18. Jacques Dupuis, S.J., *Christianity and the Religions: From Confrontation to Dialogue* (Maryknoll, NY: Orbis, 2001), 181; Dupuis, *Toward a Christian Theology of Religious Pluralism* (Maryknoll, NY: Orbis, 1997), 388; emphasis added.

could be saying new things in other religions that were not considered by the risen humanity of Jesus Christ that inspired the apostolic authors of the New Testament.

Amos Yong is one of evangelicalism's most prolific theologians of religions. He has made important contributions to theology of disability, Pentecostal understandings of science and politics, and global Pentecostalism more generally.[19] He is also a leading voice in evangelical theology of religions. His treatment of the relation between the economies of the Spirit and the Son is more ambiguous than those of Panikkar and Dupuis. He seems to want to stay within the bounds of Trinitarian orthodoxy, for he affirms that "in consistent Trinitarian fashion, all things have to be seen as the conjunction of Word and Spirit, including both the historical Jesus and the coming Christ, as well as the dynamic presence and activity of God in the world. In this framework, the Spirit is certainly the Spirit of Jesus."[20] Yet at the same time, he wants to get "beyond the impasses that have hindered developments in *theologia religionum*."[21] The chief impasse has been created, he argues, by unnecessarily restricting the economy of the Spirit to that of the Son, so that either the Spirit is considered to be at work only where people already acknowledge the lordship of Jesus Christ, or else the Spirit's presence and work are determined by using Christological criteria. Instead, it should be considered that there is "a distinction between the economy of the Word and Spirit...a relationship-in-autonomy between the two divine missions."[22] In the past, theologians of religions such as Stanley Samartha, Jacques Dupuis, and Paul Knitter have returned, after considering the universal work of the Spirit, "too quickly to Christology."[23] Instead. they should consider the work of Orthodox theologian Georges Khodr, who recognized that non-Christian

---

19. Amos Yong, *The Bible, Disability, and the Church: A New Vision of the People of God* (Grand Rapids, MI, and Cambridge, UK: Eerdmans, 2011); Yong, *The Spirit of Creation: Modern Science and Divine Action in the Pentecostal-Charismatic Imagination, Pentecostal Manifestos 4* (Grand Rapids, MI, and Cambridge, UK: Eerdmans, 2011); Yong, *Who Is the Holy Spirit? A Walk with the Apostles* (Brewster, MA: Paraclete, 2011); Yong, *In the Days of Caesar: Pentecostalism and Political Theology—The Cadbury Lectures 2009*, Sacra Doctrina: Christian Theology for a Postmodern Age Series (Grand Rapids, MI: Eerdmans, 2010); Yong, *Theology and Down Syndrome: Reimagining Disability in Late Modernity* (Waco, TX: Baylor University Press, 2007); Yong, *The Spirit Poured Out on All Flesh: Pentecostalism and the Possibility of Global Theology* (Grand Rapids, MI: Baker, 2005).

20. Yong, *Beyond the Impasse*, 47; see also 187.

21. Ibid.

22. Yong, *Discerning the Spirit(s)*, 70.

23. Ibid.

faiths should be conceived "in pneumatological terms, related but not subordinated to or redefined by the economy of the Word."[24] Khodr realized that if "the Spirit is from the Father *of* the Son, then the economy of the Son in no way limits that of the Spirit."[25] As a result, the Spirit's economy is "larger than that of the Son."[26] In Yong's discussion of Knitter's work, he suggests that "the two economies [of Word and Spirit] are distinct and perhaps autonomous."[27] In his conclusion to *Beyond the Impasse*, Yong reminds his readers that he is "certainly not arguing for a view of the economy of the Spirit as completely sovereign or unrelated to that of the Son" but that he wants "more neutral categories" than Christological ones to discern the presence and activity of the Spirit in world religions.[28] So while Yong does not want to sever the two economies too sharply, he also does not want the economy of the Spirit to be "subordinated" to that of the Word by defining the Spirit's work with Christological criteria.

To be fair, Yong has not used language of "autonomy" since his early work. Yet in his later work, he regularly downplays the usefulness of Christological criteria in discernment, and in a 2012 unpublished paper, he refers to his having wanted to "hold at bay christological categories momentarily in order to explore how pneumatological perspectives might open up other pathways of dialogue and understanding."[29] In 2004, he criticized the use of "Christian (e.g., biblical) criteria" in discernment of the Spirit in other religions because these criteria impose "our own categories on religious others who . . . have their own self-understandings."[30] In 2007, Yong criticized the "imperialist posture

---

24. Ibid., 62.

25. Yong, *Beyond the Impasse*, 87.

26. Ibid., 91.

27. Ibid., 85.

28. Ibid., 186.

29. Amos Yong, "The Holy Spirit, the Middle Way, and the Religions: A Pentecostal Inquiry in a Pluralistic World," annual missions lecture, Catholic Theological Union, March 5, 2012, copy loaned by author. This has now been published in *Evangelical Interfaith Dialogue* at http://cms.fuller.edu/EIFD/issues/Spring_2012/The_Holy_Spirit,_the_Middle_Way,_and_the_Religions.aspx, where he writes: "I affirm that ultimately for Christians, the work of the Spirit is discerned through that of the incarnational and cruciform work of the Son, and that Christian judgments regarding other faiths always be informed by these commitments. The question is whether or not the lack of explicit christological markers—which is what would be expected in other faiths—means that the Holy Spirit of Jesus is entirely absent even if the fruits of the Spirit are present" (12–13).

30. Amos Yong, "The Holy Spirit and the World Religions: On the Christian Discernment of Spirit(s) 'after' Buddhism," *Buddhist-Christian Studies* 24 (2004): 192.

of the missionaries who brought a 'better religion'" and "reduced other faiths to a secondary status of being fulfilled by Christ." Yong is no doubt wanting missionaries and other Christians engaged in interreligious dialogue to listen sympathetically to other religious perspectives, but he also suggests that the use of Christological categories and assumption of Christian dogmatic superiority are somehow illegitimate.[31] We will take up the question of criteria below.

Dividing Jesus from the Christ and the Eternal Word

If there have been efforts to divide the work of the Spirit from that of the Son among theologians of the religions, there have been similar attempts to divide the work of Jesus from that of the Christ or the eternal Word. Once again, Panikkar and Dupuis have led the way. Panikkar became convinced that Jesus was simply one manifestation of the cosmic Christ, the "Principle, Being, Logos or Christ that other religious traditions call by a variety of names and to which they attach a wide range of ideas." So when he called "this link between the finite and the infinite by the name Christ," he said he was "not presupposing its identification with Jesus of Nazareth."[32] Dupuis agreed that the man Jesus could not exhaust the meaning or work of the cosmic Christ or eternal Word: "The working of the Word goes beyond the limits which mark the working presence of the humanity of Jesus even in his glorified state, just as the person of the Word goes beyond the human being of Jesus Christ, notwithstanding the 'hypostatic union,' that is, the union in the person."[33] This must be the case, Dupuis argues, because Jesus' human consciousness was limited (because, for example, Jesus said he did not know when the Son of Man would return; Matt. 24:36) and therefore did not exhaust the divine mystery. So the revelation in Jesus Christ was not "exhaustive" of the divine mystery.[34] According to this logic, since Jesus was human, the eternal Word contains more than the incarnate Word, and the cosmic Christ is more extensive than the incarnate Christ.[35] S. Mark Heim draws a similar distinction between Jesus of Nazareth and the larger divine reality: "The Trinity teaches

---

31. Amos Yong, "The Spirit, Christian Practices, and the Religions: Theology of Religions in Pentecostal and Pneumatological Perspective," *Asbury Journal* 62 (2007): 16.

32. Panikkar, *The Trinity*, 53.

33. Dupuis, *Christianity and the Religions*, 160.

34. Ibid., 88, 22.

35. Dupuis, *Toward a Christian Theology*, 298.

us that Jesus Christ cannot be an exhaustive or exclusive source for knowledge of God [or] the exhaustive and exclusive act of God to save us."[36]

Paul Knitter also draws a sharp distinction between God's self-revelation in Jesus and God's broader revelatory activity. He claims that "it is not necessary to proclaim God's revelation in Jesus as *full, definitive,* or *unsurpassable....* In Jesus we do not possess a full revelation, as if he exhausted all the truth that God has to reveal." Knitter states: "To identify the Infinite with anything finite, to contain and limit the Divine to any one human form or mediation—has traditionally and biblically been called idolatry." Therefore, Knitter concludes that even in the incarnate Word, we do not have a definitive criterion for truth: "Nor do we boast a *definitive* Word of God in Jesus, as if there could be no other norms for divine truth outside of him."[37]

Panikkar, Dupuis, and Knitter reflect a trend in modern theology to take Enlightenment universalism more seriously than Trinitarian particularity. Dupuis illustrates this trend when he proposes, "The other religious traditions represent particular realizations of a universal process, which has become preeminently concrete in Jesus Christ."[38] This is a way of thinking that goes back to Kant, Hegel, and Schleiermacher, for whom Jesus was the prime *example* of a process that does not logically require the particularities of the historical Jesus. To make the historical Jesus necessary to salvation would violate the fundamental Enlightenment axiom that ultimate meaning must be expressed in general but not particular terms. As Lessing famously put it, "Accidental truths of history can never become the proof of necessary truths of reason."[39]

The problem for the Enlightenment, and perhaps for Panikkar and Dupuis, is that Jesus *was* one of the "accidents of history." The particularities of his life, death, and resurrection were divinely intended, of course, but they were not accessible to humanity universally. This could explain why neither Panikkar nor Dupuis ever mentions atonement by the cross, let alone suggest its

---

36. S. Mark Heim, *The Depth of the Riches: A Trinitarian Theology of Religious Ends* (Grand Rapids, MI: Eerdmans, 2001), 134.

37. Paul F. Knitter, "Five Theses on the Uniqueness of Jesus," in *The Uniqueness of Jesus: A Dialogue with Paul F. Knitter,* edited by Leonard Swidler and Paul Mojzes (Maryknoll, NY: Orbis, 1997), 7–8; emphasis in original.

38. Dupuis, *Christianity and the Religions,* 193.

39. Gotthold Ephraim Lessing, "The Proof of the Spirit and of Power," in *Lessing's Theological Writings,* edited by Henry Chadwick (London: Adam and Charles Black, 1956), 53. On this way of thinking, see Bruce Marshall, *Christology in Conflict: The Identity of a Savior in Rahner and Barth* (Oxford, UK: Blackwell, 1987), 1–14.

necessity for salvation. For the cross was another particular, occurring at a certain time and place in history, not accessible to the knowledge of all. Lessing's rule for universality may also explain why Panikkar, Dupuis, and Heim consider Jesus' human consciousness a problem for his universality. If the nature of the human predicament is insufficient knowledge of God's mystery, and salvation therefore comes by revelation that provides information about God that we can follow—as Panikkar, Dupuis, and others suggest—then Jesus' limited human consciousness is a problem. But if the human predicament is alienation from God because of sin, and salvation means reconciliation with God, then Jesus' limited consciousness is, in fact, our guarantee that God has taken to himself *our* sinful humanity with all its limitations in exchange for giving us his righteousness and Spirit. This reveals not merely information *about* God but God's own action to include sinners in his inner Trinitarian life. Thus Jesus's limited consciousness demonstrates not *partial* revelation of the divine mystery but the *full* picture of what salvation entails.

All of these theologians reason that since Jesus' consciousness was limited, he could not have filled the fullness of the eternal or cosmic Christ. But why need the first clause lead to the second? According to the doctrine of the *communicatio idiomatum* (sharing of divine and human attributes by the person of Christ), the divine person of the Logos in the Incarnation had available to himself both his limited human nature and the divine omniscience of the divine nature, even while choosing at times to restrict himself to the former. That did not prevent the Logos from inspiring apostolic reflection on the meaning of the Incarnation, so that John could say that the Holy Spirit made available to the apostles the "entire truth" (16:13), and the writer to the Colossians could declare that in Jesus Christ are hidden "*all* the treasures of wisdom and knowledge" (2:3). Dupuis asserts that the Word "is never totally contained in any historical manifestation," yet Colossians pronounces that "in Christ the fullness of the Deity lives in bodily form" (2:9).[40] The Trinitarian incarnation in one person did not prevent the other two from coinherence in the fullest way imaginable.

These theologians also separate Jesus' redemption on the cross from the work of the Christ in other religions. This is similar to the Nestorian mistake of separating the eternal Logos from the human Jesus, following Nestorius's rejection of *Theotokos* (God-bearing) as a title for Mary. While it is true that there is a distinction between the preincarnate Word and the Word incarnate in Jesus of Nazareth (John 1:1–3, 14), Karl Barth rightly warned that talk

---

40. Dupuis, *Christianity and the Religions*, 159.

of a *logos asarkos* (the Word without flesh) in abstraction from the incarnate Word is speculation about "some image of God which we have made for ourselves.... Like Godhead abstracted from its revelation and acts, it would necessarily be an empty concept which we would then, of course, feel obliged to fill with all kinds of contents of our own arbitrary invention."[41] To imagine that there is another Christ behind or beyond the Christ who was also Jesus invites speculation about some other Christ who might take a shape different from the incarnate Christ of the gospels. The only God we know is that revealed in Jesus of Nazareth; and we know that the Lamb was slain "from the foundation of the world" (Rev. 13:8).

Separating the Father from the Son

Our discussion thus far has focused on those who have separated the Son from the Spirit or Jesus from the Word or Christ. But there is a coordinate problem of minimizing the Christian Trinitarian understanding of God by separating the Father from the Son. In interreligious dialogue with other monotheistic traditions, for example, it is not unusual for Christian theologians to emphasize the divine unity and to focus on commonalities across monotheistic traditions, thereby ignoring or minimizing Christian Trinitarian distinctives.

Questions about commonalities across monotheistic traditions are part of the complex debate over continuity and discontinuity between the Christian faith and other religious traditions. Are there significant similarities between the beliefs and practices of biblical Christianity and those of other religions? Or is there radical discontinuity between what Christians profess and what we see in other religions? We touched on these questions in chapter 1. The issues relate to matters such as how we approach translation of the Bible into various languages where terms from indigenous religious traditions are often unavoidable, contextualization of the Christian gospel in local settings, and formulation of a theological understanding of God's presence and activity among all peoples, including adherents of other religions. Evangelicals have generally been careful to emphasize the differences between Christianity and other religions, but they have been less willing to acknowledge or build on similarities. Yet, as careful study of the religions indicates, there are some striking similarities along with obvious differences.

---

41. Karl Barth, *Church Dogmatics*, 4:1, translated by G. W. Bromiley and T. F. Torrance (Peabody, MA: Hendrickson, 2010), 52.

To what extent are Christian understandings of God similar to conceptions of the religious ultimate in other religious traditions? Although most would acknowledge that the Christian understanding of God is significantly different from, say, the view of *nirguna* Brahman in Advaita Vedanta Hinduism or nirvana in Buddhism or the kami in Shinto, the matter becomes more complicated—and controversial—when we consider monotheistic traditions such as Islam. Relations between Christians and Muslims have been uneasy ever since the time of Muhammad in the seventh century, but following the tragic attacks on New York and Washington on September 11, 2001, perceptions of Muslims among Western Christians have become especially negative.[42] Ongoing violence between Christians and Muslims in Nigeria, Sudan, Indonesia, and elsewhere has exacerbated tensions between the two faiths.[43] Theological issues concerning the religions are often conflated with social and political matters, making dispassionate analysis difficult.

The matter of commonalities and differences is often expressed in terms of the following question: Do Muslims and Christians worship the same God? The question as it stands is highly ambiguous and can be understood in a variety of ways. It could be taken to mean any of the following: Do Christians and Muslims agree that everything apart from the creator was created by an eternal creator God? Do Christians and Muslims agree on their respective understandings of the nature and activity of God? Do Christians and Muslims share some basic moral values and commitments? Can Muslims be saved by acting appropriately on the core Islamic teachings, apart from responding in faith to the gospel of Jesus Christ? Can one be an authentic disciple of Jesus ('Isa) while continuing to identify as a Muslim and participate in Islamic institutions and rituals? Should Arabic-speaking followers of Jesus today use "Allah" to refer to the God of the Bible? And so on. But these are very different questions that might be answered quite differently by different theologians within the broader orthodox Christian community.[44]

---

42. On Christian–Muslim relations historically, see William Montgomery Watt, *Muslim–Christian Encounters: Perceptions and Misperceptions* (London: Routledge, 1991); Alan G. Jamieson, *Faith and Sword: A Short History of Christian–Muslim Conflict* (London: Reaktion, 2006). On American Christians and Islam, see Thomas S. Kidd, *American Christians and Islam: Evangelical Culture and Muslims, from the Colonial Period to the Age of Terrorism* (Princeton, NJ: Princeton University Press, 2009).

43. For a thoughtful, but troubling, look at Christian–Muslim tensions in these areas, see Eliza Griswold, *The Tenth Parallel: Dispatches from the Fault Line between Christianity and Islam* (New York: Farrar, Strauss, and Giroux, 2010).

44. By "orthodox," we mean those believers who affirm the content, if not all the precise language, of the early creeds.

Yale theologian Miroslav Volf, an evangelical, has produced an impressive array of theological works including a creative and ecumenical ecclesiology grounded solidly in the doctrine of the Trinity.[45] More recently, he has become actively involved in dialogues with Muslims and in working to improve relations between Christians and Muslims. As part of a broader effort to counter conflict rooted in religious differences, Volf has taken on the question of whether Muslims and Christians worship the same God. In *Allah: A Christian Response*, Volf argues forcefully that Christians and Muslims do indeed "worship one and the same God, the only God."[46] He is not suggesting that Christians and Muslims agree on what the one God is like or that they simply are using different language to speak of the same reality.

To be precise, the issue is not whether Muslims and Christians have exactly the same beliefs about the one God they worship. Clearly, the answer is that they do not. Nobody disputes this. Even among themselves, Christians disagree. How would they then not disagree with Muslims? The same is also true of Muslims. Muslim and Christian beliefs about God significantly diverge at points. The issue is, rather, this question: Is the object of Christians' and Muslims' faith and love the same?[47]

Volf's answer is that despite significant differences, there is sufficient commonality among beliefs that we can answer in the affirmative.

As noted earlier, evangelicals are often reluctant to acknowledge commonalities between the Christian faith and other traditions. So Volf is to be applauded for his willingness to explore similarities between Islam and Christian faith and to build on this for more irenic relations between Christians and Muslims. Evangelicals should support efforts to establish trust and cordial relations between Christians and Muslims. Volf's *Allah* is a thoughtful and rich discussion of some difficult issues, and there is much in it with which we heartily agree. The manner in which Volf frames some of the issues, however, and the evidence he adduces for his conclusion are, in our judgment, problematic. As a result, his basic conclusion is questionable.

Although we agree with Volf that Christians should do all they can to promote better understanding and more irenic relations between Christians and Muslims, he draws an unhelpful link between theological agreement and peaceful relations. Volf claims that only if Christians acknowledge significant

45. Miroslav Volf, *After Our Likeness: The Church as the Image of the Trinity* (Grand Rapids, MI: Eerdmans, 1998), especially 191–220.

46. Miroslav Volf, *Allah: A Christian Response* (San Francisco: HarperOne, 2011), 14.

47. Ibid., 33.

common ground theologically between Muslims and Christians in their respective conceptions of God will they be able to avoid conflict: "Muslims and Christians will be able to live in peace with one another only if (1) the identities of each religious group are respected and given room for free expression, and (2) there are significant overlaps in the ultimate values that orient the lives of people in these communities. These two conditions will be met only if the God of the Bible and the God of the Qur'an turn out to embody overlapping ultimate values, that is, if Muslims and Christians, both monotheists, turn out to have 'a common God.' "[48] Volf insists that "the gaping chasm between Muslims and Christians will widen if it turns out that each community worships a profoundly different God."[49]

Where there is agreement between Muslims and Christians, this should be clearly acknowledged. And we agree with Volf that there are some significant commonalities between Muslim and Christian understandings of God. But surely it is an unhelpful overstatement to claim that peaceful coexistence between Christians and Muslims is possible only if both sides agree that they worship "a common God." The tensions between the two are rooted not simply in theological disagreement but also in centuries of social, ethnic, political, and military conflicts, and theological agreement will not necessarily eradicate these other sources of antagonism. Moreover, Volf's claim presupposes that different communities cannot live together harmoniously unless they agree on their basic views and commitments. But this is implausible. Does Volf mean to suggest that Christians and Buddhists—who deny the reality of a creator God—cannot live together without strife? Should we not rather expect that Christians, animists, polytheists, and atheists can all live together peacefully despite widely different understandings of the universe and the religious ultimate?

Volf correctly asserts that there are some significant similarities between Muslim and Christian understandings of God. In sum, he argues, Muslims and Christians agree on the following six claims about God:

1. There is only one God, the one and only divine being.
2. God created everything that is not God.
3. God is radically different from everything that is not God.
4. God is good.

---

48. Ibid., 8–9.

49. Ibid., 35.

5. God commands that we love God with our whole being.
6. God commands that we love our neighbors as ourselves.[50]

Many will acknowledge significant commonality with respect to the first three claims and similarity in the fourth. By definition, there can be only one eternal creator who creates everything else apart from the creator. Therefore, to the extent that Muslims are referring to the one creator, the only God who exists, of course, Christians and Muslims are referring to the same God. Thus, Lamin Sanneh states, "If you accept, as Muslims and Christians do, that there is only one God, then it seems imperative to say the God of one religion is none other than the God of the other."[51] But as evangelical Islamicist Dudley Woodberry observes, "In comparing Muslim and Christian beliefs it is helpful to distinguish between (1) the Being to whom we refer and (2) what we understand about the character and actions of that Being in the two faiths." Woodberry goes on to say: "As monotheists we both refer to the One and Only Creator God, but what we understand about the character and actions of God are significantly different."[52] So while Christians and Muslims will both affirm the first three claims wholeheartedly, we will see below in our discussion of love that God's goodness is understood differently by Muslims and Christians. There is similarity here, but there are perhaps even more important differences.

Volf's final two claims are more problematic. Yet these final claims are important for Volf, since they "sum up the principal commands of God," and if indeed they are common to Christians and Muslims, this further reinforces the conclusion that they worship a "common God."[53] Volf says that if Christians are to determine whether "the God whose final self-expression is found in the life and teachings of Jesus Christ [is] the same God as the God of the Qur'an," they should compare "specific but overlapping convictions about God found in the holy books of Christians and Muslims."[54] If they find that descriptions of the object of worship are "sufficiently similar," Christians can

---

50. Ibid., 110.

51. Lamin Sanneh, "Do Christians and Muslims Worship the Same God?" *Christian Century* (May 4, 2004): 35.

52. J. Dudley Woodberry, "Do Christians and Muslims Worship the Same God?" *Christian Century* (May 18, 2004): 36.

53. Volf, *Allah*, 110.

54. Ibid., 36, 98.

assume that "the object of worship is the same."[55] Most telling, he avers, are commands in the holy books: "If what God is said to command in the Bible were similar to what God is said to command in the Qur'an, then this would suggest that the character of God is similar and that Muslims and Christians have a common God."[56]

Volf thus focuses on the two great commandments of the Bible, love for God "with our whole being" and love for neighbor "as ourselves," and argues that Islam, just like Christianity, makes these commands central to worship of God.[57] In our view, however, Volf's contention is not supported by the evidence.[58] For example, his evidence for the claim that Islam teaches the first commandment—that we are to love God with our whole being—is remarkably scanty, and odd at that. He proffers only one phrase from one verse in the Qur'an—"God, One and Only" (39:45)—for support, explaining that "once you embrace the belief in the one true God and know what you are talking about when you say 'God,' you've bought into the commitment to love God with your whole being."[59] Perhaps Volf was reduced to this one phrase because our love for God is never commanded by the Qur'an and is rarely even mentioned. Only three verses appear to use unambiguously what translators render as "love" in the human response to God (2:165, 3:31, 5:54), and two more may also do so, depending on how the Arabic is translated (2:177, 76:8).[60] Yet none of these verses *commands* love—they merely describe a relation to Allah—and they are at most five out of six thousand verses.

Even Muslim scholars recognize that none of these five verses constitutes a command to love God. In his 1960 study, *God of Justice*, Daud Rahbar insisted that

the Qur'an never enjoins love for God. This is because God Himself loves only the strictly pious. To love God one must presuppose that God

---

55. Ibid., 96.

56. Ibid., 103.

57. Ibid., 110.

58. We are grateful to Gordon Nickel for conversation with him about these subjects and for his scholarship on some of these issues.

59. Volf, *Allah*, 104. Volf's translations of the Qur'an are from the English translation of Addullah Yusuf Ali.

60. See Gordon Nickel, "The Language of Love in Qur'an and Gospel," in *Sacred Text: Explorations in Lexicography*, edited by Juan Pedro Monferrer-Sala and Angel Urban (Frankfurt am Main: Peter Lang, 2009), 232.

is reciprocating the sentiment. And to presuppose that is to presume that one is perfectly pious. Such presumption the Qur'an never allows. Even the most virtuous men as prophets are constantly reminded that they are sinful creatures who must ask forgiveness of [the] smallest sins whether they are aware of them or not. Side by side with such a conception of God's unrelaxing justice[,] love for God would certainly be out of place. It is therefore very rarely that the subject of human love for God is touched on at all in the Qur'an.[61]

So, according to Rahbar and others, even if the Qur'an *mentions* love for God, it never *commands* it. Instead of love, fear of God is commanded by the Qur'an. A Muslim when he wrote this book, Rahbar argued that the central theme of the Qur'an is God's justice, and its most common exhortation is to "guard yourselves fearfully against God's wrath."[62] Norman Anderson, who for many years was a specialist in Islamic law at the University of London, concurred with this assessment: while the Bible presents God as a father or shepherd or lover to whom one returns love, "in Islam, by contrast, the constant reference is to God as sovereign Lord (*Rabb*), and man as his servant or slave (*'abd*)."[63]

If love for God is rarely mentioned and never commanded in the Qur'an, it is nevertheless important for the Sufi tradition. Joseph Lumbard has traced the development of the concept from the second through the sixth centuries of Islamic history, arguing that "love has been an integral component of Sufism from the second century AH [Hijrah year] until today."[64] Volf draws heavily on the Sufi tradition within Islam to make his case for the importance of these two love commandments and thus for similarity in "character" between the Islamic Allah and the God of the Bible.[65] For evidence of this, Volf cites the

61. Daud Rahbar, *God of Justice: A Study in the Ethical Doctrine of the Qur'an* (Leiden: Brill, 1960), 180.

62. Ibid., xiii, 5, 180, 181–183, 223, 225.

63. Norman Anderson, *God's Law and God's Love* (London: Collins, 1980), 98.

64. Joseph B. Lumbard, "From Ḥubb to 'Ishq: The Development of Love in Early Sufism," *Journal of Islamic Studies* 18, no. 3 (2007): 345.

65. In using the Arabic term *Allah* to refer to God as understood in Islam and the English term *God* to refer to God as understood in Christianity, we are not suggesting that *Allah* cannot be used of the Christian deity or that *God* cannot be used to refer to non-Christian understandings of deity. *Allah* was used by Arabic-speaking Christians before the time of Muhammad, and continues to be used today, to refer to the Christian God. Arabic translations of the Bible continue to use *Allah* to translate Hebrew and Greek terms for deity.

work of Sufi theologian Abu Hamīd al-Ghazāli (d. A.D. 1111), who he says is the "paradigmatic" Muslim and therefore representative of "the normative mainstream" of Islam.[66]

But there are problems with this use of Sufism. First, many Muslims over the centuries have denounced Sufism as a departure from orthodoxy, so it is strange to appeal to the Sufi tradition in support of mainstream Islamic teachings.[67] Furthermore, the Sufi understanding of love is different from what most Christians presume about love for God and God's love for humanity. Lumbard reports that in al-Ghazāli, love between the Muslim and God is no longer a duality but a unity in which the individuality of the human is annihilated.[68] According to another historian of Sufism, the concept "of God's love as pursuing the soul, a conception which had reached its highest development in the Christian doctrine of Redemption, was impossible to the Sufis" because for Muslims, God's transcendence meant he would not have "feelings akin to their own."[69] One of the most famous early Sufis was Rābiʿa al-'Adawiyya al-Qaysiyya (d. A.D. 801), who wrote of her love for God but said little or nothing of his love for her.[70] More recently, Murad Wilfried Hofmann has argued that "a love of God for His creation comparable to the love human beings are capable of…must be ruled out as incompatible with the very nature of God as sublime and totally self-sufficient." Hofmann, a convert to Islam, suggests that any talk of "God's love" inevitably "humanizes" and therefore distorts what is transcendent.[71]

Similarly, the English *God* is used to refer to non-Christian understandings of deity as in "Spinoza's God" or "the God of deism."

66. Volf, *Allah*, 12, 103.

67. Nickel, "The Language of Love," 241. Alluding to disputes within Islam over Sufism, Daniel Brown points out that in the modern period, Muslim reformers, "anxious for a scapegoat for the apparent weakness of Islam vis-à-vis the West, focused on Sufism as the root of passivity and conservatism in Muslim religious culture": *A New Introduction to Islam* (Malden, MA, and Oxford, UK: Blackwell, 2004), 173.

68. Lumbard, "From *Ḥubb* to *ʿIshq*," 351.

69. Margaret Smith, *Rābiʿa the Mystic and Her Fellow Saints in Islām* (Cambridge, UK: Cambridge University Press, 1924), 92.

70. Ibid., 101; see also Nickel, "The Language of Love," 246.

71. Murad Wilfried Hofmann, "Differences between the Muslim and Christian Concepts of Divine Love," 14th General Conference, Royal Aal al-Bayt Institute for Islamic Thought, September 4–7, 2007, Amman, Jordan, 5–6. http://www.bismikaallahuma.org/archives/2008/differences-between-the-muslim-and-christian-concepts-of-divine-love/.

According to both Sufi and non-Sufi Muslims, God does not have unconditional love for humans generally. Rahbar writes, "Unqualified Divine Love for mankind is an idea completely alien to the Qur'an."[72] God's love is conditional, expressed only toward those who do righteous deeds. The American Islamicist Frederick Denny agrees with Rahbar about the conditional character of the Islamic God's regard for humanity. He cites the Qur'anic verses 19:96 ("On those who believe and work deeds of righteousness") and 5:54 ("Soon Allah will produce a people whom he will love as they will love him") as examples of conditional love.[73] Denny warns that God's mercy, which is offered to all, should not be confused with love, which is offered "only to select ones."[74]

In short, the God of the Qur'an never commands his human creatures to love him. Sufis have a long tradition of recommending love for God, but their status as "normative mainstream" in Islam is debatable, and their conceptions of love for God—not to mention the absence of a sense of his love for humanity--are significantly different from Christian conceptions.

But what of Volf's second claim about the Islamic God's principal commands, that Allah commands love for neighbor as oneself? For evidence to support this claim, Volf goes not to the Qur'an but to the Hadith, written records of oral tradition about the sayings and deeds of Muhammad.[75] Volf concedes that Muslim sacred texts do not affirm love for enemies but rests his claim for Muslim neighbor-love on the oral tradition (Hadith) of Muhammad's saying, "None of you has faith until you love for your neighbor what you love for yourself."[76]

Once again, there are problems. The first is that the Qur'an contains repeated admonitions to Muslim believers not to make friends with non-Muslims. For example, 3:118 reads, "O believers, do not take as close friends other than your own people." Similar warnings include 58:22 and 60:1. In the *Encyclopedia of the Qur'an*, Denis Gril observes that "love or friendship between human beings is not fully recognized by the Qur'an unless confirmed by faith." Instead, there is conditional love: "One can truly love only

---

72. Rahbar, *God of Justice*, 172.

73. Frederick M. Denny, "The Problem of Salvation in the Qur'an: Key Terms and Concepts," in *In Quest of an Islamic Humanism: Arabic and Islamic Studies in Memory of Mohamed al-Nowaihi*, edited by A. H. Green (Cairo: American University Press, 1984), 199–200.

74. Ibid., 199.

75. Volf, *Allah*, 105.

76. Ibid., 108, 105.

believers, since love for unbelievers separates one from God and attracts one toward this world.... Adopting unbelievers as friends or allies ... is equivalent to lining up on the side of the enemies of God."[77] This is rather different from the command of Jesus to his disciples to love even their enemies (Matt. 5:43–48). Another difficulty is that, as we have already noted, there simply is no command to love one's neighbor in the Qur'an. So one can talk about love for neighbor in the Islamic *tradition* but not as something commanded by the God of the Qur'an.

We have examined in some detail Volf's claim that Islam and Christianity both teach our obligation to love God with our entire being and to love our neighbors as ourselves. We have seen that there are good reasons to believe that such obligations are not clear in the Qur'an or mainstream Islamic teaching. It is also unclear that Christians and Muslims agree in any unqualified way that God is "good" (Volf's fourth claim). For Christians, God's goodness is understood in terms of his love. Volf says rightly that "love *is* the divinity of God, and that's why only the absolute power of love deserves to be called divine."[78] Yet the Islamic God is never said to *be* love, as the Christian God is (1 John 4:16). The Allah of the Qur'an never commands his creatures to love him, and the Islamic conception of love for neighbor is different from the Christian idea. It is never commanded as such, it is mostly limited to love for other Muslims, and the enemy is not considered a neighbor.

But even if we were to reject these claims to commonality between the two faiths and recognize that his fourth claim about God's being "good" is also problematic because of the two religions' differences on love, we must acknowledge that Volf's first three claims do indicate areas of commonality. Does this then mean that we should conclude that Muslims and Christians "worship the same God"?

At one level, of course, we have to say yes, because as monotheists, we all agree there is only one God. Ontologically, there can be only one eternal creator God. But the question that Volf asks is whether Qur'anic descriptions of God are "sufficiently similar" to biblical descriptions of God, and here we must qualify our initial positive answer.

Christians and Muslims agree that there is an eternal creator God, and, as Volf notes, there is substantial agreement on some of the attributes of God (omnipotence and omniscience, etc.). But in other respects, Muslims and

---

77. Denis Gril, "Love and Affection," in *Encyclopedia of the Qur'an* edited by Jane Dammen McAuliffe (Leiden: Brill, 2003), 234, 235.

78. Volf, *Allah*, 101.

Christians clearly disagree on what this one creator God is like, and the major disagreement concerns the Christian doctrine of the Trinity with its assertion of the deity of Jesus Christ. Volf is fully aware of this difference, and he accepts the doctrine of the Trinity as an essential component of Christian faith: "The doctrine of the Trinity is central to the Christian account of God and to the Christian faith as a whole, not an optional extra. Take away the Trinitarian nature of God, and the Christian belief about Christ as the incarnation of God collapses and, with it, the whole Christian faith."[79]

There is no question that the Qur'an has been understood as rejecting the idea that Jesus Christ is divine, and there are passages that are usually taken as repudiations of the doctrine of the Trinity (see 4:171; 5:17, 109–119; 9:30–31; 23:93; 112:1–4). Certainly, most Muslims and Christians today think that the Christian teachings on the deity of Jesus Christ and the Trinity are incompatible with what the Qur'an affirms. Does this not make it impossible to claim that Christians and Muslims worship the same God? Not necessarily, according to Volf. He argues that if "we have other good reasons to believe that Muslims have a common God with Christians, then their denial of the Trinity doesn't provide sufficient grounds to say that Muslims don't believe in the same God." In rejecting the Trinity, Muslims "are misunderstanding the true nature of God."[80] Moreover, Volf maintains that what is rejected in the Qur'an is not the orthodox Christian teaching on the Trinity but rather certain aberrant, heretical views circulating at the time of Muhammad. He argues that "the rejections of the 'Trinity' in the Qur'an do not refer to normative Christian understanding of God's threeness, and that the Christian doctrine of the Trinity does not call into question God's oneness as expressed in Muslims' most basic belief that there is 'no god but God.' What the Qur'an may be targeting is misconceptions about God's nature held by misguided Christians."[81]

A number of scholars agree with Volf that what is rejected in the Qur'an seems to be a variety of heretical views common among some Christian communities at the time. Geoffrey Parrinder, for example, states: "The Qur'an denies Christian heresies of Adoption, Patripassianism, and Mariolatry. But it affirms the Unity, which is at the basis of trinitarian doctrine."[82] Similarly,

---

79. Ibid., 145.

80. Ibid.

81. Ibid., 143.

82. Geoffrey Parrinder, *Jesus in the Qur'an* (New York: Oxford University Press, 1977), 137.

Timothy Tennent notes that "some objections [to the doctrine of the Trinity] are based on a fundamental misunderstanding of what the Christian doctrine actually teaches."[83] Surah 5:116, for example, seems to assume that Christians believe that Mary, the mother of Jesus, is one of the three members of the Trinity.

But rejection of the Trinity by Muslims cannot be explained simply as a result of misunderstandings. For even when common misunderstandings are clarified, it is not unusual for Muslims to insist that the Christian belief in Father, Son, and Holy Spirit as God compromises the unity of God. At the heart of the dispute is the question of the deity of Jesus Christ.[84] Lamin Sanneh brings us to the heart of the matter: "Muslims and Christians agree on the great subject that God exists and that God is one. They disagree, however, about the predicates they use of God. Much of the Christian language about God affirms Jesus as God in self-revelation, and much of the Muslim language about God seeks exception to that Christian claim."[85]

In light of the significance of the doctrine of the Trinity for Christian faith, Volf's claim that denial of the doctrine by Muslims need not imply that Muslims and Christians do not worship the same God is problematic. As is by now apparent, the question itself needs careful clarification and cannot be given a simple yes or no answer. The relations among Father, Son, and Holy Spirit are integral to the Christian understanding of God, so that the doctrine is not simply a curious abstraction that can be set aside. The Trinitarian relations also have implications for our understanding of God as love, which is central to Volf's discussion. The Trinitarian rule (*opera Trinitatis ad extra indivisa sunt*) reminds us that the Father's works are not to be divided from the Son's. The Son helps identify the character of the Father, for the Father's character is revealed by the Son: "Whoever has seen me has seen the Father" (John 14:9). If the Son told his disciples that God loved the world (John 3:16), that they should love God with all their hearts (Matt. 22:37), and that they should love everyone including their enemies (Matt. 5:44), we can infer that the Father has said and commanded the same.

---

83. Timothy C. Tennent, *Christianity at the Religious Roundtable* (Grand Rapids, MI: Baker, 2002), 153–154. See also Kenneth Cragg, "Islam and Incarnation," in *Truth and Dialogue in World Religions,* edited by John H. Hick (Philadelphia: Westminster, 1974), 126–139; Cragg, *The Call of the Minaret,* 3rd ed. (Oxford, UK: Oneworld, 1985), 232–235, 278–289.

84. See Kenneth Cragg, *Jesus and the Muslim: An Exploration* (Oxford, UK: Oneworld, 1999); Parrinder, *Jesus in the Qur'an*; Neal Robinson, *Christ in Islam and Christianity* (Albany, NY: State University of New York, 1991).

85. Sanneh, "Do Christians and Muslims Worship the Same God?" 35.

Hence, we conclude with Sanneh that the question of whether Christians and Muslims worship the same God "def[ies] a simple dismissal or acceptance of the claim."[86] Woodberry rightly points out, "Christians, Muslims and Jews as monotheists refer to the same Being when they refer to God—the Creator God of Abraham, Ishmael, Isaac, and Jacob. But in significant ways they do not have the same understanding about him, even though they also agree in significant ways."[87] In fact, the Christian teaching on the Son transforms even the most basic predicates ascribed to God and the Father of Jesus. For example, both Christians and Muslims say that God is one. But while Muslims insist that God is numerically one without differentiation, Jesus showed and taught that oneness is also triune.

Another predicate shared by both religions is that God is all-powerful. Yet the Son's demonstration that true power is found in the weakness of the cross is emphatically rejected by Muslims.[88] Therefore, if the Father is not divided from the Son and, in fact, is revealed by the Son, even the most basic predicates of God as understood by Muslims and the biblical God are different. Thus we must agree with Sanneh that affirming the sameness of the Islamic understanding of God and the biblical God "is adequate insofar as there is only one God, but inadequate with respect to God's character, on which hang matters of commitment and identity."[89]

Setting Aside Trinitarian Criteria

How are we to recognize the presence of the Triune God in non-Christian religions? This has been a recurring question for all theologies of religions that recognize the Trinity as God's distinctive name for Christians.[90] Three approaches have been taken: setting aside the use of Trinitarian criteria, searching for abstract patterns that resemble the Trinity, and using the Trinitarian relations in their concrete expressions.

---

86. Ibid., 35.

87. Woodberry, "Do Christians and Muslims Worship the Same God?" 37.

88. This idea of the Son transforming the most basic predicates that the Islamic and Christian conceptions of God share was suggested to us by Timothy C. Tennent, *Theology in the Context of World Christianity* (Grand Rapids, MI: Zondervan, 2007), 40–41.

89. Sanneh, "Do Christians and Muslims Worship the Same God?" 35.

90. On the Trinity as God's self-given name, see Robert Jenson, *The Triune Identity* (Philadelphia: Fortress, 1982), 1–18.

The first approach has been taken by those theologians who recognize the Triune character of the Christian God but regard the use of this name in inter-religious dialogue as "imperialistic" and "condescending." They have searched for "neutral" criteria by which to discern the presence of God in other religions. Most theologians of religions have rightly warned against a triumphalist use of the Trinity where there is no serious and painstaking attempt to learn about another religion. Without serious effort to listen to what adherents of other religions actually believe and do, resulting theologies of the religions will be ineffective for Christians and unnecessarily off-putting to non-Christians who might otherwise lend an ear. Veli-Matti Kärkkäinen warns that "ignoring the self-understanding of adherents of religions means nothing less than violating their religious rights." Little wonder that such indifference has been dubbed "imperialistic" or even "intellectual Stalinism."[91]

But others worry that using Christological criteria, even perhaps after listening keenly to the testimony of religious others, will by itself prevent understanding by silencing the voice of the other. As Amos Yong puts it, "To insist on a robust Christological criterion is to mute the identity of the other and to act imperialistically toward other faiths."[92] Use of Christological categories when evaluating other religions can by their overspecificity obscure non-Christian ways of representing similar things. It is far better, he suggests, to use categories that are more "vague," as recommended by C. S. Peirce and Robert Neville, that allow "things that are perhaps otherwise starkly contrasting" to be "unified without doing violence to their integrity." In the use of these vague categories "the law of [the] excluded middle does not apply."[93] In this way, Christian theologians of religions can perhaps achieve "a truly transcultural and universal discourse and rationality," one that will avoid the "lopsided" and "less-than-neutral" categories in Christological approaches.[94] Yong recommends a three-tiered process of discernment that he hopes encapsulates those neutral terms. The first is phenomenological-experiential, using aesthetic norms to "gauge the intensity and authenticity of personal religious experiences," watching for how the experience "transforms the individual."[95] The next level is moral-ethical, once more looking for "the fruits of

---

91. Kärkkäinen, *Trinity and Religious Pluralism*, 165. The terms in quotes are from others whom Kärkkäinen is citing.

92. Yong, *Beyond the Impasse*, 103.

93. Ibid., 178–179.

94. Ibid., 73, 91, 179.

95. Yong, *Discerning the Spirit(s)*, 250–251.

the individual's change for the better," relating religious symbols to the "fruits of the Spirit."[96] Yong says this is similar to the criterion of the *humanum* proposed by Hans Küng.[97] Thus, the Christian theologian of the religions asks if lives are made whole and communal relationships are mended and strengthened.[98] The third level, theological-soteriological, asks what "transcendental reality" is the referent for the religious symbols involved. Yong warns that the demonic may be involved and that this question is answered by what is "ultimately a spiritual act that transcends purely rational ways of knowing."[99]

Yong applies this process to a case study of Umbanda, an Afro-Brazilian religious tradition that highlights spirit possession by spirit mediums. After conducting a careful analysis of the movement's history, sociology, and anthropology, he concludes with a "sympathetic understanding of the Umbandist reality."[100] "In the end," he writes, "the 'proof' of the Holy Spirit's presence and activity may lie in the positive and negative events that follow spirit possession in the long run: positively in resulting healings, material prosperity, existential serenity, etc., and negatively in the destructive consequences that are inevitably seen as punishments handed down by the gods to doubters and dissenters."[101] So while criticizing Umbanda, Yong also expresses "positive appreciation" for the Umbandist creed in which the devotee proclaims, "I believe in Umbanda as a religion of redemption which can bring us on the way of development to Orixa Father."[102] While he does not label this tradition as demonic or crypto-Christian in any simplistic manner, Yong thinks the presence of the Spirit can be detected here and in other traditions where we

---

96. Ibid., 251–252.

97. See Hans Küng, "What Is True Religion? Toward an Ecumenical Criteriology," in *Toward a Universal Theology of Religion*, edited by Leonard Swidler (Maryknoll, NY: Orbis, 1987), 231–250.

98. Yong, *Discerning the Spirit(s)*, 252–253.

99. Ibid., 254.

100. Ibid., 287.

101. Ibid.

102. Ibid. These depictions of Umbanda must be weighed alongside R. Andrew Chesnut's finding that Umbanda and other African diaspora religions in Brazil "actually offer spiritual protection to prostitutes, pimps, smugglers, traffickers, and others whose work takes them beyond the pale of the law." Umbanda and its religious cousins provide "spiritual assistance and protection for purposes and acts considered morally dubious at best and evil at worst by [their] Christian rivals and prevailing social mores," such as injuring or even murdering one's enemies. R. Andrew Chesnut, *Competitive Spirits: Latin America's New Religious Economy* (New York: Oxford University Press, 2003), 109, 116.

see law, rationality, relationality, and community; conversely, we might sense the demonic when we observe chaos, irrationality, isolation, and alienation.[103]

What are we to make of Yong's bold proposal? It is to be commended for pushing evangelicals to consider the possibility that the Holy Spirit might be at work among those whose religions have been traditionally dismissed as merely demonic. His work suggests that evangelicals must work harder to specify how we think the Spirit is at work outside the church and to specify criteria by which we can evaluate the presence and effects of the Spirit's work. Yong is also right to encourage evangelicals to be more Trinitarian and not simply Christomonist, with Christ in effect wholly replacing the Trinity.

But we would raise a number of questions. First, what might the Holy Spirit be doing in a religion such as Umbanda? Should we assume that evidence of the Spirit's presence in fostering individual and communal welfare means that this is a religion that brings its devotees to the Triune God in a saving way? In one sense, goodness wherever it appears is to be attributed ultimately to God, the source of all goodness. But it does not follow from this that any particular instance of goodness or communal well-being should be directly attributed to the activity of the Holy Spirit. Christian theology has long distinguished between common grace, in which God mysteriously works by his Spirit to bring varying degrees of wholeness to individuals and societies, and special or saving grace, in which God's Spirit brings individuals into saving fellowship with the Father through his Son.

A second question: How are we to know what is rational and relational? Or what is truly humane, as in Küng's *humanum*?[104] Küng rules out witchcraft, but Yong thinks its use in Umbanda might sometimes produce what Küng would otherwise call humane. What about cannibalism? Some theologians of the religions would think it inimical to human flourishing, but others, informed by anthropological studies, might find tribes for which its practice enhances social cohesion. In other words, criteria centered in human "transformation" are inherently subjective and ambiguous. Without the use of more concrete theological criteria, such as Christological norms, there will be no clear way to decide between differing conceptions of human flourishing. An observation by Clark Pinnock suggests that in the absence of sharper criteria, we can be deceived: "In the 1930s, for example, many intelligent Americans and Europeans were fooled when they visited Berlin and Moscow; the same

---

103. Yong, *Beyond the Impasse*, 131–132.

104. Küng, "What Is True Religion?" 240.

thing happened in China in the 1960s. These naive visitors experienced a spirit of renewal and returned home enthusiastic for regimes that later proved to be oppressive, even murderous. They thought they had glimpsed new possibilities for human life, but they were sadly and dangerously duped and deluded."[105]

We would also ask: Is it possible to have neutral criteria? What is meant by the term? Neutral in what sense? If Yong's point is simply that we should avoid arbitrary or biased criteria that prevent us from adequately assessing the religions, then we heartily agree. But he seems to be going beyond this and claiming that criteria derived from explicitly Christian sources should not be used in such assessment. If so, this is unacceptable. Surely, any genuinely Christian theological evaluation of other religions must use some criteria derived from Scripture and the Christian tradition. This means that every evaluation of another religion by a Christian—no matter how fair and neutral that Christian tries to be—will inevitably judge that religion by criteria that have been conditioned by Christian thinking.[106] Christian use of "relationality," for example, cannot avoid being influenced by Christian understandings of love and justice, even when attempts are made to find similar notions in non-Christian traditions. Therefore, if "imperialistic" means using criteria that have been shaped in part by one's own religious tradition when evaluating another tradition, no Christian theologian of the religions can avoid being "imperialistic." But of course, the same holds for any evaluation of an alternative religious perspective made by a Hindu or Buddhist or Muslim or Mormon. This does not excuse inattention and insensitivity to the particularities of the other, but it does suggest that the search for neutral criteria in theologies of religions—innocent of influence from one's own tradition—is neither desirable nor possible.

---

105. Pinnock, *Flame of Love*, 209.

106. We can accept Yong's call for neutral *categories* with which to evaluate religions but not his suggestion that a human *observer* can be neutral in his or her final comparative assessments. So we can agree with his warning that a category such as divine revelation is not useful for assessing the scriptures of nontheistic religions such as Theravada Buddhism (since revelation requires a deity who reveals) but that categories such as "scriptures" are better, since some religions such as Theravada Buddhism have scriptures but no concept of revelation. Yong, *Beyond the Impasse*, 178–179. But we disagree with his further suggestion that it is possible for Christians to transcend their Christian identities and attain a degree of neutrality such that they can experience the "realities" of another religion "to some degree 'from within.'" Amos Yong, "A P(new)matological Paradigm for Christian Mission in a Religiously Plural World," *Missiology* 33 (April 2005): 180–181.

Trinitarian Patterns

Other Christian theologians of the religions have been less reluctant to use the Trinity in their assessments of other religions. But a number of them use abstract concepts derived from the Trinity rather than the Christian Trinity itself. George Sumner thinks this started in the modern era with Hegel's Trinitarian philosophy, with its threefold movement of abstraction, alienation, and consummation.[107] Hegel believed that the Christian doctrine of the Trinity was "picture thinking" that required elucidation in philosophy, particularly his own. The result was that a philosophical construct outside of Christian theology eventually reshaped the Trinity into something at odds with the biblical narrative. For Hegel, the world determined God's shaping as Trinity, but for classical Trinitarian theology, God was Trinity before the world's creation. Sumner sees a number of contemporary Trinitarian theologies of religions as "grandchildren of Hegel."[108]

Panikkar, for example, writes that the Trinity is the Christian word for a "theandric" structure of reality that "permeates all realms of being and consciousness."[109] It represents three ways of thinking about ultimate union between the divine and the human. The first way is "iconolatry," in which the divine is rendered in human likeness; the second is "personalism," where a personal love relationship is posited between the two; the third is mystical Advaita, in which one contemplates the Absolute as the ground of everything.[110] Put in other terms, the Father represents nihilism and apophaticism, the Son suggests theism, and the Spirit stands for monism.[111] For Panikkar, then, the Trinity is a symbol for the deeper ontological pattern of nonduality (the notion that there are no ultimate distinctions).

Some see a similar method in Mark Heim's Trinitarian theology of different religious ends.[112] Yet Heim's recent proposal is far more attentive to orthodox theology than is Panikkar's. It is one of the most innovative and intriguing Trinitarian theologies of religions to have appeared in decades and so deserves fuller attention. In an earlier work, Heim had argued not only that

---

107. Sumner, *The First and the Last*, 110.

108. Ibid., 111.

109. Panikkar, *The Trinity*, xi.

110. Ibid., 9–40.

111. Ibid., 41–69.

112. Sumner, *The First and the Last*, 116–117.

the religions teach different goals or salvations but also that there may actually *be* different salvations. These different ends are not to be realized by the same person at the same time but are for different people or for the same person at different times. And this reality of different ends may be "providentially" provided by God. Ontologically, "there can be a variety of actual but different religious fulfillments, salvations."[113] In other words, Theravadin Buddhists may indeed experience nirvana, and Muslims may indeed find Paradise. So there are three types of religious fulfillment: lostness, penultimate religious fulfillment through a non-Christian religion, and communion with the triune God—the last of which only Christian faith may provide.[114] Speaking of how this might work in relation to a Buddhist, for whom nirvana is understood as the ontological ultimate, realized through release from suffering associated with the cycle of rebirths, Heim writes: "Christians can affirm an eschatological plenitude whereby, for instance, those who give themselves to the 'divine abyss' of emptiness can be seen to have realized a facet of the divine plenitude. From my Christian view, this is a secondary good, since I believe that communion with God in a fuller range of God's being is possible. But the end is neither unreal nor evil; it does truly offer release from the round of human suffering. Our place in the great tapestry of the consummation is alterable, but each one glorifies God in some measure."[115] In a later work, Heim, drawing heavily from Dante, adds a fourth end: fixation on a created good, which alone (not God) binds a soul to hell. Heim's God, like Dante's, keeps none in hell by external force. Hell is self-governed, and its demons are willing captives; its denizens complain but are unwilling to give up their sins and therefore hell.[116]

Heim's theology controls his eschatology—as it should. God, for Heim, is composed of relations, among the three persons of the Trinity and with creatures. So God's being is communion. This means that the various ends (goals) of the religions represent various dimensions of the triune God. They are different because they are isolated from the other dimensions of the Trinity and are thereby limited. Yet because non-Christians focus exclusively on one dimension of the divine, they can come to know that dimension with a purity,

---

113. S. Mark Heim, *Salvations: Truth and Difference in Religion* (Maryknoll, NY: Orbis, 1995), 131.

114. Ibid., 165.

115. Ibid.

116. S. Mark Heim, *The Depth of the Riches: A Trinitarian Theology of Religious Ends* (Grand Rapids, MI: Eerdmans, 2001), 107–114.

Heim thinks, unavailable to Christians, who are in communion with the Trinity as a whole. At the same time, Heim asserts that non-Christians cannot experience the abundant life in Christ. Other religious ends (separate from communion with the Trinity, which alone is properly called salvation) are not isolated to one person of the Trinity but represent the elevation of one dimension of the Trinity's relations with the creation.

Heim is not a pluralist along the lines of John Hick, who would have a hard time saying that any one religion is more true than others. Heim argues that even if the religions represent isolated dimensions of the triune life, they are not wholly true. The whole truth is the social Trinity, which is the true divine reality at the center of the world's religions. For example, a Theravadin Buddhist focuses on the impersonal dimension of God in which creation can be seen as "empty" at its base. Heim argues that just as human beings contain an impersonal dimension—their blood chemistry, for instance—so does God, such as when one considers the inanimate creation as not only created by God but also "in" God. When Buddhists talk about the emptiness of reality, Heim believes they point to certain truths but not in the ways Buddhists think: God *can* be said to be empty because there is no cause for God's acts; God and persons are never exhaustively revealed; and God "contracts" or withdraws in order to allow creaturely freedom and prevent our being overwhelmed by full experience of his presence. So Theravadin Buddhists are wrong when they deny a personal god, but they touch and describe the true God when they talk about the emptiness of Reality—yet not in the way they think.

Similarly, Heim does not say that nirvana is the ontological ultimate as this is understood by Theravadins but that Buddhist nirvana *is* a description of a certain dimension in God that may be seen better by Buddhists and is really experienced by Buddhists. Yet at the same time, the experience of nirvana falls short of the fullest soteriological end, which is communion with the Trinity. To cite another example, a Hindu may actually attain union with the divine—with absolute Brahman—but this is a limited and constricted experience of both reality and God.

So for Heim, while there is a sense in which the soteriological ends of other religions can be attained, in a deeper sense, the soteriological expectations of the other religions fall short. They represent, in varying degrees, failures of hope and faith. Their devotees absolutize one aspect of truth instead of seeing the fullness of truth(s) and coming into communion with the fullness of God in the Trinity. Therefore, "lostness," for Heim, means refusal to relate to others or to God. The closer one is to God in triune fullness, the greater the dimensions of relation and the greater the sense of individuality. But the soul that refuses relation will finally lose its own selfhood and identity. This is how Heim understands annihilation.[117]

We believe that Heim's theology of religions is insightful and highly creative but ultimately untenable. It is important because of its Trinitarian fullness and because it recognizes profound differences in actual religious ends, as early forms of pluralism rarely did. In an admirable way, Heim sees the uniqueness of the Christian Trinity when compared with the world of religions, yet at the same time, he links what he regards as real religious truth in the religions to that same Christian Trinity. But there are two aspects of Heim's Trinitarian theology that give us pause: its weak biblical base and its ambiguous role for Jesus Christ.

First, Heim's appeal to biblical revelation is strange and limited. It is not sufficient that a proposal merely be conceptually possible.[118] We must also ask whether Scripture gives any reason for supposing that it is, in fact, the case. Heim makes a biblical case for different soteriological ends by appealing to the variety of offices in Revelation's picture of heaven (martyrs, elders, and angels) and the variety of gifts in 1 Corinthians, Ephesians, and Romans. Yet in the biblical narrative, these offices and gifts are possessed by saints and angels in communion with the whole Trinity and not simply its isolated dimensions. Then Heim cites Paul's statement that God "will repay according to *each* one's

---

117. Ibid., 273, 286.

118. Yet even on the conceptual level, there are reasons for questioning Heim's model. Heim argues that it is possible that, for example, Christians and Buddhists both can attain their respective soteriological ends as these are envisioned within Christianity and Buddhism. But for Christians, salvation presupposes the reality of the soul, an ontologically real, enduring dimension of the person that survives the dissolution of the physical body and, in the resurrected body, enjoys the presence of the Triune God. Buddhists classically have denied the reality of such a soul or atman, and attainment of nirvana or emptiness is directly related to proper realization of this truth. Now, imagine Joe, who is born into a secular home and grows up without any religious commitments. At age eighteen, he becomes a deeply committed Christian, but in his thirties, he grows disillusioned and abandons his Christian faith. At age fifty, he begins Buddhist meditation and at fifty-two makes the vows declaring himself a Buddhist. This is an increasingly familiar spiritual narrative in today's globalized world. In Heim's scenario, what happens ontologically to Joe throughout his life? If one's ontological condition and the reality of soteriological ends depend on one's religious commitments, what are we to conclude about Joe's "person" throughout his life? Before becoming a Christian, did Joe have a soul, or does he receive a soul when he embraces Christian teachings? Presumably, he had a soul while he was a practicing Christian. What happened to it when he converted to Buddhism? Can one have a soul and then cease having a soul? While perhaps not strictly incoherent, Heim's model does have some strange and confusing implications. It is also worth noting that Heim's model is not likely to be embraced by adherents of other religions themselves, since it relegates their soteriological understandings to a penultimate status within the Christian Trinitarian framework.

deeds: to those who by patiently doing good seek glory, honor and immortality, He will give eternal life" (Rom. 2:6–7). He interprets this to mean that upright people in other traditions will not go without reward, as, in fact, Scripture hints in its depiction of pagan saints such as Abel, Enoch, Noah, Melchizedek, Abimelech, Job, and the queen of Sheba. Heim also notes that Revelation 20:13 cites two different "locations" giving up their dead: "Death" and "Hades."

Yet we would observe that Paul's statement about God's repayment according to different deeds takes place in a discourse on salvation by Christ into the triune life. More generally, Heim makes little or no attempt to wrestle with problematic texts relating to eschatology and rival religions. They deserve more than just the observation that we find "a confused system of the afterlife."[119] For example, nowhere in his Dantean portrayal of hell as a prison with no walls but the corrupt desires of the unrepentant (often satisfied) is there any grappling with the biblical imagery of torment and teeth gnashing (see Matt. 8:12, 10:28, 13:24–43, 25:31–46; Mark 9:43; Luke 16:19–31; Rev. 20:14). More troubling is Heim's role for Christ in salvation. He says on the one hand that Christ is not constitutive of other religious ends, but he also insists that Christ is always involved in overcoming sin that blocks other religious paths, not just Christian ones.[120] But if Christ is the power and wisdom of God, and there is mutual indwelling of the three Trinitarian persons—both of which claims Heim makes—how can Christ *not* be constitutive of all religious ends? The problem is not other religionists' ignorance of Christ. Heim himself points out that the resurrected Jesus was often not recognizable to his disciples—at Emmaus, on the shore of the Sea of Galilee in John 21, in his appearances to Paul and to Mary in the garden.

More to the point of this chapter, Heim asserts that "the Trinity teaches us that Jesus Christ cannot be an exhaustive or exclusive source for knowledge of God [or] the exhaustive and exclusive act of God to save us."[121] Heim does not engage closely with biblical texts (John 1:9 and 14:6 and Acts 4:12, for example) that point to Christ as mediator of all knowledge of God and the only Savior. Nor does he reconcile his implicit claim for certain kinds of salvation apart from Jesus Christ with his concomitant assertion that there is salvation only in communion with the Trinity. As we saw above with Panikkar and Dupuis, this separates the *logos asarkos* (the Logos without flesh) from the *logos ensarkos*

---

119. Heim, *The Depth of the* Riches, 93.

120. Ibid., 288, 286.

121. Ibid., 134.

(the enfleshed Logos), dividing in Nestorian fashion the eternal Logos from the human Jesus.

Heim is to be commended for a robust Trinitarianism that argues for union with the Trinity as the fullest human end. But his argument for traces or parallels of Trinitarian experience in the religions tends to isolate the persons of the Trinity one from another and separates Christ from a variety of salvations. All in all, we think that Veli-Matti Kärkkäinen cautions wisely that parallels to the Trinity are just that—parallels and not the real thing.[122] The mere use of Trinitarian models does not guarantee connection with the Christian Trinity if in so doing the economic Trinity of revelation is bypassed. We are encouraged that some theologies of religions use the Trinity as a model—this is preferable to seeking an impossibly neutral common ground with other religions—but the model must be grounded as much in biblical narrative as in speculative abstractions.[123] Or if there is theological development of biblical themes, that development must be faithful to the Trinitarian economy.

Trinity in Its Narrative Fullness

In our view, Kärkkäinen charts the directions in which evangelical Trinitarian theologies of the religions must proceed. Kärkkäinen is not afraid to use the Trinity in its narrative fullness as a framework for analysis of the religions and dialogue with theologians from other traditions. Nor does he content himself with a Trinitarian framework indebted more to a philosophical system than to revelation. He declares that there "is simply no way to proceed otherwise in Christian theology of religions."[124] For there is no knowledge of or experience with the true God apart from the God revealed in his economic relations as Father, Son, and Holy Spirit.[125] Other religionists may have some connection with God, but it is always with that tri-personal God and no other. Thus any purported experience of the divine in other religions must be scrutinized by what the self-revealing God has shown of himself in that narrative history.

---

122. Kärkkäinen, *Trinity and Religious Pluralism*, 170.

123. See the fine essay by Stephen Williams, "The Trinity and 'Other Religions,'" in *The Trinity in a Pluralistic Age*, edited by Kevin J. Vanhoozer (Grand Rapids, MI: Eerdmans, 1997), 26–40.

124. Veli-Matti Kärkkäinen, "The Uniqueness of Christ and the Trinitarian Faith," in *Christ the One and the Only: A Global Affirmation of the Uniqueness of Jesus Christ*, edited by Sung Wook Chung (Grand Rapids, MI: Baker, 2005), 115.

125. Ibid.

That narrative also reveals that the true God is divine communion, because God is love and was love among the three persons before the creation. It is because of the Trinity that most Christian theologians now accept Eastern Orthodox theologian John Zizioulas's thesis that persons exist in communion, since they are creatures of a God who *is* communion.[126]

Kärkkäinen goes on to argue that Trinitarian theology and Christology are interdependent: "Our Christology determines to a large extent our view of the Trinity and vice versa. Furthermore, the way to establish the truthfulness (or at least claim to truthfulness) of Trinitarian faith is via Christology." Kärkkäinen says there are two implications of this for theology of religions. First, our notions of Trinity must be grounded in the gospel narratives lest we come to employ a "generic concept of Trinity," such as Panikkar's concepts of Trinity and Christ, which are disconnected from the particularities of the gospels. Second, a narratival Trinity will "link talk about the Spirit to the Father and the Son and [resist] those kinds of pneumatological theologies of religions in which the Spirit is made an itinerant, independent deputy."[127]

Kärkkäinen adds that while we should not shy away from fresh and creative ways of expressing Trinitarian faith, we should nevertheless use Trinitarian criteria lest our final theologies be based on "abstract specula-tions...[or] alleged similarities among religions."[128] This would rule out, he warns, "kingdom-centered approaches (of, for example, the Catholic Paul F. Knitter) in which the advancement of the kingdom is set in opposition to or divorced from the Father, Son, and Spirit."[129] Kärkkäinen allows that the kingdom of God is larger than the visible church, but he agrees with Catholic Gavin D'Costa that the presence of the Spirit outside the church is intrinsi-cally Trinitarian and ecclesial: "It is trinitarian in referring the Holy Spirit's activity to the paschal mystery of Christ, and ecclesial in referring the paschal event to the Spirit's constitutive community-creating force under the guid-ance of the Spirit."[130] In the New Testament, he asserts, the church is the body of Christ and temple of the Spirit. Thus, whenever the Spirit is at work in a saving way, he is drawing persons toward eventual incorporation into Christ's body, the church.

---

126. John D. Zizioulas, *Being as Communion: Studies in Personhood and the Church* (Crestwood, NY: St. Valdimir's Seminary Press, 2002).

127. Kärkkäinen, "The Uniqueness of Christ," 123.

128. Ibid., 124.

129. Ibid., 126.

130. Ibid.

Furthermore, Kärkkäinen insists that Trinitarian full disclosure is actually helpful to interreligious dialogue. "Trinitarian faith and the 'scandal of particularity' are not to be thought of as opposites."[131] Here Kärkkäinen draws on the work of Sri Lankan evangelical Vinoth Ramachandra, who explains that "particularity is for the purpose of universality, not exclusion."[132] God chose one nation and one mediator in order to reach all. Jesus' uniqueness in Trinitarian faith does not impose on Asian religions but, in fact, "safeguards some of the legitimate concerns of contemporary Asian theologians,"[133] such as poverty, human equality as created in the image of God, humility, service, and self-sacrifice. Rather than handicapping Asian theologians in interreligious dialogue, the Jesus of the Trinitarian God opens up channels of communication with other religious traditions.

In the middle of the last century, Karl Barth wrote: "The doctrine of the Trinity is what basically distinguishes the Christian doctrine of God as Christian, and therefore what already distinguishes the Christian concept of revelation as Christian, in contrast to all other possible doctrines of God or concepts of revelation."[134] Since Jonathan Edwards and until very recently, evangelicals have neglected this hallmark of the Christian doctrine of God. They have regularly and consistently expressed their agreement with the doctrine of the Trinity, but they have often engaged in apologetics, for example, with a generic "theistic" idea of God rather than a Trinitarian one. Feeling compelled to leave the specifically Trinitarian teaching outside the debating hall, they have not recognized the extent to which they need a robust Trinitarian notion of God not just as a chapter in their dogmatics but as a foundational component of their apologetics. Of course, it is sometimes quite appropriate to *start* with mere theism, as Paul did at the Areopagus in Acts 17. But just as Paul then turned the discussion toward the Son of God's resurrection, apologetics should not typically *end* with theism. Evangelical theology has been pinched when it has bracketed the Trinity, particularly in its evaluations of other religions. We can be thankful that the last few decades have seen a resurgence of Trinitarian understanding among evangelicals thinking about the religions. In this chapter, we have seen some Trinitarian rules that biblical revelation

---

131. Ibid., 128.

132. Ibid.

133. Ibid., citing Vinoth Ramachandra, *The Recovery of Mission* (Grand Rapids, MI: Eerdmans, 1996), 216.

134. Barth, *Church Dogmatics*, 1:1, 301.

offers to theology of religions. We have also seen some of the problems that can develop when the Trinity's narratival specificities are ignored or replaced with abstract speculation. In the rest of this volume, we chart the ways in which the Trinitarian vision of God guides understanding of key issues in interreligious work: revelation, conversion, Christian ethics, the relationship between culture and religion, ultimate reconciliation, and mission.

3

Revelation and the Religions

THE STORY OF the economic Trinity is the history of salvation. The Father sent
the Son and the Spirit on missions to bring wayward human creatures back
to God. Another way of telling this story is to speak of the history of revelation: God saved the world by sending his Son and brought people to the Son
by *revealing* the Son and the Father through the Spirit.

As we saw in the last chapter, only God knows God fully, and so as human
beings, we can know God only to the degree that God reveals himself to us. This
chapter will take up the question of what that means, especially the question
of whether there is revelation by the tri-personal God among non-Christian
religions. But before we get to that, we must see what the Christian tradition
has meant by revelation. We will start with a definition, then look at media and
modes of revelation, next explore the nature of revelation (is it propositional
primarily? ineffable? is there revelation in nature?), and then discuss the relation of revelation to the Bible. After touching briefly on what the Bible has to
say about knowledge of God outside Israel, we will at last take up the question
of revelation in the religions.

First, however, it would be good to note that our emphasis on revelation is
a bit modern. Before the Enlightenment, there was more emphasis on "salvation" than on "revelation," reflecting the priority in both Testaments of words
expressing God's saving activity."[1] The term *revelation* has been a commonplace in theology only since the English Deists launched a frontal attack on
the notion that God had made himself known through media beyond nature
and reason. Deists argued that a God who revealed himself only to Jews and
Christians was an arbitrary monster in whom right-thinking persons could
not believe, for a just God would have made himself known to all human
beings, not just to those who fell within the ambit of the Judeo-Christian tradition. Hence, since the Enlightenment, it has been customary to refer to two

---

1. Gerald O'Collins, S.J., *Rethinking Fundamental Theology* (Oxford, UK: Oxford University
Press, 2011), 68. Alister McGrath makes a similar point, arguing that the modern Western
concern for justification departs from the Bible's greater emphasis on the larger story of
salvation history: *Iustitia Dei: A History of the Christian Doctrine of Justification*, 2nd ed.
(Cambridge, UK: Cambridge University Press, 1998), 3–16, especially 4–5.

sources of knowledge about God: general revelation through nature and reason, which are available to all, and special revelation, which is available only to those with access to Christian teaching and the Bible.[2]

The doctrine of revelation forces us to address up front a methodological issue in the theology of religions: What is the source of our information for thinking about the religions? On the one hand, part of our information comes from observing the religions themselves. So the observation and study of other religious traditions are important. But is theology of religions based on merely the observable phenomena or the reported experiences of the various religious traditions? The approach of some theologians suggests that theology of religions is to be developed from the study of the various religions, building on the experiences and teachings of the many religions.[3] But in this case, theology of religions really is little more than comparative religion.

Or do we have access to truth about God and the world that comes to us from outside of our particular sociocultural and religious contexts? Has God actually revealed himself in an intelligible manner to us? Has God spoken to us? If, indeed, God *has* spoken, then it is God's self-revelation that provides the framework for our understanding of the religious phenomena we observe around us. We are then to submit to God's revelation as truth and to allow it to control our beliefs, even where this truth may not be particularly palatable to contemporary tastes. Evangelicals, in line with the witness of Scripture, insist that God has indeed revealed himself in an authoritative manner to us in the incarnation and the written Scriptures.[4] Thus, theology of religions cannot be reduced to comparative religion. Instead, it must acknowledge the inevitability of using a framework to evaluate religious phenomena. In our case, the framework is the story of salvation as told by the Christian Scriptures and

---

2. For the Deist attack on revelation, see Gerald McDermott, "Deism," in *The Encyclopedia of Protestantism*, edited by Hans J. Hillebrand (New York: Routledge, 2004), 568–574.

3. The clearest example here is John Hick, but one finds this approach also reflected in the work of Wilfred Cantwell Smith, Paul Knitter, Raimundo Pannikkar, and Keith Ward.

4. Although religions such as Islam, Hinduism, Buddhism, Jainism, Sikhism, Daoism, and Confucianism all have authoritative scriptures, the nature and role of such texts in the respective religions vary greatly. We should not assume that they have the same status and function that the Bible does for Christians. See *The Holy Book in Comparative Perspective*, edited by Frederick M. Denny and Rodney L. Taylor (Columbia: University of South Carolina Press, 1985); John Bowker, *The Message and the Book: Sacred Texts of the World's Religions* (New Haven, CT: Yale University Press, 2011).

interpreted according to the basic agreements of orthodox Christians over the last two thousand years.[5]

Definition

Etymologically, the word *revelation*, which comes from the Latin *revelo*, goes back to the Hebrew *galâ* and the Greek *apokaluptō*, both of which mean the unveiling of something that was hidden, so that it might then be seen and known for what it is. The sense of this is conveyed in Ephesians: "the mystery of Christ, which was not made known to the sons of men in other generations as it has now been revealed to his holy apostles and prophets by the Spirit" (3:4–5).

For the authors of Scripture, then, revelation is the unveiling of a previously hidden mystery. More important, however, it is God who uncovers the mystery. God has taken the initiative to disclose his plans, character, and very being to his human creatures. God has shown himself and his ways to selected human beings, who in turn have passed down to us what they have seen, heard, and experienced: "That which was from the beginning, which we have heard, which we have seen with our eyes, which we looked upon and have touched with our hands, concerning the word of life—the life was made manifest, and we have seen it, and testify to it and proclaim to you the eternal life, which was with the Father and was made manifest to us—that which we have seen and heard we proclaim also to you, so that you may have fellowship with us; and indeed our fellowship is with the Father and with his Son Jesus Christ" (1 John 1:1–3). As this passage makes clear, revelation for the biblical authors was not the product of human seeking or imagination but a divine gift to creatures who otherwise have only distorted ideas about the divine: we were "dead" in our sins and "darkened" in our understanding of God when God took the initiative to open our eyes and ears to see his reality and redemptive designs (see Matt. 11:25–27, 16:17; 2 Cor. 4:6; Eph. 2:1, 4:18). Apart from revelation, our speculations about the divine are only "foolishness" and, in fact, contradict true knowledge of God (Rom. 1:21; 1 Cor. 2:14). Even if sin were not a barrier to knowing the divine, there is still the vast ontological gulf between us and the transcendent realm. God is so far from humanity in his mode of being that human beings can neither see him (John 1:18; 1 Tim. 6:16; Exod.

5. By "basic agreements" we mean the consensus over "mere Christianity" sketched by C. S. Lewis in the book with that title, articulated in evangelical fashion in such works as *The Oxford Handbook of Evangelical Theology*, edited by Gerald R. McDermott (New York: Oxford University Press, 2012).

33:20) nor find him by searching (Job 11:7, 23:3–9) nor guess his thoughts (Isa. 55:8–9). As Kierkegaard famously expressed it, there is an "infinite qualitative distinction between God and man."[6] It is for these reasons that Pascal said that only "God speaks rightly of God."[7]

The word *revelation* refers not only to the process of God disclosing his purposes and being but also to the knowledge of God that results from that disclosure. This knowledge then reveals the meaning of all the rest of reality. As Thomas Oden has put it, receiving and understanding God's revelation is an experience through which we see all the rest of experience.[8] Lesslie Newbigin has compared it to Kepler's discovery of his third law. In Kepler's words, "At last I have brought it to light and recognized its truth beyond all my hopes...the pure Sun itself of the most marvellous contemplation has shone forth." Newbigin adds that while Kepler proclaimed, "I have brought it to light," the biblical prophets testified, "God spoke to me."[9] If the provenance of revelation was different, the result was similar: it is an event that makes all other events intelligible.

This is the way revelation worked for the Israelites and early Christians. Human experience took on cosmic meaning when seen through the prism of revelatory events captured by Scripture. In Exodus, we read, "When in time to come your son asks you, 'What does this mean?' you shall say to him, 'By a strong hand the LORD brought us out of Egypt, from the house of slavery'" (Exod. 13:14). When the first Christians were persecuted for their faith or saw miraculous healings, it was the death and resurrection of Christ that explained these events (Acts 1–5). In other words, the content of revelation was a God whose character and nature were revealed primarily in narratives about his work of redemption, which began in the counsels of the godhead in eternity and will continue until the eschatological establishment of a kingdom headed by the Son. It is this story, which began with Adam and Abraham and the Jews and continued through the incarnation, that demonstrates to all the cosmos God's holiness, faithfulness, and sovereignty. It shows that in the Trinity, God is a society of love and that Jesus was God's last revelation to

6. Søren Kierkegaard, *Training in Christianity*, in *A Kierkegaard Anthology*, edited by Robert Bretall (New York: Modern Library, 1946), 391.

7. Pascal, *Pensées* (New York: Modern Library, 1941), no. 798.

8. Thomas C. Oden, *The Living God*, in *Systematic Theology*, 3 vols. (San Francisco: Harper & Row, 1987), 1:333.

9. Lesslie Newbigin, *The Gospel in a Pluralist Society* (Grand Rapids, MI: Eerdmans, 1989), 59.

humanity. For he was the image of God, in whom all the divine fullness dwells (2 Cor. 4:4; Col. 1:15; Heb. 1:3).[10]

If revelation conveys knowledge, it is not merely information providing new insight. The divine disclosure demands wholehearted *trust* in what is revealed; it inspires a faith that if properly received entails *obedience* (Rom. 1:5, 16:26). Those who receive this revelation are called not to mere mental assent but to an openness that is self-involving and transforming. In the absence of that openness, true revelation has not been received.

Media and Modes

Through what media or modes does revelation come? According to the biblical witness, they are many and varied. God spoke through the casting of lots (1 Sam. 10; Acts 1:24–26), visions (1 Kings 22:17–23), audible voice (1 Sam. 3:1–14), dreams (Gen. 28:10–17), interpretation of dreams (Gen. 40–41), angels (Judg. 13:15–20), inspiration of prophecy (Jer. 1), wisdom (Proverbs), historical events (such as the Exodus), metaphors (Ps. 18:2), parables (Matt. 13:1–50), and stories (the gospel accounts of Jesus's life, passion, and resurrection).

Sometimes the biblical text says simply that God revealed himself—to Jacob (Gen. 35:7, 9) and Samuel (1 Sam. 3:21), for example. God appeared in human form to Abraham (Gen. 18:1–19:1), and Jacob wrestled with God (Gen. 32:24–30). Moses saw his back (Exod. 33:21–23), but according to the text, he sometimes spoke with God "face to face" (Num. 12:8; Deut. 34:10).

In the New Testament, we are told that knowledge of God involves all three divine persons. Jesus chose those to whom he reveals the Father (Matt. 11:27). He spoke in parables both to reveal the nature of the kingdom to his disciples and to keep its mysteries hidden from those not ready or able to hear (Matt. 13:11–15). But it was his very person that is the fullest revelation of God (John 1:1). Now the Word had become a human being (John 1:14), so to know Jesus was to know God (John 14:9). God had revealed himself in "many and various ways" during the Old Testament era, but the history of revelation culminated in Jesus himself (Heb. 1:1–2). The Holy Spirit was sent to continue the revelatory function of the Son through the inspired writings of the apostolic generation (John 14:25–26, 16:12–15).

---

10. For a theological understanding of this narrative, see Jonathan Edwards, *A History of the Work of Redemption*, edited by John F. Wilson (New Haven, CT: Yale University Press, 1989), 111–530.

Revelation in Nature?

In twentieth-century theology, Karl Barth initiated a debate over whether God also reveals himself through nature in what is sometimes called "natural revelation."[11] Barth called into question the traditional interpretation of Scripture where it seems to testify that nature provides knowledge about God. For example, the psalmist declares that "the heavens declare the glory of God, and the sky above proclaims his handiwork" (Ps. 19:1). Luke reports Paul's saying at Lystra that God gave a witness to himself in his provision of nature's seasons, rain, and food (Acts 14:17); then at Athens, Paul proclaimed that God created the earth's seasons and geography so that human beings would "seek God, in the hope that they might feel their way toward him and find him" (Acts 17:26–27). In his letter to the Romans, Paul wrote that "what can be known about God is plain" to those who suppress the truth, "because God has shown it to them. For his invisible attributes, namely, his eternal power and divine nature, have been clearly perceived, ever since the creation of the world, in the things that have been made" (1:19–20).

It was on the basis of these and similar passages that John Calvin and Jonathan Edwards argued that God has given objective revelation of himself in nature. Calvin said that God the Creator (not God the Redeemer, who is known only through Christ) can be known by reflection on the created order, which is a mirror or theater for the display of God's presence, nature, and attributes.[12] Calvin also believed that the historical process itself gives witness of God. He pointed to such biblical passages as those in the prophets, where Isaiah and Habakkuk, for example, discerned God working through Assyria and the Chaldeans (Isa. 10:5–6; Hab. 1:5–6).[13] Edwards used revelation in nature as a foundation for cosmological (based on the notion that all contingent things require a cause for their existence) and teleological (inferring a designer responsible for the design of the cosmos) arguments for the existence of God.[14]

---

11. Of course, this was not a new subject in the history of theology, but Barth made it particularly compelling in the last century.

12. John Calvin, *Institutes of the Christian Religion*, edited by John T. McNeill (Philadelphia: Westminster, 1960), 1.5.

13. Ibid., 1.18.

14. Jonathan Edwards, *Freedom of the Will*, edited by Paul Ramsey (New Haven, CT: Yale University Press, 1957), 181–182; see also Gerald McDermott, *Jonathan Edwards Confronts the Gods: Christian Theology, Enlightenment Religion, and Non-Christian Faiths* (New York: Oxford University Press, 2000), chap. 3.

Both Calvin and Edwards were impressed from Paul's second chapter in Romans that the human conscience contains divinely implanted testimony to God's moral law: the Gentiles "show that the work of the law is written on their hearts, while their conscience also bears witness" (Rom. 2:15). For Calvin, this was part of his grounding for what he called a *sensus divinitatis* found in every human being, a sense of the divine that points the human being to God.[15] Edwards also wrote of an innate, prereflective awareness of God, a natural inclination that prejudices the soul to believe in God: "That secret intimation and sort of inward testimony that men have upon occasion of the being of God."[16] For this eighteenth-century theologian, nature was chock-full of evidence for God: "There is nothing else that we behold or converse with but that the being of God is evident from it. The very being of any of them [is evidence]: creation, daily providences, sun, moon, [and] stars."[17]

Edwards agreed with Calvin that nature points only to God the Creator, not God the Redeemer, and that knowledge of only the former is insufficient for salvation. The American theologian asserted that knowledge of God the Creator reveals to humanity something of what it must do to please God but not how to find God after it has displeased him. So nature shows that there is a God who makes moral demands but not how sinners can be restored to that God after they have failed to meet those demands. Nature reveals God, he wrote, but no one has ever come to God through nature alone. Even if some had come to God through nature, they still would not know whether God wanted to save them or damn them.[18] Edwards also claimed that while nature can tell us something about the truth of God—that he exists and is all-powerful—it does not tell us that God is triune and wants to save us. So for neither Calvin nor Edwards is revelation in nature a basis on which to build a comprehensive theology—which must come by special revelation about Christ in a manner qualitatively different from what has been revealed through nature. Nor does natural revelation mean that humanity has an innate capacity for finding God apart from grace. Only the action of the Holy Spirit on and in a person can

---

15. Calvin, *Institutes*, 1.3.1.

16. Jonathan Edwards, *The Miscellanies, a–500*, edited by Thomas A. Shafer (New Haven, CT: Yale University Press, 1994), 373.

17. Jonathan Edwards, "Practical Atheism," in *Sermons and Discourses, 1730–1733*, edited by Mark Valeri (New Haven, CT: Yale University Press, 1999), 55.

18. Jonathan Edwards, *The Miscellanies, 1153–1360*, edited by Douglas A. Sweeney (New Haven, CT: Yale University Press, 2004), 259. See also McDermott, *Jonathan Edwards Confronts the Gods*, chap. 3.

reveal the Father by shining light on the Son; apart from this work, that person is dead in his or her sins.

As mentioned above, another way of putting this has been to differentiate between general and special revelation, a distinction widely accepted by evangelicals.[19] The former is given to all human beings through nature and conscience (Rom. 1:18–20, 2:14–15), while the latter has come through God's dealing with the people of Israel and the incarnation in Jesus Christ and is contained in the canonical Scriptures. Special revelation therefore has been made known only to those who have had access to these special events or the written Scriptures. The former reveals God's existence, power, and moral demands, while only the latter shows how we can find relief for our inevitable failure to meet those demands. There is value in this distinction and the language used to describe it. The distinction shows us that while many do not have full knowledge of the way of salvation, all have access to some knowledge of God. It also suggests that we may be able to discover some of God's truth in the wider world outside the sphere of special revelation. The language of "revelation" used for both sides of the distinction affirms that knowledge of God given to non-Christians has been *revealed* by God. It may not be enough for salvation, but it is nevertheless true knowledge about God given by the triune God himself.

Karl Barth protested that the biblical passages typically used to support knowledge of God in nature have been misinterpreted by generations of readers, particularly since the Enlightenment. In fact, he alleged, the Old Testament passages show no knowledge of God apart from knowledge of the God of Israel (those outside of Israel use nature only for idolatrous purposes), and Paul indicates that this knowledge of God gained through nature leads only to condemnation.[20] In Barth's famous battle with Emil Brunner over natural revelation, Barth accused Brunner of the error of *analogia entis*, by which (according to Barth) we seek knowledge of God by extrapolating from the perfection of human attributes. For Barth, the biblical way was the *analogia relationis*, by which we know ourselves only by relationship to God through Jesus Christ. Therefore testimonies of God in nature are not revelation, because

---

19. See Bruce A. Demarest, *General Revelation: Historical Views and Contemporary Issues* (Grand Rapids, MI: Zondervan, 1982).

20. Karl Barth, *Church Dogmatics* 2:1 (Edinburgh: T. and T. Clark, 1957), 130–133.

they are invariably misunderstood; they falsify rather than illumine. The only knowledge we have of God is in the face of Christ (2 Cor. 4:6).[21]

In our judgment, Barth was right to insist that saving knowledge of God requires not just objective knowledge of God but also subjective understanding of and response to that knowledge. But in his attempt to defend Christian revelation against the German Christian religion based on blood and soil (with which he associated Brunner's natural theology), he overreacted. He argued, for example, that the voices of the cosmos in Psalm 19 are dumb because the text says their "voice is not heard" (19:3).

Yet on closer inspection, it seems the psalmist probably meant that there is no *audible* voice, for he goes on to say that that voice "goes out through *all* the earth (*bəkol-hā ʾāreṣ*), and their words to the *end* of the world" (*ûḇiqṣēʰtēḇēl*; 19:4; emphasis added). This seems to speak of God's revelation going to those who have *not* heard of the Lord of Israel, not just to Israelites, as Barth had suggested. Furthermore, Paul made it clear that the revelation of God's law is made to *every* human heart (Rom. 2:14). In Romans 1:19–21, he used six words to emphasize that God's revelation is seen and heard even by those who rebel against him: "For what can be *known* [*gnōstòn*] about God is *plain* [*phanerón*] to them, because God *has shown* [*ephanérōsen*] it to them. Ever since the creation of the world his eternal power and divine nature, invisible though they are, have been *understood* and *seen* [*nooúmena kathorâtai*] through the things he has made. So they are without excuse; for though they *knew* [*gnóntes*] God, they did not honor him as God or give thanks to him."

Barth accurately noted that many biblical writers suggest that these voices are not heard properly. But the passages from Psalm 19 and Romans 1–2, and others besides, nevertheless indicate that there is genuine disclosure of God given through the cosmos and the human person, even if that disclosure is not properly understood by many. Condemnation is indeed the result of some of this revelation (Rom. 1:20), but Scripture also hints that the Spirit uses this revelation, no doubt in conjunction with others, to lead some closer to God (Rom. 2:15; Acts 17:27). As G. C. Berkouwer put it, Barth's interpretation seems to be special pleading: Barth's exegesis "is more the result of an a priori view of revelation than an unprejudiced reading of the text itself."[22]

---

21. Karl Barth, *Nein! Antwort an Emil Brunner* (Munich: Chr. Kaiser Verlag, 1934); English translation in Karl Barth and Emil Brunner, *Natural Theology: Comprising "Nature and Grace"* (London: G. Bles, Centenary Press, 1946).

22. G. C. Berkouwer, *General Revelation*, translated from the Dutch edition (Grand Rapids, MI: Eerdmans, 1983), 154.

Is Revelation an Event or a Proposition?

Debate has raged not only over the question of whether genuine revelation is given by God through nature. Scholars and other interpreters have also contested the nature of the truth conveyed by revelation. This argument—or, more accurately, series of arguments—has concerned three questions. First, is revelation an event or a proposition expressed in words?[23] Second, is God's truth capable of being conceptualized, or is it ineffable? Third, what is the relationship between revelation and Scripture?

The first question is whether God's revelation is more properly described as an event in history that is described by human words or as God's speech conveyed to human subjects in verbal and propositional form. Those who favor the first view argue that truth in Scripture refers primarily to the Christ event: God's self-revelation to humanity as the Christ in the person of Jesus. For the biblical writers, truth is something that *happens*. Truth is not a series of statements but a train of events in history such as the Exodus and a person in history named Jesus of Nazareth. Borrowing Calvin's language of accommodation, these interpreters say that God has accommodated himself to our capacity by revealing himself in our history through these historical events. Revelation, then, is first and foremost a historical event. As Barth put it, revelation demands historical predicates.

This view can be corroborated to some extent by Scripture, which represents God as manifesting his presence to human beings in a variety of ways and instances, many of which can be described as events. He revealed his presence to Abraham, Isaac and Jacob, Moses, Paul, and many others (Gen. 35:7; Exod. 6:3; Num. 12:6–8; Gal. 1:15–16). There were the theophanies at the burning bush, Mount Sinai, and the river Chebar (Exod. 3:2, 19:11–20; Ezek. 1). The angel of the Lord seems to have been a manifestation of Yahweh himself (Gen. 16:10; Exod. 3:2; Judg. 13:9–23). John said, "The Word became flesh and lived among us" (John 1:14). There is no doubt that, as we have already seen, Scripture portrays Jesus as God's paramount revelation. All of these manifestations of God's presence were events and not simply messages.

But it is equally clear that for the biblical writers, revealed truth was not only something that happened but also something that was *told*. In Scripture, God also revealed himself by *speaking* his *purposes* to his people. This divine

---

23. By "proposition" we mean the cognitive meaning expressed by a statement or assertion. Scripture contains much more than statements and assertions, such as questions, exclamations, expressions of praise or regret, and so on. But it also includes implicit and explicit assertions or claims about what is the case, and these are what we mean by "propositions."

speech was historical insofar as it was communicated to human beings who lived in history and received these communications at a given place and time. The reception of the message and the consequent reiteration of the message in human words can thus be considered as a historical event. But the revelation itself is better characterized as a message from God than as merely an event in history.

Consider, for example, God's frequent statements of his purposes—that is, his communication of his character, plans, and demands. He spoke to Noah, Abraham, and Moses not only of his plans and purposes for them but also of his ultimate purposes for his people and the rest of humanity (Gen. 6:13–21, 12:1, 15:13–21, 17:15–21, 18:17; Exod. 3:7–22).[24] Then he declared to Israel the laws and promises of his covenant (Exod. 20–23; Deut. 6:13; Deut. 28; Ps. 78:5, 147:19). He told Amos that he would do nothing without revealing his purposes to his prophets (Amos 3:7). Christ told his disciples all he heard from his Father and promised he would send the Spirit to complete his instruction to them (John 15:15, 16:12). Paul said that God revealed to him the mystery of his eternal purpose in Christ (Eph. 1:9, 3:3–11), and John testified that Jesus revealed to him what would come to pass shortly (Rev. 1:1).

The biblical evidence, then, shows that to overemphasize the distinction between revelation as event and revelation as word produces a false dichotomy. Both are prominent in Scripture. In fact, neither is complete without the other. Words interpret events, and events fulfill promises made with words. The Exodus was interpreted by words that sought to use Israel's liberation as a reminder of God's grace and motivation to keep the terms of the covenant. The prophets' words promising a messiah and a new covenant were fulfilled by Jesus and his kingdom.

Is Revelation in Words or beyond Words?

A second question has concerned the intelligibility of revealed truth: is it capable of being communicated with words, or is it ineffable? Certain Hindu, Buddhist, and Daoist traditions are well known for their suspicion of attempts to put religious truth into words. The Buddhist *Lankavatara Sutra* says:

> Therefore let every disciple take good heed not to become attached to words as being in perfect conformity with meaning, because Truth is

---

24. This and the next paragraph are indebted to J. I. Packer, "Revelation," in *The New Bible Dictionary*, edited by J. D. Douglas (Grand Rapids, MI: Eerdmans, 1962).

not in the letters. When a man with his finger-tip points to something to somebody, the finger-tip may be mistaken for the thing pointed at; in like manner the ignorant and simple-minded, like children, are unable even to the day of their death to abandon the idea that in the finger-tip of words there is the meaning itself. They cannot realize Ultimate Reality because of their clinging to words which were intended to be no more than a pointing finger.[25]

Similarly, the Daoist classic *Dao de Jing* begins with the enigmatic statement, "The way [Dao] that can be spoken of is not the constant way; the name that can be named is not the constant name." The Dao, or the Way, is said to be "forever nameless." The suspicion of verbal expressions of the highest truth is reflected in the claim, "One who knows does not speak; one who speaks does not know."[26]

Early in the twentieth century, Rudolf Otto published what has now become a classic, *Das Heilige*, in which he (rightly) argued that as much attention ought to be paid to the nonrational (distinct from irrational) dimension of religion as to the rational. But he also claimed that the otherness of the divine, which he called the "numinous," "completely eludes apprehension in terms of concepts."[27] It can be experienced only as an intuition; no coherent description of it can be formulated in language.

In a later version of what could be called the ineffability thesis, the Swiss theologian Emil Brunner proposed that revelation should not be construed in terms of communication of information about God but rather as a dynamic, dialectical encounter between God and humans. The truth of revelation is not propositional but existential and can be expressed only in terms of a personal encounter of the human "I" with God's "Thou" in Jesus Christ.[28]

More recently, the Harvard historian of religion Wilfred Cantwell Smith distinguished between the external "cumulative tradition" of religious communities and the inner faith of the religious believer. Only the latter, he claims, constitutes significant religious truth. Therefore, we should think of religious truth not in terms of propositional statements about God, self,

---

25. *Self-Realization of Noble Wisdom: The Lankavatara Sutra*, compiled by Dwight Goddard (Clearlake, CA: Dawn Horse, 1932), 92.

26. *Lao Tzu: Tao te Ching*, translated by D. C. Lau (New York: Penguin, 1963), 57, 91, 117.

27. Rudolf Otto, *Das Heilige*, originally published 1917, translated by J. Harvey as *The Idea of the Holy* (New York: Oxford University Press, 1950), 5–6.

28. Emil Brunner, *Truth as Encounter*, 2nd ed. (Philadelphia: Westminster, 1964).

or world but rather as indicators of personal integrity, sincerity, faithfulness, authenticity of life, and one's success in appropriating certain beliefs in one's life and conduct.[29]

The first problem with this position is that the biblical testimony indicates, as we have already seen, that God often spoke his purposes, plans, and demands to his people. He communicated in rational terms, or at least through messages that were then expressed in rational terms, to human beings. The term used in John 1 to refer to the incarnate Son—*logos*—is a term associated with the notions of reason and word. So while it is clear from Scripture that there is more to revelation than simply propositions (Jesus was a person, not a proposition), we cannot eliminate the verbal and propositional dimension from divine revelation.

Is divine revelation ineffable? Much depends on what one means by "ineffable." If one means that literally nothing can be said about it and revelation cannot be expressed in words at all, then clearly, divine revelation, as understood by classical Christian theologians, is not ineffable. As we have seen, the Christian Scriptures present God as speaking to human beings, and the Scriptures themselves are a written record of God's self-revelation. Yet even within the Scriptures, we find hints of realities that defy verbal expression. In what many commentators take to be a reference to Paul's own experience, Paul speaks of one being caught up to the "third heaven" and hearing things that cannot be expressed (2 Cor. 12:2–4).

Whether we speak of God or of God's revelation, there is an important distinction to be made between two different senses in which we say that God is "wholly other."[30] The distinction is evident in the ways each answers the question, Can God coherently be described in human language as ordinarily used? Those adopting strict ineffability maintain that no coherent descriptions of God or his activity can be formulated in language. This not only contradicts much that is stated or implied by the Christian Scriptures and the classical theological tradition, but it also results in theological agnosticism.[31]

A different response, however, claims that coherent descriptions of God and his activity can be expressed in human languages, although such

---

29. Wilfred Cantwell Smith, *The Meaning and End of Religion* (New York: Harper & Row, 1962).

30. See the seminal essay by W. D. Hudson, "The Concept of Divine Transcendence," *Religious Studies* 15 (1979): 197.

31. On the incoherence of a strict ineffability thesis, see Keith E. Yandell, *The Epistemology of Religious Experience* (Cambridge: Cambridge University Press, 1993), chapters 3–5.

expression has its limitations and must be interpreted appropriately. To be sure, language used of God is always limited, and we must remember that there is much about God that we cannot know and that cannot be expressed in human language. Thus, Paul said the love of Christ "surpasses knowledge" (Eph. 3:19). But the fact that we cannot have exhaustive knowledge of the love of Christ does not mean that we cannot have some understanding of Christ's love. The very concept of revelation suggests that God has made some dimensions of his being and ways known to us. Hence we can know something of God *ad nos*. As Aquinas argued, our language about God is neither univocal nor equivocal but analogical. The terms we use for God, taken from ordinary language, are not fully adequate to portray God, but they do convey meaning. Similarly, while our understanding of God, derived from God's revelation, is partial and limited, it still is knowledge. We see through a glass darkly, but we do see.[32]

Another way of putting this is to say that Scripture and theology provide us with models or images of God. A model is never the same thing as what it represents. But by understanding it, the mind can grasp something of the reality to which it points. For example, the stories of Jesus in the gospels do not give us the full reality of Jesus, but they nevertheless provide us with something of his person, character, and teaching.[33] Therefore, by grasping the words and images of revelation in Scripture, we can grasp something of the reality of God himself. This applies not only to the words and symbols of Scripture but also to the historical events described therein. No historical account is an exact reconstruction but is always an interpretive picture. Yet because the historical accounts in Scripture were superintended by the Holy Spirit's inspiration, they can show us something of both the character and the purposes of God. When the objective content of Scripture is illuminated by the Holy Spirit (which we will discuss below), the reader can encounter the divine.

Therefore, we *can* know something about God, and it can be expressed in rational terms. For the economic Trinity is the immanent Trinity. The Trinity as made known to us through redemption (economic) is not a different Reality from the inner life of the triune God (immanent). The knowledge of God that

---

32. Thomas Aquinas, *Summa Theologica*, I, q. 13, art. 1–6, 12. For a helpful discussion of the issues in the use of ordinary language to speak of God, see William P. Alston, *Divine Nature and Human Language: Essays in Philosophical Theology* (Ithaca, NY: Cornell University Press, 1989).

33. Colin Brown, "Revelation," in *The New International Dictionary of New Testament Theology*, 3 vols., edited by Colin Brown (Grand Rapids, MI: Zondervan, 1978), 3:336–337.

we have been given through revelation is not simply a human construction, although our understanding and formulation of revelation will always be conditioned by our finite and fallen perspectives. Our knowledge of God is not so broken that we can know nothing of who God is and what he is like.

Revelation and the Bible

The third question, which asks whether the Bible is revelation or merely the witness to revelation, is related to the first question concerning revelation as event or word. Those who have said, following Barth, that revelation is always event, have also said, following Barth, that the Bible is not revelation in itself but the witness to revelation. This view of the Bible is based on Barth's motif of actualism, which thinks in terms of events and relationships rather than things or substances. God's being, Barth taught, is always a being in act. Just as our relationship to God is never possessed once and for all but is continually established anew by the ongoing activity of grace, so revelation is always an event or happening and never a thing.[34] Therefore, the Bible, which is a book, can never be identified with the Word of God, which is continually established anew according to God's good pleasure. The Spirit often uses it to communicate a dynamic and living Word to a person who reads it or hears it, but apart from that dynamic illumination of the Spirit, the Bible is not the Word or revelation of God.

Barth's understanding of the relation of revelation to Scripture is too occasionalist to do justice to the Scripture's own witness to itself. New Testament authors regard Old Testament passages—the written text of the Hebrew Scriptures, not just the events to which the texts refer—as authoritative utterances of God (Matt. 19:4–5; Acts 4:25–26; Heb. 1:5, 3:7). The question "Have you not read...?" is virtually the equivalent of "Do you not know that God has said..." (Matt. 12:3, 21:16, 22:31; Mark 2:25, 12:10, 12:26; Luke 6:3). And the phrase "it is written" carries the full weight of divine authority (Matt. 11:10, 21:13, 26:24, 26:31; Mark 9:12–3, 11:17, 14:21, 14:27; Luke 7:27, 19:46). Occasionally, "God" and "Scripture" are used interchangeably (Rom. 9:17; Exod. 9:16; Gal. 3:8; Gen. 12:3; Matt. 19:4–5; Gen. 2:24).

So while Scripture claims that its *written* deposit was inspired by the Spirit (2 Tim. 3:16; 2 Pet. 1:20–21, 3:2, 3:15–16; 1 Tim. 5:18), Barth connects inspiration

---

34. See George Hunsinger, *How to Read Karl Barth: The Shape of His Theology* (New York: Oxford University Press, 1991), 30–32, 76–102; Barth, *Church Dogmatics* 2:1, 257–321.

only with the responsive state of the believer. Geoffrey W. Bromiley, chief translator of Barth's *Church Dogmatics*, concludes that Barth stressed the present ministry of the Holy Spirit at the expense of the once-for-all work of the Spirit in
the authorship of Scripture.[35] Edwards, in contrast, provided a more (biblically)
balanced way to incorporate both the objective character of revelation in the Bible
and the need for subjective illumination to the believer.[36]

---

35. Geoffrey W. Bromiley, *Historical Theology: An Introduction* (Grand Rapids, MI: Eerdmans, 1978), 420–421.

36. For Edwards, the biggest part of interpretation is opening the eyes of the believer to the Reality behind Scripture and to which Scripture points. Thus, reading the words alone is not enough, even if one believes the Bible is divine revelation. Edwards said that words have no natural power to open up the divine Reality. They have the capacity to convey to the mind the notions that are the subject matter of the Word, but only the Spirit can convey what Edwards called the "sense of the heart" that alone can shine light on divine realities. Jonathan Edwards, "A Divine and Supernatural Light," *Sermons and Discourses, 1730–1733*, edited by Mark Valeri (New Haven, CT: Yale University Press, 1999), 405–426.

Even intellectual apprehension of, and assent to, the truths of Christ's redemption are insuf-
ficient for salvation. What is needed is a vision of the *beauty* of God in Christ, which for Edwards involved a personal knowledge and appreciation for the love that God the Father showed in the incarnation and passion of his son. This is a recognition—which comes only by the illumination of the Holy Spirit—that "God is God, and distinguished from all other beings, and exalted above 'em, chiefly by his divine beauty, which is infinitely diverse from all other beauty." Jonathan Edwards, *Religious Affections*, edited by John E. Smith, vol. 2 in *The Works of Jonathan Edwards* (New Haven, CT: Yale University Press, 1959), 298.

It is this vision of the divine beauty that makes divine realities seem not only true but real. For Edwards, that spelled the difference between what might be called familiar and personal knowledge of a person. We can be familiar with Barack Obama by the many newspaper and magazine articles we have read about him and the television news programs we have watched. On the basis of this input, we can say that we are familiar with Obama and believe that certain things said about him are true. But if we actually meet him and spend several hours with the man, then we might say, in Edwards's sense of the word, that what we *thought* was true we now *know* to be real. This is approximately the distinction that Edwards made between believing that certain divine things are true and being convinced of their reality. Edwards himself used the analogy of knowing that honey is sweet. Until we have actually tasted honey, we can believe the sweetness of honey to be true because of universal reports we have heard about it. But when we taste it for ourselves for the first time, then we know not only that honey's sweetness is true but also that it is real. It has become *real* for us.

Edwards insisted that without this seeing of the divine beauty, which comes only by the illu-
mination of the Holy Spirit, revelation has not been truly revealed to us: "Unless this is seen, nothing is seen.... This is the beauty of the godhead, and the divinity of Divinity...without which God himself (if that were possible to be) would be an infinite evil: without which, we ourselves had better not have been; and without which there had better have been no being. He therefore in effect has nothing, that knows not this." Edwards, *Religious Affections*, 274.

Therefore, we think Edwards did a better job of balancing the subjective and objective poles in revelation than Barth did. Barth rightly stressed the subjective pole, in reaction against, among other things, dry and sterile orthodoxies that seem to presume that mental assent to Christian doctrine is sufficient. The Swiss theologian properly emphasized God's dynamic

Evangelicals have long been known for their commitment to the full authority of God's special revelation, the Bible. Alister McGrath places the authority of Scripture first among his six fundamental convictions that define evangelicalism. Evangelicals affirm the "supreme authority of Scripture as a source of knowledge of God and a guide to Christian living."[37] This commitment is also reflected in the Lausanne Covenant (1974), widely adopted throughout the world as an expression of evangelical identity: "We affirm the divine inspiration (2 Tim. 3:16; 2 Pet. 1:21), truthfulness and authority of both Old and New Testament Scriptures in their entirety as the only written word of God, without error in all that it affirms, and the only infallible rule of faith and practice.... Through it the Holy Spirit still speaks today. He illumines the minds of God's people in every culture to perceive its truth freshly through their own eyes (Eph. 1:17, 18) and thus discloses to the whole Church ever more of the many-coloured wisdom of God."[38]

While an evangelical theology of religions draws on material from a variety of sources, including the history and phenomenology of religions, it is an orthodox understanding of the divinely inspired Scriptures that provides the normative framework for understanding and assessing the religions.

Models of Revelation

So far, we have used opposing terms to describe revelation (event or proposition, rational or ineffable, objective or subjective) and have suggested that each pair is a false dichotomy. Revelation comprehends both events and propositions about those events; it both transcends the limitations of human linguistic and conceptual categories and is capable of expression in such categories; and it involves both an objective content of knowledge about God and

---

activity of the Spirit, by which the human subject sees and acts by repeated acts of grace, rather than looking solely to a realm and a book that were completed two millennia ago. But Barth marginalized the inspiration of Scripture and failed to give proper attention to the work of the Spirit in superintending the writing and selection of the biblical canon. In contrast, Edwards highlighted both the work of the Spirit in producing an authoritative Scripture and the work of the Spirit in the church to open the eyes of readers and hearers to the realities to which Scripture points so they may participate in those realities. Michael J. McClymond and Gerald R. McDermott, *The Theology of Jonathan Edwards* (New York: Oxford University Press, 2012), 130–148.

37. Alister McGrath, *Evangelicalism and the Future of Christianity* (Downers Grove, IL: InterVarsity, 1995), 55.

38. "The Lausanne Covenant," in *New Directions in Mission and Evangelization 1: Basic Statements 1974–1991*, edited by James A. Scherer and Stephen B. Bevans (Maryknoll, NY: Orbis, 1992), 254.

a process or activity of the Spirit. Yet even this does not go far enough. To stop here would give a narrow and unnecessarily limited view of revelation. It is far better to say that revelation involves not one or two but many dimensions. Catholic theologian Avery Dulles has helpfully outlined five models of revelation that survey the range of ways in which God has revealed himself to his creation.[39]

The models are not mutually exclusive but complementary, like theories of light as both particle and wave. All theological models are somewhat deficient representations of limited aspects of the mysteries of faith, and they are not of equal value. But the combination of the five taken together presents a fuller and more nuanced description of revelation as found in Scripture than the three polarities we have just discussed:

1.*Revelation as doctrine.* This way of looking at Scripture sees it as containing clear, propositional statements that are the data from which church doctrines can be derived. It sees the events of Scripture as interpreted only by the words of Scripture. This view does not entail a dictation theory of inspiration but emphasizes the propositional content of revelation. It asserts that faith is not blind but a reasonable act of trust that rests on both external and internal validations of the Bible.

2.*Revelation as history.* This view claims to return to Semitic historical concreteness in a flight from Greek metaphysics, which is thought to dominate the first view. Revelation, it is claimed, is not a collection of doctrines but a story. Proponents of this view are correct in emphasizing the importance of narrative in Scripture but not at the expense of the nonnarrative sections, such as the wisdom literature (Proverbs, James, and other biblical books). Dulles suggests mediating these first two views by saying that the historical event in Scripture is the material element in revelation, while the word that interprets it is the formal element. Revelation is complex, which means that the next three models are also needed.

3.*Revelation as inner experience.* This considers revelation as an interior experience of grace or communion with God, in which spiritual perception is immediate to the individual. Some proponents of this view would say it is not necessarily dependent on Christ, while others hold that in this sense, revelation is merely the heightening of the normal and universal experiences of the moral and mystical life. We contend that in order for it

---

39. Avery Dulles, S.J., *Models of Revelation* (Garden City, NY: Doubleday, 1983). See also C. Stephen Evans, "Faith and Revelation," in *The Oxford Handbook of Philosophy of Religion*, edited by William J. Wainwright (New York: Oxford University Press, 2005), 323–343.

to be Christian revelation, it must be mediated by Christ and that there is a fundamental discontinuity between natural experience and supernatural revelation. So while some versions of this view conflict with an evangelical understanding of revelation, it nevertheless reminds the evangelical that the apprehension of revelation contains not only an objective pole (models 1 and 2 above) but also a subjective pole, in which the objective content of revelation is personally appropriated by the believer through the work of the Spirit.

4. *Revelation as dialectical presence.* This is the notion that God is not an object to be known by inference from nature or history, by direct perception, or simply by propositional teaching. God is utterly transcendent; he encounters the human subject only when it pleases him by a word in which faith recognizes him to be present. Therefore, the word of God both reveals and conceals God. Just as Jesus was not recognized as God by most of his contemporaries, so, too, the Word of God is not seen for what it is unless God in his pleasure decides to reveal it as such. While this view could restrict the objective content of revelation when used in isolation from these other four views and by itself can be understood as denying general revelation of God among all peoples, it is a potent warning that illumination of the Word by the Spirit is a necessary part of revelation and that evangelicals run the danger of domesticating the divine when they forget this. Hence the need to keep to a Trinitarian understanding of revelation.

5. *Revelation as new awareness.* Proponents of this last view worry that the four preceding views can be too individualistic and otherworldly. They maintain that revelation is an expansion of consciousness or a shift in perspective that engages people to join in works of social liberation. It is a presentation of paradigmatic events that stimulate the imagination to restructure one's experience. Truth is practical and salvational and has no fixed content. Evangelicals, by contrast, insist that revelation has content indeed, but they can agree that the illumination of the Spirit works on the written revelation of Scripture to bring about a new consciousness. And this new awareness will be concerned not only with individual salvation but also with the material and social well-being of others.

Why have we introduced Dulles's five models of revelation? It could be argued that they are contradictory—some refer to revelation as a body of knowledge, while others see revelation as a process of knowing. The first stoutly affirms revelation as propositional, but the last argues for awareness that includes but transcends propositions. But our point is that revelation is multidimensional. It must be, if it is the self-manifestation of the tri-personal

God, who is the infinite fountain of all being and beauty. God necessarily subsumes all of reality, so it stands to reason that his revelation of himself would include every dimension of reality.

Therefore, while each of these models is incomplete when taken in isolation from the others, each contributes to our understanding of the polydimensional phenomena gathered under the word *revelation*. Like everything else about God, revelation is always distorted when considered from only one perspective. Since it is *God's* revelation, we must expect that it will be at least as complex and multidimensioned as the most profound temporal realities we experience. And then some! So even the ideas we glean from these five models don't begin to exhaust the meaning of God's revelation. But they do begin to open us to the multiple meanings for the word. And they suggest that when we ask about revelation in other religions, we must be open to a variety of ways in which that might happen.

Knowledge of God outside Israel and the Church

Before we address the question of revelation in the religions more directly, it will be helpful to recognize that in the Bible, people outside Israel and the church seem to have some knowledge of the true God. This is not to say they had saving knowledge of God; in some cases, it was clear that wicked people such as Balaam had some knowledge of the true God (Num. 22–24). But it is nevertheless important to acknowledge that there was knowledge of the true God among those outside the people of Israel and the church, even among people who were clearly not in the kingdom of God. We may recall from chapter 1 that Melchizedek had some sort of knowledge of the God who manifested himself as the Holy One of Israel (Gen. 14:18–20). In some way that we do not know, true knowledge of God apparently came to Melchizedek and, as far as we can tell from the Genesis story, apart from revelation given through the Abrahamic lineage.[40] Chris Wright observes that regardless of how Melchizedek came to possess his knowledge of the one true God, this

---

40. Daniel Strange argues that Melchizedek and other "holy pagans" gained their knowledge of the true God by special revelation from Yahweh and usually came into contact with Israel or the church. Perhaps, but in the case of Melchizedek, we do not know this from the text. Moreover, one thinks of Job, who seems to have had no contact with Israel, thus rendering less than conclusive Strange's suggestion that Old Testament saints "were never pagans but confessed Christ albeit in an embryonic way." Daniel Strange, *The Possibility of Salvation among the Unevangelized: An Analysis of Inclusivism in Recent Evangelical Theology* (Eugene, OR: Wipf and Stock, 2002), 195, 179–189.

awareness of God was expressed in linguistic terms with which he was already familiar.

> What we have here, then, is a situation where the living God is known, worshipped, believed and obeyed, but under divine titles which were common to the rest of contemporary semitic culture, and some of which at least, according to some scholars, may originally have belonged to separate deities or localizations of El....The living God who would later reveal the fullness of his redemptive name, power, and purpose, prepared for that fuller revelation by relating to historical individuals and their families in terms of religious rites, symbols and divine titles with which they were already culturally familiar—i.e. accommodating his self-revelation to their existing religious framework, but then bursting through that framework with new and richer promises and acts.... So the patriarchal experience allows us to believe that God does address and relate to men in terms of their existing concept of deity (as, e.g., in the case of Cornelius). But we must presume that such initiative is preparatory to bringing them to a knowledge of his historic revelation and redemptive acts (which, in our era, means knowledge of Christ). It does not allow us to assert that worship of other gods is in fact unconscious worship of the true God, [or] to escape from the task of bringing knowledge of the saving name of God in Jesus Christ to men of other faiths.[41]

The Old Testament is replete with Gentiles who knew something of the true God. Pharaoh's magicians, for example, told Pharaoh after the (third) plague of gnats, "This is the finger of God" (Exod. 8:19). There is no indication that they had saving knowledge of God, but the text states that they recognized at this point that he, and not some other agent, was at work. Although the New Testament condemns Balaam's errors (2 Pet. 2:15; Jude 11), the Old Testament historian records that Balaam made accurate prophecies of the future of Israel, presumably under the inspiration of the Holy Spirit (Num. 24). Rahab the Canaanite prostitute recognized that the God of the Israelites was the true God and became an example of faith for Jewish Christians in the New Testament era (Josh. 2:10–11; Heb. 11:31). King Huram of Tyre told Solomon that he knew it was the God of Israel who made the heaven and the earth (2 Chron. 2:11–12). Other people outside the Jewish tradition who knew and sometimes "walked

---

41. C. Wright, "The Christian and Other Religions," *Themelios* 9, np. 2 (January 1984): 67.

with" the true God include Abel, Enoch, Noah, Job, Abimelech, Jethro, Ruth, Naaman, and the queen of Sheba.

The Old Testament also includes numerous foreign officials who recognize the sovereignty of the God of Israel. Pharaoh, for example, more than once acknowledged that he had sinned against Yahweh (Exod. 9:27, 10:16). After he was healed of leprosy, Naaman confessed, "Now I know that there is no God in all the earth except in Israel" (2 Kings 5:15). Nebuchadnezzar made a similar confession after Daniel interpreted his dream, and then again after Shadrach, Meshach, and Abednego emerged unscathed from the fiery furnace. Then when he gained his sanity after mental illness, he again testified to the sovereignty of the God of Israel (Dan. 2:46–47, 3:28, 4:34–37). When Daniel was saved from the lions, Darius issued a decree commanding people "in all my royal dominion" to tremble and fear before the God of Daniel: "For he is the living God, enduring forever; his kingdom shall never be destroyed, and his dominion shall be to the end. He delivers and rescues; he works signs and wonders in heaven and on earth, he who has saved Daniel from the power of the lions" (6:25–27).

Some of this knowledge of God by Gentiles came from encounters with followers of Yahweh, the God of Israel. Nebuchadnezzar, for example, was no doubt informed by the testimony of the three Hebrew young men, Shadrach, Meshach, and Abednego. So this does not count as knowledge coming from outside the Jewish tradition. Nor does knowledge of the true God necessarily mean saving knowledge. Many of these people, such as Pharaoh's magicians and Balaam, apparently never came to know and cling to Yahweh as their savior. Nonetheless, they knew something about the true God.[42]

As we saw in chapter 1, the apostle Paul quotes approvingly two pagan poets, Epimenides and Aratus (sixth and third centuries b.c.): " 'In him we live and move and have our being'; as even some of your own poets have said, 'For we too are his offspring' " (Acts 17:28).[43] Apparently, Paul believed these pagan thinkers had some insight into religious truth. New Testament scholar N. B. Stonehouse observes that these pagan writers "as creatures of God confronted with the divine revelation were capable of responses which were valid so long as and to the extent that they stood in isolation from their pagan systems. Thus, thoughts which in their pagan contexts were quite un-Christian and

---

42. For some like Rahab, however, it may have.

43. See F. F. Bruce, *Commentary on the Book of the Acts* (Grand Rapids, MI: Eerdmans, 1980), 359–360.

anti-Christian, could be acknowledged as up to a point involving an actual apprehension of revealed truth."[44]

We can draw some parallels with aspects of world religions today, for they teach some things with which Christians resonate. For example, Islam teaches that all that exists apart from God was created by an eternal creator God. Muslims, like Christians, teach that God is one and not many and that he is a moral Being. Spiritism of all sorts teaches that ultimate reality is not simply material. Most of the great religions teach a moral code that is very similar to the second table of the Ten Commandments. None of the great religions teaches that selfishness is a good thing. All teach that we exist for the sake of what is beyond us and that we have obligations both to other human beings and to whatever they call ultimate reality. We find clear statements of the Golden Rule (albeit in a negative form) twice in the *Analects* of Confucius, and the ethical principle underlying the Golden Rule is expressed in less clear form in the sacred texts of many religions.

Some religious traditions even teach something similar to what Christians call grace. In the Hindu *bhakti* tradition, for example, devotees believe they reach the divine by a gift of the deity (Krishna or Vishnu) and not through their own efforts. The Pure Land traditions of Mahayana Buddhism teach that rebirth in the Pure Land, the soteriological goal, comes not through our own efforts but rather through the gracious activity of Amida (Amitabha) Buddha on our behalf. The Japanese Buddhist Shinran (1173–1262), the founder of Jodo-Shin-Shu ("Pure Land True Sect"), rejected all "ways of effort" in the search for salvation and preached that we must rely on "the power of the other," which for him was Amida Buddha, who would bring to the Pure Land all who have faith in his power.[45]

Similarities and Differences

What are we to make of these remarkable similarities? Do they represent revelation from God? Before we try to answer that, we must clarify the similarities

---

44. Ned Barnard Stonehouse, *The Areopagus Address* (London: Tyndale, 1949), 37, as cited in Bruce, *Commentary*, 360.

45. "Shinran's Confession," in *Buddhism: A Religion of Infinite Compassion: Selections from Buddhist Literature*, edited by Clarence H. Hamilton (Indianapolis: Bobbs-Merrill, 1952), 141–142. For a penetrating study of the Hindu *bhakti* and Buddhist Pure Land traditions in relation to Christian theology, see John B. Carman, *Majesty and Meekness: A Comparative Study of Contrast and Harmony in the Concept of God* (Grand Rapids, MI: Eerdmans, 1994).

by noting the degree to which these notions are similar to Christian ideas. That is, we must also note the differences amid the similarities.

As we saw in chapter 2, Muslims, for example, also teach God's oneness, but the Christian God's oneness is a differentiated oneness made up of Father, Son, and Holy Spirit. Muslims would object that the Christian sense of oneness is therefore profoundly different, and Christian theologians would agree with this. Other examples of dissimilarity within similarity can be found in the moral codes of the great religions. They are indeed similar to the Ten Commandments that refer to neighbor relations, but at the same time, Christian understandings of each commandment are clarified by Jesus's gospel story, which only Christians accept. This can be seen, for instance, in relation to Buddhist ethics. Although Buddhist and Christian ethics agree on important principles (that stealing, lying, the killing of innocent life, and sexual misconduct are wrong and that compassion and sympathy are imperative), they differ on the relationship of moral values and principles to ultimate reality. For Gautama Buddha and Theravadins, the ethical life is a provisional raft that takes us to the other shore of nirvana, where it can then be discarded, for on the level of ultimate reality, differences between good and evil no longer prevail. For Christians, by contrast, the distinction between right and wrong, good and evil, is part of the fabric of reality and will persist into eternity.[46]

The differences are also important when it comes to other religions' concepts of "grace." While both Hindu *bhakti* and Pure Land Buddhism depict a kind of grace, in neither of these traditions is the absolute holiness of the divine depicted with such clarity as in the Christian tradition; and while the gift of salvation is given by the Hindu and Buddhist deities somewhat gratuitously, the God of Jesus confers the gift only at infinite cost to himself. Moreover, the ontologies of Christianity and Mahayana Buddhism, within which the language of grace functions, are radically different. For Christianity, God, the eternal creator who is holy and morally pure, is the ontological ultimate, and everything else apart from God—including humankind—is both contingent and ontologically distinct from God. In Mahayana Buddhism, the ontological ultimate is not an eternal creator but a reality variously termed

---

46. The contrast between Christian and Jewish understandings of moral distinctions and that of Zen Buddhism is brought out nicely in the Japanese Buddhist Masao Abe's essay "Kenotic God and Dynamic Sunyata" and the accompanying responses by Jewish and Christian theologians. See the essays in *The Emptying God: A Buddhist-Jewish-Christian Conversation*, edited by John B. Cobb Jr. and Christopher Ives (Maryknoll, NY: Orbis, 1990). See also Masao Abe, "The Problem of Evil in Christianity and Buddhism," in *Buddhist-Christian Dialogue: Mutual Renewal and Transformation*, edited by Paul Ingram and Frederick J. Streng (Honolulu: University of Hawaii Press, 1986), 139–154.

nirvana, sunyata (emptiness), the Dharmakaya (the Buddha Law), or the all-pervasive Buddha essence (*tathagatagarbha*). Shinran's thought reflects the East Asian Mahayana Buddhist emphasis on the universal Buddha nature or Buddha essence inherent in all beings. Paul Williams expresses concisely the Buddhist assumptions underlying the language of "other power" in Pure Land Buddhism. Williams notes that *shinjin*, or the attitude of sincere trust and self-abandonment to the "other power" of Amida,

> is not a volitional belief in something, but an articulation of our Buddha-nature. This is crucial, and places Shinran's thought squarely within the development of East Asian Buddhist theory.... We can become enlightened because we are already enlightened—as Dogen said, only Buddhas become Buddhas. We cannot enlighten ourselves, for the ego cannot bring about egolessness. Only Other Power can help us. This is because within us all, at our very core, is Other Power itself, or the Buddha-nature which is Amitabha.... We can only have self-abandonment because self-abandonment is a shining forth of our innate Buddha-nature, which is Amitabha himself. All can be saved through self-abandonment, for all have the Buddha-nature, and all that is required is to stop striving and allow the Buddha-nature to radiate self-abandonment.[47]

Furthermore, there are significant differences between the historicity of the life, teachings, death, and resurrection of Jesus Christ and the mythological nature of the Bodhisattva Dharmakara, who is said to have become the Amida Buddha. "Shinran's faith is in the words of a human being who through the accumulation of merit created his own paradise named the Pure Land and made a vow that can 'take away the karma of the world' and allow others to be reborn into this Land."[48] Karl Barth was aware of the formal similarities between Pure Land Buddhism and Protestant Christianity. Since Pure Land Buddhism also teaches that there is nothing that we can do to earn enlightenment or rebirth in the Pure Land, what then is distinctive about the Christian gospel? Barth concluded that only one thing is decisive in setting the Christian faith apart from Pure Land Buddhism: the name of Jesus Christ.

---

47. Paul Williams, *Mahayana Buddhism: The Doctrinal Foundations*, 2nd ed. (New York: Routledge, 2009), 262–263.

48. Timothy C. Tennent, *Theology in the Context of World Christianity* (Grand Rapids, MI: Zondervan, 2007), 158.

Only Jesus Christ was a God-man who died to save sinners from sin, death, and the devil.[49]

These differences are what led Jannie Du Preez to conclude, after a study of Shinran and Protestant theology, that "at a deeper level... it becomes crystal clear that a difference of such magnitude exists between the two religions that injustice is done to both when an attempt is made to interpret one in terms of the other. As David Bosch has said, 'We are dealing with different worlds.' "[50]

Du Preez realized what many scholars of the religions have discerned when comparing Christian truth to similar ideas in other religions. Every particular notion is shaped profoundly by the broader narrative in which it is found. So Shinran's grace is shaped by the story of Amida Buddha, in which the controlling ideas are not sin, guilt, and damnation but karma and liberation from rebirth in samsara. The human predicament for Shinran is not rebellion against a personal God but the weight of impersonal karma. Therefore, the solution involves not forgiveness from a holy God but release from an inevitable cycle of life, death, and rebirth. The overall story changes what "grace" means, so that Christian grace is finally of a fundamentally different nature from Buddhist grace.

Revelation in the Religions?

In spite of the cautions noted above about acknowledging the real differences between Christian teachings and practices and what we find in other religions, there is still the question of striking similarities between Christian faith and other traditions.[51] How should we explain these? Do these similar notions in other religions represent revelation from God? Where do these similarities come from?

The first thing we must say is that insofar as these teachings or practices are fundamentally different from Christian perceptions of how God has saved and is saving through Jesus Christ by his Spirit, they cannot be direct revelations from the triune God. God is truth, and so God would not suggest ways to

---

49. Karl Barth, *On Religion: The Revelation of God as the Sublimation of Religion*, translated by Garrett Green (London and New York: T. and T. Clark, 2006), 102–106.

50. Jannie Du Preez, "A Buddhist Form of Salvation by Grace Alone?" *Missionalia* 21, no. 2 (August 1993): 183; quoted in Tennant, *Theology*, 159.

51. Part of the difficulty in addressing this question is a result of the ambiguity of the term *religions*. Whether we can speak of God's revelation "in the religions" depends in part on what we mean by "religions." Issues relating to our understanding of the category "religion" are addressed in chapter 6.

liberation from rebirth for a Buddha when salvation from sin and death come by the life and death of Jesus—even if both teachings have a surface similarity of "other power" to assist helpless humans. The first is a real history of the God-man in space and time, while the second is a narrative disconnected from genuine history. The two religions cast the human predicament differently and provide solutions that are radically different. So it is only in cases where there is a genuine similarity between the teachings or practices of the Christian faith and another religious tradition that it makes sense to raise the question of God's revelation and other religious traditions.

In what follows, we will consider three ways in which Christian thinkers have attempted to account for what seem to be genuine similarities between Christian faith and other traditions. Some evangelicals will no doubt feel more comfortable with one explanation than with another, but each has merit and deserves consideration. First, a common answer to the question among evangelicals is that to various degrees, some of these similarities come from human reflection on God's general revelation and the fact that human beings are created in God's image with some capacity to know certain things about God.[52] Psalm 19 and Romans 1 both speak of God's revelation of himself in nature, and Romans 2 points to God's revelation of his moral law in the human conscience. Paul told the crowds at Lystra that "God did not leave himself without witness" but showed his goodness through the blessings of nature (Acts 14:17). This general revelation can explain the prevalence in many religions of belief in an eternal creator God; belief that something about this world is terribly wrong; belief that life does not end with the dissolution of the physical body; agreement on many ethical principles such as condemnation of murder, stealing, sex outside marriage, and selfishness and praise for altruism, compassion, and mercy; and the widespread sense that we humans have violated moral and spiritual law and that we must do something to make up for what has been done wrong.

Reflection on general revelation can also explain phenomena in world religions such as the Confucian "negative golden rule": Do not do to others what you do not want done to yourself.[53] Confucius was a Gentile who, as Paul put it five hundred years after the Chinese thinker's death, "show[ed] that the work of the law is written on [Gentiles'] hearts" (Rom. 2:15). Confucius seems to

---

52. See Harold Netland, *Encountering Religious Pluralism* (Downers Grove, IL: InterVarsity, 2001), 330–337.

53. Confucius, *The Analects*, translated and edited by D. C. Lau (Hammondsworth, UK: Penguin, 1979), 15.24.

have sensed in his heart the obligation to do to our neighbor what we would like done to ourselves.

Thomas Aquinas (1225–1274) used the Romans 2 text ("the work of the law is written on their hearts") as a basis for his doctrine of "natural law," which he said was the human participation in God's eternal law.[54] Thomas taught that since God's moral law is written on every human heart, humans can derive by reason aspects of God's moral truth. Thus, Confucius was using rational reflection to discern in negative form what Jesus would teach five hundred years later in positive form.

A variation of the general revelation theme is found in the work of the Austrian anthropologist Wilhelm Schmidt (1868–1954). Schmidt wrote a twelve-volume catalog of data on the early religions in which he argued that there are certain commonalities with respect to conceptions of deity that can be found in early religious traditions in various parts of the world. Schmidt was struck by what he claimed was an original monotheism in the earliest religions—belief in a benevolent creator god, or a "high god." As a Christian, Schmidt maintained that this belief in original monotheism was a result of God's general revelation given to all humankind, and he suggested that the world religions developed in part by reflection on that revelation.[55] Schmidt's critics said that the notion of a sky god in the earliest religions was only a dim personification of the physical heavens, so that worship of nature preceded true monotheism. But Schmidt retorted that "a being who lives in the sky, who stands behind the celestial phenomena, who must 'centralize' in himself the various manifestations [of thunder, rain, etc.] is not a personification of the sky at all" and came before worship of the sky itself.[56] While later historians of religions found evidence of early monotheism alongside more abstract notions of divinity, the mere presence of early belief in a beneficent high god across many cultures suggests that a principal source of religious truth in the religions was reflection on general revelation.[57] Winfried Corduan is an evangelical who has developed a theology of religions that draws on general

---

54. Thomas Aquinas, *Summa Theologica*, I–II, pp. 90–106.

55. Wilhelm Schmidt, *Der Ursprung der Gottesidee*, 12 vols. (Münster: Aschendorff, 1912–1955 1921–1955).

56. W. Schmidt, *The Origin and Growth of Religion: Facts and Theories* (New York: Cooper Square, 1972), 211.

57. Edward Evans-Pritchard, *Theories of Primitive Religion* (New York: Oxford University Press, 1987), 104–105.

revelation and Schmidt's notion of original monotheism to explain common-alities across religious traditions.[58]

Appeals to general revelation and natural law as a source for transreligious truth continue today. Recently, three scholars invoked what we would call general revelation to defend the traditional notion of marriage (as between one man and one woman) as a religious insight common to the great religions. Sherif Girgis, Robert P. George, and Ryan T. Anderson argued that "the demands of our common human nature have shaped (however imperfectly) all of our religious traditions to recognize this natural institution. As such, marriage is the type of social practice whose basic contours can be discerned by our common human reason, whatever our religious background."[59] These scholars contend that reflection on human moral nature—which Christian thinkers since Paul have typically said is part of general revelation—has led most of the great religions to insist that marriage between a man and woman is not only best suited to procreation and child-rearing but is also a truth given by the divine.

Jonathan Edwards (1703–1758) was among those Christian students of world religions who have proposed a second source for truth in the religions: contact with special revelation. Edwards received and developed a tradition called the *prisca theologia* (Latin for "ancient theology"), which attributed truth in the religions to indirect contact with revelation coming from Noah's sons or later Israel. The *prisca theologia* was developed first by Philo, Justin Martyr, Clement of Alexandria, Origen, Lactantius, and Eusebius to show that the greatest philosophers had stolen from the Chosen People and then in the Renaissance by Marsilio Ficino and Pico Della Mirandola to synthesize Neoplatonism and Christian dogma.[60] In his own appropriation of the *prisca theologia*, Edwards said that the heathen learned these truths by what could be called a trickle-down process of revelation. In the "first ages" of the world, the fathers of the nations received revelation of the great religious truths, directly

58. Winfried Corduan, *A Tapestry of Faiths: The Common Threads between Christianity and World Religions* (Downers Grove, IL: InterVarsity, 2002).

59. Sherif Girgis, Robert P. George, and Ryan T. Anderson, "What is Marriage?" *Harvard Journal of Law and Public Policy* 34:1 (Winter 2010): 247. See their more recent book, *What Is Marriage? Man and Woman: A Defense* (New York: Encounter, 2012).

60. Even Augustine seems to have been influenced by this tradition: "What is now called Christian religion has existed among the ancients, and was not absent from the beginning of the human race, until Christ came in the flesh: from which time true religion, which existed already, began to be called Christian" (1.12.3). Saint Augustine, *The Retractions* (Washington, DC: Catholic University of America Press, 1968), 52.

or indirectly, from God himself.[61] These truths were then passed down, by tradition, from one generation to the next. Unfortunately, there was also a religious law of entropy at work. Human finitude and corruption inevitably caused the revelation to be distorted, resulting in superstition and idolatry.

In *Notes on the Scriptures,* one of his private commentaries on selected biblical passages, Edwards recapitulated this drama: "The knowledge of true religion was for some time kept up in the world by tradition. And there were soon great corruptions and apostasies crept in, and much darkness overwhelmed great part of the world." By the time of Moses, most of the truth that had previously been taught by tradition was now lost. So "God took care that there might be something new, [which] should be very public, and of great fame, and much taken notice of abroad, in the world heard, that might be sufficient to lead sincere inquirers to the true God." Others of the ancient Near East heard about the exodus of the Jews from Egypt, the miracles God performed for them in the wilderness, Joshua's conquests of the Canaanites, and the sun standing still. The defeated Canaanites fled to Africa, Asia, Europe, and the isles of the sea "to carry the tidings of those things ... so that, in a manner, the whole world heard of these great things."[62]

After these wondrous acts of God, knowledge of true religion was maintained for several generations. But by the time of David, much had been forgotten and distorted again. So God acted once more, this time for David and Solomon, "to make his people Israel, who had the true religion, [be] taken notice of in the heathen [nations]." The diaspora after the Babylonian captivity spread knowledge of the true God even farther abroad, so that "the heathen world had opportunity by ... the Jews dispersed abroad in the world ... to have come to the knowledge of the true God."[63]

And if it were not enough for God to send out news of these great events, he saw to it that pagan philosophers came looking for news. Gentile "wise men" and "philosophers" obtained "scraps of light and truth ... by travelling from

---

61. *Works of Jonathan Edwards* (henceforth WJE), vol. 20, edited by Amy Plantinga Pauw (New Haven, CT: Yale University Press, 2002), 222–226, 309–311, 308. Usually, Edwards was ambiguous about the location of the original deposit of revelation. Only occasionally did he pinpoint Adam; in his private notebooks, he said that Adam learned the moral law from God and taught it with great clarity to his descendants. WJE, 20:142–143. In *Original Sin,* he wrote that Adam "continued alive near two thirds of the time that passed before the flood," so that most people alive until the flood heard from Adam what "passed between him and his Creator in paradise." WJE, 3:170. Most often, however, he simply referred to the fathers of the nations as identical to or descended from Noah's sons.

62. Ibid., 15:369–372.

63. Ibid., 15:371–372.

one country to another," especially Judea, Greece, and Phoenicia. Edwards noted that Plato, for instance, had come to Egypt to learn what he could of the Jewish religion.[64]

There is little historical evidence for most of this *prisca theologia* tradition. The details cannot be substantiated, particularly when it comes to the earliest events in this account involving God, the first human beings, Noah and his sons, and even relations between Israel and its neighbors. The Greek geographer and historian Strabo wrote that Plato visited Egypt, but the few references to Egypt in Plato's writings reveal little.[65] Augustine was familiar with the legend that Plato had encountered the Old Testament prophet Jeremiah while in Egypt, but he concluded that the chronological history of the two men made this impossible: "On that journey of his, therefore, Plato could neither have seen Jeremiah, who had died so long before, nor read those same Scriptures, which had not yet been translated into the Greek language in which he was fluent."[66]

Yet the general theses of this tradition should not be rejected out of hand. Israel was at the crossroads of many ancient civilizations, and so it is plausible that its neighbors learned of its religious heritage. We cannot know with precision what ideas in other religions came from contact with Israel before the Christian era, but there is little doubt that Islam, for example, arose as a response to both Judaism and its offshoot, Christianity. Muhammad was a trader whose work brought him into contact with a variety of Jewish and Christian ideas. Many scholars have observed that Islam's monotheism (*tawḥīd*) was shaped largely by Judaism, whose followers were more numerous than Christians in seventh-century Arabia.[67]

Historians have also concluded that Indian Christians have plausible claims to a first-century planting of Christian churches on the Asian subcontinent. Strabo reported that on a visit to Egypt about the time of Christ, he found as many as 120 ships a year sailing for India from the Egyptian head of the Red Sea. Jerome tells us of a mission to India in 180 or 190 by Pantaenus "to preach Christ to the Brahmans and philosophers there." Pantaenus was

---

64. Ibid., 19:713, 23:447.

65. Strabo, *Geographica*, 17.29.

66. Augustine, *The City of God against the Pagans*, translated by R. W. Dyson (Cambridge, UK: Cambridge University Press, 1998), VIII.11, 327–328.

67. Richard Bell, *The Origin of Islam in Its Christian Environment* (Oxford, UK: Routledge, 1968; original edition 1926); Abraham Katsch, *Judaism in Islam*, 3rd ed. (Lakewood, NJ: Intellectbooks, 2009).

the great Jewish-Christian scholar of Alexandria and founder of its renowned theological school. It is little wonder that Clement and Origen, his pupils, demonstrate knowledge of the Buddha, Indian Brahmans, and "gymnosophists."[68] This evidence for early inroads of Christian teachings to the Indian subcontinent is significant because it would have made possible the influence of Christian ideas on the later development of both Hindu and Buddhist traditions. Generally, we have little proof of this sort of religious crossbreeding in the next fifteen centuries, but the presence of these traditions living side-by-side for centuries makes such influence plausible. It is much easier to show Christian influence on modern Hindu schools of thought such as the Brahma Samaj and the Ramakrishna movement.[69]

A third possible explanation for Christian similarities in non-Christian religions was first advanced by Justin Martyr (d. ca. 165), the early Christian apologist who concluded that truth found in pagan philosophers could be explained in part by the work of the Logos, the eternal Word. As we saw above, Justin was an early proponent of the *prisca theologia*. He, too, believed that Plato had learned from Jews he met in Egypt. Specifically, he thought, Plato had learned from the books of Moses that the world is not eternal (as Aristotle taught) but was created at some point in time. This explained the creation account in the *Timaeus*. Justin went on to teach that from messianic hints in the Hebrew Bible, Plato determined that there is a power next to God that is placed crosswise in the universe, and from other clues, he figured that there must be a third entity in the divine. Plato did not understand these things well, Justin thought, but he believed it was by studying the Greek translation of the Hebrew Bible that Plato could see things that Christians later realized were pointing to Christian realities.[70]

Learning from the Jews was only one explanation for what Justin saw as the remarkable religious truth among the philosophers and even among some popular religious myths and rites. Justin advanced another explanation that was more novel: pagans were learning from Christ himself in his role as the Logos or Word of the cosmos. Here Justin developed an idea first suggested by the apostle John, that Jesus is the Logos, who not only created the world

---

68. Samuel Hugh Moffett, *A History of Christianity in Asia*, Vol. 1: *Beginnings to 1500* (San Francisco: HarperSanFrancisco, 1992), 25–39. See also Robert Eric Frykenberg, *Christianity in India: From Beginnings to the Present* (Oxford, UK: Oxford University Press, 2008), 91–115.

69. Robert D. Baird and Alfred Bloom, *Indian and Far Eastern Religious Traditions* (New York: Harper & Row, 1971), 107–114; see also *Neo-Hindu Views of Christianity*, edited by Arvind Sharma (Leidin: Brill, 1988).

70. Justin, *First Apology*, 59, 54.

and holds it together moment-by-moment but "enlightens every man." John 1:9, to which Justin is referring, is ambiguous, and scholars disagree on its meaning. Many believe that John was trading on the Stoic concept of a Logos or rational principle that gave form to all creation and is discernible because it is present in the human mind—but that John went further by attributing personhood to what Stoics regarded as an abstract principle. Later theologians agreed with Justin that the Logos was not only a person but also the primary person in the Trinity responsible for revealing God to his creatures. After all, as Edwards observed, Jesus said he was the light of the world (John 8:12) and that no one knows the Father unless the Son reveals the Father to that person (Matt. 11:27). Edwards asked, "Who can be so properly appointed to be [the] revealer of God to the world, as that person who is God's own perfect idea or understanding of himself?"[71]

Justin pushed this Johannine concept further by relating it to the religious philosophers. He argued, in effect, that Christ the Logos was speaking when the philosophers of the ancient world taught truth. Socrates, he said, knew Christ in part because he had part of the Logos. Christ "was and is the Logos who is in every man" and so inspires whatever truth we find in the world. Therefore, "whatever things were rightly said among all men, are the property of us Christians."[72]

Drawing on Jesus's parable of the sower, Justin contended that the Stoics, the poets, and the historians all "spoke well in proportion to the share [they] had of the seminal divine Logos" (*tou spermatikou theiou logou*). They were all "able to see realities darkly through the sowing of the implanted words that was in them."[73] So the Word of Christ, speaking to non-Christians, explains whatever truth there is among pagan thinkers. It also explains why there is error in their thought: "Because they did not know the whole Logos, which is Christ, they often contradicted themselves."[74] With only part of the Logos, they could not see the whole picture. They had access to truths taken out of their broader context.

It is important to clarify what Justin was *not* saying. He did not say these philosophers had full knowledge of God through Jesus Christ. That came only through *epignosis*, or deep knowledge, which came only through possession

---

71. Jonathan Edwards, *Discourse on the Trinity*, WJE, 21:121.

72. Justin, *Second Apology*, 10, 13.

73. Ibid., 13.

74. Ibid., 10.

of the whole Logos, which in turn is possible only through personal faith in Christ. Since that required conscious faith in Jesus of Nazareth as the Christ, pagans with no knowledge of the gospel were lacking in this respect. According to Justin, they would need to come into personal contact with Jesus Christ, which was possible (for those already dead, such as Socrates and Plato) only through the descent of Christ to the dead.[75]

So participation in part of the Logos was qualitatively different from possession of the person of the Logos himself. As Justin put it, "The seed and imitation imparted according to capacity is one thing, and quite another is the thing itself." The good pagan could be moral and know all sorts of truth from the Christ. But he could never have the faith of the Christian, which comes only from possession of the full Logos. Without the latter, he could never "know God, the maker of all things through Jesus the crucified." There were righteous pagans who, though uncircumcised and failing to keep the Sabbath, were yet "pleasing to God." But they did not possess Christian *grace*, which is the presence of the person of the Logos.[76]

For Justin, then, truth, wherever it is found, is a gift of Christ the Logos. The presence of a truth in another philosophy or religion did not mean that the teacher or pupil or worshipper possessed the Logos, only that the truth itself, insofar as it was true, came from the principle of truth, Jesus Christ. Truth is not something that humans find on their own, for they wander in darkness. If they glean truth by reflecting on general revelation, it is because the Logos is enabling them to interpret that revelation in nature and the human person. If by chance there is truth amid the error in other religions, it is there because the Logos has guided some to see some aspect of what is real.

Edwards said that one truth to which the Logos led many of the world religions was the practice of sacrifice. Nearly all religions have made sacrifices for sin and in so doing have recognized that sin breaks fellowship with God and demands some sort of atonement. We could say that it was simply human reflection on the empirical evidence for human depravity and then the recognition that we cannot save ourselves from that depravity that have brought billions through the ages to recognize their need for some recompense for their

75. Chrys Saldanha argues that Justin and other fathers such as Clement of Alexandria believed that the Christian tradition's stories of Christ's descent to the dead (Matt. 27:52; 1 Pet. 3:19, 4:6) meant a postmortem opportunity for salvation for some but only through personal and explicit faith in Christ. Saldanha, *Divine Pedagogy: A Patristic View of Non-Christian Religions* (Rome: LAS, 1984), 163–167.

76. Justin, *Second Apology*, 13; *Dialogue with Trypho* 34, 19, 92, 46.

sins. We could also say, with Justin and Edwards, that it was only by the work of Christ the Logos in human minds that they made the connection between depravity and the need for sacrifice. Edwards said God used this general revelation and the work of the Logos to prepare entire peoples for the later special revelation of Jesus as the final, perfect sacrifice.[77]

It is clear that if one follows Justin and Edwards in positing an active role for the Logos in bringing about some recognition of truth among adherents of other religious traditions, there is a certain tension that results. For on the one hand, we saw above that every so-called truth in the religions is similar and yet also dissimilar to its counterpart in Christian faith, because the non-Christian expression is shaped by the non-Christian story in which it is found. Yet now we are talking about Christ the Logos being responsible for the "truth" that is somewhat distorted by its non-Christian narratival context. How can Christ the Logos provide "truth" that is in some ways different from Christian truth?

The answer seems to be twofold. First, the true teaching in another religion—similar and yet also dissimilar to its Christian counterpart—was permitted by the Logos to prepare people to receive its proper or more complete expression in the gospel. Therefore, second, the partial or incomplete truths found in other traditions can be understood fully or most adequately only in relation to Jesus Christ, the Logos who took on human nature to save sinners and who sums up all things in himself. This is why, for example, from a Christian perspective, the idea of sacrifice in most world religions is always broken and partial unless it is seen as a preparation for understanding the perfect sacrifice in Christ.

We have looked briefly at three ways in which Christian thinkers have attempted to explain the apparent commonalities between the Christian faith and other religions or the presence of some truth and goodness in other religions. Some are more speculative than others, but each has important insights for us to consider. Scripture provides certain basic themes and examples of God's interactions with various peoples in diverse settings. Beyond this, we are left with unanswered questions, and we must attempt cautiously and responsibly to bring the biblical testimony to bear on the empirical realities we encounter in our world. We know from Scripture that God has purposely revealed himself to all human beings through nature and conscience. We can also know with certainty that God has revealed his work to save his people and form them into a family in fellowship with the triune society through

---

77. On Edwards and sacrifices, see McDermott, *Jonathan Edwards Confronts the Gods*, 125–126.

Israel, Jesus Christ, and the church. But whenever we encounter beauty or goodness or truth in other religions, we must compare it to what we find in Jesus Christ in order to distinguish deeper differences from surface similarities and to bring out the richness of what God has revealed to us. We must also be humble when we speculate about *how* that truth or goodness came to be recognized and displayed. Was it by human reflection on general revelation? By contact with special revelation? By the work of the Logos opening eyes and enlightening minds and hearts? Perhaps just one of these answers applies in some cases; perhaps two or even all three might be appropriate in others. We cannot always be sure. But we can know that all truth is God's truth. There is no sphere of human knowing in which human beings by their own unaided powers speculate accurately about the divine. At the end of the day, as it were, there is no way apart from the tri-personal God's self-revelation to come to know the true God—or even a part of his truth, beauty, or goodness.

4

Salvation and Conversion

RELIGIONS TRADITIONALLY HAVE assumed that humankind, and perhaps the cosmos at large, is at present in an unsatisfactory state and that a more desirable state is possible. Each religion offers a particular path to this preferred state, referred to alternatively as salvation or liberation or enlightenment. Picking up on a medical analogy used in some religions, Keith Yandell observes that "a religion proposes a diagnosis of a deep, crippling spiritual disease universal to non-divine sentience and offers a cure."[1] Each religion typically regards its own diagnosis and cure to be accurate and effective, and the proposals of other religions have generally been dismissed as inadequate at best. Only by following the prescribed path can one attain the desired state. Thus, Christians have traditionally insisted that only by responding appropriately, by God's grace, to Jesus Christ as Lord and Savior can one overcome the effects of sin and attain salvation. But such "exclusivism" is increasingly rejected today as intellectually and morally untenable.

For many, the dogmatic and absolute claims associated with religious exclusivism are directly linked to religious violence. Charles Kimball states: "It is somewhat trite, but nevertheless sadly true, to say that more wars have been waged, more people killed, and these days more evil perpetrated in the name of religion than by any other institutional force in human history." According to Kimball, one of the most significant indicators that a religion is becoming evil and conducive to violence is its commitment to "absolute" truth claims: "When particular interpretations of these claims become propositions requiring uniform assent and are treated as rigid doctrines, the likelihood of corruption in the tradition rises exponentially. Such tendencies are the first harbingers of the evil that may follow."[2] Similarly, Stanley Samartha asserts: "At a time when the histories of different nations are increasingly

---

1. Keith Yandell, "How to Sink in Cognitive Quicksand: Nuancing Religious Pluralism," in *Contemporary Debates in Philosophy of Religion*, edited by Michael L. Peterson and Raymond J. Van Arragon (Oxford: Blackwell, 2004), 191.

2. Charles Kimball, *When Religion Becomes Evil: Five Warning Signs* (New York: HarperCollins, 2002), 41, 1.

being drawn together, when different communities of faith are in dialogue with each other as never before, and when people of the world, for good or bad, share a common future, the exclusive claims of particular communities generate tensions and lead to clashes."[3] Monotheistic religions—Christianity in particular—are said to be especially problematic in insisting that only by adopting *their* distinctive teachings and practices can one attain salvation.

Doctrines, we are told, are divisive and therefore should not be emphasized. What really matters in religion is not doctrine but basic moral values and principles that the religions are said to share. A chorus of well-meaning voices informs us that evangelism and conversion only produce further tensions; the time for competition among religions for the souls of humankind is past, and the agenda for the twenty-first century is peaceful coexistence and cooperation in eradicating the many problems in our world.

There is much to be said for these concerns. There is no question that religions can and do contribute to violence, and surely leaders of all religions should commit to work for peaceful coexistence and alleviation of our many problems. But while the long and tragic history of violence in religion should not be minimized, neither should it be exaggerated.[4] Religions are complex, and it is not always clear—despite sometimes strident religious rhetoric—when instances of bigotry, violence, or war are caused by religious rather than other social, ethnic, economic, or political factors.

In this chapter, we will consider some of the issues stemming from the doctrine of Christian salvation. Drawing on the teachings of the Bible, Christians traditionally have insisted that salvation is found only in Jesus Christ and that

---

3. Stanley Samartha, "The Lordship of Jesus Christ and Religious Pluralism," in *Christ's Lordship and Religious Pluralism*, edited by G. H. Anderson and T. F. Stransky (Maryknoll, NY: Orbis, 1981), 22.

4. While secular critics are often simplistic in their easy equation of religion with violence, evangelical Christians often minimize the role of religion in social and political conflicts. What is needed here is careful and honest assessment of the historical record and the range of factors involved in instances of violence. Moreover, religious violence is not limited to the monotheistic traditions. Each of the major religions has its own dark side. Even Buddhism, long regarded as the epitome of a peaceful religion, has a legacy of sanctioning violence and warfare. See *Buddhist Warfare*, edited by Michael K. Jerryson and Mark Juergensmeyer (New York: Oxford University Press, 2010); Mark Juergensmeyer, *Terror in the Mind of God: The Global Rise of Religious Violence* (Berkeley: University of California Press, 2000); Juergensmeyer, *Global Rebellion: Religious Challenges to the Secular State, from Christian Militias to Al Qaeda* (Berkeley: University of California Press, 2008); William T. Cavanaugh, *The Myth of Religious Violence: Secular Ideology and the Roots of Modern Conflict* (New York: Oxford University Press, 2009); *Belief and Bloodshed: Religion and Violence across Time and Tradition*, edited by James K. Wellman Jr. (New York: Rowman and Littlefield, 2007).

all people—including sincere followers of other religious ways—are to repent of their sin and acknowledge Jesus as Lord and Savior. Not only has this conviction been central to the church throughout the centuries, but it also has been a basic assumption behind the modern Christian missionary movement. But this claim is deeply offensive to many today. Many contend that it is precisely this kind of exclusivism, with the accompanying insistence on the need for conversion, that provokes mistreatment of others and even religious violence.

Thus we begin the chapter by looking briefly at two influential figures today who call for a basic unity among the religions rather than ongoing competition over the souls of humankind. We will argue that when such unity comes at the expense of minimizing or distorting the distinctive teachings that have characterized the religions over the centuries, then we fail to take the religions seriously on their own terms. Basic disagreements among the religions over soteriology cannot be so easily dismissed. We will then look at Christian teaching on salvation and Jesus Christ as the only Savior for humankind, including some brief observations about conversion and culture. We conclude with a response to the growing popularity of soteriological universalism in some evangelical circles.

From Competition to Unity among the Religions

No one has been a more powerful and effective symbol of unity among peoples of different faiths than Tenzin Gyatso (b. 1935), the Dalai Lama and spiritual leader of the Geluk (dGe lugs) school of Tibetan Buddhism. The Dalai Lama has become one of the most recognized and respected spiritual leaders today, and he speaks passionately of the need for harmony and mutual acceptance among the religions:

> One area where peaceful coexistence has been hugely problematic in the history of humankind is in the relations between the world's religions. In the past, conflicts generated by religious differences may have been significant and regrettable, but they did not threaten the future of the planet or the survival of humanity. In today's globalized world, where extremists have access to vast technological resources and can draw on the immense emotive power of religion, a single spark could ignite a powder keg of truly frightening proportions. The challenge before religious believers is to genuinely accept the full worth of faith traditions other than one's own. This is to embrace the spirit of pluralism.[5]

5. His Holiness the Dalai Lama, *Toward a True Kinship of Faiths: How the World's Religions Can Come Together* (New York: Doubleday Religion, 2010), ix.

The stakes are high, for the Dalai Lama claims that "harmony between the world's religions is one of the essential preconditions for genuine world peace.... [W]ithout the emergence of a genuine spirit of religious pluralism, there is no hope for the development of harmony based on true inter-religious understanding."[6]

Religions become obstacles to peace when religious believers assume that "one's own religion [is] the only legitimate faith" and that other religions are evil and false.[7] The Dalai Lama emphasizes that we should focus on what the religions have in common and not their differences: "All of the different religious faiths, despite their philosophical differences, have a similar objective. Every religion emphasizes human improvement, love, respect for others, sharing other people's sufferings. On these lines, every religion has more or less the same viewpoint and the same goal." Rather than trying to convert others to their own faith, religious believers ought to respect religious others and work with them for the common good. "I am not interested in converting other people to Buddhism but in how we Buddhists can contribute to human society, according to our own ideas."[8] The precondition for world peace lies in acknowledging the religions' common commitment to the value of compassion and then acting on this for the global common good.

> It is the task of all human beings with an aspiration to spiritual perfection—not just the leaders of the world religions but also every individual believer—to affirm the fundamental value of the compassion that lies both at the heart of human nature and at the core of the ethical teachings of all the world's major religions..... [The religions] use different words, invoke different images, root themselves in different concepts. But what they have in common is far more than what divides them, and their differences form the potential for a tremendously enriching dialogue, rooted in a marvelous diversity of experience and insight.[9]

---

6. Ibid., x, 146.

7. Ibid., ix.

8. His Holiness the Dalai Lama, "'Religious Harmony' and the Bodhgaya Interviews," in *Christianity through Non-Christian Eyes*, edited by Paul J. Griffiths (Maryknoll, NY: Orbis, 1990), 163, 165.

9. Dalai Lama, *Toward a True Kinship*, xii.

One might conclude from these statements that the Dalai Lama is a thorough pluralist, who believes that all major religions are equally "true" and that no particular religious perspective should take priority over others. But this would be misleading, for he is a committed Buddhist who is convinced that the Buddhist perspective is true and efficacious in ways that other worldviews are not.[10] And yet although he is a devoted Buddhist, the Dalai Lama also is representative of many today who minimize religious teachings and doctrines as irrelevant to what is supposed to be the true heart of religion: compassion for others and working to make this a better world for everyone. In a speech concluding the 1993 Parliament of the World's Religions in Chicago, the Dalai Lama stated: "We should look at the underlying purpose of religion and not merely at the abstract details of theology or metaphysics. All religions make the betterment of humanity their primary concern. When we view the different religions as essentially instruments to develop a good heart—love and respect for others, a true sense of community—we can appreciate what they have in common."[11]

On one level, there is much to affirm in the Dalai Lama's statements. It is true that religions are concerned with compassion and the "betterment of humanity," and undoubtedly, there is much that the different religions have in common. Evangelical Christians can and should work together with religious leaders from other faiths to tackle the many problems we face globally. But nagging questions remain. Are human improvement, love, and respect for others *all* that the religions are concerned with? Are these even the most significant concerns of the religions? Do the religions agree on what constitutes human improvement? Can metaphysics and "abstract theology" so easily be discarded if we are to be faithful to the religions themselves? There is

---

10. For example, the Dalai Lama rejects the Christian teaching about a creator God as false. Comparing Christianity and Buddhism, he states: "Now from the philosophical point of view, the theory that God is the creator, is almighty and permanent, is in contradiction to the Buddhist teachings. From this point of view there is disagreement. For Buddhists, the universe has no first cause and hence no creator, nor can there be such a thing as a permanent, primordially pure being. So, of course, doctrinally there is conflict. The views are opposite to one another." The Dalai Lama, "Buddhism and Other Religions," in *Philosophy of Religion: Selected Readings*, 4th ed., edited by Michael Peterson et al. (New York: Oxford University Press, 2010), 578. See also His Holiness the Dalai Lama, *The Good Heart: A Buddhist Perspective on the Teachings of Jesus*, edited by Robert Kiely and translated by Geshe Thupten Jinpa (Boston, MA: Wisdom, 1996), 82; and Dalai Lama, *Toward a True Kinship*, 133–134.

11. His Holiness the Dalai Lama, "The Importance of Religious Harmony," in *The Community of Religions: Voices and Images of the Parliament of the World's Religions*, edited by Wayne Teasdale and George Cairns (New York: Continuum, 1996), 216.

an obvious tension in the Dalai Lama's statements between the basic incompatibilities among religious teachings and the need to genuinely accept other religions as authentic ways of being religious. As he puts it, "The challenge is to find a way in which the followers of these traditions can, despite remaining true to their doctrinal standpoints, revere one another as representing legitimate paths to God."[12] The Dalai Lama does not explain how this tension is to be resolved.

Religious Pluralism and Soteriology

As we saw in chapter 1, philosopher and theologian John Hick (1922–2012) has provided a model of religious pluralism that acknowledges the differences among religions while also affirming the major religions as alternative ways of responding to the one divine reality, which he calls the Real. Our concern here is not with the details of Hick's complex and much-discussed model. But we will consider his assertion that basic disagreements over doctrinal issues do not matter and his claim that there is a common soteriological structure to the religions—namely, moral transformation from self-centeredness to Reality-centeredness: "The great world faiths embody different perceptions and conceptions of, and correspondingly different responses to, the Real from within the variant ways of being human; and that within each of them the transformation of human existence from self-centeredness to reality-centeredness is taking place. These traditions are accordingly to be regarded as alternative soteriological 'spaces' within which, or 'ways' along which, men and women find salvation/liberation/enlightenment."[13]

Christians might wonder why Hick replaces "God" with "the Real." Not all religions are theistic, accepting the reality of a creator God, so "the Real" is used in an effort to include both nontheistic and theistic religions. But why suppose that theistic and nontheistic religions are referring ultimately to the same reality? Hick postulates the Real as the ultimate reality because of what he regards as a common experience of moral transformation in the

---

12. Dalai Lama, *Toward a True Kinship*, 134. The reference to God should not be taken as indicating the Dalai Lama's belief in God: "even though my own faith tradition, Buddhism, is not theistic, nothing stops me from developing deep admiration and reverence toward the theistic teachings that provide so much inspiration and solace to so many of my fellow humans—and that have enabled the spiritual development of so many saints and spiritually evolved beings" (134).

13. John Hick, *An Interpretation of Religion*, 2nd ed. (New Haven, CT: Yale University Press, 2004), 240.

religions: "My reason to assume that the different world religions are referring, through their specific concepts of the Gods and Absolutes, to the same ultimate Reality is the striking similarity of the transformed human state described within the different traditions as saved, redeemed, enlightened, wise, awakened, liberated. This similarity strongly suggests a common source of salvific transformation."[14] Hick claims that "the production of saints, both contemplative and practical, individualistic and political, is thus one valid criterion by which to identify a religious tradition as a salvific response to the Real." This criterion enables us to conclude "that each of the great world faiths constitutes a context for salvation/liberation: for each has produced its own harvest of saints."[15]

How do we know when such transformation has taken place? Those whose lives have been authentically transformed and have abandoned "self-centeredness" for "Reality-centeredness" manifest qualities such as compassion and love for others, strength of soul, purity, charity, inner peace and serenity, and radiant joy.[16] According to Hick, this moral transformation is occurring roughly to the same extent across the major religions.[17]

Hick is well aware of the many conflicting truth claims among the religions, but he does not regard this as a decisive problem. In order to defuse the problem of conflicting truth claims, he makes a basic distinction between what he calls literal truth and mythological truth. The understanding of truth that we ordinarily use is literal truth: "The literal truth or falsity of a factual assertion (as distinguished from the truth or falsity of an analytic proposition) consists of conformity or lack of conformity to fact: 'it is raining here and now' is literally true if and only if it is raining here and now." But Hick argues that this notion of truth is not applicable to the disputes between the religions over basic metaphysical teachings. Religious claims concerning these matters should not be understood in terms of literal truth but rather mythological truth: "A statement or set of statements about X is mythologically true if it is not literally true but nevertheless tends to evoke an appropriate dispositional attitude to X."[18] Mythological truth does not depend on an objectively existing state of affairs but rather on the effect that accepting a particular belief has on

14. John Hick, *A Christian Theology of Religions: The Rainbow of Faiths* (Louisville, KY: Westminster John Knox, 1995), 69.

15. Hick, *An Interpretation of Religion*, 307.

16. Ibid., 301–302.

17. John Hick, *Problems of Religious Pluralism* (New York: St. Martin's, 1985), 86–87.

18. Hick, *An Interpretation of Religion*, 348.

an individual or communities. Thus, a basic teaching such as "There is no God but Allah, and Muhammad is his prophet" is said by Hick to be true not because in fact Allah is the only God and Muhammad is God's prophet but because belief in this statement tends to bring about an "appropriate dispositional attitude" toward the Real among Muslims.[19] And the same holds for basic teachings of all the religions.

A full response to Hick's proposal is impossible here, but some brief comments are in order.[20] While it is true that the major religions are all concerned in some way with moral transformation and there is considerable agreement among religions regarding the moral qualities defining a saint, none of the religions would agree that such moral transformation *by itself* constitutes what is essential in religion. For each religion situates its moral teachings within a broader metaphysical system that gives the moral imperatives their meaning and significance. The moral injunctions cannot be appreciated apart from their relation to broader teachings on the nature of the cosmos, the religious ultimate, and our relation as persons to these larger realities.

In other words, Hick has reduced the specific soteriological claims of the religions to an abstract general formula. On a general level, Hick is correct in observing that all the major religions share a certain formal soteriological structure. Each religion claims that the cosmos as we now experience it is not as it should be and thus that humankind suffers from some undesirable condition. And each offers a way to overcome the present predicament and attain a superior state.

But when it comes to filling in this formal soteriological structure with specific meanings, the fundamental disagreements among the religions are obvious. It is not as though the religions all have a common goal in view and simply disagree on the best way to attain this goal. They disagree on the nature

---

19. In his notion of mythological truth, Hick clearly was influenced by Wilfred Cantwell Smith's proposal concerning personal truth in religion. See Wilfred Cantwell Smith, *The Meaning and End of Religion: A Revolutionary Approach to the Great Religious Traditions* (San Francisco: Harper & Row, 1962); Smith, "A Human View of Truth," in *Truth and Dialogue in World Religions: Conflicting Truth Claims*, edited by John Hick (Philadelphia: Westminster, 1974), 20–44.

20. There are enormous problems confronting any attempt to formulate a coherent model of religious pluralism. See Harold Netland, "Religious Pluralism as an Explanation for Religious Diversity," in *Philosophy and the Christian Worldview*, edited by David Werther and Mark D. Linville (New York: Continuum, 2012), 25–49; Keith Yandell, "Some Varieties of Religious Pluralism," in *Inter-Religious Models and Criteria*, edited by James Kellenberger (New York: St. Martin's, 1993), 187–211; *The Philosophical Challenge of Religious Diversity*, edited by Philip L. Quinn and Kevin Meeker (New York: Oxford University Press, 2006).

of the current predicament and the preferred alternative to our problematic world. This is brought out clearly in the following extensive quote from Harold Coward's *Sin and Salvation in the World Religions*:

> "Salvation" is a term which arises most clearly in the Christian tradition—the idea that God's love through Jesus Christ will save humans from their sinful state. However, other religions have parallel concepts. Rather than salvation, Jews speak of "redemption" for individuals, for Israel and indeed for all nations. In Islam the closest parallel is found in the term *najat* which means "escape or deliverance from the fires of hell to pleasures of paradise by following God's guidance." In Judaism, Christianity, and Islam the human condition from which we all begin is one of sin and disobedience to God, and it is from that state that we need to be saved. When we turn to Hinduism and Buddhism, however, it is human ignorance rather than sin that is our baseline human experience. Our ignorance traps us in a seemingly unending series of lives —of birth, aging, sickness, and death repeated over and over. This apparently endless series of suffering, death and rebirth is the human condition that leads one to long for "release from rebirth"—the Hindu and Buddhist functional parallel to the idea of salvation. "Release" for Hindus is referred to as *moksa*, while Buddhists call it *nirvana*.[21]

Although Hindu, Jain, and Buddhist traditions identify the root problem with ignorance, they disagree over the nature of this ignorance and the ways to overcome it. Chinese religious traditions such as Daoism locate the problem in a fundamental imbalance or disharmony between cosmic and moral forces, and Japanese Shinto appeals to a vague notion of impurity and failure to properly respond to the ubiquitous kami. Thus, religious studies scholar Stephen Prothero states: "What the world's religions share is not so much a finish line as a starting point: And where they begin is with this simple observation: something is wrong with the world.... Religious folk worldwide agree that something has gone awry. They part company, however, when it comes to stating just what has gone wrong, and they diverge sharply when they move from diagnosing the human problem to prescribing how to solve it."[22]

---

21. Harold Coward, *Sin and Salvation in the World Religions* (Oxford, UK: Oneworld, 2003), 2–3.

22. Stephen Prothero, *God Is Not One: The Eight Rival Religions That Run the World—and Why Their Differences Matter* (New York: HarperCollins, 2010), 11.

Given the very different diagnoses of the problem, it is hardly surprising that Christians, Hindus, Buddhists, and Jains offer very different ways of overcoming this predicament.

These differences were regarded traditionally as matters of great importance, for it was believed that unless one diagnoses the nature of the problem correctly, the proposed cure will not be effective. Traditional Hindus, Jains, and Buddhists, for example, assumed that unless one understood properly the way things actually are and the causal conditions driving rebirth, there is little hope for release from the endless cycle of rebirths. Representatives of the three traditions thus criticized each other vigorously over metaphysical questions about Brahman (the Supreme Being) and the reality of the individual soul or atman.[23] Hindus and Jains believed in the reality of the soul; Buddhists denied this. Buddhists and Jains denied the reality of Brahman, while most Hindus affirmed this. The great Hindu theologian Shankara (d. 820), architect of Advaita Vedanta Hinduism, forthrightly states that "if the soul…is not considered to possess fundamental unity with Brahman—an identity to be realized by knowledge—there is not any chance of its obtaining final release."[24] In other words, only if one accepts Shankara's perspective, as expressed in Advaita Vedanta, can one be liberated. Similarly, a text from the Jaina Sutras, the authoritative texts of Jainism, bluntly informs us: "Those who do not know all things by Kevala (knowledge), but who being ignorant teach a Law (of their own), are lost themselves, and work the ruin of others in this dreadful, boundless Circle of Births. Those who know all things by the full Kevala knowledge, and who practicing meditation teach the whole Law, are themselves saved and save others."[25] In other words, those who accept Jain doctrine can be enlightened and liberated from rebirths—but without this doctrine, one cannot be enlightened.

---

23. See Richard King, *Indian Philosophy: An Introduction to Hindu and Buddhist Thought* (Washington, DC: Georgetown University Press, 1999).

24. Sankara, "The Vedanta Sutras, with Commentary by Sankaracarya," IV.3.14, translated by George Thibaut, Part II, in *Sacred Books of the East*, edited by F. Max Müller, Vol. 38 (Delhi: Motilal Barnarsidass, 1968 [1904]), 399–400. Consider Shankara's assessment of the teachings of the Buddha: "Buddha, by propounding the three mutually contradictory systems, teaching respectively the reality of the external world, the reality of ideas only, and general nothingness, has himself made it clear either that he was a man given to make incoherent assertions, or else that hatred of all beings induced him to propound absurd doctrines by accepting which [people] would become thoroughly confused." Sankara, "The Vedanta Sutras," II.2.32, Part I, Vol. 34, 400, 428.

25. "Jaina Sutras," translated by Hermann Jacobi, in *Sacred Books of the East*, edited by F. Max Müller, Vol. 45 (Curzon: Richmond, Surrey, 2001), 418.

Moving to the contemporary period, consider the Dalai Lama's response to the question of whether only the Buddha can provide "the ultimate source of refuge": "Here, you see, it is necessary to examine what is meant by liberation or salvation. Liberation in which 'a mind that understands the sphere of reality annihilates all defilements in the sphere of reality' is a state that only Buddhists can accomplish. This kind of *moksha* or *nirvana* is only explained in the Buddhist scriptures, and is achieved only through Buddhist practice."[26] Understanding the relevant doctrines is thus directly linked to attaining the soteriological goal. Contrary to Hick's contention, doctrinal beliefs do matter, and proper acceptance of the relevant teachings is regarded by the religions as essential for attaining the soteriological goal.

Moreover, Hick's attempt to bypass the problem of conflicting truth claims by interpreting religious claims in terms of mythological truth is also problematic.[27] This is not how religious believers typically understand the claims that they affirm. Furthermore, the notion of mythological truth only makes sense if it is combined with a logically prior understanding of literal truth in religion. To say that "God raised Jesus from the dead" is mythologically true, because its acceptance evokes appropriate dispositional responses to the Real on the part of Christians, presupposes that there are *some* statements about the Real—what the Real is like and what an appropriate response to the Real would be—that are true in a nonmythological, or literal, sense. For example, Hick says that an appropriate response to the Real is to act in an altruistic way to our neighbor and to refrain from thinking only of our own interests. This is to speak in a literal way about how we are to treat our neighbor. Otherwise, we are unable to know when a statement evokes an appropriate response to the Real, and the notion of mythological truth becomes vacuous. So the idea of literal truth in religion cannot be so easily disposed of, and with it, we are back to the problem of conflicting truth claims in religion.

Sin

The major religions acknowledge that the present world is not as it should be. But, as we have seen, they offer very different views about the nature of

---

26. Dalai Lama, "'Religious Harmony,'" 169.

27. See Harold Netland, *Encountering Religious Pluralism* (Downers Grove, IL: InterVarsity, 2001), 227–246; Brian Hebblethwaite, "John Hick and the Question of Truth in Religion," in *God, Truth and Reality: Essays in Honour of John Hick*, edited by Arvind Sharma (New York: St. Martin's, 1993), 124–134.

the present malady, its causes, and what is required for attaining a more desirable state. John Hick's appeal to a common soteriological structure among the religions simply ignores the specificity of the teachings of the religions, reducing them to an abstract, lowest-common-denominator moral principle. Christopher Wright astutely observes: "I find it a frustrating exercise reading the work of religious pluralists because they tend to be so vague and inadequate on what salvation actually is. And that in turn seems to me largely because they ignore the Hebrew Bible's insight on the nature and seriousness of sin."[28]

Christianity offers not an abstract, generic soteriology but rather a rich and very particular understanding of salvation. Moreover, the Christian teaching on salvation must be understood within the context of what the Scriptures have to say about the fundamental problem confronting humankind: sin. Sin must be distinguished from simple moral failure. All the religions acknowledge moral failure on the part of humankind, and they offer different analyses of the significance and consequences of such failure. But sin is more than merely our failure to act morally as we ought. At its core, sin is rebellion against and rejection of God and God's righteous ways. Cornelius Plantinga observes: "In biblical thinking, we can understand neither shalom nor sin apart from reference to God. Sin is a religious concept, not just a moral one."[29] Thus, the notion of sin must always be understood within the context of a holy and righteous God. Although nontheistic religions speak of moral failure, it makes little sense to ascribe a doctrine of sin to religions that deny the reality of a holy and righteous God.

Plantinga very helpfully situates the biblical teaching on sin in relation to the great Old Testament theme of shalom: "The webbing together of God, humans, and all creation in justice, fulfillment, and delight is what the Hebrew prophets call *shalom*..... In the Bible shalom means *universal flourishing, wholeness, and delight*—a rich state of affairs in which natural needs are satisfied and natural gifts fruitfully employed, a state of affairs that inspires joyful wonder at its Creator and Savior and opens doors and welcomes the creatures in whom he delights. Shalom, in other words, is the way things ought to be."[30]

---

28. Christopher J. H. Wright, "The Unique Christ in the Plurality of Religions," in *The Unique Christ in Our Pluralistic World*, edited by Bruce Nicholls (Grand Rapids, MI: Baker, 1994), 39.

29. Cornelius Plantinga Jr., *Not the Way It's Supposed to Be: A Breviary of Sin* (Grand Rapids, MI: Eerdmans, 1995), 12. See also Henri A. G. Blocher, "Sin," in *The Oxford Handbook of Evangelical Theology*, edited by Gerald R. McDermott (New York: Oxford University Press, 2010), 129–145.

30. Plantinga, *Not the Way It's Supposed to Be*, 10; emphasis in original.

But sin has distorted God's creation, removing shalom. Scripture teaches that the choice of the first humans to reject God introduced the cancer of sin to all humankind (Gen. 2:16–17; Gen. 3; Rom. 5:12). Sin is a pervasive condition of the heart that affects all aspects of our being, including our thoughts, desires, dispositions, and actions. Sin involves not only our inner constitution but also our relationships with others. Plantinga describes sin as "any spoiling of *shalom*, whether physically (e.g., by disease), morally, spiritually, or otherwise."[31] Sin also is depicted in Scripture as a breach of God's moral order or standard, or "any activity or stance opposed to God, or any rejection of God's claims by humans bent on going their own way."[32] Millard Erickson defines sin as "any lack of conformity, active or passive, to the moral law of God. This may be a matter of act, of thought, or of inner disposition or state."[33] Sin is characterized in Scripture as unrighteousness (Rom 1:18), lawlessness (1 John 3:4), disobedience (2 Tim. 3:2), transgression (Gal. 3:19), wickedness (John 3:20), evil (Rom. 12:9), and ungodliness (Rom. 1:18).

According to Scripture, all human beings are sinners. As a result of the initial rebellion against God (Gen. 3), there is no one who is righteous and consistently does what is right (Ps. 14:2–3; Isa. 53:6; Rom. 3:10–18, 23). People commit sin because they are by nature sinful. Sinful acts are the product of a sinful heart (Gen. 6:5; Isa. 29:13; Jer. 17:9; Matt. 15:18–20). Sin is both personal and social in its manifestations; its effects are evident both in individuals and collectively in human societies and cultures. There is a sense in which sin has adversely affected the entire natural order, resulting in the "groaning of creation" as it awaits its release from "its bondage to decay" (Rom. 8:19–22).

The consequences of sin are profound. Scripture presents God as holy, righteous, and morally pure in all his ways (Lev. 11:44–45, 20:26; Ps. 77:13, 99:3, 99:5; Isa. 6:1–4, 40:25, 57:15; 1 Peter 1:15–16; Rev. 4:8). Our sin results in our guilt before God (Rom. 1:18–3:23). Sin ruptures our relationships with others, producing suffering and pain. Most significantly, sin results in alienation from God our creator (Isa. 59:2). Sin brings with it death (Rom. 6:23), and all persons, unless saved by God's mercy and grace, face God's righteous wrath and eternal condemnation for sin (John 3:36; Rev. 20:11–15). Jesus warned repeatedly of the judgment to come for those who do not repent (Matt. 11:20–24, 12:41–42, 13:36–43, 25:31–46; Mark 9:42–49; Luke 13:22–30,

---

31. Ibid., 14.

32. Marguerite Shuster, "Sin," in *Global Dictionary of Theology*, edited by William A. Dyrness and Veli-Matti Kärkkäinen (Downers Grove, IL: InterVarsity, 2008), 818.

33. Millard Erickson, *Christian Theology*, Vol. 2 (Grand Rapids, MI: Baker, 1984), 578.

16:19–31; John 3:18, 3:36, 12:47–48). God hates sin and cannot allow sin to go unpunished: "God hates sin not just because it violates his law but, more substantively, because it violates shalom, because it breaks the peace, because it interferes with the way things are supposed to be....God is for shalom and therefore against sin."[34] Scripture teaches that there is nothing that we can do in and of ourselves to overcome our sinful condition and its effects; apart from God's special intervention on our behalf, we are helpless, "dead in our sins" (Eph. 2:1–3). It is against the background of this very bleak picture that we must appreciate the biblical teaching on salvation.

Salvation

Here we confront one of the great mysteries in Scripture. In his mercy and love, God has taken the initiative and provided a way for sinful persons to be forgiven and reconciled to God. Evangelical Christians frequently use the word *salvation* to refer to God's provision for repentant sinners resulting in forgiveness of sin, reconciliation with God, and eternal life both now and in heaven. And this is certainly a dominant theme in Scripture. But it is also important to see that biblical salvation involves more than this. Just as the effects of sin on the created order are many and diverse, so, too, God's work in defeating sin and its consequences has many implications.

The first thing to observe about salvation in Scripture is that it is always God who saves. Christopher Wright observes: "Salvation belongs to God, is initiated by his grace, achieved by his power, offered on his terms, secured by his promises, guaranteed by his sovereignty. God is the subject of the act of saving us....Salvation is the result of no action of ours other than that of asking and accepting it from God."[35] In Scripture, God's act of saving takes many forms. God delivers his people from slavery, enemies, anxiety, injustice, illness, guilt, shame, danger, idolatry, demonic oppression, and hopelessness. Another way to put this is to say that God saves people from the power and consequences of sin. Just as the entire cosmos has been affected by sin, so, too, God's salvation results in the defeat of sin and evil and the restoration of the created order, culminating in the "new heavens and new earth" (Rom. 8:19–22; Rev. 21:1–4).

---

34. Plantinga, *Not the Way It's Supposed to Be*, 14.

35. Christopher J. H. Wright, "Salvation Belongs to Our God," *Evangelical Interfaith Dialogue* 1, no. 4 (Fall 2010): 3.

But a dominant theme throughout Old and New Testaments is the salvation of human beings from the guilt of sin and the reconciliation of sinful humanity to God. Although a variety of terms are used in the New Testament to speak of salvation, the most common term used by the apostle Paul is the verb *sōzō*.[36] The term and its cognates are used in various ways, so that on some occasions it speaks of rescue from immediate physical danger (as in Matt. 8:25, 14:30; Acts 27:20, 31). *Sōzō* is also sometimes used in reference to physical healing of disease (as in Matt. 9:21–22, 14:36; Mark 10:52; Luke 7:3, 8:48; Acts 4:9). *Soteria* can mean physical healing or spiritual salvation, and at times, it can include both meanings, as in Peter's declaration in Acts 4:12 after the healing of the crippled man: "There is salvation [*soteria*] in no one else, for there is no other name under heaven given among men by which we must be saved." But in general, "'salvation' refers to what Christ has done in his great saving act for sinners.... Salvation is a comprehensive word bringing out the truth that God in Christ has rescued people from the desperate state that their sins had brought about."[37]

God is a merciful and gracious God, who deeply loves all people and desires their salvation (John 3:16; Eph. 2:4–10; 1 John 4:8). God's salvation of sinful human beings is rooted in the incarnation of the Son of God, for "Christ Jesus came into the world to save sinners" (1 Tim. 1:15). In announcing the birth of Jesus, the angel instructed Joseph, "You shall call his name Jesus, for he will save his people from their sins" (Matt. 1:21).[38] Jesus saw his mission as providing salvation. Speaking of himself, he declared, "For the Son of Man came to seek and to save the lost" (Luke 19:10). Jesus' entire life is at the center of God's saving work by meriting eternal life for us, but it is especially in the cross and the resurrection that God's victory over sin and evil is accomplished. God's wrath against sin and unfathomable love for sinners come together in a mysterious way in the life, death, and resurrection of Jesus of Nazareth, the eternal Word become man. For in the incarnation in Jesus—an utterly unique event in which the eternal creator assumed humanity and took upon himself the sins of the world (2 Cor. 5:21)—God provided a way for sinful humanity

---

36. See I. Howard Marshall, "Salvation," in *Dictionary of Jesus and the Gospels*, edited by Joel B. Green, Scot McKnight, and I. Howard Marshall (Downers Grove, IL: InterVarsity, 1992), 720–724; Leon Morris, "Salvation," in *Dictionary of Paul and His Letters*, edited by Gerald F. Hawthorne, Ralph P. Martin, and Daniel G. Reid (Downers Grove, IL: InterVarsity, 1993), 858.

37. Morris, "Salvation," 862.

38. The original Hebrew for "Jesus" was *Yeshua*, derived from the verb meaning "to deliver or rescue or save."

to be reconciled to himself (John 3:14–18; Eph. 2:4–5; 1 Pet. 3:18). God's mercy and love are manifest in the cross, as the Son suffered and died as our substitute to pay the penalty for sin (John 3:14–16; 1 John 4:9–10). Thus, salvation is based on the sinless person and atoning work of Jesus Christ on the cross (Rom. 3:25; 2 Cor. 5:18–19, 21; Heb. 2:17; 1 John 2:2, 4:10).[39] According to the Scriptures, salvation is a gift of God's grace, is based on the person and work of Jesus Christ in his life and on the cross, and comes through an exercise of faith in God (Rom. 3:25; 2 Cor. 5:18–19, 21; Heb. 2:17; 1 John 2:2, 4:10). Salvation is totally the work of God's grace and is not the result of human effort or good works (Eph. 2:8–10).

A variety of terms and images are used throughout Scripture to speak of the many ways in which God delivers humankind, and indeed the creation at large, from the ravages of sin. Brenda Colijn notes: "From one angle, the human predicament is rebellion against God. Salvation looks like living under God's universal reign. From another angle, the human predicament is bondage to both internal and external forces. Salvation looks like freedom from those sources. From yet a third angle, the human predicament looks like alienation from God, from other people, from creation and even from one's own best self. Salvation looks like the restoration of those relationships."[40]

Theologians use various terms to speak of aspects of God's saving work on our behalf. But three concepts in particular—atonement, regeneration, and justification—are at the heart of biblical teaching on salvation. Atonement refers to the work of Jesus Christ on the cross that makes possible a reconciled relationship with God, which had been broken due to sin. That it is the death of Jesus Christ on the cross that results in the reconciliation of sinful humanity to God is a recurring theme in the New Testament (Matt. 20:28; John 3:13–16; Rom. 3:21–25, 5:1–2, 5:6-11; 1 Cor. 15:3–4; Gal. 2:20; Col. 1:20, 2:13–14; 1 Tim. 2:5–6; Heb. 10:19–22; 1 Pet. 3:18; 1 John 4:9–10).

Throughout the history of the church, there has been considerable debate over just how it is that Christ's death brings about reconciliation with God.[41] The various theories of the atonement fall into three broad categories. One view, which was influential during the first millennium of Christian history, understands Christ's work largely in terms of his conflict with and triumph

---

39. See John R. W. Stott, *The Cross of Christ* (Downers Grove, IL: InterVarsity, 1986).

40. Brenda B. Colijn, *Images of Salvation in the New Testament* (Downers Grove, IL: InterVarsity, 2010), 14.

41. For a helpful overview, see *The Nature of the Atonement: Four Views*, edited by James Beilby and Paul R. Eddy (Downers Grove, IL: InterVarsity, 2006).

over Satan and the demonic forces that hold sinful humankind captive. In the cross and resurrection, Christ defeats the kingdom of darkness and rescues sinful humanity. A variation on this theme is found in the influential work of the Swedish theologian Gustaf Aulén, *Christus Victor*. Aulén argued that central to this model is "the idea of the Atonement as a Divine conflict and victory; Christ—Christus victor—fights against and triumphs over the evil powers of the world, the 'tyrants' under which mankind is in bondage and suffering."[42]

Another perspective on the atonement is the "objective" view, which sees the atonement as addressing a necessary demand on God's part for reconciliation to take place. The atonement is viewed as substitutionary and sacrificial, as Jesus took the place of sinful humanity and bore the penalty for human sin. Salvation of sinful human beings requires a sacrifice—not the sacrifice of animals but that of a perfect person (Heb. 10:4, 9:26, 10:5–10). Jesus puts himself forward as the sacrifice of atonement in our place. A key text here is 2 Corinthians 5:21: "For our sake he made him to be sin who knew no sin, so that in him we might become the righteousness of God." Similarly, Romans 3:23–25 states: "Since all have sinned and fall short of the glory of God; they are now justified by his grace as a gift, through the redemption that is in Christ Jesus, whom God put forward as a sacrifice of atonement by his blood, effective through faith." One of the more influential thinkers here is the medieval theologian Anselm (1033–1109), whose *Cur Deus Homo* (Why God Became Man) sets out the classic statement of the satisfaction theory of the atonement. Variations of the objective perspective, such as the penal substitution and satisfaction theories, have been influential among evangelicals.

A third perspective holds that the change brought about by the atonement is not so much in God but in humans. Jesus' death on the cross is held up as a moral example for us. "But God demonstrates his own love for us in this: while we were still sinners, Christ died for us" (Rom. 5:8). We are to have the same love and humility that Christ demonstrates in his willingly submitting to the horrors of death on the cross (Phil. 2:5–11). Peter Abelard (1079–1142) was an exponent of the view that Christ's work on the cross was primarily a demonstration to the world of God's amazing love for sinful humanity. The moral influence theory, as this view is sometimes called, has been especially influential in modern liberal theology. All three perspectives—the *Christus Victor*, objective substitutionary, and moral influence theories—have

---

42. Gustaf Aulén, *Christus Victor: An Historical Study of the Three Main Types of the Idea of Atonement*, translated by A. G. Hebert (New York: Macmillan, 1969), 4.

important insights, and a robust, biblical understanding will include each of these perspectives.

Another term that is basic to Christian understandings of salvation is *regeneration.* J. I. Packer states: "Regeneration, or new birth, is an inner recreating of fallen human nature by the gracious sovereign action of the Holy Spirit."[43] The redemption of sinful humanity involves a transformation, or re-creation, of the soul through the supernatural work of the Holy Spirit. Jesus, in the gospel of John, speaks of this as the "new birth," without which one cannot enter the kingdom of God (John 3:5–8). The image of new birth is powerful and striking, for what is in view here is not simply becoming morally better people than we were but rather a radical break with the past inaugurated by a special work of the Spirit (John 1:12–13; Titus 3:4–6). Thus, the apostle Paul states that "if anyone is in Christ, he is a new creation" (2 Cor. 5:17). Packer explains: "The regenerate person has forever ceased to be the person he or she was; the old life is over and a new life has begun; he or she is a new creature in Christ, buried with him out of reach of condemnation and raised with him into a new life of righteousness (see Rom. 6:3–11; 2 Cor. 5:17; Col. 3:9–11)."[44] Those who are made regenerate by the Spirit are to "walk by the Spirit," living in submission to the Spirit so that their lives manifest love, joy, peace, patience, kindness, goodness, faithfulness, gentleness, and self-control (Gal. 5:22–23, 25).

God's salvation of sinful humanity also involves its justification. Central to the biblical understanding of salvation is the idea that God pardons and accepts believing sinners (Ps. 32:1–5; Isa. 55:6–7; Luke 7:41–50, 18:9–14; Acts 10:42–43; 1 John 1:8–9). Justification is the doctrine that speaks to God's provision for human guilt before God for having failed to respond appropriately to God's expectations. As Erickson explains, "Justification is God's action pronouncing sinners righteous in his sight."[45] It is because of the substitutionary sacrifice of Jesus Christ on the cross that God declares believing sinners righteous: "In the New Testament, justification is the declarative act of God by which, *on the basis of the sufficiency of Christ's atoning death*, he pronounces believers to have fulfilled all of the requirements of the law which pertain to them. Justification is a forensic act imputing the righteousness of Christ to

---

43. J. I. Packer, "Regeneration," in *Evangelical Dictionary of Theology*, 2nd ed., edited by Walter A. Elwell (Grand Rapids, MI: Baker, 2001), 1000.

44. Ibid.

45. Millard Erickson, *Christian Theology*, Vol. 3 (Grand Rapids, MI: Baker, 1985), 954. For current debates on issues relating to justification, see *Justification: Five Views*, edited by James K. Beilby and Paul Rhodes Eddy (Downers Grove, IL: InterVarsity, 2011).

the believer; it is not an actual infusing of holiness into the individual. It is a matter of declaring the person righteous, as a judge does in acquitting the accused."[46] But if justification is essentially a declarative judgment made by God on the basis of Christ's work external to the believer, it is also integrally connected to the pouring out of the Holy Spirit *into* the believer, as Paul suggests by speaking of both justification and the indwelling Spirit in the same paragraph: "Therefore, since we have been justified by faith, we have peace with God through our Lord Jesus Christ... and hope does not put us to shame, because God's love has been poured into our hearts by the Holy Spirit who has been given to us" (Rom. 5:1, 5). The reformers, while insisting on justification by grace alone through faith alone, also emphasized the inextricable connection between justification and internal renewal. For Luther, when God forgives in justification, he also confers the real presence of Christ, so that there is no sharp distinction between an extrinsic pronouncement and an intrinsic process: "Christ *in nobis* is also Christ *extra nos*."[47] Calvin placed regeneration before justification in logical order, insisting that justification is based on union with Christ.[48] As Donald Bloesch has put it, "For the mainstream Reformers, sanctification and justification are two sides of the one redeeming work of grace, which results in an ontological change in a person's inner being....The miracle of grace is a verdict of acquittal pronounced on us from on high and also a transformative presence that mitigates the power of sin to enslave us."[49]

The New Testament speaks of salvation as a past, present, and future reality. It is the atoning work of Christ on the cross that produces justification, regeneration, and reconciliation with God; believers are continually being saved from the power of sin as they grow in Christ-likeness; and yet we await the final redemption of creation and glory of life in the presence of God.

Atonement, regeneration, and justification are concepts that speak of what God has done to provide for salvation of sinful humanity. Sinners are called

---

46. Erickson, *Christian Theology*, 956.

47. Tuomo Mannermaa, *Christ Present in Faith: Luther's View of Justification* (Minneapolis: Fortress, 2005), 25.

48. John Calvin, *Institutes of the Christian Religion*, edited by John T. McNeill (Philadelphia: Westminster, 1960), 3.2.10; Bruce McCormack, "What's at Stake in Current Debates over Justification: The Crisis of Protestantism in the West," in *Justification: What's at Stake in the Current Debates*, edited by Mark Husbands and Daniel Treier (Downers Grove, IL, and Leicester, UK: InterVarsity and Apollos, 2004), 101–102.

49. Donald G. Bloesch, "Justification and Atonement," in *The Oxford Handbook of Evangelical Theology*, edited by Gerald McDermott (New York: Oxford University Press, 2010), 224.

to respond, by God's enabling grace, to what God has provided and thus to appropriate for themselves God's gift of salvation. Throughout the Scriptures, we find people challenged by Jesus and the apostles to repent of their sin (Mark 1:14–15; Luke 13:3; Acts 2:38, 3:19, 17:30, 26:20) and believe in the gospel of Jesus Christ (John 1:12, 3:15–16, 3:36, 8:24, 20:31; Rom. 3:21–22; Gal. 3:22). In response to the query by the Philippian jailer, "Sirs, what must I do to be saved?" the apostle Paul declares, "Believe in the Lord Jesus and you shall be saved, you and your household" (Acts 16:30–31).

Salvation is a rich concept in the Old and New Testaments, having many facets and described through the use of various images. Brenda Colijn reminds us, however, that "despite their rich variety, the New Testament images of salvation tell a single story—the story of God's love for his broken creation, his desire for covenant relationship, and his patient shaping of a people who would reflect his love to one another and to the world."[50]

Jesus the Only Savior

The New Testament consistently presents Jesus Christ as the unique incarnation of God, the only Lord and Savior for all humankind. Christopher Wright observes that although the Greek term *soter* (savior) was common in the classical world and was applied to human kings, military deliverers, and mythological deities, in the New Testament, the term is used of God (eight times) and of Jesus (sixteen times) but never of anyone else.[51]

Jesus' life must be understood within the broader context of the Hebrew Scriptures and Jewish monotheism. For Jesus' sayings and deeds appear within a framework that took for granted the reality of the God of Abraham, Isaac, and Jacob, of the Hebrew Scriptures' teaching on human sin and the need for reconciliation with God, and the anticipation of God's provision for salvation. The New Testament proclaims that it is in Jesus of Nazareth that God has provided the Way to reconciliation with God.

The comprehensive witness of the New Testament is that God was present and active in Jesus of Nazareth in a decisive and utterly unique way. Jesus is not portrayed as simply one among other great religious figures. The incarnation—the eternal Word, God, becoming man in Jesus of Nazareth—forms the apex of God's self-revelation to humankind. The gospel of John identifies

---

50. Colijn, *Images of Salvation*, 313.

51. Wright, "Salvation Belongs," 4.

Jesus with the preexistent Word (the Logos), who "was with God and who was God" and through whom "all things were made," and then asserts that "the Word became flesh and made his dwelling among us" (John 1:1–4, 1:14). The letter to the Hebrews states: "In the past God spoke to our forefathers through the prophets at many times and in various ways, but in these last days he has spoken to us by his Son, whom he appointed heir of all things and through whom he made the universe" (Heb. 1:1–2).

Throughout the New Testament, sometimes explicitly but often implicitly, Jesus is placed in an unprecedented relationship of identity with Yahweh, the everlasting creator God of the Old Testament. Jesus is presented as claiming the authority to do things that only God can do, such as forgive sins (Mark 2:5–11), judge the world (Matt. 19:28, 25:31–46), and give life, even to the dead (John 5:21, 5:25–29, 11:17–44). Jesus states that anyone who has seen him has seen the Father (John 14:9)—a remarkable claim in the context of Jewish monotheism. Jesus identifies himself with the I AM of Exodus 3:14 and in so doing is understood by his contemporaries to be identifying himself with God (John 8:58). The apostle Paul asserts that all of the "fullness" (*pleroma*) of God is present in the human person of Jesus (Col. 1:19, 2:9). Understood within the context of first-century Jewish monotheism, the assertion that in Jesus of Nazareth the one eternal God has become man is unique in its audacity and is unparalleled in other religions.[52]

The question of Jesus constitutes the great divide in theologies of religion. Christians have traditionally maintained that the Bible presents Jesus as God incarnate, the only Savior for all of humankind; no one is reconciled to God except through Jesus Christ (John 3:16, 3:36, 14:6; Acts 4:12; 1 Tim. 2:5). If this

---

52. This, of course, presupposes that the New Testament presents an accurate account of the sayings and deeds of Jesus of Nazareth. The issues concerning the reliability of the New Testament accounts are complex and controversial and cannot be explored here. While fully aware of the critical issues, however, we are convinced that there are good reasons to accept the reliability of the New Testament portrayal of Jesus. For helpful discussion, see Paul Barnett, *Is the New Testament Reliable?* 2nd ed. (Downers Grove, IL: InterVarsity, 2003); N. T. Wright, *The New Testament and the People of God: Christian Origins and the Question of God*, Vol. 1 (Minneapolis: Fortress, 1992); N. T. Wright, *Jesus and the Victory of God: Christian Origins and the Question of God*, Vol. 2 (Minneapolis: Fortress, 1996); Richard Bauckham, *Jesus and the Eyewitnesses: The Gospels as Eyewitness Testimony* (Grand Rapids, MI: Eerdmans, 2006); Larry Hurtado, *Lord Jesus Christ: Devotion to Jesus in Earliest Christianity* (Grand Rapids, MI: Eerdmans, 2003); Paul Rhodes Eddy and Gregory A. Boyd, *The Jesus Legend: A Case for the Historical Reliability of the Synoptic Jesus Tradition* (Grand Rapids, MI: Baker, 2007). Helpful discussion of the some of the theological and philosophical issues in the doctrine of the incarnation are found in Oliver D. Crisp, *Divinity and Humanity* (Cambridge, UK: Cambridge University Press, 2007); *The Incarnation*, edited Stephen T. Davis, Daniel Kendall, S.J., and Gerald O'Collins, S.J. (New York: Oxford University Press, 2002).

is correct, then it is impossible to regard Jesus as just one—even the greatest—among many great religious leaders. This is acknowledged even by John Hick, who admits that if the traditional understanding of Jesus Christ is correct, then religious pluralism is untenable:

> Traditional orthodoxy says that Jesus of Nazareth was God incarnate—that is, God the Son, the Second Person of a divine Trinity, incarnate—who became man to die for the sins of the world and who founded the church to proclaim this to the ends of the earth, so that all who sincerely take Jesus as their Lord and Savior are justified by his atoning death and will inherit eternal life. It follows from this that Christianity, alone among the world religions, was founded by God in person. God came down from heaven to earth and launched the salvific movement that came to be known as Christianity. From this premise it seems obvious that God must wish all human beings to enter this new stream of saved life, so that Christianity shall supersede all the world faiths.... Christianity alone is God's own religion, offering a fullness of life that no other tradition can provide; it is therefore divinely intended for all men and women without exception.[53]

Hick, together with all pluralists, rejects the orthodox view of Jesus as God incarnate and proposes instead a metaphorical understanding of the incarnation: "We see in Jesus a human being extraordinarily open to God's influence and thus living to an extraordinary extent as God's agent on earth, 'incarnating' the divine purpose for human life."[54] But this does not make Jesus unique, for Hick claims that not only Jesus but also Moses, Gautama, Confucius, Zoroaster, Socrates, Muhammad, and Nanak "have in their different ways 'incarnated' the ideal of human life in response to the one divine Reality."[55] While Christians need not abandon their commitments to Jesus as *their* Lord, traditional claims about Jesus as the *only* Savior for all humankind should be rejected.

Similarly, Paul Knitter argues that it is time to reject the idea that "Jesus is the *only* mediator of God's saving grace in history." Knitter distinguishes Jesus

53. John Hick, "A Pluralist View," in *Four Views on Salvation in a Pluralistic World*, edited by Dennis L. Okholm and Timothy R. Phillips (Grand Rapids, MI: Zondervan, 1996), 51–52.

54. John Hick, *The Metaphor of God Incarnate: Christology in a Pluralistic Age* (Louisville, KY: Westminster John Knox, 1993), 12.

55. Ibid., 96, 98.

being *truly* a Savior from his being the *only* Savior: "As a pluralist Christian, even though I do not feel it possible or necessary to affirm that Jesus is the *only* Savior, I still experience him to be so *truly* a Savior that I feel compelled to cast my lot with him."[56] He acknowledges that "much of what the New Testament says about Jesus is…*exclusive*, or at least *normative*."[57] But he argues that the "one and only" language should be understood as "confessional" or "love" language, not as making ontological claims about Jesus as the only Savior.[58] When Peter, for example, states that salvation is found in no one else, "for there is no other name…by which we must be saved" (Acts 4:12), or when Jesus is called the "one mediator between God and man" (1 Tim. 2:5), we should not understand these statements as metaphysical claims that rule out the possibility of there being other saviors. The purpose of such "love language" is to express total, personal commitment of the Christian community to Jesus. As far as the early disciples are concerned, Jesus is the one and only. But this is compatible with our recognizing today that other religious communities can also have their own, equally legitimate saviors.

In light of such revisionist perspectives, it is hardly surprising that Lutheran theologian Carl Braaten states: "We are facing a conflict in Christology as great as the ancient controversies over the three persons of the Godhead (Nicaea) and the two natures of Christ (Chalcedon)." The critical question is this: "Does Jesus model the salvation that God is working universally through all the religions? Or is what happens in Jesus the sole constitutive cause of the salvation that God delivers to the world?"[59] The New Testament and the orthodox tradition insist that it is the latter, not the former.

It is not as though the first-century world was unaware of other religious figures and traditions. Early Christians were familiar with the popular religious movements of the day—the cults of Asclepius or Artemis-Diana; the "mystery religions" of Osiris and Isis, Mithras, Adonis, or Eleusis; the cult of the Roman emperor; and the many versions of Stoicism, Cynicism, and Epicureanism were available. It was widely accepted in the ancient Mediterranean world that

---

56. Paul F. Knitter, "Five Theses on the Uniqueness of Jesus," in *The Uniqueness of Jesus: A Dialogue with Paul F. Knitter*, edited by Leonard Swidler and Paul Mojzes (Maryknoll, NY: Orbis, 1997), 7, 15; emphasis in original.

57. Paul F. Knitter, *No Other Name? A Critical Survey of Christian Attitudes toward the World Religions* (Maryknoll, NY: Orbis, 1985), 182.

58. Ibid., 182–186.

59. Carl Braaten, *No Other Gospel! Christianity among World Religions* (Minneapolis: Fortress, 1992), 8.

the same deity could be called by different names in different cultures. Had the writers of the New Testament wished to say merely that Jesus was *their* Lord but that he was only one among many alternative lords and saviors, they certainly could have done so. Not only did they not do this, but they insisted that Jesus was, in fact, the Lord of lords (1 Cor. 8:5–6).

Furthermore, Paul Knitter's reinterpretation of the exclusive claims of Jesus is also problematic. Surely Knitter is correct in noting that the New Testament includes "love language" or expressions of commitment to Jesus Christ. But he draws a misleading exclusive disjunction between expressions of commitment and ontological claims, as if language cannot include both. Language, in fact, serves many functions simultaneously. Knitter provides no reason for concluding that exclusive statements as found in John 3:16, John 14:6, and Acts 4:12 cannot be both expressions of adoration and statements with significant ontological implications. Christological language in the New Testament is full of ontological implications. Even if we accept John 14:6 or Acts 4:12 as expressing "love language," we must ask what it was about the nature of Jesus that evoked this unusually expressive language of love and commitment. And answering *this* will result in unpacking the ontological implications of the New Testament understanding of Jesus the Son and his unique relation to God the Father. The conclusion of the early followers of Jesus was that, in an admittedly mysterious and paradoxical sense, the human Jesus is to be identified with the eternal creator: Jesus is God in human flesh.

The radical nature of the New Testament portrayal of Jesus is seen in the fact that it presents Jesus not as simply teaching the way to reconciliation with God but rather as claiming that he himself *is* the Way to salvation (John 14:6). Many religious leaders claim to have discovered teachings or practices leading to salvation or enlightenment. But that is not what Jesus does. The New Testament does not present Jesus merely as teaching the way to salvation; Jesus claims to *be* the Way to the Father. It is not simply that Jesus has discovered the truth and that if we follow his teachings, we, too, can find the way for ourselves. Jesus called upon others to believe in him and to find salvation in him (John 5:24, 6:35–58). It is because of who he is and what he has done for us in his sinless life, on the cross, and in the resurrection that Jesus is himself the Way, the Truth, and the Life. Thus, the truth of Jesus's teachings cannot be separated from the ontological grounding of this truth in the person of Christ as the incarnate Word of God.[60]

---

60. See further James R. Edwards, *Is Jesus the Only Savior?* (Grand Rapids, MI: Eerdmans, 2005); Carl E. Braaten, *Who Is Jesus? Disputed Questions and Answers* (Grand Rapids, MI: Eerdmans, 2011).

The Question of the Unevangelized

The emphasis on Jesus Christ as the only Savior naturally raises questions about the scope of salvation and the destiny of those who do not hear the gospel. Although there has been some disagreement on the issue since the second century, the subject has become especially pressing and controversial since the voyages of discovery in the sixteenth century, as the extent of the world beyond the reach of the Christian church became evident. The question gained widespread attention from evangelicals in the West in the 1990s.

Evangelicals generally agree that the biblical witness is clear on the following points: (1) All peoples in all cultures, including sincere followers of other religions, are sinners and face God's just condemnation for sin. (2) Salvation is available only on the basis of the sinless person and atoning work of Jesus Christ. All who are saved are saved only through Jesus Christ. (3) No one is saved merely by being sincere or by doing good works or by being devout in following a particular religion. (4) Salvation is always only by God's grace and must be personally accepted through faith. (5) Ultimately, not everyone will be saved. Some, probably many, will be eternally lost. (6) God is entirely righteous, just, and fair in his dealings with humankind. No one who is condemned by God is condemned unjustly. (7) Both out of a sense of obedience to the Lord and compassion for the lost, the church is to be actively engaged in making disciples of all peoples, including adherents of other religions. Moreover, most evangelicals agree that the clear pattern in the New Testament is that people first hear the gospel and then, through the work of the Holy Spirit, respond in faith to the gospel and are saved.

But is it possible for some who have never heard the gospel of Jesus Christ also to be saved? Before looking at some responses to the question, we should note the comments of Lesslie Newbigin, one of the more influential twentieth-century missiologists. Newbigin had little patience for what he regarded as "increasingly fruitless questions about who will and will not be saved":

> When Jesus was asked the question about whether few or many would be saved he declined to answer it but sternly warned the questioner to strive to enter by the narrow door that leads to life. His often repeated words about the reversal of expectations (the first shall be last and the last first) and the parables which suggest that those who are confident will find themselves excluded and those who never expected it find themselves welcomed, all point in the same direction. There is a kind of confidence which leads to complacency, and there is a kind of

anxiety which leads to selfish efforts to save oneself. It seems to me clear from the whole New Testament that the Christian life has room both for a godly confidence and for a godly fear.[61]

Newbigin is critical of those with clear answers to the question about the unevangelized, either positive or negative: "I must confess...that I find it astonishing that a theologian should think that he has the authority to inform us in advance who is going to be 'saved' on the last day."[62] The issue about who ultimately will be saved "is a question which God alone will answer, and it is arrogant presumption on the part of theologians to suppose that it is their business to answer it. We have to begin with the mighty work of grace in Jesus Christ and ask, How is he to be honored and glorified? The goal of missions is the glory of God."[63]

Newbigin's statements serve as a healthy caution. Surely we must acknowledge that the ultimate goal of missions is the glory of the triune God. Jesus does warn against a presumptuous arrogance with respect to God's judgment (Matt. 7:21–23, 25:31–46; Luke 13:23–30). There will be surprises when we realize just who is–and who is not–accepted by God, so some theological humility is necessary here. Nevertheless, the concern with salvation cannot simply be dismissed, for it is a central theme of the Scriptures. Certain conditions for salvation are set out in the Scriptures, and, given our awareness of other religions today, the question of the destiny of those who never hear the gospel cannot simply be thrown out. Some response is necessary.

There has long been some disagreement among evangelicals on the question of the unevangelized. In reviews of the literature, Christopher Morgan identifies nine distinct positions on the question, while Daniel Strange delineates twelve.[64] We will briefly consider several responses to the question. It is important to see that the differences between these positions concern not the means of salvation (for example, grace versus works) but rather the amount of

---

61. Lesslie Newbigin, *The Gospel in a Pluralist Society* (Grand Rapids, MI: Eerdmans, 1989), 88.

62. Lesslie Newbigin, *The Open Secret* (Grand Rapids, MI: Eerdmans, 1978), 196.

63. Newbigin, *The Gospel*, 180.

64. See Christopher W. Morgan, "Inclusivisms and Exclusivisms," in *Faith Comes by Hearing: A Response to Inclusivism*, edited by Christopher W. Morgan and Robert A. Peterson (Downers Grove, IL: InterVarsity, 2008), 26; Daniel Strange, *The Possibility of Salvation among the Unevangelized* (Waynesboro, GA: Paternoster, 2002), 304–331.

knowledge necessary for a saving response to God and the means of acquiring such knowledge.[65]

The first perspective maintains that only those who hear the gospel and explicitly respond in faith to Jesus Christ in this life can be saved. Sometimes referred to as restrictivism, this position insists that explicit knowledge of the gospel of Jesus Christ is necessary for salvation, and there is no hope for those who die without having heard the gospel.[66] Restrictivists claim that texts such as John 3:16, John 3:36, John 14:6, Acts 4:12, and Romans 10:13–17 make it clear that only those who respond explicitly to the gospel can be saved. Veteran missiologist David Hesselgrave states: "Only by hearing and believing in Christ during this life can men and women be saved."[67] The collection of essays in *Faith Comes by Hearing* makes up a sophisticated and nuanced defense of the view that "Jesus Christ is the only Savior of the world and that one must believe in God's special revelation that culminates in the gospel of Christ in order to be saved."[68]

Frequently, advocates of this position make a distinction between the degree of explicit knowledge of Christ's gospel required for saving faith in the time of the Old Testament and that required since the incarnation. While Old Testament saints could be saved apart from explicit knowledge of the gospel of Christ, this is no longer possible. This is the case with dispensational theologians such as Ramesh Richard, who states: "A dispensational reading of the biblical history of salvation provides adequate theological resources to (1) preserve Old Testament salvation outside explicit knowledge of Christ, and

---

65. For helpful discussion of the relevant biblical and theological issues in the debate, see D. A. Carson, *The Gagging of God: Christianity Confronts Pluralism* (Grand Rapids, MI: Zondervan, 1996); Millard J. Erickson, *How Shall They Be Saved? The Destiny of Those Who Do Not Hear of Jesus* (Grand Rapids, MI: Baker, 1996).

66. In addition to the essays in *Faith Comes by Hearing*, edited by Christopher W. Morgan and Robert A. Peterson (Downers Grove, IL: InterVarsity, 2008), see John Piper, *Let the Nations Be Glad!* (Grand Rapids, MI: Baker, 1993); Ronald Nash, *Is Jesus the Only Savior?* (Grand Rapids, MI: Zondervan, 1994); Ramesh Richard, *The Population of Heaven: A Biblical Response to the Inclusivist Position on Who Will Be Saved* (Chicago: Moody, 1994); R. Douglas Geivett and W. Gary Phillips, "A Particularist View," in *Four Views on Salvation in a Pluralistic World*, edited by Dennis L. Okholm and Timothy R. Phillips (Grand Rapids, MI: Zondervan, 1996), 211–245; Christopher Little, *The Revelation of God among the Unevangelized: An Evangelical Appraisal* (Pasadena, CA: William Carey, 2000).

67. David Hesselgrave, *Paradigms in Conflict: 10 Key Questions in Christian Missions Today* (Grand Rapids, MI: Kregel, 2005), 65.

68. Robert A. Peterson, "Introduction," in *Faith Comes by Hearing*, edited by Christopher W. Morgan and Robert A. Peterson (Downers Grove, IL: InterVarsity, 2008), 12.

(2) insist that explicit knowledge of Christ is an exclusive, universal condition for salvation in the present epoch. If the historical and hermeneutical distinctions between the dispensations are eliminated, a broadened condition for salvation could become evangelically viable."[69] For Richard, then, the exclusive faith requirement is a function of a dispensational hermeneutic.[70] But even those not committed to dispensationalism often make the same distinction. Consider the comments of John Piper: "Saving faith was once focused on the mercy of God known in His redemptive acts among the people of Israel, and in the system of animal sacrifices and in the prophecies of coming redemption. Outside Israel we hear of Melchizedek (Genesis 14) who seems to know of the true God apart from connection with special revelation in the line of Abraham. But now the focus of faith has narrowed down to one Man, Jesus Christ, the fulfillment and guarantee of all redemption and all sacrifices and all prophecies. It is to his honor now that henceforth all saving faith shall be directed to him."[71]

We should also mention two related variations of restrictivism that, while never dominant within the church, have been adopted by some leading theologians, both in the early church and today. One perspective, sometimes referred to as the postmortem evangelism view but which Gabriel Fackre prefers to call the divine perseverance view, maintains that while responding explicitly to the gospel of Jesus Christ is necessary for salvation, those who die without hearing the gospel receive an opportunity to respond to it after death.[72] An early expression of this view was suggested by the church father Irenaeus, who proposed that those who died without hearing the gospel would be raised during the millennium so that they could respond to the gospel.[73] Proponents of this

---

69. Richard, *The Population of Heaven*, 123.

70. Dispensationalism is the theological approach that emphasizes the different dispensations or stewardship arrangements God used in various stages of history to mediate his salvation. In one sense, these different stages or economies were taught by Paul, who said on Mars Hill that in former times, God overlooked pagan ignorance but that once Christ came, God was commanding everyone to repent (Acts 17:30). The nineteenth-century English pastor John Nelson Darby sharply separated God's dispensation for Israel from that for the church, which began on Pentecost. Revision of this view can be seen in Craig Blaising and Darrell L. Bock, *Progressive Dispensationalism* (Wheaton, IL: BridgePoint, 1993).

71. Piper, *Let the Nations*, 163.

72. Gabriel Fackre, "Divine Perseverance," in *What About Those Who Have Never Heard?* edited by John Sanders (Downers Grove, IL: InterVarsity, 1995), 71–106.

73. See Terry Tiessen, *Irenaeus on the Salvation of the Unevangelized*, ATLA Monograph 31 (Metuchen, NJ: Scarecrow, 1993); Gerald McDermott, *God's Rivals: Why Has God Allowed Different Religions?* (Downers Grove, IL: InterVarsity, 2007), 110–115.

view, like other restrictivists, maintain that Romans 10:9 provides a necessary condition for salvation: "If you confess with your mouth that Jesus is Lord and believe in your heart that God raised him from the dead, you will be saved." They contend that the author of these words, Paul, is the same apostle who wrote in the same letter about Gentiles who do not have the law but "show that the work of the law is written on their hearts" (Rom. 2:14–15). Paul, they suggest, apparently thought that even Gentiles who had not heard of Moses (or, presumably, of Jesus) must hear the gospel and confess their adherence to it in order to be saved. They also point to the near-universal testimony of the early fathers to the view that explicit confession of Christ is necessary for salvation and the fact that the fathers of the first few Christian centuries lived in pagan cities where some died without hearing the gospel.

A related but distinct proposal suggests that it is at the point of death itself—not after death—that those who did not hear the gospel in this life are confronted by Jesus Christ and given opportunity to respond. Those who did not hear the gospel during their lives might receive special revelation from God at the point of death. Clark Pinnock, who also advocates the "wider hope" inclusivism noted below, appeals to texts such as 1 Peter 3:19 and 4:6 in support of the claim that "death is the occasion when the unevangelized have an opportunity to make a decision about Jesus Christ."[74] Most evangelicals today, however, reject as lacking in biblical warrant the idea that those who do not hear the gospel in this life might encounter Jesus Christ and the gospel either at the point of death or in some manner after death. But it is important to acknowledge that this is a perspective that was more widely accepted in the early history of the church and even today has respected defenders.

A rather different perspective from restrictivism is that of the "wider hope" or "inclusivism," which maintains that we can expect that large numbers of those who have never heard the gospel will nevertheless be saved. Although Jesus Christ is the one Savior for all people and salvation is possible only because of Christ's atoning work on the cross, one need not know explicitly about Jesus Christ and the cross in order to be saved.[75] John Sanders, for

---

74. Clark Pinnock, "Is Jesus the Only Way?" *Eternity* 27 (December 1976): 34; Pinnock, *A Wideness in God's Mercy: The Finality of Jesus Christ in a World of Religions* (Grand Rapids, MI: Zondervan, 1992), 168–172. See also Donald Bloesch, *Essentials of Evangelical Theology*, Vol. 2 (San Francisco: Harper & Row, 1978), 224, 227; Terrance L. Tiessen, *Who Can Be Saved? Reassessing Salvation in Christ and World Religions* (Downers Grove, IL: InterVarsity, 2004); Fackre, "Divine Perseverance."

75. John Sanders, *No Other Name: An Investigation into the Destiny of the Unevangelized* (Grand Rapids, MI: Eerdmans, 1992), 215.

example, anticipates that many will be saved apart from hearing and responding explicitly to the gospel.[76]

Clark Pinnock grounds inclusivism on two foundational axioms.[77] First,
God is a God of limitless love and mercy who has acted for the salvation of
humankind in a decisive manner in the life, death, and resurrection of Jesus
Christ. Second, Jesus Christ is the unique incarnation of God, the only Savior
for all people, including sincere followers of other religions. But Pinnock contends that the second axiom is compatible with "an optimism of salvation"
that anticipates many people being saved apart from actually hearing and
responding to the gospel of Jesus Christ: "What has to be said forthrightly
is that a biblically based Christology does not entail a narrowness of outlook
toward other people. The church's confession about Jesus is compatible with
an open spirit, with an optimism of salvation, and with a wider hope. . . . There
is no salvation except through Christ, but it is not necessary for everybody to
possess a conscious knowledge of Christ in order to benefit from redemption
through him."[78]

Sanders states: "Salvation for the unevangelized is made possible only by
the redemptive work of Jesus, but God applies that work even to those who are
ignorant of the atonement. God does this if people respond in trusting faith
to the revelation they have."[79] Inclusivists are optimistic about the numbers of
those who might be saved apart from hearing and responding to the gospel.

Many evangelicals, however, find themselves somewhere between restrictivism and inclusivism, convinced that each goes beyond what the biblical
data affirm. Those in this group admit that in principle God might save some
who have never explicitly heard the gospel, but they add that we simply do not
know whether this occurs or, if so, how many might be saved in this manner.
John Stott, for example, states that on the basis of Scripture, we know that

> Jesus Christ is the only Saviour, and that salvation is by God's grace
> alone, on the ground of Christ's cross alone, and by faith alone. The
> only question, therefore, is how much knowledge and understanding
> of the gospel people need before they can cry to God for mercy and

76. John Sanders, "Inclusivism," in *What About Those Who Have Never Heard?* edited by
John Sanders (Downers Grove, IL: InterVarsity, 1995), 55.

77. See Pinnock, *A Wideness*, chaps. 1 and 2. See also Amos Yong, *Beyond the Impasse: Toward
a Pneumatological Theology of Religions* (Grand Rapids, MI: Baker, 2003), chap. 5.

78. Pinnock, *A Wideness*, 74–75.

79. Sanders, "Inclusivism," 36.

be saved. In the Old Testament people were "justified by faith" even though they had little knowledge or expectation of Christ. Perhaps there are others today in a similar position, who know that they are guilty before God and that they cannot do anything to win his favour, but who in self-despair call upon the God they dimly perceive to save them. If God saves such, as many evangelical Christians believe, their salvation is still only through Christ, only by faith.[80]

Commenting on this possibility, J. I. Packer states: "We may safely say (i) if any good pagan reached the point of throwing himself on his Maker's mercy for pardon, it was grace that brought him there; (ii) God will surely save anyone he brings this far (cf. Acts 10:34f; Rom. 10:12f); (iii) anyone thus saved would learn in the next world that he was saved through Christ. But what we cannot safely say is that God ever does save anyone in this way. We simply do not know."[81]

Those embracing this view are not suggesting that general revelation somehow saves the unevangelized; strictly speaking, neither special nor general revelation saves anyone. Salvation is always the gift of God the Father's grace, is based on Christ's atoning work on the cross, and is mediated by the Spirit. The issue here is simply the degree of understanding of God and his saving ways that is necessary for salvation and the means by which this understanding can be attained.

Is it possible that some might understand enough about God through his general revelation and respond by God's grace to this knowledge with appropriate faith? Restrictivists deny this possibility. General revelation, they contend, provides some knowledge of God, so that all people are without excuse before God, but such knowledge is in principle insufficient for saving faith. Only the understanding of the gospel provided by special revelation is sufficient for salvation. Many, however, point out that it is difficult to understand what it means to be "without excuse" on the basis of general revelation if, indeed, those without access to special revelation could not even in principle have responded appropriately to God on the understanding they have through general revelation. Millard Erickson, for example, asks, "How can people who

---

80. John Stott, *The Authentic Jesus* (London: Marshall Morgan and Scott, 1985), 83.

81. J. I. Packer, *God's Word: Studies of Key Bible Themes* (Downers Grove, IL: InterVarsity, 1981), 210; see also Packer, "Evangelicals and the Way of Salvation," in *Evangelical Affirmations*, edited by Kenneth S. Kantzer and Carl F. H. Henry (Grand Rapids, MI: Zondervan, 1990), 121–123.

have not heard the gospel be without excuse if they could not possibly have believed and if such belief is indispensable to salvation?"[82] Similarly, David Clark observes: "The claim that natural [general] revelation renders one without excuse but cannot save is not required by Romans 1:18–23, although it is consistent with it. Romans 1:18–23 is also consistent with the claim that natural revelation fails to bring salvation to those who are rebellious and wicked, but potentially leads to salvation for those who respond to it."[83]

In an early essay, Erickson suggests that there are five elements that constitute "the essential nature of the gospel message" and are in principle available through general revelation. These include "(1) The belief in one good powerful God. (2) The belief that he (man) owes this God perfect obedience to his law. (3) The consciousness that he does not meet this standard, and therefore is guilty and condemned. (4) The realization that nothing he can offer God can compensate him (or atone) for this sin and guilt. (5) The belief that God is merciful, and will forgive and accept those who cast themselves upon his mercy." Erickson then asks: "May it not be that if a man believes and acts on this set of tenets he is redemptively related to God and receives the benefits of Christ's death, whether he consciously knows and understands the details of that provision or not? Presumably that was the case with the Old Testament believers. Their salvation was not based upon works. It was, as with all who are saved, a matter of grace. The grace, in turn, was manifested and made available through the death of Jesus Christ. The Old Testament saints, however, did not know the identity of the Redeemer or the details of the accomplishment of salvation."[84]

The optimism of the "wider hope" inclusivism of Pinnock and Sanders, noted above, goes well beyond the cautious acknowledgments of Stott, Packer, and Erickson. For, as Erickson points out, "There are no unambiguous instances in Scripture of persons who became true believers through responding to general revelation alone. Scripture does not indicate how many, if any, come to salvation that way."[85]

---

82. Erickson, *How Shall They Be Saved?* 63–64.

83. David Clark, "Is Special Revelation Necessary for Salvation?" in *Through No Fault of Their Own?* edited by William V. Crockett and James Sigountos (Grand Rapids, MI: Baker, 1991), 40–41.

84. Millard Erickson, "Hope for Those Who Haven't Heard? Yes, but...," *Evangelical Missions Quarterly* 11 (April 1975): 125. See also Erickson, *Christian Theology*, Vol. 1 (Grand Rapids, MI: Baker, 1983), 172.

85. Erickson, *How Shall They Be Saved?* 158.

The issue of the unevangelized was vigorously discussed by participants at the 1992 World Evangelical Fellowship conference in Manila on "The Unique Christ in Our Pluralistic World." The Manila Declaration, a thoughtful and carefully crafted statement produced by the conference, acknowledges a lack of consensus on the issue:

> Is it possible that [those who do not hear the gospel of Jesus Christ] also might find salvation through the blood of Jesus Christ although they do not consciously know the name of Jesus? We did not achieve a consensus on how to answer this question. More study is needed. We did agree that salvation is to be found nowhere else than in Jesus Christ. The truth to be found in other religious teachings is not sufficient, in and of itself, to provide salvation. We further agreed that universalism (that all people without exception will be saved) is not biblical. Lastly, we agreed that our discussion of this issue must not in any way undercut the passion to proclaim, without wavering, faltering, or tiring, the good news of salvation through trust in Jesus Christ.[86]

The issues in the debate are significant and should be addressed, to the best of our ability, on the basis of the clear and comprehensive witness of the Scriptures, not through proof texting, emotional appeals, or pragmatic considerations. Disagreements on the issue are not simply a result of differences over exegesis of texts such as John 14:6 or Acts 4:12. Other broader theological commitments can influence how we approach the texts. For example, various theological systems (e.g., covenant or dispensational) approach the question of the relation between the Old and New Testaments differently. The different systems adopt different perspectives on the degree to which knowledge of the coming Christ and the cross were necessary for salvation in Old Testament times and the implications of this for those living after the incarnation. Similarly, theological frameworks will differ over the nature and extent of divine election, or the extent and effect of God's prevenient or common grace, or how we should understand the relation between God's justice and mercy. These broader differences can affect how one interprets particular biblical texts.

In our judgment, "wider hope" inclusivists go beyond what the Scriptures clearly support in maintaining that we can be confident about the salvation of

86. "The WEF Declaration," *The Unique Christ in Our Pluralistic World*, edited by Bruce J. Nicholls (Grand Rapids, MI: Baker, 1994), 15.

many who never hear the gospel. The clear pattern in the New Testament is for people first to hear the gospel and then to respond by God's grace to Jesus Christ in saving faith. At the same time, we believe that restrictivists also go beyond the clear teaching of Scripture in excluding the possibility that God might save those who do not explicitly hear and respond to the gospel of Jesus Christ. Texts such as John 14:6 or Acts 4:12 are compatible with restrictivism but are not necessarily demanded by it. In our judgment, the wisest response to the issue is to acknowledge the possibility that some who never hear the gospel might nonetheless, through God's grace, respond to what they know of God through general revelation and turn to him in faith for forgiveness. We concur with Christopher Wright: "While I strongly affirm that people can only be saved by Christ, and that the normal way that God brings salvation is through those who know Christ witnessing to those who do not yet and leading them to repentance and faith (i.e. evangelism), I cannot take the further step of saying that God is somehow unable or unwilling to save anybody at any time in human history, unless and until a Christian reaches them with an intelligible explanation of the story of the gospel."[87] But to speculate about how many, if any, are saved in this manner is to go beyond what the Scriptures affirm. Surely, all evangelicals can agree that regardless of disagreement on some points, they must continue to proclaim the good news of salvation through trust in Jesus Christ. Out of obedience to the clear command of the Lord (Matt. 28:18–20; John 20:21) and a desire that all peoples give glory to God and worship him appropriately (Ps. 67, 96; Isa. 45), they must urge all peoples, including sincere followers of other religions, to acknowledge Jesus Christ as their Lord and Savior.

Salvation through Other Religions?

A question that emerges here is whether God's saving grace is made available to people through non-Christian religions. That is, if one acknowledges the possibility of salvation for those who have not heard and responded explicitly to the gospel, is salvation in such cases to be understood as being mediated somehow through the religions or in spite of other religions? This, of course, is not an issue for restrictivists. But those who acknowledge the possibility of salvation apart from explicit response to the gospel, whether only cautiously or confidently, need to address the question of the role of the religions in salvation.

---

87. Christopher J. H. Wright, *Salvation Belongs to Our God* (Downers Grove, IL: InterVarsity, 2007), 168.

As we saw in chapter 1, the Roman Catholic Church at Vatican II affirmed the possibility of salvation for those who have not heard the gospel of Jesus Christ or become members of the church. But is such salvation mediated through the other religions, or is it somehow made available to individuals apart from the religions themselves? There has been some disagreement over the implications of Vatican II on the issue. Karl Rahner, an influential voice at Vatican II, held that the question of whether the religions themselves are salvific was not directly addressed by Vatican II.[88] But Rahner's own writings on "anonymous Christians," which speak of non-Christian religions in certain circumstances as "lawful religions," imply that God's saving grace is available through the social and religious matrix of other religions.[89] Rahner affirms that in appropriate circumstances, the religions can be "grace-filled" ways of salvation and are "positively included in God's plan of salvation."[90] Rahner suggested that the religions are potentially "salvific" by the mysterious work of Christ through them.

In a 1967 essay, Hans Küng reversed the more common formula, which regarded the church as the ordinary means of salvation and the other religions as, at best, an extraordinary vehicle of salvation: "As against the 'extraordinary' way of salvation which is the Church, the world religions can be called—if this is rightly understood—the 'ordinary' way of salvation for non-Christian humanity."[91] Later Catholic theologians such as Jacques Dupuis affirmed the religious traditions of others as "indeed for them a way and means of salvation." Through the religions, the "mystery of salvation...is present in an implicit, concealed manner."[92] World religions represent "particular

---

88. See Karl Rahner, "On the Importance of the Non-Christian Religions for Salvation," in *Theological Investigations*, Vol. 18, translated by Edward Quinn (London: Darton, Longman, and Todd, 1984), 288–295.

89. Karl Rahner, "Christianity and the Non-Christian Religions," in *Theological Investigations*, Vol. 5, translated by Karl-H. Kruger (Baltimore: Helicon, 1966), 115–134; Rahner, "Anonymous Christians," in *Theological Investigations*, Vol. 6, translated by Karl-H. Kruger and Boniface Kruger (Baltimore: Helicon, 1969), 390–398.

90. Rahner, "Christianity and the Non-Christians Religions," 118, 122, 131–134; Rahner, "Anonymous Christians," 390–395. See also Paul Knitter, "Roman Catholic Approaches to Other Religions: Developments and Tensions," *International Bulletin of Missionary Research* (April 1984): 50–54.

91. Hans Küng, "The World Religions in God's Plan of Salvation," in *Christian Revelation and World Religions*, edited by Joseph Neuner (London: Burns and Oates, 1967), 51–52.

92. Jacques Dupuis, *Toward a Christian Theology of Religious Pluralism* (Maryknoll, NY: Orbis, 1997), 319.

realizations of a universal process, which has become preeminently concrete in Jesus Christ."[93]

Many today within the mainstream Roman Catholic tradition, however, are more cautious on the question of salvation through other religions. Gavin D'Costa, for example, argues that neither the documents of Vatican II nor the official statements of the church since then regard other religions themselves as means of salvation.[94] By this, he means not that "elements of [non-Christian] religious cultures" cannot mediate grace but that "the religions as a whole, rather than in their parts, or systematically, rather than atomistically, cannot be 'salvific' per se in so much as they do not preach Christ crucified and God's Trinitarian action of redemptive love."[95] Thus, although other religions can be affirmed for the truth and goodness evident within them, "they can only be seen as part of God's plan in so much as they provide a *praeparatio* to the gospel, but not in themselves as a means of salvation."[96] Paul Knitter, in response, chides D'Costa for being "a rooster out of tune with the rest of the choir." Knitter claims that the "Catholic theological choir is pretty unanimous in recognizing the religions as conduits of God's saving action."[97]

Yet it seems that it is Knitter who is out of step with mainstream Catholic teaching on this point. While Vatican II documents do speak of the Holy Spirit offering "to every man...in a manner known only to God...the possibility of being associated with [the] paschal mystery,"[98] they also say that the religions serve only as *praeparatio evangelica*, a preparation for the fullness of the gospel, and stop short of claiming that the religions themselves mediate

93. J. S. O'Leary, *La vérité chrétienne à l'âge du pluralism religieux* (Paris: Cerf, 1994), 253; approvingly cited by Dupuis in *Toward a Christian Theology*, 328.

94. See Gavin D'Costa, *The Meeting of Religions and the Trinity* (Maryknoll, NY: Orbis, 2000), 99–142; D'Costa, "Christianity and World Religions: A Theological Appraisal," in Gavin D'Costa, Paul Knitter, and Daniel Strange, *Only One Way? Three Christian Responses on the Uniqueness of Christ in a Religiously Plural World* (London: SCM, 2011), 7–36.

95. Gavin D'Costa, "Gavin D'Costa Re-responds to Daniel Strange and Paul Knitter," in Gavin D'Costa, Paul Knitter, and Daniel Strange, *Only One Way? Three Christian Responses on the Uniqueness of Christ in a Religiously Plural World* (London: SCM, 2011), 197.

96. D'Costa, "Christianity and World Religions," 35.

97. Paul Knitter, "Knitter Responds to Gavin D'Costa and Daniel Strange," in Gavin D'Costa, Paul Knitter, and Daniel Strange, *Only One Way? Three Christian Responses on the Uniqueness of Christ in a Religiously Plural World* (London: SCM, 2011), 156. See also Knitter, *Introducing Theologies of Religions* (Maryknoll, NY: Orbis, 2002), 81–84.

98. *Gaudium et Spes* 22, in Walter M. Abbott, S.J., *The Documents of Vatican II* (New York: Guild, 1966).

salvation.[99] Moreover, *Dominus Iesus*, the significant statement issued by the Congregation for the Doctrine of the Faith in 2000, asserts that "it would be contrary to the faith to consider the Church as *one way* of salvation alongside those constituted by other religions." The religions may have "religious elements which come from God," but they also contain rituals that "constitute an obstacle to salvation." Therefore, devotees of other religions are in danger: "*Objectively speaking* they are in a gravely deficient situation in comparison with those who, in the Church, have the fullness of the means of salvation."[100]

Some evangelical theologians have also been intrigued by the thesis that God's saving grace is mediated through other religions. Amos Yong, for example, asks how "it is possible to assert the Spirit's presence [in the religions and among non-Christians] while denying that saving grace is active throughout the world of the religions."[101] For if non-Christian religious experience is so transformative as to lead devotees to fulfilling their created purposes in authenticity and integrity, with greater and greater degrees of harmony, it seems that "non-Christian faiths can be regarded as salvific in the Christian sense when the Spirit's presence and activity in and through them are evident as hereby defined."[102]

The potentially salvific nature of the religions was also addressed by Clark Pinnock, although his writings are more ambivalent. He speaks of the religions as mixed, containing goodness and truth and also falsehood and much that is evil.[103] Although he maintains that we can expect that many who have never heard the gospel will be saved, Pinnock is reluctant to state categorically that God's saving grace is mediated through the other religions. He says that because God is present in the whole world, "God's grace is also at work in some way among all people, possibly even in the sphere of religious life." Thus, "religion may play a role in the salvation of the human race, a role preparatory

99. Veli-Matti Kärkkäinen, *Trinity and Religious Pluralism* (Burlington, VT: Ashgate, 2004), 32.

100. *Dominus Iesus* 22; emphasis in original; http://www.vatican.va/roman_curia/congregations/cfaith/documents/rc_con_cfaith_doc_20000806_dominus-iesus_en.html.

101. Amos Yong, *Beyond the Impasse: Toward a Pneumatological Theology of Religions* (Grand Rapids, MI: Baker, 2003), 125.

102. Amos Yong, *Discerning the Spirit(s): A Pentecostal-Charismatic Contribution to Christian Theology of Religions* (Sheffield, UK: Sheffield Academic, 2000), 312.

103. See Clark Pinnock, "Toward an Evangelical Theology of Religions," *Journal of the Evangelical Theological Society* 33, no. 3 (September 1990): 364–365; Pinnock, *A Wideness*, 81–113.

to the gospel of Christ, in whom alone fullness of salvation is found."[104] We should think of "the Spirit as graciously present in the world among all peoples, even in non-Christian religious contexts."[105] And yet Pinnock says that the "cautious inclusivism" he espouses "stops short of stating that the religions themselves as such are vehicles of salvation."[106] He writes that

> religions provide a window of opportunity for the Spirit to engage people, because—in spite of a measure of deceptive activity, the mystery of evil—God is also mysteriously present and working. The Spirit is not limited to the boundaries of churches but also gives life to the whole creation. The Spirit is ever at work setting in motion the plan of redemption revealed in the gospel.
>
> This does not make religions salvific as such, however. The Spirit is the power of God unto salvation, not to religion. God *may* use elements in them as a means of grace, even as God may use the moral dimension, the celestial bodies, or social interaction to lead people to himself. We must be alert to the possibility that God is effectively at work in the religious dimension in a given instance, but there are no guarantees of it. Religions as such do not mediate salvation.[107]

It seems that Pinnock is trying to distinguish between the Spirit's work in the world in general, which includes the religions, and the Trinity's special work of drawing men and women into salvation: "It is one thing to be attentive to the Spirit at work in a religious context and to be thankful if a religion helps inculcate holiness and virtue. It is another thing to claim that other religions are vehicles of grace and salvation."[108] This, it seems to us, is an important distinction.

Let us draw some of these difficult matters together. Although we acknowledged above the possibility of salvation by God's grace of some who do not hear the gospel, we do not think that God's *saving* grace in these cases is mediated through the teachings and practices of other religions. Here it is instructive

---

104. Clark Pinnock, "An Inclusivist View," in *Four Views on Salvation in a Pluralistic World*, edited by Dennis L. Okholm and Timothy R. Phillips (Grand Rapids, MI: Zondervan, 1996), 98.

105. Ibid., 100.

106. Ibid., 99.

107. Ibid., 116.

108. Clark Pinnock, *Flame of Love* (Downers Grove, IL: InterVarsity, 1996), 207.

to consider again the early church father Justin Martyr, who is often appealed to as an example of an early Christian theologian who accepted adherents of other religions as potentially Christians. Although he was willing to say that earlier Greek thinkers "who lived reasonably are Christians," he nevertheless insisted that such thinkers had only part of the Logos and would need to possess the full Logos by personal contact with Jesus Christ.[109] As we have seen in previous chapters, because of God's creation, general revelation, and common grace, there is an important sense in which we can and should speak of aspects of truth, goodness, and beauty in other religious traditions. But even if one acknowledges the possibility of salvation for some apart from explicitly hearing the gospel, we do not think that in such cases God's salvation should be construed as coming through the religions. Because Jesus Christ is the Savior, and none of the other religions preaches Jesus Christ or contains Jesus Christ, they cannot mediate salvation. They might advance truth and goodness and beauty that point to various aspects of Jesus and his gospel, but only by the triune God himself working through the gospel is any human being saved. They can prepare people for the gospel, but they cannot bring the gospel of Jesus Christ and therefore salvation.

Conversion

Evangelicals have been known for their emphasis on conversion.[110] Great evangelists such as John Wesley, George Whitefield, Charles Finney, and Billy Graham called people to turn from sin to a personal commitment to Jesus Christ as their Savior. Evangelicals in America in the twentieth century popularized the view of conversion as essentially a personal experience in which one "believes in Jesus" and thus is granted eternal life. Evangelical missionaries in Asia and Africa called for conversion to Christianity, often leaving it unclear whether conversion meant embracing the biblical Jesus or

---

109. Justin, *First Apology* 46, in *The Writings of Justin Martyr and Athenagoras*, edited by Marcus Dods et al. (Edinburgh: T. and T. Clark, 1879). Justin and other fathers such as Clement believed that the Christian tradition's stories of Christ's descent to the dead (Matt. 27:52; 1 Pet 3:19, 4:6) meant a postmortem opportunity for salvation for some but only through personal and explicit faith in Christ. See Chrys Saldanha, *Divine Pedagogy: A Patristic View of Non-Christian Religions* (Rome: Libreria Arteneo Salesiano, 1984), 163–167; Gerald Bray, "Explaining Christianity to Pagans: The Second-Century Apologists," in *The Trinity in a Pluralistic Age: Theological Essays on Culture and Religion*, edited by Kevin J. Vanhoozer (Grand Rapids, MI: Eerdmans, 1997), 9–25; McDermott, *God's Rivals*, 93–96.

110. See David Bebbington, *Evangelicalism in Modern Britain: A History from the 1730s to the 1980s* (Grand Rapids, MI: Baker, 1989), 5–17.

Western patterns of life. In considering Christian salvation, we must briefly also discuss what is—and what is not—included in a biblical understanding of conversion.

Although *salvation* and *conversion* are sometimes used as synonyms, it is important to maintain a distinction between them. Failure to do so can result in the kind of confusion all too evident in the history of Christian missions, when certain patterns of behavior from European or American cultures were identified as essential markers of salvation. Gordon Smith helpfully distinguishes conversion from salvation, arguing that salvation "is the work of God," whereas conversion "is the human response to the work of God." Whereas salvation is entirely the work of God, conversion involves "both divine action—salvation—and human response to the saving work of God.... Conversion is a personal response to the saving work of God in Christ Jesus."[111] Salvation involves regeneration, justification, sanctification, and glorification. That entire sequence is begun at a point in time by the Holy Spirit on the basis of the atoning work of Jesus Christ. Conversion is the human side of the beginning of that sequence; it is the human response to God's saving work and also the beginning of a process in which believing sinners are transformed into the image of Jesus Christ, becoming progressively Christlike (Rom. 8:29).

While it is important for cultural reasons to distinguish conversion as the beginning of salvation from the entire process of salvation and in doing so to emphasize conversion as human response, it is also important to remember that even that human response is enabled by a work of God. Jesus said, "You did not choose me, but I chose you," and "No one comes to me unless the Father draws him" (John 15:16, 6:44). Paul suggested that every human movement toward or for God is also God's work: "It is God who works in you, both to will and to work for his good pleasure" (Phil. 2:13). Yet although the soul's movement toward God is initiated and sustained at each stage by God's grace, there is also an important sense in which the individual is involved in repentance, turning to God and, under the power of the Holy Spirit, progressively manifesting Christlike qualities (Col. 3:1–17; Gal. 5:16–26). There is great mystery here, and theologians have struggled for centuries with how to articulate precisely the relationship between the divine and the human in this process. What is clear from Scripture, however, is that even though it is a special work of God that initiates the process, enables one to turn in repentance toward

God, and brings about moral and spiritual transformation, the individual is also responsible for responding appropriately to God's grace in his or her life.

Two New Testament Greek terms are central to the biblical idea of conversion.[112] The first is *epistrephō*, which includes the notion of turning around or reversing direction. Conversion to Christ involves turning away from one's former, sinful way of life and following the way of Jesus. The apostle Paul was sent by God to the Gentiles "to open their eyes, so that they may turn from darkness to light and from the power of Satan to God, that they may receive forgiveness of sins and a place among those who are sanctified in [Jesus]" (Acts 26:18). In his encounter with the folk religionists at Lystra, Paul urged them "to turn from these vain things to a living God, who made the heaven and the earth and the sea and all that is in them" (Acts 14:15).

The second term is *metanoeō*, to repent or have a change of heart. John the Baptist called the people to repentance, "for the Kingdom of heaven is at hand" (Mark 3:2). Jesus, too, began his public ministry by saying, "Repent, for the kingdom of heaven is at hand" (Matt. 4:17). The gospel of Mark portrays Jesus declaring, "The time is fulfilled, and the kingdom of God is at hand; repent and believe in the gospel" (Mark 1:15). The early apostolic preaching included a clear call to repentance: in the sermon on the day of Pentecost, Peter urged the people, "Repent and be baptized every one of you in the name of Jesus Christ for the forgiveness of your sins" (Acts 2:38; see also Acts 3:19, 17:30). The proclamation of Christ's kingdom and the call to repentance are integral parts of proclaiming the gospel. For, as Johannes Verkuyl observes: "To everyone of whatever religious persuasion the message must be repeated: 'The Kingdom of God is at hand; repent and believe in the Gospel.' In no circumstances may the Evangel be proclaimed in a neutral way. The Gospel always involves decision....A theology and missiology informed by the biblical notion of the rule of Christ will never fail to identify personal conversion as one of the inclusive goals of God's Kingdom."[113]

In turning in repentance, by the grace of God, from a life dominated by sin and rebellion against God to a life increasingly lived under the power of the Holy Spirit, one progressively manifests the qualities associated with the Lord Jesus himself. The disciples of Jesus are to manifest the qualities set

---

112. See "Conversion," in *The New International Dictionary of New Testament Theology*, Vol. 1, edited by Colin Brown (Grand Rapids, MI: Zondervan, 1975), 353–362.

113. Johannes Verkuyl, "The Biblical Notion of Kingdom: Test of Validity for Theology of Religion," in *The Good News of the Kingdom*, edited by Charles Van Engen, Dean S. Gilliland, and Paul Pierson (Maryknoll, NY: Orbis), 72–73.

out in the Sermon on the Mount (Matt. 5–7) and the Great Commandment (Matt. 22:34–40). They are to exemplify the fruit of the Spirit (Gal. 5:22–23) and the humility and service found in Christ (Phil. 2:5–11). They are not to be overcome with evil but rather to overcome evil with good (Rom. 13:21). Richard Peace states: "Christian conversion involves repentance from sin, turning to Jesus, and it results in life transformation."[114]

The notion of conversion is controversial today. Conversion is often identified with overly zealous, unscrupulous missionaries who are concerned primarily with increasing the numbers of their flock and who understand conversion as little more than adopting the missionaries' appearance and behavior. The perceived link between missionaries and Western colonialist empires in the late nineteenth and early twentieth centuries provoked bitter reactions. Christianity in China was dismissed as foreign and incompatible with Chinese culture, so that when a Chinese person professed faith in Jesus Christ, the response was often, "One more Christian, one fewer Chinese!" But perhaps the sharpest critique of Christian conversion came from Indian nationalists at the height of the British Empire.

Mahatma Gandhi (1869–1948), for example, was a persistent critic of conversion. Although he had many friends among the missionaries in India, Gandhi repeatedly urged them to abandon their evangelistic efforts intended to convert Hindus into Christians. In part, this was because Gandhi perceived Indian Christians as having abandoned their Indian heritage and identity: "As I wander throughout the length and breadth of India, I see many Christian Indians almost ashamed of their birth, certainly of their ancestral religion, and of their ancestral dress. The aping of Europeans on the part of Anglo-Indians is bad enough, but the aping of them by Indian converts is a violence done to their country and shall I say, even to their new religion."[115]

But Gandhi's dislike for conversion also was based on his conviction concerning the essential unity of the religions. In Gandhi's view, it was not a matter of there being one true religion that alone provides salvation; all religions are, in their own way, true and beneficial. There is therefore no need for conversion. On one occasion, when asked by a missionary why he shouldn't engage in evangelism among Hindus and others, Gandhi replied, "Because…you cannot possibly say that what is best for you is best for all.…Your difficulty lies in your considering the other faiths as false or so adulterated as to amount

114. Richard V. Peace, "Conversion," in *Global Dictionary of Theology*, edited by William A. Dyrness and Veli-Matti Kärkkäinen (Downers Grove, IL: InterVarsity, 2008), 196–197.

115. *Gandhi on Christianity*, edited by Robert Ellsberg (Maryknoll, NY: Orbis, 1991), 38–39.

to falsity. And you shut your eyes to the truth that shines in the other faiths and which gives equal joy and peace to their votaries."[116] Gandhi went on to say that all the religions are roughly equally imperfect manifestations of the one true Religion: "Personally, I do not regard any of the great religions of the world as false. All have served in enriching mankind and are now even serving their purpose.... Even as a tree has a single trunk, but many branches and leaves, so is there one true and perfect Religion, but it becomes many, as it passes through the human medium. The one Religion is beyond all speech. Imperfect men put it into such languages as they can command, and their words are interpreted by other men equally imperfect."[117] Gandhi's comments raise many important issues that cannot be pursued in detail here. We have already discussed other versions of this approach—generally called "pluralism"—in earlier chapters. What is relevant here, however, is Gandhi's perception concerning conversion and Indian cultural identity. Although we cannot explore the issues in any depth, we will note briefly five general principles that characterize biblical conversion and its relation to culture.

First, biblical conversion, although it includes participation in the church, is not simply a matter of joining a new religion, Christianity. It is turning away from a life under the control of sin to a qualitatively new life as a disciple of Jesus Christ. Now, to be sure, conversion does not occur in a vacuum. It is not abstract, generic human beings who are converted; it is actual men and women, rooted in complex ethnic, social, historical, religious, and cultural settings, who are transformed by God's saving grace. It is in this connection that the relation between conversion and one's culture becomes so significant. Salvation and conversion do not entail extraction from the broader social setting, but they do involve a transformed relationship to this context. As Smith observes: "A conversion is an experience of deep continuity and discontinuity. Although through conversion we are certainly not called to abandon the world or escape from it—Jesus insists on this in his prayer of John 17 (see v. 15)— we nevertheless recognize that there is a profound discontinuity between the values and mores of the world and those of the reign of Christ. The whole process and experience of conversion is one of moving out from under this foreign authority and moving under the reign of Christ, the cosmic Lord and head of a new humanity (cf. Col. 1:13-14)."[118]

---

116. Ibid., 55.

117. Ibid., 23, 62.

118. Smith, *Transforming Conversion*, 33.

Growing in maturity as a disciple of Jesus Christ is not something that is done in isolation. It involves becoming an active participant in a community of believers, in worship, service, instruction, and accountability. And it is true that the patterns of life stemming from such involvement produce what we identify empirically as the Christian religion. But conversion itself is not simply a matter of engaging in these religious activities; it is turning to Jesus Christ and making him Lord of one's life.

Second, given the nature of the gospel, conversion to Jesus Christ can, in principle, occur within any given linguistic, ethnic, social, or cultural framework. There is no particular culture, ethnicity, or language that is distinctively Christian and to which all other cultures must conform. Andrew Walls has expressed this in terms of what he calls "the indigenizing principle" of the gospel.[119] The gospel of Jesus Christ can be expressed in any language and become "at home" in any culture; followers of Jesus do not need to abandon their cultural or ethnic identity when converting to Christ: "There can be no single Christian civilization; the Christian Scriptures are not, like the Qur'an, the Word of God only when delivered in the original languages. In Christian understanding the Word of God can be spoken in any language under heaven."[120]

Conversion thus involves the dialectical tension between what we are becoming—the new humanity in Christ—and the familiar patterns that have shaped us. While conversion does involve a clear break with aspects of our past way of life, it does not entirely negate the social and cultural framework in which we find ourselves. Our identity, even after conversion, continues to be shaped by our past: "Our past is the clue to our identity. It has made us what we are, and without it we would not know ourselves."[121] In becoming a disciple of Jesus Christ, then, a Chinese person does not cease being a Chinese. He or she can be authentically Chinese and a follower of Jesus.

Third, although conversion does not require a total break with one's social and cultural past, it does involve a new identity as a disciple of Jesus, which in turn demands modification of aspects of one's culture. While the gospel can be expressed in any culture, it also judges every culture. Turning to Christ, becoming increasingly Christlike, involves a profound transformation of one's

---

119. Andrew F. Walls, *The Missionary Movement in Christian History: Studies in the Transmission of Faith* (Maryknoll, NY: Orbis, 1996), 7–8.

120. Ibid., 47. See also Lamin Sanneh, *Translating the Message: The Missionary Impact on Culture,* 2nd ed. (Maryknoll, NY: Orbis, 2009).

121. Walls, *The Missionary Movement,* 45.

beliefs, desires, values, actions, and relationships. This implies a complex, dynamic relationship between the transformative effects of the gospel of Jesus Christ and local societies and cultures. Walls speaks of this as "the pilgrim principle," which "creates within the Christian community the sense that it is not fully at home in this world, so that it comes into tension with its society from its loyalty to Christ."[122] Conversion to Christ involves living as a community of Christ's disciples in the ongoing tension between the indigenizing and the pilgrim principles: "The one [principle] tends to localize the vision of the Church, the other to universalize it. The two principles are recurrent because each springs directly out of the Gospel itself. On the one hand God accepts us in Christ just as we are, with all our distinctives—even the things which mark us off from others—still on us. On the other he accepts us in order that we may become something different; that we may be transformed out of the ways of this world into the image of Christ."[123] Living within the dynamic tension between the two principles should be the reality for all communities of Christians, in the West and also in Asia, Africa, and Latin America.

Fourth, Christians around the world must be encouraged to develop patterns of living that reflect their identities both as genuine disciples of Jesus Christ and as authentic members of their own ethnic, social, and cultural communities. Since the 1960s, this concern has been discussed under the rubric of contextualization. We might think of contextualization as the process through which the gospel of Jesus Christ is expressed in appropriate local linguistic and cultural patterns and particular Christian communities live out their commitments as disciples of Christ within such cultural contexts.[124]

Finally, since genuine conversion is an expression of one's religious conscience, societies around the world should be encouraged to promote and protect the freedom of religious choice. The twentieth century witnessed the rise of the some of the most totalitarian and despotic regimes in human history, but, ironically, it also produced an unprecedented emphasis on the dignity of the human person and the importance of preserving human rights.[125]

---

122. Ibid., 54.

123. Ibid.

124. Helpful introductions to contextualization include Paul Hiebert, "Critical Contextualization," *Missiology* 12, no. 3 (July 1984): 287–296; Darrell Whiteman, "Contextualization: The Theory, the Gap, the Challenge," *International Bulletin of Missionary Research* 21, no. 1 (January 1997): 1–7; A. Scott Moreau, *Contextualization and World Missions* (Grand Rapids, MI: Kregel, 2012).

125. See Lynn Hunt, *Inventing Human Rights: A History* (New York: W. W. Norton, 2007).

In 1948, at the founding of the United Nations after World War II, member nations signed the Universal Declaration of Human Rights. Among the rights enumerated in the declaration is the right to freedom of religion. Article 18 states: "Everyone has the right to freedom of thought, conscience and religion; this right includes freedom to change his religion or belief, and freedom, either alone or in community with others and in public or private, to manifest his religion or belief in teaching, practice, worship and observance."[126]

It goes without saying that there are today many places in the world—including among many of the signatory nations—where such freedom of religious expression is not tolerated. The lack of freedom for religious choice in many Islamic societies is well known, and those who come to faith in Jesus Christ in such contexts often pay a heavy price for conversion. It is important that as we strive for the protection of human rights worldwide, we also encourage respect for the religious conscience and genuine freedom of religious expression.

But Is There Universal Salvation?

One last question must be considered before we conclude this chapter on salvation and conversion: whether all are eventually saved. For if they are, the evangelical emphasis on conversion would appear to be seriously misguided. Why go to such effort and expense trying to persuade people that Jesus is the only Way if they all will eventually be saved anyway? Why risk offending people—especially believers in other religious traditions—with the contention that their way is insufficient without knowledge of Jesus Christ if we will all one day enjoy the full truth in peace and joy?

Before we look at contemporary claims for universalism, it would be good to sketch its history briefly.[127] Overall, it is a short one. That is, the notion that

---

126. "Universal Declaration of Human Rights," Article 18, in ibid., 226. From our vantage point today, it is easy to forget that the idea of religious toleration or freedom of conscience was not always accepted even in the West but became increasingly accepted only after the eighteenth century. See Perez Zagorin, *How the Idea of Religious Toleration Came to the West* (Princeton, NJ: Princeton University Press, 2003).

127. One of the best comprehensive reviews of this history is Laurence Malcolm Blanchard, "Universalism: Its Historic Development and Its Contemporary Expression in Western Theology" (PhD dissertation, Fuller Theological Seminary, 2007). Much of the bibliography and thinking in these pages on universalism is indebted to the forthcoming analytical history of universalism, *The Devil's Redemption: An Interpretation of the Christian Debate Over Universal Salvation* (Grand Rapids: Baker Academic), by Michael J. McClymond, which he kindly shared with us.

all will or might be saved has come into vogue among a significant number
of major theologians only since the mid-twentieth century. There was not a
hint of universalism in the first two centuries of Christianity. Then, in the
next three centuries, there were some noted proponents of the notion, but
they were in the minority. Many Greek fathers, such as Irenaeus (d. ca. 200),
Basil (d. ca. 379), and Cyril of Jerusalem (d. ca. 387), said that hell would be the
destiny for most human beings.

Origen (d. ca. 254), in his doctrine of *apokatastasis* (the restoration of all
beings to their original state in God), seems to imply a rudimentary form of
universalism.[128] Theophilus of Alexandria (d. 412) took issue with Origen's
teaching, and Basil the Great rejected the version of the same by his brother
Gregory of Nyssa (d. ca. 394).[129] Augustine (d. 430) attacked it with gusto
in *City of God*, and in the anathemas published after the Fifth Ecumenical
Council at Constantinople (553), it was condemned in no uncertain words: "If
anyone says or thinks that the punishment of demons and of impious men
is only temporary, and will one day have an end, and that a restoration
[ἀποκατάστασις] will take place of demons and of impious men, let him be
anathema."[130]

Church creeds from the early Middle Ages through the Reformation and
into the modern era regularly affirmed the eternal punishment of the wicked.
A sampling would include the *Athanasian Creed* (early sixth century); the
Fourth Lateran Council, Canon 1 (A.D. 1215); the *Augsburg Confession*, chapter 17
(A.D. 1530); the *Second Helvetic Confession*, chapter 26 (A.D. 1564), the *Dordrecht
Confession*, article 18 (A.D. 1632); and the *Westminster Confession*, chapter 33
(1646)—along with many later denominational statements of faith from the

128. See Frederick W. Norris, "Universal Salvation in Origen and Maximus," in *Universalism
and the Doctrine of Hell*, edited by Nigel M. de S. Cameron (Grand Rapids, MI: Baker,
1992), 35–72.

129. Richard Bauckham, "Universalism: An Historical Survey," *Themelios* 4 (1978): 47–54;
Avery Cardinal Dulles, "The Population of Hell," *First Things* (May 2003): 36–41.

130. Augustine, *City of God*, Book XXI; for the anathemas of the Fifth Council (Constantinople
II), see *The Seven Ecumenical Councils of the Undivided Church*, edited by Henry Percival, in
Nicene and Post-Nicene Fathers, series 2 (Grand Rapids, MI: Eerdmans, 1991), 14:318–320; this
quote from 320. Some have claimed this condemnation applied only to the doctrine's association with the preexistence of souls, as is suggested by other anathemas, but the language in
this anathema undermines that claim. Others complain that these anathemas are to be dis-
counted because they were added later to the text of the council proceedings, but Blanchard
notes that the universal church nevertheless drew from these anathemas the conclusion
that universal salvation had been officially proscribed. Blanchard, "Universalism," 68–69.

seventeenth century onward.[131] The reality of hell and eternal punishment was thought to be as basic to Christian belief as Trinity and incarnation.

There were ripples of interest in universalism in the seventeenth and eighteenth centuries when Socinians, Deists, and Enlightenment *philosophes* doubted the traditional doctrine of hell. Then, in the nineteenth century, the father of liberal Protestant theology, Friedrich Schleiermacher (1768–1834), challenged the teaching on hell by suggesting that divine election was corporate, not individual. Anticipating Barth, Schleiermacher intimated that all human beings were elected for salvation.[132] Later in the nineteenth century, Scottish novelist and poet George MacDonald (1824–1905) suggested that the fire of God's love would burn away sin and impurity in some sort of purgatorial state after death. Significantly, MacDonald's disciple C. S. Lewis elected not to follow his master's lead.[133]

Already by the mid-twentieth century, fewer people in the West accepted traditional teaching on hell, so that the atheist philosopher Bertrand Russell was able to observe, "Hell is neither so certain nor so hot as it used to be."[134] Prominent theologians, too, rejected the idea of eternal damnation and began to teach various forms of universalism. The most influential has been Karl Barth (1886–1968), the great Reformed theologian from Switzerland. Barth taught that all human beings were both damned and elected in Christ and that the damnation took place on the cross. The mystery of salvation is not

---

131. See Bauckham, "Universalism," 47, n. 2.

132. Friedrich Schleiermacher, *The Christian Faith* (Philadelphia: Fortress, 1976), 548–551, 720–722.

133. George MacDonald, "The Consuming Fire" (18–33), "It Shall Not Be Forgiven" (45–66), "The Last Farthing" (259–274), "Justice" (501–540), "Righteousness" (577–592), "The Final Unmasking" (593–606), "The Inheritance" (607–619), in *Unspoken Sermons: Series I, II, and III in One Volume* (Whitethorn, CA: Johannesen, 1997 [1867, 1885, 1889]). For a secondary account, see David M. Kelly, "The Treatment of Universalism in Anglican Thought from George Macdonald (1824–1905) to C. S. Lewis (1898–1963)" (PhD dissertation, University of Ottawa, 1989). In Lewis's *The Great Divorce*, after the narrator finds MacDonald in heaven and reminds him that he had been a universalist while on earth, MacDonald indicates that he has changed his mind. The problem with universalism, Lewis's MacDonald now advises, is that it removes "freedom, which is the deeper truth of the two." The other truth of the two is predestination, "which shows (truly enough) that external reality is not waiting for a future in which to be real." C. S. Lewis, *The Great Divorce* (New York: Macmillan, 1946), 124–125. By "deep truth" Lewis seems to have meant the idea that there will always be some who want nothing to do with a God who invites them to confess their sins, serve persons other than themselves, and worship someone other than themselves. As Milton put it, "The choice of every lost soul can be expressed in the words, 'Better to reign in Hell than serve in Heaven.'" John Milton, *Paradise Lost*, line 263; quoted in Lewis, *The Great Divorce*, 69.

134. Bertrand Russell, *Why I Am Not a Christian* (New York: Simon & Schuster, 1957), 195.

that some are saved, as Augustine and the Reformers taught, but that some sin against grace and reject salvation. Yet we have reason to hope for the salvation of all, because there is always more grace in God than sin in us. Barth insisted that we cannot say that all are saved, because such a statement is a theological abstraction divorced from the particularities of the biblical witness to Jesus Christ.[135] Yet most of Barth's interpreters conclude that Barth's theological logic points to universalism, and this was exactly the conclusion reached by those influenced by Barth: John A. T. Robinson, Jacques Ellul, Jan Bonda, Eberhard Jüngel, and Jürgen Moltmann.[136]

From a quite different perspective, theologian and philosopher John Hick advocated universalism as the only credible response to the vexing problem of evil and suffering: only if ultimately all are saved can we believe in a God of love.[137]

Some twentieth-century Catholic theologians also questioned the traditional Catholic doctrine of hell. Jacques Maritain speculated that there might be a limbo (without punishment) for the damned. Karl Rahner said that we have no clear revelation that anyone is damned forever and that we must uphold God's universal salvific will. Hans Urs von Balthasar opined that we have an obligation to hope for the salvation of all. Even Pope John Paul II speculated that hell is not a punishment but a condition of those who separate themselves from God and that we do not know if humans are actually damned in the ways conceived of by traditional belief.[138] Yet more recent Catholic statements from the Vatican have shown greater adherence to traditional eschatology. *Dominus Iesus* (2000) warned that those in other religions who do not accept the gospel face an "obstacle to salvation" that puts them "in a gravely deficient situation."[139] The *Catechism of the Catholic Church* teaches "the

---

135. Karl Barth, *Church Dogmatics* 4:2 (Edinburgh: T. and T. Clark, 1958), 520; George Hunsinger, *How to Read Karl Barth: The Shape of His Theology* (New York: Oxford University Press, 1991), 134; Barth, *Church Dogmatics* 2:2 (Edinburgh: T. and T. Clark, 1958), 417–418.

136. John A. T. Robinson, *In the End God: A Study of the Christian Doctrine of the Last Things* (London: James Clarke, 1950); Jacques Ellul, *What I Believe* (Grand Rapids, MI: Eerdmans, 1989); Eberhard Jüngel, "The Last Judgment as an Act of Grace," *Louvain Studies* 15 (1990): 389–405; Jan Bonda, *The One Purpose of God: An Answer to the Doctrine of Eternal Punishment*, translated by R. Bruinsma (Grand Rapids, MI: Eerdmans, 1998 [1993]); Jürgen Moltmann, *The Coming of God: Christian Eschatology*, translated by M. Kohl (Minneapolis: Fortress, 1996), especially 235–255.

137. See John Hick, *Death and Eternal Life* (New York: Harper & Row, 1976); Hick, *Evil and the God of Love*, 2nd ed. (San Francisco: Harper & Row, 1977).

138. Dulles, "The Population of Hell," 38–39.

139. *Dominus Iesus*, paras. 21, 22.

existence of hell and its eternity" and that those who die in a state of mortal sin "suffer the punishments of hell, 'eternal fire.'"[140] Commenting on statements such as these, the late Cardinal Avery Dulles remarked on the "thoughtless optimism" of previous and contemporary theologians.[141]

In Eastern Orthodoxy, the story has been similar. For most of its history, its official documents have taught two destinations for humans: heaven and hell. Only since the 1970s have two Orthodox theologians—Kallistos Ware and Metropolitan Hilarion Alfeyev of Russia—begun to call for a revised view.[142]

Evangelicals and Pentecostals are newcomers to this conversation. Robin Parry, sometimes under the pen name of Gregory MacDonald, has brought out a number of volumes dedicated to "evangelical universalism," which includes several varieties all of which agree that God ultimately will save all through the work of Christ.[143] Parry argues that neither orthodoxy nor evangelicalism need preclude universalism; in other words, an evangelical and orthodox Christian can embrace universalism without a sense of theological incoherence. Yet in what is perhaps his most interesting volume, Parry edits a variety of essays on universalists who are theologically unorthodox (Schleiermacher, Robinson, and Hick, for example) or unevangelical (Julian of Norwich, Barth, Balthasar, and Moltmann).[144] Thomas Talbott is an evangelical philosopher whose work on universalism has attracted wide attention.[145] In 2012, megachurch pastor Rob Bell's book *Love Wins*, which implicitly recommends a hopeful universalism (like Balthasar's: we can hope without knowing for sure), sparked a perfect storm of controversy both within and outside the evangelical world.[146]

---

140. *Catechism of the Catholic Church* (Liguori, MO: Liguori, 1994), sect. 1035.

141. Dulles, "The Population of Hell," 40.

142. Kallistos Ware, *The Inner Kingdom* (New York: St. Vladimir's Seminary Press, 2000), 193–215; Hieromonk Hilarion Alfeyev, *Christ the Conqueror of Hell: The Descent into Hades from an Orthodox Perspective* (New York: St. Vladimir's Seminary Press, 2009).

143. In *Universal Salvation? The Current Debate*, edited by Robin A. Parry and Christopher H. Partridge (Grand Rapids, MI: Eerdmans, 2003), xv–xxvii. See also Gregory MacDonald (pseudonym for Robin Parry), *The Evangelical Universalist* (Eugene, OR: Cascade, 2006).

144. *"All Shall Be Well": Explorations in Universal Salvation and Christian Theology from Origen to Moltmann*, edited by Gregory MacDonald (Eugene, OR: Cascade, 2011). The volume also contains essays on a few universalists, such as George MacDonald, who are closer to evangelical sensibilities.

145. Thomas Talbott, *The Inescapable Love of God* (n.p.: Universal, 1999); see also *Universal Salvation? The Current Debate*, edited by Robin A. Parry and Christopher H. Partridge, whose first three chapters are written by Talbott.

146. Rob Bell, *Love Wins: A Book about Heaven, Hell, and the Fate of Every Person Who Ever Lived* (New York: HarperOne, 2012).

Time magazine featured the book on one of its covers. If evangelicals had not known that some of their theologians and pastors had been challenging traditional eschatology, this new book made them suddenly aware.

How do universalists make their case? It might be helpful first to examine three ways in which they have interpreted the many biblical texts that speak of eternal punishment and banishment from God's presence. Some of these are overlapping, but all three represent different ways of interpreting problem texts. A first group has believed that these texts mean something other than what appears on the surface. Clement of Alexandria and Origen, for example, believed that texts about the fires of hell mean the fire of God's love, which will purge sinners of their impurities over the course of many lives.[147] Karl Rahner maintained that "hell" is simply a metaphor for lostness. Emil Brunner thought that texts talking about two destinations for sinners are not intended to give theoretical information but are existential invitations to sinners to come out of a state of perdition.[148] For Brunner and others, these are threats, not predictions—like the exasperated mother warning her son, "If you don't clean up your room right now, I'll kill you!"

A second group of universalist interpreters has thought that the biblical authors really did mean that there would be two destinations and eternal punishment for the wicked, but they concluded that these authors were simply mistaken. They were benighted by what Schleiermacher called the "alleviating influence of custom" and so were prevented from seeing straight.[149] Ancient culture was not as clear-eyed as modern sensibility. If the ancient authors had really understood the implications of what they *did* see about God's love, they would not have sketched eschatology as they did.

A last group sees two different themes in Scripture and regards them as paradoxical. Barth, as we have seen, taught that Scripture teaches both that God elected all in Christ and that some reject that election, which is the greatest mystery of all. It is a paradox that we can hope God finally resolves. For German Lutheran theologian Paul Althaus, the paradox of God's damnation of some and universal will to save must remain an open question. For Emil Brunner, these two conflicting strands of teaching are incompatible. John

147. See, for example, *Origen: On First Principles*, translated by G. W. Butterworth (New York: Harper & Row, 1966), 145.

148. Karl Rahner, "Hell," in *Encyclopedia of Theology: The Concise Sacramentum Mundi*, edited by Karl Rahner (New York: Continuum, 1975), 603; Emil Brunner, *The Christian Doctrine of the Church, Faith, and the Consummation*, translated by David Cairns, in *Dogmatics* (Philadelphia: Westminster, 1960), 421–424.

149. Schleiermacher, *The Christian Faith*, 720.

A. T. Robinson said that universal restoration and final division are the New Testament's two eschatological myths, the reconciliation of which is paradoxical.[150] In the end, God's omnipotent love will break the deadlock by forcing everyone to a free choice prompted by that love. Philosophers John Kronen and Eric Reitan assert that the "plain sense" of some biblical passages supports universalism, while the plain sense of other passages teaches eternal destruction, so the two sets of texts are "at odds." We must find what is "central" in the biblical narrative as a hermeneutical key and thus interpret some texts in ways that deviate from or override their plain sense.[151]

If these are three basic ways of construing texts that pose problems for universalism, there are also three kinds of positive arguments universalists use: philosophical, theological, and biblical. The philosophical is best represented by evangelical Thomas Talbott, who sets out three philosophico-theological axioms: (1) that God is love and therefore must love all his creatures, not just some; (2) that if God is love, he must will the salvation of all he loves, which means all his human creatures; and (3) that since God is all-powerful, he will achieve all his purposes, among which is included the salvation of all. Talbott considers the objection that this might override the freedom of those creatures but responds that once they are fully informed of God's offer, all humans will realize that to reject the offer would be irrational. Thus, they will accept freely, without coercion.[152] Parry adds that those in hell must have a second chance to repent, since a God of love would not refuse one who repents and calls for help, no matter where that one is.[153] Kronen and Reitan argue that God will eliminate "salvation inhibitors" such as delusions and bad habits and provide such clear vision of himself that it will not be possible, given enough time, for any sinner to cling to his false beliefs. None

---

150. Paul Althaus, *Die letzen Dinge,* 10th ed. (Gütersloh: G. Mohn, 1970 [1922]); Brunner, *The Christian Doctrine,* 423; Robinson, *In the End God.* As we saw above, Brunner resolves this incompatibility by means of a metaphorical understanding.

151. John Kronen and Eric Reitan, *God's Final Victory: A Comparative Philosophical Case for Universalism* (London: Continuum, 2011), 54, 58, 66. It is worth noting that this way of interpreting Scripture was explicitly proscribed by the Reformers' principle of Scripture interpreting Scripture, which hermeneutic refused to countenance a reading that would pit one part of Scripture against another. As it was stated in the *39 Articles of Religion,* "Neither may [the church] so expound one place of Scripture, that it be repugnant to another" (Art. XX); *Book of Common Prayer* (New York: Church, 1979), 871.

152. *Universal Salvation? The Current Debate,* edited by Robin A. Parry and Christopher H. Partridge (Grand Rapids, MI: Eerdmans, 2003), chaps. 1–3.

153. Ibid., xxiv.

will continue to choose ignorance or remain in bondage to bad desires. With unrelenting application of God's efficacious grace, there is "mathematical certainty" that every soul will freely accept salvation.[154]

Universalists' theological warrants are various, but nearly all of them come down to an argument from divine love. This is very similar to the philosophical arguments for universalism, but whereas Talbott argues that logic forbids an eternal hell, Parry and others focus on the meaning of love for theological understandings of God's nature. As Parry puts it, "Any view of hell as *purely* retributive punishment brings God's justice and wrath into serious conflict with God's love and is in danger of dividing the divine nature." But even when Parry considers that traditional eschatology might attribute other reasons for hell than simply retribution, the fact that it includes eternal conscious torment makes it "very hard to square with God's love for the damned."[155] The only way that some universalists can accept hell is to think of it as therapeutic and therefore temporary, progressive and restorative rather than punitive and final. For God's compassion and love, they aver, would never permit a soul's final exclusion from the company of the redeemed.

Kronen and Reitan insist that an eternal hell allows sin to "reign forever victorious." In retributive doctrines of hell, God "cannot" save the damned without compromising his justice, and in classical doctrines, God "deliberately withhold[s]" efficacious grace from the damned. In either case, "God is *less* loving or *less* powerful than he might be...[and] is needlessly denied His final and triumphant victory over sin."[156] All such traditional views of hell mean that God ultimately fails to achieve what is best.[157]

Universalists believe the Bible supports their view. They point to a number of biblical texts that seem to predict the salvation of all, such as Jesus' claim that "when I am lifted up from the earth, I will draw all people to myself" (John 12:32) and Paul's declaration that "at the name of Jesus every knee should bow, in heaven and on earth and under the earth" (Phil. 2:10).[158] They also proffer New Testament texts that seem to announce God's intention to save all (1 Tim. 2:4; 2 Pet. 3:9) and others that they see linking the cross of Christ to the

---

154. Kronen and Reitan, *God's Final Victory*, 42, 44, 136–148, 177, 179.

155. Robin Parry, "Evangelical Universalism: Oxymoron?" *Evangelical Quarterly* 84, no. 1 (2012): 9.

156. Kronen and Reitan, *God's Final Victory*, 24, 27, 47.

157. Ibid., 106.

158. Other Scriptures they use to support this claim are Acts 3.21; Rom. 5.18, 11.32; 1 Cor. 15.22–28.

salvation of all, such as Hebrews 2:9: "But we see him who for a little while was made lower than the angels, namely Jesus, crowned with glory and honor because of the suffering of death, so that by the grace of God he might taste death for everyone."[159]

Now let us critically examine these arguments for universal salvation. A full response is impossible here, and in any event, we must tread carefully, since there is much we simply do not understand about God's love and mercy, not to mention his wrath and judgment. There is mystery here, and we must avoid speculation that conflicts with what Scripture clearly attests. But several brief comments are in order.

First, Talbott's argument from God's love to universal salvation is problematic in its assumption that all people will freely respond positively to God's love. Why should we accept this assumption? Many have argued that significant freedom must include the freedom ultimately to reject God, thereby choosing for oneself the terrible reality of hell.[160] Philosopher Jerry Walls provides a thoughtful response to Talbott's argument for universalism in *Hell: The Logic of Damnation*. Walls argues that "a person can so deceive himself into believing evil is good, or at least holds sufficient advantage to be gained, that he comes to the point where he consistently and thoroughly prefers evil to good."[161] In such cases, it is plausible to believe that God will allow the person the evil reality he prefers, an awful reality apart from God's presence, or hell. Kronen and Reitan cannot imagine that anyone would ever cling to false beliefs if God provides vision of himself. But we must regard this as speculation, unsupported by the biblical witness. Besides, the notion that everyone will inevitably accept salvation if given enough information suggests a mechanistic view of the human person—that with the proper input, this entity will inevitably respond in this way—which is inconsistent with their assertion of human autonomy. We can have mathematically certain outcomes of a machine but not of a free person.[162]

Similarly, the theological argument based on love has come under fire from assorted critics for abstracting that divine attribute from others such

---

159. They also point to 2 Corinthians 5:19, Titus 2:11, and 1 John 2:2.

160. See, for example, Richard Swinburne, "A Theodicy of Heaven and Hell," in *The Existence and Nature of God*, edited by Alfred J. Freddoso (Notre Dame, IN: University of Notre Dame Press, 1983), 49.

161. Jerry L. Walls, *Hell: The Logic of Damnation* (Notre Dame, IN: University of Notre Dame Press, 1992), 138.

162. Kronen and Reitan, *God's Final Victory*, 143, 145, 148.

as justice. No good reason is given for preferring love to justice in the order of divine attributes, except the modern sentimentalist presumption that love must finally prevail over justice. Besides, some argue, the very idea that love prevails over justice misunderstands the nature of God and replaces the biblical vision of divine love with a modern sentimentalist one. Moreover, if the biblical authors are right, divine love is very different from human love. It is a love that is fiercely holy and not averse to punishment. The same Jesus who emphasizes the importance of love also says, "These will go away into eternal punishment, but the righteous into eternal life" (Matt. 25:46).

Kronen and Reitan argue that an eternal hell would cause those in heaven to be "forever saddened" by the privations of the lost and "God's ultimate failure to achieve what is best." But N. T. Wright, C. S. Lewis, and others have suggested that hell gradually dehumanizes its residents as they grow in their hatred for God. They reach a state that is "beyond pity." The saved realize that sin no longer has dominion over God's kingdom, because it has been punished and contained. It is like a memory that has lost its power to make us frightened or angry.[163] Contrary to Kronen and Reitan's suggestion, the combination of the new heaven and earth, with healing for the nations, and a hell that has finally put away evil underscores God's triumph.

Karl Barth was right to reject theological abstractions in eschatology that are divorced from the concrete revelation of God in Christ. But when he rests his hopeful universalism (we may or should hope for the salvation of all) on the knowledge that there is always more grace in God than in us and that God is free to enlarge "the circle of redemption," he embraces his own sort of abstraction: that God's freedom and election will always prevail over human resistance. Barth compared willful blindness and deafness to a dam against a rising and surging stream: "But the stream is too strong and the dam too weak for us to be able *reasonably* to expect anything but the collapse of the dam and the onrush of the waters."[164] Barth's point here seems to be similar to that of Talbott noted above and thus faces the problem articulated in Walls's response to Talbott. Moreover, it seems to be at odds with the actual biblical witness, a witness that Barth insisted should direct theology. To this witness we now turn.

---

163. Ibid., 106; N. T. Wright, *Surprised by Hope: Rethinking Heaven, the Resurrection, and the Mission of the Church* (New York: HarperOne, 2008), 182; Wright, *Evil and the Justice of God* (Downers Grove, IL: InterVarsity, 2006), 141–144.

164. Barth, *Church Dogmatics*, 2:2, 418; 4:3, 355–56 (emphasis added).

We have seen that universalists stress the restorative function of God's justice. They also highlight Old Testament biblical texts that emphasize repentance and mercy after threats of judgment. So, for example, some point to Jonah's delivery of God's message that Nineveh would be overturned in forty days. The result was not destruction but restoration. Nineveh repented, and the promised destruction never ensued—at least, at that time.[165] Others point to Judah's exile to Babylon, which led eventually to repentance and return to both God and the land.[166] They also cite Egypt, Assyria, and Elam; all of these were judged with punishment but were later given or promised mercy and blessing.[167]

But traditional eschatologists point out that the Old Testament contains hundreds of stories and passages that feature judgment, illustrating vividly that the God of Israel is "judge of all the earth" (Gen. 18:25). The prophets regularly spoke of two different outcomes, depending on the behavior of Israel and the nations. Rewards were contingent on obedience. Judah and the nations mentioned above received mercy along with judgment, but there were others, such as Babylon and Edom, that received only judgment. They were said to be perpetual wastes, symbols of eternal destruction.[168] Therefore, some judgments in the Old Testament led to softening of the heart and restoration. But other judgments hardened hearts, and the fate of those hearts mirrored that of the generation of Jews who came out of Egypt and "fell" in the wilderness because they never changed in repentance. They were like those Jeremiah criticized for refusing "to take correction . . . they have refused to repent" (5:3). As a result, God "struck them down" (5:3).

The gospels present a similar eschatology of two different outcomes. The evidence is overwhelming. As New Testament scholar Richard Bauckham wrote in his survey of universalist thought, "Few would now doubt that many New Testament texts clearly teach a *final* division of mankind into saved and lost, and the most that universalists now commonly claim is that alongside

---

165. The prophecy of Nahum suggests that judgment eventually came at some point to Nineveh.

166. The Israelites returned to God and the land after their exile to Babylon. After their earlier conquest by Assyria, some were deported and, it seems, never returned.

167. Jeremiah writes of Elam: "But in the latter days I will restore the fortunes of Elam, declares the Lord" (Jer. 49:39 [ESV]). Much the same is written of Moab, too (Jer. 48:47). On Egypt and Assyria, see Isa. 19:24–25.

168. Jeremiah compares the destruction of Bozrah—the Edomites' capital city—to the destruction of Sodom and Gomorrah (Jer. 49:18); on Babylon, see Rev. 17, 18.

these texts there are others which hold out a universalist hope (e.g., Eph. 1:10; Col. 1:20)."[169] I. Howard Marshall, another New Testament scholar, has shown that the New Testament authors both teach and assume that there is a double outcome for humanity, and this outcome is final.[170] Jesus said he would deny before the Father those who denied him during their lives (Matt. 10:33) and that many would seek to enter the kingdom but would not be able (Luke 13:24). In his parables of the wheat and the tares and the dragnet, he said some would be excluded from his kingdom (Matt. 13:24–30, 36–43, 47–50). He taught that there is an eternal sin that cannot be forgiven (Mark 3:28–30). The foolish bridesmaids and those indifferent to the needy would be given chilling sentences: "I do not know you.... Depart from me, you cursed, into the eternal fire prepared for the devil and his angels" (Matt. 25:12, 41). Luke says that Jesus stressed repentance and warned that some would knock but be told by the master of the house, "Depart from me, you workers of evil" (Luke 13:25–28).

Was the judgment proclaimed by Jesus only temporary and thus restorative? In Matthew 25:41, Jesus says he would send the goats to the same place he would send the devil and his angels: "the eternal fire." Orthodox Christians have always believed and taught that all of Scripture is inspired by the same Spirit, so that the book of Revelation is divinely inspired just as the gospels are. Revelation speaks of the smoke of the fire of hell that goes up "forever and ever" (Rev. 14:11, 20:10). Universalists object that the word for "forever"— *aiōnios*—means only "age-long." Yet it is used in the gospels in the phrase "eternal life," where clearly the meaning is life that goes on forever.[171] *Aiōnios* is also used in the gospel phrases "eternal weight of glory," "eternal glory," "eternal covenant," and "eternal gospel," all of which seem to denote things that go on without end. The author of Revelation declares that the damned will be tormented "unto the ages of the ages," just as the devil and his lieutenants will be tormented "day and night unto the ages of ages" (Rev. 14:11, 20:10). "Day and night" seems to refer to ceaseless activity that endures forever, for it is used also for the worship of the saints in heaven: "They are before the throne of God and worship him day and night in his temple" (7:15). "Unto the ages of ages" (*eis tous aiōnas tōn aiōnōn*) is also used of the saints' reign in 22:5. So the

---

169. Bauckham, "Universalism," 52; emphasis in original.

170. I. Howard Marshall, "The New Testament Does *Not* Teach Universal Salvation," in *Universal Salvation? The Current Debate*, edited by Robin A. Parry and Christopher H. Partridge (Grand Rapids, MI: Eerdmans, 2003), 55–76.

171. On issues relating to interpreting the language used of hell, see D. A. Carson, *The Gagging of God: Christianity Confronts Pluralism* (Grand Rapids, MI: Zondervan, 1996), 515–536.

parallelism is persistent; the Greek phrases used to depict the unending reality of heaven are also used for hell. In the words of the early-nineteenth-century scholar Moses Stuart, "We must either admit the endless misery of hell or give up the endless happiness of heaven."[172] We concur with Scot McKnight in his conclusion that Jesus clearly taught "punishment in an individual, eternal, sense."[173] As Wright puts it, the Bible contains passages that "appear to speak unambiguously of a *continuing* state for those who reject the worship of the true God." In Romans, Wright points out by way of example, Paul "is quite clear that there will indeed be final condemnation for 'those who are factious and disobey the truth, but obey wickedness.' "[174]

Other parts of the New Testament also undermine universalism. The gospel of John never mentions hell, but the theme of judgment is pervasive throughout (see John 3:19–21, 3:18, 3:36, 17:3). Judgment begins now when people fail to believe the gospel message; they bring judgment on themselves. Jesus evokes two responses: welcome from those who embrace him and refusal from those who reject him or are indifferent to him. Faith is needed to come into the eternal life he offers in his person; there is no automatic entry.

The Pauline epistles are more challenging, for they have always offered to universalists more apparent support than any other part of the Bible. Yet at the same time, the Pauline epistles contain eighty references to divine judgment.[175] Nevertheless, universalists point to the texts that use "all," such as Romans 5:18, one of their favorites: "Therefore, as one trespass led to condemnation

172. Moses Stuart, *Exegetical Essays on Several Words relating to Future Punishment* (Andover, MA: Codman, 1830), 62.

173. Scot McKnight, *A New Vision for Israel: The Teachings of Jesus in National Context* (Grand Rapids, MI: Eerdmans, 1999), 38.

174. Wright, *Surprised by Hope*, 182, 183; emphasis in original.

175. Francis Chan and Preston Sprinkle, *Erasing Hell: What God Said about Eternity, and the Things We Made Up* (Colorado Springs, CO: David C. Cook, 2011), 98. For "death" and "die" in Paul's letters, see Rom. 1:32; Rom. 5:12, 14, 15, 17, 21; Rom. 6:16, 21, 23; Rom. 7:5, 9, 10, 11, 13; Rom. 8:2, 6, 13; 1 Cor. 15:21, 22; 2 Cor. 2:16; 2 Cor. 3:6, 7; 2 Cor. 7:10; Eph. 2:1. For "perish," "destroy," and "destruction," see Rom. 2:12; Rom. 9:22; Rom. 14:15, 20; 1 Cor. 1:18; 1 Cor. 15:18; 2 Cor. 2:15; 2 Cor. 4:3; Gal. 6:8; Phil. 1:28; Phil. 3:19; 1 Thess. 5:3; 2 Thess. 1:9; 2 Thess. 2:10; 1 Tim. 6:9. For "wrath," see Rom. 1:18; Rom. 2:5, 8; Rom. 3:5; Rom. 5:9; Rom. 9:22; Eph. 2:3; Eph. 5:6; Col. 3:6; 1 Thess. 1:10; 1 Thess. 2:16; 1 Thess. 5:9. For "condemn," "condemnation," or "judge," see Rom. 2:1, 2, 3, 5, 12; Rom. 3:7, 8; Rom. 5:16, 18; Rom. 8:1; 1 Cor. 11:32; 2 Cor. 3:9; 2 Thess. 2:12; 1 Tim. 5:24. For "curse" or "cursed," see Rom. 9:3; 1 Cor. 12:3; 1 Cor. 16:22; Gal. 1:8, 9; Gal. 3:10, 13. For "punish," see 1 Thess. 4:6; 2 Thess. 1:8–9. References taken from Douglas J. Moo, "Paul on Hell," in *Hell Under Fire: Modern Scholarship Reinvents Eternal Punishment*, edited by Christopher W. Morgan and Robert A. Peterson (Grand Rapids, MI: Zondervan, 2004), 92–93.

for all men, so one act of righteousness leads to justification and life for all men." The interpretive problem in the whole passage, which runs from verses 12 to 21, is that Paul uses two different terms for the same group: both "many" (15, 16, 19) and "all" (12, 18). So "all" are also "many," not a conclusive case for universalism. Paul was probably using "all" in the way the author of Joshua did when he wrote that "all Israel stoned Achan" (7:25). A small representative portion of Israel participated in the stoning.

Another favorite for universalists is Philippians 2:19–11: "Therefore God has highly exalted him and bestowed on him the name that is above every other name, so that at the name of Jesus every knee should bow, in heaven and on earth and under the earth, and every tongue confess that Jesus is Lord, to the glory of God the Father." It seems to affirm universal salvation in its depiction of every knee bowing to the lordship of Jesus. But it is important to recognize that this is almost a direct quote from Isaiah 45:22–25: "Turn to me and be saved, all the ends of the earth! For I am God and there is no other. By myself I have sworn; from my mouth has gone out in righteousness a word that shall not return: 'To me every knee shall bow, every tongue shall swear allegiance.' Only in the Lord, it shall be said of me, are righteousness and strength; to him shall come and be ashamed all who were incensed against him. In the Lord all the offspring of Israel shall be justified and shall glory." The context in Isaiah is a speech by Yahweh declaring his reality against the unreality of the gods of the nations. Those of Israel who trust in him shall not be put to shame (17), but those who trust in other gods will be ashamed (24). These are people who are "incensed against him" (24). This was a familiar picture to residents of the ancient world. Conquering kings and generals would return from battle with their prisoners of war, who would be forced to bend their knees in subjection to the victor. The native subjects of those kings and generals would also bend the knee but in joyous submission. Yahweh's speech ends with a prediction of destructive fire for those who do not submit to his reality and reign (47:14–15). The language in Philippians 2 about every knee bowing and every tongue confessing Jesus as Lord must be understood in light of the background to Isaiah 45. In the New Testament in general and in the Pauline letters in particular, then, there is a prediction of future universal submission that takes place in two different ways: voluntary submission for some and involuntary submission for others. It seems, then, that universalism rests on the neutral logic of a system that is at odds with the complex realities of scriptural testimony.

Two other notes are instructive for this brief discussion. First, the declaration that God desires all to be saved in 1 Timothy 2:4 is qualified by warnings in the same epistle that faith is necessary for salvation (1:16, 4:10). Second, the eternal destruction of the wicked in 2 Thessalonians 1 is retributive, not restorative or remedial. Why will the wicked "suffer the punishment of eternal destruction, away from the presence of the Lord and from the glory of his might" (9)? Two reasons are given. "God considers it just to repay with affliction those who afflict you" (6). Furthermore, the punishment inflicts "vengeance on those who do not know God and on those who do not obey the gospel of our Lord Jesus" (8). Robin Parry acknowledges that this text is a problem for universalists.[176] This punishment is said to be both eternal and vindictive. No restoration is in sight.

The book of Revelation adds to the problems for universalists. The God portrayed in these apocalyptic dramas does not try to persuade unbelievers, waiting forever until they accept his loving offer, as many universalist accounts suggest. Instead, the God of Revelation attacks, defeats, and subjugates his enemies. Nor do we read, as some universalists claim, that every tribe is redeemed. It is only some *from* (*ek*) every tribe who are redeemed (Rev. 5:9, 7:9). This is what Michael McClymond calls "representative universalism," which is the pattern many have observed in the Old Testament: people from all the nations (but not all the people in all the nations) will join Israel in the latter days to worship the true God.[177]

For the biblical and especially New Testament authors, hell is not a problem but a solution. It helps answer the question of why God permits evil to continue unpunished. Rather than creating a problem for theodicy, as it does for moderns, hell for the ancients was a solution to difficult problems of theodicy. People of God in biblical books such as Habakkuk, Job, and Revelation—not to mention Matthew—struggle with God's patience in permitting sin and wickedness but seldom with his judgment on evildoers. For them, the ultimate horror of the universe is not the suffering of the wicked but the suffering of the innocent because of the oppression of the wicked.

We must conclude that universalism is attractive to many because of modern presumptions about love and justice that were not shared by the biblical authors. The philosophical and theological underpinnings of universalism do not survive careful scrutiny, and the biblical witness is to an eschatology that flatly contradicts it.

---

176. MacDonald, *Evangelical Universalist*, 151–155.

177. From McClymond's draft; see note 1 above.

5

The Christian Life

IF ORTHODOX CHRISTIANITY is true, then based on the New Testament, we would expect Christians to be markedly different from other people in the spiritual and moral quality of their lives. After all, 2 Corinthians 5:17 promises that "if anyone is in Christ, he is a new creation. The old has passed away; behold the new has come." It is not simply that those "in Christ" live morally better lives than previously. Because of the supernatural work of the Spirit, there is an important sense in which believers are actually "new creations," ontologically different from before. Although previously we "were dead in our trespasses," God in his mercy and love "made us alive together with Christ." Because of this work of God in us, we are God's "workmanship, created in Christ Jesus for good works, which God prepared beforehand, that we should walk in them" (Eph. 2:4–5, 10).

According to the New Testament, this new life is to manifest itself in an identifiably different manner of living. Evangelicals are well known for their emphasis on the Great Commission of Matthew 28:19–20, with its command to "make disciples" of all peoples. What tends to receive the most attention in evangelical use of this passage is the idea of verbal proclamation of the gospel message to those who have never heard the good news. This, of course, is crucial, but it is also important to see that in the text, disciple making includes teaching people to obey all that Jesus has commanded (Matt. 28:20). This means all of Jesus' teachings in the gospel of Matthew—in the great discourses such as the Sermon on the Mount and the parables of the kingdom—and in the other gospels. In other words, a disciple of Jesus is someone who lives his or her life in accordance with the teachings of Jesus, who follows what Jesus has commanded. Among other things, disciples of Jesus are to follow the Great Commandment of Matthew 22:34–40: they are to love God with their entire beings and to love their neighbors as they love themselves. Among the more significant of Jesus' many instructions to his disciples is the so-called Golden Rule in Matthew 7:12: "So whatever you wish that others would do to you, do also to them, for this is the Law and the Prophets." Jesus' disciples are to treat others the way they would themselves want to be treated.

This ethical principle has tremendous implications for how Christians are to live among followers of other religions.

Contrary to common perceptions, therefore, "fulfilling the Great Commission" involves much more than simply transferring information about salvation to those who have yet to hear; it includes bringing about, through the work of the Spirit, genuine disciples whose lives are characterized by ongoing obedience to what Jesus has commanded for his followers. In the Sermon on the Mount, Jesus uses the metaphors of salt and light to character- ize the witness of his disciples in the world around them (Matt. 5:13–15). The moral quality of his disciples' lives should be noticeably different, so that in letting their "light shine before others," the result will be that others "may see your good works and give glory to your Father who is in heaven" (Matt. 5:16). What is to distinguish Jesus' followers is, among other things, their love for one another (Rom. 12:9–10; 1 John 3:11, 4:7–11) and for others, even to the point of loving their enemies (Matt. 5:43–48; 22:34–40); their doing good to those who mistreat them (Matt. 5:10–12; Rom. 12:14–21; 1 Pet. 2:11–12, 15; 1 Pet. 3:9– 17); sexual purity in conduct and disposition (Matt. 5:27–30; 1 Cor. 5–7; Gal. 5:19; 1 Thess. 4:3–7); and dispositional attitudes of "love, joy, peace, patience, kindness, goodness, faithfulness, gentleness, self-control," and humility (Gal. 5:22–23; Phil. 2:5–11; 1 Pet. 5:6–7). Clearly, then, Christ's followers are to be different from others.

But for many today, Christians do not seem to be any different from others when it comes to the moral quality of their lives. As people in the West become personally acquainted with Buddhists, Muslims, Hindus, and others, they are often struck by their moral integrity. Whereas during the period of Western colonialism, especially in the late nineteenth century, it was often taken for granted in the West that Christians (which usually meant Westerners in gen- eral) were morally superior to peoples in Asia, Latin America, and Africa, this is no longer the case. It is widely accepted today that there is a rough moral parity across religious traditions, with good and bad elements manifest in fol- lowers of all the religions.

John Hick, for example, speaks for many when he says that as he became personally acquainted with Jews, Buddhists, Hindus, and Muslims, he did not sense that adherents of any particular religion were obviously morally supe- rior to the rest: "Coming to know both ordinary families, and some extraor- dinary individuals, whose spirituality has been formed by these different traditions and whose lives are lived within them, I have not found that the people of the world religions are, in general, on a different moral or spiritual level from Christians. They seem on average to be neither better nor worse than the Christians."[1] Hick acknowledges that this judgment is personal and anecdotal: "We can only go on personal observation and the reports of others, both contemporary and historical, and on this basis form a global impression, though one that we cannot claim to prove." Indeed, how could one possibly assess the moral quality of believers in all the major religious traditions over the past centuries, compare them objectively, and determine which tradition, if any, produces a greater number of saints? Hick writes: "My own global impression, based inevitably on having known a limited number of families and individuals and having read a limited amount of history and travelers' accounts, is that the virtues and vices seem to be spread more or less evenly among human beings, regardless of whether they are Christians or—to confine ourselves for the moment to the 'great world religions'—Jews, Muslims, Hindus (including Sikhs), or Buddhists."[2] Shifting the focus from the lives of individual believers to the cultures and civilizations associated with particular religions does not help matters: "I want to suggest that it is entirely possible that there is an ethical ranking of religious civilizations, with one rightly appearing at the top of the list. But I also want to suggest that we are not in fact able to make the comparative assessment which might lead to such a result."[3]

Hick appeals to this apparent moral parity across religions to undermine the claim about the uniqueness of salvation in Christianity and to support his model of religious pluralism:

> But is this what we would expect if Christians have a more complete and direct access to God than anyone else and live in a closer relationship to him, being indwelt by the Holy Spirit? Should not the fruit of the Spirit, which according to Paul is "love, joy, peace, patience, kindness, goodness, faithfulness, gentleness, self-control" (Gal. 5:22–23), be more evident in Christian than in non-Christian lives? It would not, of course, be fair to expect that any randomly selected Christian be morally superior to any randomly selected non-Christian. But surely the *average* level of these virtues should be noticeably higher among Christians than among non-Christians. Yet it does not seem to me that

1. John Hick, "A Pluralist View," in *Four Views on Salvation in a Pluralistic World*, edited by Dennis L. Okholm and Timothy R. Phillips (Grand Rapids, MI: Zondervan, 1996), 39.

2. Ibid., 40–41.

3. John Hick, *Problems of Religious Pluralism* (New York: St. Martin's, 1985), 84.

in fact Christians are on average noticeably morally superior to Jews, Muslims, Hindus, Sikhs, or Buddhists.[4]

Hick raises a very important point, one that evangelicals tend to dismiss too quickly, although his attempt to establish religious pluralism on this basis is highly problematic.[5] Nevertheless, we agree with Hick that there are many adherents of other religious traditions (and also explicit atheists) who lead morally exemplary lives, and we rejoice whenever and wherever we find examples of moral virtue. Moreover, Hick is surely correct in noting the difficulty of evaluating the historical legacy of religious civilizations. Nevertheless, while not attempting a complete response to Hick's challenge here, several points can be briefly noted.

Hick readily admits the impressionistic and anecdotal nature of his judgment about the rough parity of moral virtue among the religions. Others, however, based on *their* experiences, might have quite different impressions. So we should acknowledge the limitations of such impressionistic observations. Yet, although one might question the generalizability of Hick's conclusion in this manner, surely the fact that Hick and others can raise this as a plausible objection to the claims of orthodox Christianity is an indictment of the Christian community's failure often to live up to the expectations that Jesus sets out for his followers.

Christians might respond to Hick's claims by making several observations. First, just who is to count as Christian when we make such assessments? Those who are "in Christ" and who are expected to manifest the fruit of the Spirit to which Hick refers are those who have been spiritually transformed by a supernatural work of the tri-personal God. Not everyone who self-identifies as a Christian is necessarily in this category. Jesus himself reminds us that not everyone who claims to follow Christ is an authentic disciple. One of the most haunting verses in Scripture is Jesus' statement in Matthew 7:21–23: "Not everyone who says to me, 'Lord, Lord' will enter the kingdom of heaven, but the one who does the will of my Father who is in heaven. On that day many will say to me, 'Lord, Lord, did we not prophesy in your name, and cast out demons in your name, and do many mighty works in your name?' And then I will declare to them, 'I never knew you; depart from me, you workers of

---

4. Hick, "A Pluralist View," 41.

5. For a critique of Hick's model, see Harold Netland, *Encountering Religious Pluralism* (Downers Grove, IL: InterVarsity, 2001), 212–246.

lawlessness.'" So we cannot assume that all who call themselves Christians are necessarily genuine disciples of Jesus Christ.

Moreover, the spiritual and moral transformation that accompanies regeneration through the Holy Spirit often is a process that takes place over time. There are, of course, cases of dramatic transformation, in which one's life is profoundly and visibly changed in a short span of time as one submits to the work of the Holy Spirit in one's life. But for many Christians, the transformation is a long process of progressive submission to the Spirit and ongoing conformity into the image of Jesus Christ (Rom. 8:29).

What Hick criticizes in the observable lives of many Christians can be linked to the Christian church in the West embracing what Dietrich Bonhoeffer called "cheap grace." Bonhoeffer was bothered by the cultural, nominal Christianity so evident in Europe in the early twentieth century. "Cheap grace is the deadly enemy of our Church," he wrote in his classic work, *The Cost of Discipleship*.[6] Cheap grace is the idea that as long as we believe Jesus died for our sins or we have had an emotional experience after seeing the terror of hell, we can do as we please. After all, it is often thought, Jesus freed us from the law (this despite the fact that the New Testament never claims this, only that Jesus freed us from being saved by the law): "Cheap grace means the justification of sin without the justification of the sinner. Grace alone does everything, they say, and so everything can remain as it was before."[7] Or, as we are told by those who defend this perspective, if we insist that true faith will do good works, then we turn salvation into a matter of works. In what follows, rather than respond further to Hick's charge, we will explore briefly the relation between faith and works in Christian theology and then make some observations about moral conduct and religious diversity.

Law in the West

Evangelicals and Lutherans are among many Christians who have tended to think of law as a burden from which Christ has set us free. Part of the problem has been the New Testament's use of *nomos* or "law" to translate *torah*, the latter of which is better translated as "teaching to guide hearers to a wise and happy life." There is also a cultural problem. While ancients might have seen law as something that protects society against chaos, Westerners accustomed

---

6. Dietrich Bonhoeffer, *The Cost of Discipleship*, rev. ed. translated by R. H. Fuller (New York: Macmillan, 1963), 45.

7. Ibid., 46.

to civil order think instead of a police car pulling them over for a traffic ticket or governmental regulation that seems to grow by the year.

Protestantism, which protested late-medieval Catholic presumptions that obedience to the law could save, has tended to regard biblical law with suspicion. An early example of this was one of Luther's close associates, Johannes Agricola, who notoriously proclaimed that the Ten Commandments "belong in a courtroom, not in a pulpit."[8] Much later, the Lutheran theologian Paul Tillich said that law is a gift but only because it shows our estrangement. In the second volume of his *Systematic Theology*, he warned that "this situation of estrangement, in which the law becomes commandment, is just the situation in which the law cannot be fulfilled." For this reason, Christ, in whom "the law has ceased to be law," is the "end of the law" (Rom. 10:4). Here Tillich took "end" to mean "doing away with" instead of the more likely "climax" or "purpose." Tillich associated freedom in Christ with the absence of commandments: "Where there is New Being, there is no commandment and no judgment."[9]

Roman Catholic biblical scholar Jerome Murphy-O'Connor is more emphatic in his biography *Paul: His Story*. He writes that in "Paul's antinomian stance," the law "had no place in the life of a Christian." Paul believed that love was the "sole binding imperative" in Christ's new law. There was "no place . . . in any shape or form" for Jewish law "in any of Paul's communities."[10]

Evangelical megachurch pastor and theologian Greg Boyd takes a similar approach. Jewish law is not binding on Christians, he argues, for, among other reasons, the God of the Old Testament is strikingly different from the God of the New Testament. "Jehovah" was "positively hateful" and "merciless" at times in the narrative of Israel's history. He showed a "violent strand" that reflects "warrior nationalistic Canaanite deities," not the true God of Jesus. The Old Testament "never revealed God's true character or true heart."[11]

---

8. This prompted the Formula of Concord (1577) to argue against antinomianism in Articles V and VI, teaching that the third use of the law is "that regenerate men . . . may have some certain rule after which they may and ought to shape their life." *The Formula of Concord*, in *The Creeds of Christendom*, Vol. 3, edited by Philip Schaff (Grand Rapids, MI: Baker, 1983), 131.

9. Paul Tillich, *Systematic Theology*, Vol. 2 (Chicago: University of Chicago Press, 1957), 81, 119.

10. Jerome Murphy-O'Connor, *Paul: His Story* (New York: Oxford University Press, 2004), 119, 116, 115.

11. Greg Boyd, video of lecture at the Meeting House in Toronto, May 16, 2010, http://vimeo.com/12080925; this lecture apparently was based on his forthcoming book, *Crucifixion of the Warrior God* (Downers Grove, IL: InterVarsity, forthcoming).

It is little wonder that so much of today's Western church teaches a peculiarly Christian antinomianism: since Christ allegedly freed us from the law, it would be wrong to live by a set of commandments. This is despite the fact that Jesus and Paul and the other apostles issued what one scholar has counted to be more than eight hundred different commandments in the New Testament.[12] It is also no surprise that members of non-Christian religious communities have drawn the conclusion that Christians have no concern for ordered moral life and, in fact, regularly flout what most other religions consider to be moral law. As the great Islamic scholar Seyyed Hossein Nasr puts it, "Islam criticizes Christianity for not having a Divine Law, a *Shar'iah*, in the strict sense of the term, and does not understand why Christianity did not follow Mosaic Law or bring a law of its own."[13] At the end of the twentieth century, for example, African Muslims pointed to liberal American churches' support for gay marriage and acceptance of partnered gay ministers as illustrative of Christian disregard for common morality. Furthermore, they argued, high rates of divorce, substance abuse, abortion, and pornography in this "Christian" nation proved to them that Christian faith is irrelevant to and unconcerned with moral life. Muslims in Asia have made similar charges. In 2005, Islamic officials in Malaysia issued a fatwa (ruling in Muslim law) warning young people not to participate in Valentine's Day because the day promotes immoral activities that come from its roots in "elements of Christianity."[14]

The Intrinsic Connection of Dogmatic Theology to Moral Theology

America is not Christian in anything but a sociological sense, which means that every year, roughly 70 percent of Americans tell pollsters they look to Jesus Christ as their savior or role model. We lament the antinomianism (resistance to religious law and restraint) so prevalent in this nation and contend that it is theologically mistaken. Rather than dogmatic theology being disconnected from moral theology, as this antinomianism would suggest, they are fundamentally interwoven. In biblical language, true faith and

---

12. Michael McClymond has shown us a list of commandments in many different categories that he has compiled for use in a future manuscript.

13. Seyyed Hossein Nasr, "The Islamic View of Christianity," in *Christianity through Non-Christian Eyes*, edited by Paul J. Griffiths (Maryknoll, NY: Orbis, 1990), 130.

14. "PAS Wants to Stop Valentine's Day Celebration," The Star Online, February 7, 2012, http://thestar.com.my/news/story.asp?file=/2012/2/7/nation/10686706&sec=nation.

good works are inseparable. One cannot exist without the other—unless one or the other is a cheap imitation. True faith will always work when it has a chance, but works that are not inspired by faith do not please God (Heb. 11:6).

Paul wrote that true faith "works by love" (Gal. 5:6). Its nature is to produce works of love. A Christian believer's faith will naturally produce a lifestyle of loving service. Paul told the church at Ephesus that this is why God created us, so that we would do "good works" inspired by faith: "For we are his workmanship, created in Christ Jesus *for good works*, which God prepared beforehand, that we should walk in them" (Eph. 2:10).

Luther, who coined the term *faith alone* in an effort to combat the notion that we are saved by good works, nevertheless insisted that true faith always results in good works because it is the nature of true faith to produce good works: "Our faith in Christ does not free us from works but from false opinions concerning works, that is, from the foolish presumption that justification is acquired by works."[15] Although justification comes through faith in Christ, those who are thus justified manifest their faith through a life of service for others: "O, it is a living, busy, active, mighty thing, this faith. It is impossible for it not to be doing good works incessantly. It does not ask whether good works are to be done, but before the question is asked, it has already done them, and is constantly doing them."[16]

Not only does true faith work, but it keeps working until the end. Jesus said, "The one who endures to the end will be saved" (Matt. 10:22, 24:12–13). In the parable of the sower and the seed, only the seed that endured through trouble, persecution, the cares of the world, and the lure of wealth was pronounced "good" (Matt. 13.4–8). In another parable, Jesus declared, "Blessed are those servants whom the master finds awake when he comes" (Luke 12:37). And in John's gospel, Jesus teaches, "If you *continue* in my word, you are truly my disciples" (8:31; our translation).

Jesus also teaches that works are the best evidence of true faith to our own conscience. At the end of the Sermon on the Mount, he distinguishes true from false disciples by their practice: "Everyone then who hears these words of mine and does them will be like a wise man.... And everyone who hears these words of mine and does not do them will be like a foolish man" (Matt.

---

15. Martin Luther, "The Freedom of a Christian," in *Martin Luther: Selections from His Writings*, edited by John Dillenberger (New York: Anchor, 1961), 81.

16. Martin Luther, *Works of Martin Luther* (Philadelphia: Concordia and Muhlenberg, 1960), 35:370.

7:24, 26). So we can know, in part, what kind of disciples we are by looking at our works.

In John's gospel, Jesus teaches the same: "If you love me, you will keep my commandments... If anyone loves me, he will keep my words.... Whoever does not love me does not keep my words.... By this my Father is glorified, that you bear much fruit and so prove to be my disciples.... You are my friends, if you do what I command you.... If you continue in my word, you are truly my disciples" (John 14:15, 23–24; 15:8, 14; 8:31; our translation).

Salvation by Works?

Does this imply that we are saved by our good works? Does it rob glory from Christ by placing so much emphasis on our actions? Is this inconsistent with the grand Protestant doctrine of justification by grace through faith alone? We don't think so, for two reasons.

First, this emphasis on works might suggest these things if the basic point were not taught by the Scriptures that works are not the price of God's favor but instead the *sign* of faith and therefore God's favor. The Scriptures we have quoted above, when placed in the context of the whole biblical message of salvation, teach us that works are the sign of true faith. They are what faith *does*, not what we do to gain faith or favor.

If one of us were to give a student a dollar bill simply because we feel like it, he would look at the dollar in his hand as a sign of our generosity. His possession of the dollar says nothing about him. We could have given it just as easily to the student sitting beside him. And it says nothing about his character—whether he is studious or lazy, friendly or obnoxious. But it does say something about us. It says that either we are generous or we just wanted to make a point to our class that day.

Similarly, the presence of works in believers' lives does not mean that they are better than unbelievers or more deserving or that those works have earned them a place in God's kingdom. It simply indicates that God has freely poured his grace on them. The result of that grace is faith, which in turn has produced works. For faith is always active and will produce Christlike character.

In theological terms, this is the idea of justification without works. We are justified (accepted by God and received into his kingdom) only by the righteousness of Christ, not by our own righteousness. In other words, we are saved by Christ's works, not by our own. But once we are saved, we are filled with the Holy Spirit, who enables us to do works pleasing to God.

Second, if justification by grace through faith alone is contradicted by the necessity of works as a sign of true faith, then it is also contradicted by the necessity of *anything* as a sign of true faith—joy, love, gratitude, a softened heart, conviction of sin, or any kind of holy practice. Any one of these can be regarded as human work that earns salvation. But just as a believer typically will see these spiritual experiences as signs of (not payments for) grace, the believer when properly instructed will see works as signs of grace.

Faith, then, cannot be separated from works of obedience. To emphasize the fact that we are saved by a free gift, evangelicals say that we are saved by faith and not by works. But as we have argued, all true faith produces works. If faith does not produce works, it is not true faith. Bonhoeffer explained: "From the point of view of justification it is necessary thus to separate [faith and works], but we must never lose sight of their essential unity. For faith is only real when there is obedience, never without it, and faith only becomes faith in the act of obedience."[17]

Christian Moral Theology and Other Religions

This has implications for Christian theology of religions in several ways. First, it helps us understand not only biblical Christianity but perhaps also the nature of most great religions, that they are not simply ways of looking at reality but also ways of being in the world. Beliefs about God or ultimate reality are inextricably tied to ways of living, particularly in relation to other human beings. The great religions animate the center of a person and therefore will enliven not only his or her thinking but also his or her choosing and feeling. Any religion that speaks to the whole of life—and almost all the world's great religions do—will involve beliefs and also ways of worshipping or reverencing (in the case of a nontheistic religion) and rules or paradigms for moral behavior. When Christians look at another religion, they must therefore examine not only its beliefs about ultimate reality but also its religious and ethical practices. Its prescriptions for the moral life may help us evaluate its beliefs about reality. If a religion orders its devotees to kill those who don't share its vision of reality or to discriminate against a person of another color or class, there is then more reason to look for theological problems that might produce such problematic prescriptions.

This can help us realize that even within religions, there are huge differences in perspectives. As Pope Benedict XVI said in his Regensburg address, there are destructive and diseased forms of religion and other forms that are

---

17. Bonhoeffer, *The Cost of Discipleship,* 69.

constructive and healing.[18] Christians must concede that there are diseased forms of Christianity, such as that which underwrote South African apartheid. But there was also Martin Luther King's Christianity, which taught nonviolent resistance to violence in the name of Jesus Christ and led middle-class white America to a reconsideration of race. Then there was the Christianity of Archbishop Oscar Romero in El Salvador, who condemned terror and death squads, defending the rights of poor peasants against powerful landowners. For that, he was shot through the heart while saying Mass on March 24, 1980.

Therefore, examination of moral teachings can help us distinguish among different forms of religions. When we speak of Islam, are we talking about Sufi Islam, which tends toward peace? Or Wahhabi Islam, which suggests that non-Muslims and certain other Muslims should be killed? And what about Hinduism? Are we talking about the militant sects that deny religious freedom to Muslims and Christians and sometimes kill them? Or the peaceful and constructive Hindu traditions that promote the tolerance that Mahatma Gandhi taught? Because of the unity of the human person and the intrinsic connection between views of ultimate reality and conceptions of ethics, Christians studying other religions can learn much about a religion—and the differences within each—by exploring this dogmatic-moral connection.

A second implication of the integral connection between dogmatic and moral theology is that it helps Christians understand the problems in their own theology. The shallow easy-believe-ism and frequent moral failures among Christian leaders at the end of the last century caused many Christians, including theologians, to reassess their theology. Many have come to conclude that they have so stressed faith and experience that the importance of moral law and doctrine has been eclipsed. They have come to see that their stress on grace and feeling without their connection to theology and obedience has produced several generations of Christians who think that Christian morality is optional and Christian doctrine unimportant as long as they have warm feelings for Jesus. The combination of notorious moral failure and public proclamations of antinomian theology prevents many non-Christians from taking Christianity seriously. Just as we suspect the beliefs of a religion that produces hatred and violence, they think there must be something wrong with a Christian faith that seems to excuse moral failure and produce moral insouciance.

---

18. Pope Benedict XVI, "Three Stages in the Program of De-Hellenization," September 12, 2006, Regensburg, Germany, http://www.zenit.org/en/articles/papal-address-at-university-of-regensburg.

Yet this can be a blessing in disguise. Non-Christian criticism of Christian conduct and teaching can, in fact, be the canary in the coal mine that alerts Christians to problems in their theology. Muslims in the global South have caused Christians in those regions to clarify their convictions about sex and marriage, which in turn has encouraged Christians in Europe and America to reexamine their own moral theologies. Partly as a result of these fresh inquiries, churches in the West have rediscovered marriage as the principal metaphor in both biblical Testaments for God's relation to his people and are reassessing the connections between their views of God and their views of the moral life.[19] In this curious way, Muslims are helping Christians to address problems in their own theologies and construct better ones. Oddly, then, non-Christians—and sometimes the ones who are most opposed to Christian theology—are playing a role in strengthening Christian theology. This, in turn, has led to deeper understanding by Christians of Muslims and their faith. In a roundabout way, Muslim criticism has helped Christians see the moral teaching of the Bible and Christian tradition at a deeper level.

Theological Differences but Moral Similarities

It is important for Christians to understand that while Jesus Christ is absolutely unique when set against the background of the other great religious leaders, and while historic Christian doctrine is radically different from that of other religions in significant ways, the moral teaching of the Christian tradition is nevertheless similar in many important ways to the moral teachings of the great religions.

The theological differences are great indeed. No other religious founder claimed to be the one eternal God in the flesh. The Christian church's central claim—that the crucified Jesus rose from the dead—is unparalleled in the world religions. Although it is not something that can be proven conclusively by historical research, we have the testimony of Jesus's followers that they thrust their fingers into the holes in the body of the risen Christ and shared with him a breakfast of fish and bread (1 John 1:1–3; John 20:27, 21:13). Neither ghosts nor hallucinations eat fish and bread. No other religious founder came even close to promising salvation from sin, death, and the devil by a crucified God who draws believers up into the life of a triune community of divine love.

---

19. On the influence of the church in the global South on the churches in the North, especially in regard to sex and marriage, see Philip Jenkins, *The New Faces of Christianity: Believing the Bible in the Global South* (New York: Oxford University Press, 2006), 178–193.

Jesus also gives unique answers to the problem of pain. The Buddha taught his followers to escape suffering, whereas Jesus showed the way to conquer suffering by embracing it. This is why Buddhists look to a smiling Buddha seated on a lotus blossom while Christians worship a suffering Jesus nailed to a cross. The *Dao De Jing* portrays ultimate reality as an impersonal Something requiring resignation and accommodation to minimize or perhaps escape suffering. In contrast, Jesus said that ultimate reality is a tri-personal community who sent the Son to take up suffering into himself. Finally, Jesus unveils an unparalleled intimacy with God. The Qur'an relates that God is closer to us than our jugular vein, but it never calls God "Father."[20] Jesus, on the other hand, addressed God as "Daddy" (a translation of the Aramaic *Abba*) and promised that he would lift believers up into that same intimacy.

Yet the moral similarities among the religions are startling. Ronald Green observes:

> One of the most striking impressions produced by the comparative study of religious ethics is the similarity in basic moral codes and teachings. The Ten Commandments of Hebrew faith, the teaching of Jesus in the Sermon on the Mount and of Paul in his epistles, the requirements of *sadharana*, or universal *dharma*, in Hinduism (Laws of Manu, 10:63), Buddhism's Five Precepts, and Islam's Decalogue in the Qur'an (17:22–39), constitute a very common set of normative requirements. These prohibit killing, injury, deception, or the violation of solemn oaths.[21]

No great religion has ever taught that it is morally permissible to lie, cheat, steal, commit adultery, or take the life of an innocent person. All the religions have agreed on at least the second table of the Ten Commandments.[22] All teach that it is moral to live for others and for God (or whatever they call ultimate reality) and less than moral or immoral to live primarily for oneself.[23] Although they

---

20. Qur'an 50:16.

21. Ronald M. Green, "Morality and Religion," in *The Encyclopedia of Religion*, edited by Mircea Eliade (New York: Macmillan, 1987), 10:99.

22. The second table pertains to our relations with other human beings, commanding honor for parents and forbidding murder, adultery, theft, false witness, and coveting.

23. Some religions, such as most Buddhist schools, teach that morality is a provisional "raft" we take to get us to the "other shore" of nirvana, and so moral distinctions are not ultimate; yet even these Buddhist agree that in this life, these moral rules are mandatory.

interpret and apply them differently, the religions nevertheless agree on the basic principles behind the commandments. For example, Muslims believe that a man can have as many as four wives, but they believe marriage is sacred and regard adultery against any wife to be gravely wrong. Buddhists believe that even killing an animal is wrong, and many believe that any killing of any humans is always wrong, even in self-defense. Most Christians would disagree with these applications of the principle behind the Fifth Commandment (for the majority of the Christian tradition has accepted in principle the legitimacy of just war and capital punishment), but all Buddhists and all Christians would agree that taking the life of the innocent is a grave moral wrong. The religions disagree on who is innocent, especially when their practitioners are caught up in national and civil conflicts, but all agree in the abstract that it is moral to protect the lives of innocents.

Therefore, disagreement over specific practices need not indicate different underlying moral principles:

> While ethicists do acknowledge the truth of "cultural relativism," the view that accepted or prohibited modes of conduct vary among cultures, they have pointed out that this does not necessarily mean that fundamental principles are dissimilar. Different technical and social situations can cause common basic principles to yield different results in specific circumstances. For example, a general principle of respect for parents may produce a stringent ban on parricide in a technologically advanced civilization but may lead to a custom of abandoning infirm or elderly parents in hunter-gatherer cultures where there is no provision for sustaining the disabled and where dependency is regarded by all as shameful.[24]

So the oft-repeated adage that all the great religions teach essentially the same thing but that the world's cultures teach wildly different moral systems is wrong on both scores. The religions teach very different things about ultimate reality and how to achieve a proper relationship with it. But they display remarkable convergence when it comes to the moral life. As C. S. Lewis once put it, if we traveled to a great library looking to compare the moral teachings of the great religions, after three days, we would be bored. For we would find, as he demonstrated in his famous compilation "Illustrations of the Tao," that

---

24. Green, "Morality and Religion," 94.

they all said similar things but expressed the same basic principles in different ways.[25]

Of course, even this must be qualified. While Muslims and Christians agree that it is wrong to steal, for example, we hear and apply this admonition in the context of different faiths and understandings of what is expected of us. A Muslim is told that stealing is prohibited by one of Allah's commandments, and obedience to the commandments is the requirement for entrance to Paradise. Allah is also "the Compassionate, the Merciful," as is stated at the beginning of every surah in the Qur'an except for one, and so most Muslims also rely on Allah's mercy. But at the same time, the idea that obedience of the believer is the primary requirement for Paradise is far more central in Islam than in Christian faith. Christians believe it is the obedience of Jesus Christ in *his* perfect obedience to the Law during his life and surrender to death that saves them and that their own obedience is not only infinitely less than what is required for union with God but only real when the Spirit of Jesus lives it out within them. So while Islam teaches that only Muslims and deserving "people of the Book" reach Paradise, Christians believe none of them deserves salvation. Furthermore, the Christian *telos* or end that Christian believers seek is union with the God who is the loving triune community itself, in fellowship with the saints throughout the ages.[26] Muslims, on the other hand, seek entrance into a Paradise under the rule of a distant Lord, whose relationship with his subjects is far more a matter of submission and resignation than love. Thus, while a Muslim strives not to steal by his own power in order to be accepted by a transcendent Master, a Christian asks Jesus Christ to practice loving stewardship of goods through him or her, with the hope of being caught up into the fellowship of the tri-personal God with all his saints forever. Therefore, Christians and Muslims agree that stealing is a moral wrong forbidden by a moral God, but they think in very different ways about why to obey, how to obey, and what results from obeying.

---

25. C. S. Lewis, *The Abolition of Man* (New York: Collier, 1962), 93–121.

26. While Christian faith teaches union with the triune God, it does not mean absorption into God such that the human self is dissolved. Just as Jesus said that he is one with the Father while still being distinct from the Father (John 17:22–23), so, too, believers are one with Jesus while remaining distinct members of his body (Eph. 3:6; 1 Cor. 12:12–27).

Working Together for the Common Good

Should Christians work together with devotees of other religions on issues of common moral concern? They had better! If not, Christians will lose valuable allies in a common struggle for the future of civilization. As many have said, the heart of civilization is culture, and the strength of culture is its moral vision. Another way to put it is to say that every great moral tradition grows out of a religious vision of the way things are and how we are to live in light of this fact. Muslims have strong views of what it is to be moral because of the strength of their religious commitment. Buddhists find the ability to practice nonviolence because of their vision of life taught by the Buddha. Christians testify that they believe in Jesus's moral teachings because of the faith he and the Father have given them and can practice it only by the power of the Spirit. Attack religion successfully, and you will cripple morality.

It is something of a truism today that moral relativism—or the notion that there are no final moral moorings—is common in the West. But it is not as readily recognized that even while Christians disagree with Muslims, for example, on many things theological, Islam shares the classical Christian conviction that there are eternal moral rules given by God for all of humanity to follow and that divine judgment falls on individuals and civilizations that forget them. Islam, in other words, can be a potent ally for Christian orthodoxy in its struggle to combat a radical skepticism and relativism. According to many today, we can no longer claim that anything is actually morally wrong, only that some people *think* it is wrong. And by the same token, if certain people think something is right for *them*—despite millennia of moral consensus saying otherwise—then it *is* right for them.

A casual relativism is often discernible in the media, university classrooms, courtrooms, and legislatures. While there is still a large consensus that agrees that rape, incest, murder, and terrorism are morally wrong, a sizable percentage of students who walk into university undergraduate classrooms are convinced moral relativists. They are fairly sure that religion and morality are simply matters of opinion and that they have their own views of these things because they have been socialized in homes and communities that have taught them these beliefs. If they had been raised elsewhere, they tell us, they probably would believe differently. So how can they criticize anyone who believes differently?

Muslims, by contrast, insist that there are morally objective principles and values that obtain regardless of one's particular attitude toward such principles. For God has made his existence and moral character known through what the Qur'an calls "signs" in creation. The trees and stars and ocean and even the human body testify to the beautiful Mind that created this cosmos and rules it by his moral law. No one has any excuse for missing the signs and proceeding in life as if things were *not* clear.

Evangelicals may not want to affirm with so little qualification the clarity of these signs, but we should recognize the power of the Muslim response to moral relativism. Some people today are undoubtedly converting to Islam for precisely that reason: in a world that is morally confused, Islam offers simple and clear answers. Although evangelicals will disagree with Muslims on important matters in theology, they will find thoughtful Muslims to be allies in the struggle for moral objectivism in a relativistic culture.

For some of these reasons, Roman Catholics and Muslims joined arms in 1995 to fight an abortion-rights initiative led by a hard-edged U.S. delegation to an international conference. Only by their united efforts was the notion of enshrining abortion-on-demand as an internationally recognized human right abandoned by its proponents. In 2012, Muslim leaders allied with Roman Catholics and Presbyterians in Scotland to resist the redefinition of marriage that would legally recognize gay weddings.[27]

The chances of evangelicals and other Christians winning similar battles in the future on other social and moral issues will be increased by our willingness to work with people of other religions who agree with us on basic principles of the moral life. Evangelicals should be willing to work with Buddhists and Hindus and Sikhs and Muslims to defend the idea that marriage is between a man and a woman and that children do best when they have both a mother and a father. Most followers of the world religions agree that the family is the most fundamental building block of society and that it must be protected against disintegration coming from divorce, pornography, materialism, and commercialism. Together with believers from other religions, we can defend the rights of the poor, attack sexual slavery, protect the ecosystem, and advance social justice—without compromising our respective faith allegiances.

Learning from Other Religions?

It is one thing to work together with other religionists on issues of common moral concern that do not affect our theological beliefs. It is quite another to think that we could learn from other religions' moral practices. How could that be, if the Christian tradition is based on revelation from the one tri-personal

---

27. The Christian Institute (January 13, 2012), http://www.christian.org.uk/news/former-scottish-tory-leader-dismisses-same-sex-marriage/?e130112

God of Israel and the complete revelation of God in Jesus Christ, as suggested in chapters 2 and 3?

We would suggest two answers. First, we must remember that the full meaning of the Christian faith is greater than our perception of it, and the lives of outsiders can sometimes help us see better what actually is inside. The revelation of Jesus Christ and all that he means for the church and the world far exceeds human comprehension. It has taken three thousand years for Jews and Christians to unpack the meaning of it, and none who take it seriously would say we have come to the end of our understanding of it. The Christian church has always said that the Spirit continuously illuminates our understanding of revelation, so that we are always seeing deeper implications of it and new applications to new situations. We reject the notion that the Spirit gives us new truths that contradict biblical revelation and the best of the Great Tradition of the historic church. But we affirm the orthodox teaching that the Spirit helps the church grow in its understanding of the original deposit of revelation in Israel and Jesus Christ. On this basis, the church in recent centuries has come to affirm moral principles with a clarity it did not have in earlier centuries on issues such as slavery, racism, and women's rights.

Our second answer is that Jesus himself was not averse to pointing to those outside Israel as moral exemplars. The Good Samaritan had a faith that was related to Israel's but was clearly beyond the pale of Jewish orthodoxy (Luke 10:25–37). Yet this man from another religious culture and ethnicity (the possibility that he was fictional is irrelevant, for Jesus deliberately used a Samaritan to teach a lesson) has helped teach Christians for thousands of years what it means to be a good neighbor. In our day, the Dalai Lama has also helped many Christians to understand better what Jesus meant by forgiveness. The Tibetan Buddhist teacher does not often refer to Jesus, but his willingness to forgive a nation that has murdered one million of his people and destroyed the vast majority of Tibetan Buddhist monasteries is a powerful illustration of refusal to be embittered by one's enemy.

Confucianism's Single-Minded Devotion to Moral Virtue

In short, other religions can remind us of treasures in our own tradition that have been obscured by our own cultural prejudices. Teachers or texts from other religions can help us see what our own cultures have prevented us from seeing in our own texts and traditions. Let us close with one example: Confucius and the tradition that has taken his name. This Chinese wise man has been wrongly dismissed as "simply" a moral teacher with little relevance to religion founded on faith in a transcendent dimension. Those who have spoken this way have not read Confucian texts carefully.

Confucius was convinced of the reality of the divine world. For Master K'ung, as the Chinese called him (Confucius is the Latin rendering), Heaven was the author of his virtue and object of his prayers.[28] He felt understood by Heaven alone and regarded the success of his cultural efforts as dependent on Heaven's sovereign ordering.[29] He stood in awe of Heaven's decrees and considered the movements of nature to be under its control.[30] While there is reason to believe that Confucius treated Heaven as something like a personal god, for Mencius (371–289 B.C.), the next-greatest teacher in the Confucian tradition, Heaven was more immanent and impersonal.[31] But even Mencius said that Heaven reveals itself through acts and deeds, decreeing things to happen in the absence of human agency.[32]

Confucius and Mencius can help evangelicals and other Christians better understand what we discussed earlier in this chapter: the integral connection between dogmatic and moral theology. They do so by displaying a remarkable commitment to virtue in the presence of suffering, poverty, and the threat of death. Reflection upon some Confucian themes can help evangelicals recover an understanding of moral virtue that has been lost to American Christian consciousness: the Edwardsean tradition of disinterested benevolence.

In Jonathan Edwards's theological masterpiece, *The Religious Affections*, his second reliable ("positive") sign of true religion is attraction to God and God's ways for their own sake ("the first objective ground of gracious affections, is the transcendently excellent and amiable nature of divine things, as they are in themselves; and not any conceived relation they bear to self, or self-interest").[33] In other words, true spirituality is not rooted in self-interest.

---

28. Confucius, *The Analects*, translated and edited by D. C. Lau (Hammondsworth, UK: Penguin, 1979), 7.23, 3.13, 7.35.

29. Ibid., 14.35, 9.5.

30. Ibid., 16.8, 10.25.

31. Julia Ching, "Confucianism: Ethical Humanism as Religion?" in Hans Küng and Julia Ching, *Christianity and Chinese Religions* (New York: Doubleday, 1989), 71–72. For an intriguing comparison between Mencius and Aquinas on virtue and courage, see Lee H. Yearley, *Mencius and Aquinas: Theories of Virtue and Conceptions of Courage* (Albany: SUNY Press, 1990).

32. *Mencius*, translated and edited by D. C. Lau (Hammondsworth, UK: Penguin, 1970), V A.5, V A.6.

33. Jonathan Edwards, *The Religious Affections* (New Haven, CT: Yale University Press, 1959), 240.

Natural love, or love of this world, is based on what returns one will get for one's love. But Jesus, Edwards pointed out, suggested that supernaturally inspired love is oblivious to its returns: "If you love those who love you, what credit is that to you? For even sinners love those who love them" (Luke 6:32). When Satan suggested to God that Job was good only because God had bribed him with riches and the comforts of family life, God took up Satan's challenge. He agreed to let Satan take away all that Job had, in the hope of proving that Job's faith was *not* based simply on self-interest. Notice the intriguing implication: God conceded Satan's assumption that spirituality based only on self-interest is worthless.

Edwards said that the primary reason saints love God is not the benefits that will accrue but the shining magnificence, beauty, and glories of God as he is in himself. They are attracted to God's Son, God's works, and God's ways, particularly the beauty of the tri-personal God's plan for the salvation of sinful human beings. Benefits come to saints from God but only after and as a fruit of their first being drawn to God by a vision and taste of God and his ways as they are in and of themselves.[34] Immanuel Kant's categorical imperative is similar: the inner principle of human morality is the unconditional rule that we should act only on the maxim that we can will to be a universal law. We are not to ask about consequences either for ourselves or others but only determine to obey this duty. We are drawn, as it were, by the inherent beauty of this maxim. Thus, Kantian ethics is called nonconsequentialism.

Now, there are significant differences between Edwards and Kant. Kant believed that attention to rewards would undermine ethical seriousness, while Edwards saw nothing wrong with consideration of heavenly rewards during the process of sanctification, as long as our relationship to God is based primarily on the beauty of the Trinity. But both agreed with the Confucian tradition that we should do the good not so much because of benefits we will thereby receive but because the Good has prior claims on us. Implicit in Confucius and Mencius is the notion that we will receive inner satisfaction from following the Way even when following means suffering, but that attention to any rewards besides inner satisfaction will corrupt our following.

This is akin to the corruption of religion that, in C. S. Lewis's words, takes place when we pursue not God but the thrill that God brings. It is "the first and deadly error, which appears on every level of life and is equally deadly on

---

34. See Michael J. McClymond and Gerald R. McDermott, *The Theology of Jonathan Edwards* (New York: Oxford University Press, 2012), 311–320.

all, turning religion into a self-caressing luxury and love into auto-eroticism."[35]
The first months and perhaps year of Lewis's Christian experience were without any belief in a future life. It would strike many evangelicals as strange
that Lewis considered it one of his "greatest mercies" to attempt obedience
"without even raising that question:"[36]

> My training was like that of the Jews, to whom He revealed Himself
> centuries before there was a whisper of anything better (or worse)
> beyond the grave than shadowy and featureless *Sheol*....I had been
> brought up to believe that goodness was goodness only if it were dis-
> interested, and that any hope of reward or fear of punishment con-
> taminated the will. If I was wrong in this (the question is really much
> more complicated than I then perceived) my error was most tenderly
> allowed for. I was afraid that threats or promises would demoralise me;
> no threats or promises were made. The commands were inexorable,
> but they were backed by no "sanctions." God was to be obeyed simply
> because he was God. Long since, through the gods of Asgard, and later
> through the notion of the Absolute, He had taught me how a thing can
> be revered not for what it can do to us but for what it is in itself. That
> is why, though it was a terror, it was no surprise to learn that God is to
> be obeyed because of what He is in Himself. If you ask why we should
> obey God, in the last resort the answer is, "I am." To know God is to
> know that our obedience is due to Him. In His nature His sovereignty
> *de jure* is revealed.[37]

Lewis went on to say that to think of heaven and hell as anything other than
the presence or absence of God (in other words, as reward or punishment for
certain kinds of life on earth) is to corrupt the doctrine of both "and corrupts
us while we so think of them."[38]

While neither Edwards nor Lewis discounts entirely the notion of rewards
as motivation for the ethical life, both dismiss it as corrupting if it is the principal framework in which the ethical life is constructed. Confucius and Mencius
provide us with vivid illustrations of that principle. They were dedicated to

---

35. C. S. Lewis, *Surprised by Joy: The Shape of My Early Life* (London: Geoffrey Bles, 1955), 160.

36. Ibid., 217.

37. Ibid., 218.

38. Ibid., 219.

the life that looks neither to right nor left but only straight ahead to the Way. It is happy with eating coarse rice and drinking only water if that is all that is provided by following the Way, for it is concerned not with profit but what is right.[39] It seeks neither a full belly nor a comfortable home but is worried about the Way rather than poverty.[40] Sages cannot be led into excesses when wealthy and honored or deflected from their purposes when poor and obscure.[41] Nor can they be made to compromise principle before superior force.[42] Hence the virtuous never abandon righteousness (*yi*) in adversity and do not depart from the Way in success.[43] They refuse to remain in wealth or a prestigious position if either was gained in a wrong manner.[44] Even for one basketful of rice, they would not bend.[45] If it had been necessary to perpetrate one wrong deed or kill one innocent person in order to gain the empire, no virtuous person would consent to doing either.[46] True virtue (*te*) is unconcerned with what others think and recognizes that it is better to be disliked by bad people than to be liked by all.[47] It is ready to give up even life itself if that is necessary to follow the way of benevolence.[48]

Confucius resigned the most prestigious position of his life because he felt that his lord's acceptance of a gift of dancing girls had compromised his integrity.[49] When he was offered another position in the state of Chen and found that the official who invited him was in rebellion against his chief, Confucius refused to become a party to the intrigue.[50] When he was traveling in southern China and his disciples realized that their master would never again have an opportunity to put his principles into practice (as a minister of state), they wanted to know how he felt. They asked him about two ancient sages who

---

39. *Analects*, 7.16, 14.12, 16.10, 19.1, 4.11.

40. Ibid., 1.14, 15.32.

41. *Mencius*, III B.2.

42. Ibid.

43. Ibid., VII B.9.

44. *Analects*, 4.5.

45. *Mencius*, III B.4.

46. Ibid., II A.2.

47. *Analects*, 12.6, 13.24.

48. Ibid., 19.1

49. Ibid., 18.4.

50. Huston Smith, *The World's Religions: Our Great Wisdom Traditions* (San Francisco: HarperSanFrancisco, 1991), 156.

under bad kings had died of starvation. Confucius replied that they were true men—something he rarely said of anyone past or present. So a disciple asked him again, "Do you think they had any regrets?" Master K'ung responded firmly, "Why, they wanted *jen* (benevolence), and they achieved it. Why should they regret it?"[51]

Mencius told similar stories exemplifying single-minded devotion to the Good. The sage Liu Hsia Hui was one of his favorites. According to Mencius, when Liu was passed over for a position or his virtues went unnoticed, Liu harbored no grudges. Nor was he distressed in difficult circumstances. For he was content to find his happiness in following the Way of the Good.[52] Mencius said that he would not have compromised his integrity "for the sake of three ducal offices."[53]

While we moderns might find this ideal both daunting and a tad depressing, Confucius and Mencius found it a source of joy. In the *Analects*, Confucius often remarks on the joy he finds in *jen* and *yi* even when deprived of what we would call necessities of life. One can have joy, he said, living on a bowlful of rice and a ladleful of water in a run-down hut:[54] "In the eating of coarse rice and the drinking of water, the using of one's elbow for a pillow, joy is to be found. Wealth and rank attained through immoral means have as much to do with me as passing clouds."[55] He was described by his disciples as one who neglected his meals in a spell of work, forgot his worries when overcome by joy, and was so absorbed in the joy of the Dao that he was unaware that old age was coming on.[56] Mencius remarked that he had no greater joy than to find on self-examination that he was true to himself. A man, he said, delights in three things: that his parents are alive and his brothers well, that he is not ashamed to face Heaven or men, and that he has the most talented pupils.[57]

Let us sum up now with the import of these reflections on the Christian life for Christian theology of religions. We have argued that Christians must not let orthodox moral theology become detached from dogmatic theology when trying to understand other religions and dialogue with devotees of those

51. Lin Yutang, *From Pagan to Christian* (Melbourne, Australia: Heinemann, n.d.), 80.

52. *Mencius*, V B.1.

53. Ibid, VII A.28.

54. *Analects*, 6.11.

55. Ibid., 7.16.

56. Lin, *From Pagan to Christian*, 70.

57. *Mencius*, VII A.4, A.20.

religions. Because historic orthodox theology has always treated moral and dogmatic theology as one integral whole, both moral and dogmatic theologies are distorted when one is separated from the other. People of other faiths have helped Christians in this regard. Their criticisms of Christian moral teaching have helped Christians reexamine both the connection between the two kinds of theology and the shape of each.

Another implication of this integral connection between faith and morality is twofold: that Christians misrepresent their own faith when they disconnect theology from ethics, and they misunderstand other religions when they study the theology or metaphysics of other religions without also examining their moral teachings.

Finally, we have proposed that evangelicals can cooperate with other religionists on common moral and social concerns without compromising their theological convictions and that in some cases, other religions can help Christians understand their own moral teachings more deeply.

6

Religion(s) and Culture(s)

THEOLOGY OF RELIGIONS involves proper understanding in two areas of inquiry. As an exercise in *theology*, it must include adequate biblical and theological understanding. In particular, as an exercise in *Christian* theology it must develop a Trinitarian understanding of God as Father, Son, and Holy Spirit, probing the relations of the triune God to the world in which we live.

But since it is theology *of religions*, it also requires proper understanding of the religions. But what do we mean by religion or the religions? Is the difference between the singular and the plural here significant for theology of religions? Although it is easy to suppose that we all know what we mean by religion, closer examination indicates that the concept is more complicated. In some ways, the notion of religion is closely related to that of culture, although, as we shall see, the two are not identical. Therefore, developing an adequate theology of religions involves not only responsible treatment of the biblical and theological themes but also adequate understanding of the lived realities of human communities to which the concepts of culture and religion refer. In this chapter, we will not focus so much on the theological themes for understanding religions but rather explore how we should understand the concept of religion itself and actual religious traditions we encounter in our world.

Whereas missiologists and theologians have given considerable attention to a Christian understanding of culture, developing nuanced and sophisticated understandings of the relation of the Christian gospel to culture, the same has not yet happened with religion. It is often assumed, for example, that there is a clear distinction between culture and religion, so that a particular practice or term can be identified as either cultural or religious. Moreover, whereas cultures are commonly regarded as including a mixture of good and evil and having the potential of being redeemed by the gospel, religions are often thought of merely as expressions of sin and rebellion against God. Particular religions are dismissed as little more than manifestations of falsehood and evil. Thus, discussions about the contextualization of the gospel often assume that if the meaning associated with a given activity or term is strictly cultural, then, in principle, its use can be acceptable for Christians. But if the meaning is religious, then it is unacceptable.

But is this the right way to think about these matters? Writing in 1991, missiologist Charles Taber challenged some common assumptions:

> [W]hat is the relationship between culture and religion? Is religion merely one chapter in the description of a culture, or does it have any sort of autonomy? Does religion pervade all of a culture, or is it compartmentalized? Is the relationship always the same, regardless of what kind of culture or what kind of religion we are dealing with? From a traditional missiological perspective, is religion the domain where idols rule and which must therefore be addressed directly by the gospel, while other domains are good or neutral? Or is it conceivable that idols could rule in domains other than the religious?[1]

Evangelicals generally avoid language of God's presence and activity "in" other religions out of a legitimate concern to preserve the uniqueness of God's self-revelation in the Christian Scriptures and Jesus Christ as the one Lord and Savior for all humankind. More pluralistic thinkers, by contrast, see God's presence in the religions in ways that minimize God's self-revelation in the Scriptures and incarnation. In both cases, however, there seems to be confusion over the relation between religion and culture. Evangelicals are willing to acknowledge the presence and activity of the triune God in the realm of culture but not religion and in so doing make a sharp distinction between the two domains. Pluralists often conflate the religious and sociocultural domains, regarding the religions as little more than historically and culturally shaped human responses to the one divine reality. Both approaches, while very different in their conclusions, depend on assumptions about religion and culture that need to be reexamined.

In this chapter, we will probe further some of the issues Taber sets out by exploring the concept of religion and its relation to culture. While we do not attempt to present a comprehensive model for understanding culture and religion, we will make some suggestions that we hope will clarify some issues in the theology of religions. But before we examine the concepts of culture and religion, we will consider briefly some ways in which assumptions about the nature of religion can affect discussions in the theology of religions and missiology.

---

1. Charles R. Taber, *The World Is Too Much with Us: "Culture" in Modern Protestant Missions* (Macon, GA: Mercer University Press, 1991), 21.

Contextualization and Religion

Since the 1950s, evangelical missiologists have given a great deal of atten-tion to the relation of the Christian gospel to culture. This has been reflected in the prominence of contextualization debates within missiology. We might think of contextualization as the process through which, under the guidance of the Holy Spirit, the gospel of Jesus Christ is expressed in appropriate local linguistic and cultural patterns and the ways in which particular Christian communities live out their commitments as disciples of Christ within such cultural contexts.[2]

One cannot proceed far, however, in discussions of contextualization before confronting questions about how we should understand religious phe-nomena. A particular approach to contextualization presupposes a perspective about the nature of religion in both general and particular religious beliefs and practices. A key assumption in many discussions of contextualization is the idea that if a practice, term, or institution is cultural, then it is in principle acceptable for followers of Jesus Christ; but if it is religious, it is unaccept-able. Yet this presupposes that there is a clear distinction between the cultural and religious meanings and that we can identify clearly into which domain a particular practice or term falls. Often this is not so easily done. Moreover, is it really the case that religious phenomena are inherently more problematic theologically than cultural values, beliefs, or practices?

One set of issues that has received extensive debate since the 1980s con-cerns the degree to which Muslim-background believers must break with their Islamic context in order to be faithful disciples of Jesus Christ. The debate has its parallels in earlier disputes over the degree to which Jewish follow-ers of Jesus could retain their Jewish identity as disciples of Jesus Christ and Confucian followers of Jesus could continue some of their Confucian prac-tices (see below). Evangelicals have largely accepted the idea of "Messianic Jews," who reject an overtly "Christian" identity and maintain their Jewish identity, so long as this does not clearly conflict with what it means to be a follower of Jesus.[3] Can the same approach apply to Muslims today who follow

---

2. Helpful introductions to contextualization include Paul Hiebert, "Critical Contextualization," *Missiology* 12, no. 3 (July 1984): 287–296; Darrell Whiteman, "Contextualization: The Theory, the Gap, the Challenge," *International Bulletin of Missionary Research* 21, no. 1 (January 1997): 1–7; A. Scott Moreau, *Contextualization and World Missions* (Grand Rapids, MI: Kregel, 2012).

3. Of course there are important differences between Jewish-background believers and Muslim-background believers. Jews but not Muslims use a Scripture which Christians

Christ? Can Muslims trust in Jesus Christ as Lord and Savior, believe that Christ died for their sins and rose again from the dead, and still retain their identity as Muslims and participate in many Muslim practices? Or does being a disciple of Jesus Christ mean a radical departure from most of what is associated with being a Muslim?

The issues became especially prominent in missiological circles with the publication of an essay in 1998 by John Travis proposing a spectrum of six different ways in which "Christ-centered communities" might relate to the broader Muslim world around them.[4] Extensive—and sometimes acrimonious—debate developed over what Travis advocates as C5 communities. C5 believers in Jesus meet regularly with other believers for instruction and support, but they remain legally, socially, and culturally within the Islamic context. Although aspects of Islamic teaching and practice that are clearly incompatible with biblical teaching are rejected and they openly acknowledge Jesus ('Isa) as the Messiah, C5 believers continue to call themselves Muslims and to participate actively within the Muslim community. They do not call themselves Christians; they regard themselves, and are viewed by other Muslims, as Muslims who follow 'Isa the Messiah.[5] C4 communities, by contrast, do not explicitly identify as Muslims (but they may use designations other than "Christian" to identify themselves), although they use culturally appropriate forms for worship and self-expression whenever possible. The issues are complicated and, given the great diversity among Muslim societies, defy easy, one-size-fits-all generalizations about what is appropriate. For our purposes, however, it is worth noting that at the heart of these debates lie unresolved questions about religion, culture, and identity: What does "Christian" mean in the relevant contexts? What does "Muslim" mean? Does it have the same meaning for all communities, or can its meaning vary with context? Is "Muslim" primarily a religious designation, or does it also have cultural, social, ethnic, or political meanings? Can one separate the religious from the

---

accept. So nothing in the Jewish Scripture would be unacceptable, in principle, to Christians. This would not be the case for the Qur'an.

4. John Travis, "The C1 to C6 Spectrum: A Practical Tool for Defining Six Types of 'Christ-centered Communities' (C) Found in Muslim Contexts," *Evangelical Missions Quarterly* 34, no. 4 (1998): 407–408. See also Travis, "Must All Muslims Leave Islam to Follow Jesus?" *Evangelical Missions Quarterly* 34, no. 4 (1998), 411–415. There has been an extensive debate over the issues raised by C4 and C5 communities in *Evangelical Missions Quarterly* and the *International Journal of Frontier Missions*. A useful and concise summary of the debate is found in Joseph Cumming, "Muslim Followers of Jesus?" *Christianity Today* (December 2009): 32–35.

5. Travis, "The C1 to C6 Spectrum," 408.

cultural or ethnic dimensions of the term? Given the changing circumstances of modern life and the variety among Muslim communities, who decides the meaning of such terms?

Several years ago, after one of the authors of this book had given a talk at a church, an elderly Japanese woman came up to him and somewhat nervously said she had a question. She was a new Christian, and she explained that she was having trouble understanding the Japanese Christians' attitude about something. As a grandmother, she enjoyed taking her grandchildren to local Japanese festivals. In particular, the children liked to join in dancing with the crowds as a *mikoshi*, a portable shrine or palanquin, was carried about on the shoulders of several men. But she quickly discovered that the Japanese Christians at church disapproved of their doing so. The *mikoshi* has traditionally been understood as a kind of sacred palanquin in which kami (deities or spirits) repose during a festival. Traditionally, it was said that whenever the *mikoshi* is carried about during a festival, a divine purifying power permeates the area, protecting people from evil and spreading blessings. Thus, Japanese Christians traditionally have regarded the dancing processions accompanying the public display of the *mikoshi* as enmeshed in a system of false beliefs and idolatrous practices, and participation has been strongly discouraged.

This grandmother understood the religious background to the *mikoshi*, but she said that for many Japanese today, carrying the *mikoshi* about is not a religious ritual but simply part of a cultural festival. Her grandchildren did not believe that actual kami inhabit the *mikoshi*; they simply liked the excitement of the celebration, and the grandmother thought it was silly to tell them they could not participate in the festival along with their friends. Why, she asked, was the church so strict on this issue?

Is participation in the festival unacceptable for Japanese Christians? Those who insist that such participation is syncretism or idolatry do so because carrying the *mikoshi* has traditionally been understood as a religious act, celebrating the local kami in a public ritual. But the meanings of acts and rituals change over time. Simply because carrying the *mikoshi* in the festival had overtly religious meanings at one time does not necessarily mean that it always has religious meanings. Could the meanings of the *mikoshi* and the festival be changing, so that today they are largely cultural and not particularly religious? Who determines the meaning of a public ritual? To make things even more confusing, can the meanings of the ritual vary with individuals and communities?

Without attempting to settle the C4/C5 debate or the question of the meanings of the *mikoshi* in the festival, we suggest that the most significant question in such cases is not whether a given term or practice is religious or cultural but rather whether its adoption facilitates or hinders individuals or communities in becoming mature disciples of Jesus Christ. Whether something is religious or cultural is then a secondary matter. But, of course, determining whether something facilitates or hinders becoming a follower of Christ will require navigating the religious and cultural issues within the relevant community and their impact on one's understanding of God and growth in Christlikeness. So questions about how we understand religion and culture are unavoidable.

Religion and Culture: A Historical Example

Debates over the relation between the gospel and local contexts have a long history in Asia, where the distinctions between culture and religion can be especially difficult to discern. Before the modern era, the issues were given extensive treatment during the remarkable encounter between Jesuit missionaries and the Chinese from the seventeenth to the eighteenth centuries.[6]

Europeans at the time were struggling with the unsettling implications of the voyages of "discovery" to the Americas, Africa, and Asia. Although most Europeans regarded the peoples of the new worlds as clearly inferior to European "Christian" civilization, the Jesuits adopted an attitude of respect for the Chinese. This was the approach of Matteo Ricci (1552–1610), an Italian scholar with an unusual gift for languages who arrived in China in 1583. Ricci realized that the long-term success of Christianity in China depended on the Christian gospel being expressed in Chinese linguistic and cultural forms and the basic assumptions of Christian faith being embraced by the Chinese intellectual elite. Ricci regarded his own life work in China as an investment in preparing the intellectual and cultural foundation for future generations of Chinese Christians. He devoted himself to an intensive study of Chinese intellectual and religious traditions. Initially, Ricci adopted the dress and appearance of the Chinese Buddhist clergy, but as he became convinced that Buddhism was neither compatible with the Christian faith nor the key to the cultural elite, he abandoned it. Instead, he patterned himself after the mandarins, adopted the dress of the Chinese literati, and became an acknowledged

---

6. See R. Po-Chia Hsia, *A Jesuit in the Forbidden City: Matteo Ricci, 1552–1610* (New York: Oxford University Press, 2010); Andrew Ross, *A Vision Betrayed: The Jesuits in Japan and China, 1542–1742* (Maryknoll, NY: Orbis, 1994); *East Meets West: The Jesuits in China: 1582–1773*, edited by Charles E. Ronan and Bonnie B. C. Oh (Chicago: Loyola University Press, 1988); Liam Matthew Brockey, *Journey to the East: The Jesuit Mission to China, 1579–1724* (Cambridge, MA: Harvard University Press, 2007).

expert on the Confucian Classics and early Confucianism. At a time when there were no reliable Western studies of Confucianism or grammars or dictionaries for the study of Chinese, Ricci mastered not only contemporary but also classical Chinese. Andrew Ross notes that Ricci "had become such a master of Chinese and the Confucian Classics that the literati as a class could treat him as if one of themselves."[7]

Through his studies, Ricci became convinced that early Confucianism had been monotheistic and that the deity of ancient times, Tian (Heaven) or Shangdi (Lord on High), could be identified with the transcendent creator God of the Bible.[8] Ricci argued that later generations of Chinese intellectuals had corrupted this original monotheism with a more ambiguous and problematic metaphysic. Just as Thomas Aquinas, several centuries earlier in his native Italy, had drawn on Aristotelian philosophy to explicate Christian truth for Europeans, so, too, Ricci thought, might Christians use Confucian categories to express Christian faith for Chinese. In 1603, Ricci published *On the True Meaning of the Lord of Heaven*, an influential work that made use of Confucian terms and assumptions in arguing for the reality of the Christian God: "Ricci was setting out to show that there was a belief in a transcendent God contained in what he insisted was original Confucianism, and that this transcendent Lord of Heaven and the God of the Bible were the same. What is so extraordinary was that in the eyes of a large number of literati he succeeded in proving his point."[9] Even those scholars who disagreed with him acknowledged his interpretation as a legitimate possibility.

However, the Jesuit experiment with the contextualization of the gospel was cut short because of controversy over interpretations of certain Chinese terms and ritual practices. The Jesuits were strongly criticized by Dominican and Franciscan missionaries for what was perceived as their excessive accommodation to Confucianism. The dispute among the missionaries eventually involved the highest levels of the Vatican and even the Chinese emperor. The Rites Controversy, as the dispute came to be known, involved complicated questions about the translation of Christian terms into Chinese, Chinese ancestral rituals, and the general relation between Christian faith and Confucianism. The Jesuit use of the Chinese terms *Shangdi* and *Tian* to refer to the Christian

7. Ross, *A Vision Betrayed*, 135.

8. See Julia Ching, *Confucianism and Christianity: A Comparative Study* (Tokyo: Kodansha International, 1978), 20; Ross, *A Vision Betrayed*, 148.

9. Ross, *A Vision Betrayed*, 147.

God was criticized as syncretistic. Chinese rituals regularly practiced in public and within the family—such as sacrifices to Heaven; rituals directed to Confucius; rituals honoring (worshipping?) the spirits of mountains and rivers, local deities, and spirits; and rituals for honoring the ancestors—became the centers of controversy.

The Dominicans and Franciscans worked primarily among illiterate peasants, who generally gave heavily religious meanings to such rituals, and they accused the Jesuits of syncretism and compromise with an idolatrous religion, Confucianism. Ricci and his colleagues, by contrast, worked among the educated elite, for whom the rituals had more ambiguous meanings and served primarily social functions. The Jesuits maintained that some of the rituals for honoring the dead were not necessarily religious and thus could be embraced by Christians.

The Rites Controversy erupted in the 1630s, after the death of Ricci, and lasted until 1742, when a papal bull by Benedict XIV ruled against the accommodationist approach of Ricci. Over the course of the next century, the debate continued not only among the missionaries in China but also within the Congregation for the Propagation of the Faith (Propaganda Fide) and the papal office in Rome. In 1645, the Propaganda Fide issued a document with the approval of Pope Innocent X that condemned the practices of the Jesuits.[10] The Jesuits then requested that the Kangxi emperor issue a ruling on whether the ancestral rituals were civil or religious. After consulting with leading Confucian scholars in 1700, the emperor wrote his report endorsing the view of the Jesuits and sent it to Rome. One historian summarizes the Emperor's conclusion as follows:

> [The Emperor] approved [the Jesuits'] statements that Confucius was honoured as a teacher; that "performance of the ceremony of sacrifice to the dead is a means of showing sincere affection for members of the family and thankful devotion to ancestors of the clan"; that the tablets of deceased ancestors were honoured as a remembrance of the dead rather than as an actual residence of their souls; that t'ien [*tian*] and shang-ti [*shangdi*] are not identified with the physical sky but are "the ruler and lord of heaven and earth and all things"; and that ching

---

10. The text of the Decree of the Congregation for the Propagation of the Faith can be found in Robert A. Hunt, *The Gospel among the Nations: A Documentary History of Inculturation* (Maryknoll, NY: Orbis, 2010), 73–76.

t'ien [*jing tian*] in the inscription bestowed on the Jesuit Church meant "revere Heaven" in this sense.[11]

The debate continued, however, until in 1715, Pope Clement XI formally ruled against the Jesuits' and the Chinese emperor's interpretations.[12] The emperor in turn responded in 1717 by forbidding Christianity in China, expelling foreign missionaries, and closing churches. The Rites Controversy was finally formally brought to an end by the Roman Catholic Church in 1939, when the Propaganda Fide issued an instruction, with the approval of Pius XII, that acknowledged that the rituals and ceremonies were civil and not religious and thus were open to Christian participation.[13]

The entire episode is both tragic and instructive, and illustrates some of the central questions that emerge from the encounter between the Christian gospel and Asian cultures shaped by Confucianism. The questions at the heart of the Rites Controversy remain highly relevant (and controversial) in Asia today. To what extent, if any, can Christians participate in the traditional ancestral rites or in Buddhist funerals? Can indigenous religious terms be used to translate key Christian concepts? To what extent is there continuity between Christian teachings and values and those of other religious traditions?

The missionaries, the Vatican hierarchy, and the Chinese imperial court were all discussing issues that are central to cultural anthropology, religious studies, and missiology, although at least two centuries were to pass before any of these disciplines would be established. Both the Jesuits and the officials in Rome apparently made a crucial distinction between what we today call the domains of culture and religion, although these concepts were not systematically analyzed at the time. Moreover, both parties seem to have accepted an assumption central to modern missiological debates over contextualization, namely, that if a phenomenon is clearly cultural and not religious, then, in principle, it can be adopted as an expression of Christian meanings, whereas if it is clearly religious, then it cannot.[14] This is implicit in the opening statement of the 1939 instruction *Plane compertum est* by Propaganda Fide, which granted approval for participation in the Confucian rites: "Everyone knows

---

11. The summary is from Paul Rule, as quoted in Ross, *A Vision Betrayed*, 192.

12. For the text of Clement XI's Bull *Ex illa die*, see Hunt, *The Gospel among the Nations*, 76–80.

13. Ibid., 80–81.

14. See Stephen B. Bevans and Roger P. Schroeder, *Constants in Context: A Theology of Mission for Today* (Maryknoll, NY: Orbis, 2004), 202.

that some ceremonies in Oriental countries, although in earlier times they were tied in with pagan rites, now that customs and minds have changed with the flow of the centuries, merely preserve civil expression of devotion toward ancestors, or of patriotism, or of respect for fellow countrymen."[15] In other words, both groups agreed that if the ancestral rituals in question were primarily religious, and not merely civil or social, then participation in them constituted idolatry and was inappropriate for Christians. The dispute centered on whether they were inherently religious or merely social or cultural. The Rites Controversy helps us to see more clearly a central issue in missiology and the theology of religions: Can we always identify a clear and unambiguous distinction between the religious and the cultural domains? Even if we can, should we assume that the cultural is neutral with respect to the Christian faith and that the religious is inherently unacceptable?

But before we can respond to such questions, we need to have a clearer understanding of what we mean by culture and religion. Although the terms *culture* and *religion* are widely used today, it is notoriously difficult to define them precisely. In thinking about either culture or religion, one is tempted to echo the perplexed musings of Saint Augustine, as he reflected on the nature of time: "What is time? Who can explain this easily and briefly? Who can comprehend this even in thought so as to articulate the answer in words? Yet what do we speak of, in our familiar everyday conversation, more than of time? We surely know what we mean when we speak of it. We also know what is meant when we hear someone else talking about it. What then is time? Provided that no one asks me, I know. If I want to explain it to an inquirer, I do not know."[16] Similar frustration awaits anyone attempting to define culture or religion. Nevertheless, some attempt at clarification is necessary.

Culture(s)

The concept of culture, as understood today, is a modern one. This does not mean, of course, that what the term *culture* denotes did not exist before the modern era. As far back as history takes us, people have lived together in communities in patterned and ordered ways. Since ancient times, various groups have been characterized by different languages, beliefs, customs, and institutions. Ancient peoples were very much aware of these differences. But during

---

15. Hunt, *The Gospel Among the Nations*, 80.

16. Saint Augustine, *Confessions*, XI.xiii.17, translated by Henry Chadwick (New York: Oxford University Press, 1991), 230.

the nineteenth and twentieth centuries, the notion of culture became widely adopted as a way of explaining these differences.

There are at least two ways in which the concept of culture has been understood in the modern West. On the one hand, there is the tradition that thinks of culture as something that only a select, elite subgroup manifests: "the sum total of superior, morally and spiritually edifying human accomplishments."[17] During the nineteenth century, culture (*kultur* in German) was identified with sophisticated or refined habits of living deriving from a proper education (notably in literature and the arts) which reflected the expectations for proper social interaction. On this view, not all people have culture; it is a special quality that is available only to the privileged or elite.

But during the twentieth century, another way of thinking about culture became widely accepted. Because of the influence of anthropology, there developed an understanding of culture that was based on the observed lived realities of ordinary people in actual communities. Tomoko Masuzawa calls this the "culture as a complex whole" perspective. It presents culture as "expressly holistic, rather than narrowly discriminating, descriptive rather than evaluative, and...[it] presupposes the multiplicity of cultures and does not imply obvious 'standards of excellence.' "[18] On this view, culture is no longer the possession of just the elite, for all communities have culture. Moreover, culture can no longer be thought of in the singular, as a general, cumulative human construction. Since human societies are different, culture appears differently among various peoples. The idea of a particular culture as something observable within a specific, local community emerged, and it became common to speak in terms of many cultures (plural). It is this latter, anthropologically informed sense of culture that is of interest to us as we explore the relationships among the gospel, cultures, and religions.

Christian missionaries have had an ambivalent relation to cultures. On the one hand, missionaries were instrumental in developing the modern understanding of culture. For it was the careful collection of ethnographic data by missionaries as they lived among diverse peoples in Asia, the Americas and Africa that provided the material out of which our current understanding of culture was formed.[19]

---

17. Tomoko Masuzawa, "Culture," in *Critical Terms for Religious Studies*, edited by Mark C. Taylor (Chicago: University of Chicago Press, 1998), 73–74.

18. Ibid., 77.

19. See Robert J. Priest, "Anthropology and Missiology: Reflections on the Relationship," in *Paradigm Shifts in Christian Witness*, edited by Charles E. Van Engen, Darrell Whiteman, and J. Dudley Woodberry (Maryknoll, NY: Orbis, 2008), 23–28; Taber, *The World*, chaps.

At the same time, however, many missionaries adopted simplistic and misleading views of culture, often identifying Western practices and values with the Christian gospel and dismissing "native" cultures as largely domains of darkness and demonic influence. The superiority of European or American culture was taken for granted, and mission was understood to include introducing "primitive" peoples to the blessings of Christianity, commerce, and civilization. Indigenous practices and institutions were rejected as not only uncivilized but also evil. It is easy, of course, from our vantage point today, to condemn the failure of earlier missionaries to appreciate local cultures or to distinguish adequately their own cultural influences from the Christian gospel itself. As Lesslie Newbigin reminds us, "[I]t is much more pleasant and relaxing to confess the sins of one's ancestors than to be made aware of one's own."[20] Moreover, we must also acknowledge that not all missionaries were so insensitive. David Bosch correctly observes, "It is simply inadequate to contend that mission was nothing other than the spiritual side of imperialism and always the faithful servant of the latter.... Even during the high imperial era (and particularly in its early stages), some missionaries and mission societies were very skeptical about an alliance between nation and mission."[21]

Since the mid-twentieth century, however, there has been a basic consensus among evangelical missiologists about the need to disentangle the Christian gospel from Western cultural patterns, to affirm local cultural expressions whenever possible, and to encourage appropriate expression of the gospel in the local idiom. Missiology insists that a proper understanding of culture is central to the theory and effective practice of mission. As a result of the work of linguists such as Eugene Nida and anthropologists such as Charles Taber, Charles Kraft, and Paul Hiebert, since the 1970s, evangelical missiologists have used the social sciences to explore appropriate contextualization of the gospel in local settings.[22]

2–4; Patrick Harries, "Anthropology," in *Missions and Empire*, edited by Norman Etherington (New York: Oxford University Press, 2005), 239–260.

20. Lesslie Newbigin, *A Word in Season: Perspectives on Christian World Missions* (Grand Rapids, MI: Eerdmans, 1994), 122.

21. David Bosch, *Transforming Mission: Paradigm Shifts in Theology of Mission* (Maryknoll, NY: Orbis, 1991), 310–311.

22. See Taber, *The World*; Paul G. Hiebert, "The Social Sciences and Missions: Applying the Message," in *Missiology and the Social Sciences*, edited by Edward Rommen and Gary Corwin (Pasadena, CA: William Carey Library, 1996), 184–213; Priest, "Anthropology and Missiology." The interest in culture was reflected in the 1978 Consultation on Gospel and Culture held at Willowbank, Bermuda, sponsored by the Lausanne Committee's Theology and Education Group. Thirty-three theologians, anthropologists, linguists, missionaries,

But what do we mean by the term *culture*? Paul Hiebert speaks of culture as "the integrated system of learned patterns of behavior, ideas and products characteristic of a society."[23] Similarly, Clifford Geertz defines culture as "an historically transmitted pattern of meanings embodied in symbols, a system of inherited conceptions expressed in symbolic forms by means of which men communicate, perpetuate, and develop their knowledge about and attitudes toward life."[24]

The concept is rather vague, so that we can think of culture in a very broad or a narrowly restricted sense. We can, for example, speak broadly of American culture or Bolivian culture. But we can also think in more restricted terms, so that second-generation Korean-Americans in Chicago can be said to manifest a distinctive culture. Moreover, an individual can simultaneously be a part of several different cultures—one can be part of American culture, second-generation Chinese-American culture in Chicago, and Midwestern evangelical Christian culture. Furthermore, the boundaries separating cultures are fluid and imprecise, so that it is not always clear where one culture ends and another begins. Cultures are not hermetically sealed, self-contained entities cut off from outside influences. Consider, for example, the difficulty in clearly demarcating the boundaries between American culture and Canadian culture or between first-generation Korean-American culture and second-generation Korean-American culture.

Finally, cultures involve symbolic meanings that help to define a group of people, establish boundaries, and provide normative expectations for behavior. In times of significant change, these symbolic meanings are often contested, with competing subgroups attempting to define the meanings in ways that advance their own objectives. Thus, while culture provides cohesion and identity for a group, it can also produce deep internal tensions and conflict.

Missiologists and theologians have developed a theological framework for understanding culture as both the gift of God's grace in creation and revelation on one hand and the product of human sin and distortion of what God has created on the other.[25] The possibility of our engaging in the activities and

---

and pastors from six continents gathered to study the relation between the gospel and culture. The Consultation papers, along with the Willowbank Report, were published in *Down to Earth: Studies in Christianity and Culture*, edited by John R. W. Stott and Robert Coote (Grand Rapids, MI: Eerdmans, 1980).

23. Paul Hiebert, *Cultural Anthropology*, 2nd ed. (Grand Rapids, MI: Baker, 1983), 25.

24. Clifford Geertz, *The Interpretation of Cultures* (New York: Basic, 1973), 89.

25. See D. A. Carson, *Christ and Culture Revisited* (Grand Rapids, MI: Eerdmans, 2008); Paul G. Hiebert, *Anthropological Reflections on Missiological Issues* (Grand Rapids, MI: Baker,

institutions identified with culture is itself a gift of God's grace, and the many good and positive things we find in the diverse cultures of the world reflect the goodness of the creator. Wherever we find truth and goodness in patterns of human community, these are ultimately the results of the creative, revelatory, and enlightening activity of the triune God—Father, Son, and Holy Spirit. For God is the source of all goodness and truth. Nevertheless, every culture is also affected profoundly by sin, on both the individual and institutional levels. Specific questions about contextualization of the gospel in particular cultural settings presuppose this dialectic between what is good and acceptable and what is to be rejected or modified. But Christian thinkers generally maintain that there is nothing about culture itself that is inherently theologically problematic. As W. Dyrness puts it, "Culture...is a reflection of the call that God has put in [sic] creation, especially as this comes to expression in the commission given to the human creation: be fruitful, have dominion."[26]

As the Christian faith moves into new social contexts worldwide, the church is forced to grapple with the relation of the gospel of Jesus Christ to different cultural and religious patterns. And here a distinctive of the Christian faith emerges. As we saw in chapter 4, Andrew Walls and Lamin Sanneh have drawn attention to the "translatability" of the Christian gospel into diverse cultural settings. Walls speaks of the "indigenizing principle," which reflects the fact that all Christians (including those within the first-century New Testament church) are embedded within particular historical, linguistic, and cultural settings and that it is within these cultural contexts that God encounters people.[27] Thus, the gospel of Jesus Christ can become "at home" within any particular linguistic or cultural setting. Similarly, Sanneh has written eloquently of the translatability of the Christian gospel into multiple linguistic and cultural contexts and of the positive effects of translation of the Bible into local languages.[28] Unlike Arabic and Islam, there is no "Christian language" or "Christian culture" that is normative for all believers.

1994); William A. Dyrness, *The Earth Is God's: A Theology of American Culture* (Maryknoll, NY: Orbis, 1997), chaps. 1–2.

26. Dyrness, *The Earth Is God's*, 71.

27. Andrew Walls, "The Gospel as Prisoner and Liberator of Culture," in Walls, *The Missionary Movement in Christian History: Studies in the Transmission of Faith* (Maryknoll, NY: Orbis, 1996), 3–15.

28. See Lamin Sanneh, *Translating the Message: The Missionary Impact on Culture*, rev. ed. (Maryknoll, NY: Orbis, 2009).

But the translatability of the gospel and the indigenizing principle must be balanced with what Walls calls the "pilgrim principle." While the gospel can be authentically expressed within any cultural setting, it cannot simply be identified with any culture. The gospel of Jesus Christ transcends and challenges all cultures, reminding believers that they are not to be completely at home in any earthly culture. Much of missiology, and discussions of contextualization in particular, involves navigating between the indigenizing and pilgrim principles.

Religion as a Modern Concept

The academic study of religion—or, better, of religions—is relatively young, emerging only in the late nineteenth century. It was the pioneering efforts of thinkers such as Edward Burnett Tylor (d. 1917), James G. Frazer (d. 1941), Max Müller (d. 1900), Émile Durkheim (d. 1917), and Max Weber (d. 1920), among others, that produced the methodological framework for the modern study of religions. A variety of approaches was adopted, with some emphasizing historical studies and others exploring psychological, sociological, phenomenological, or structural dimensions of the religions. As with anthropology, religious studies as an academic discipline developed in part on the basis of the extensive reports produced by Christian missionaries, along with explorers and traders, in Asia, Latin America, and Africa.[29] Early missionaries were often careful ethnographers, recording rich descriptions of people in distant lands. They also served as brokers between the Old World and the New Worlds, not only translating the Bible into local languages but also making available to the West through translation the sacred texts of other religions. But in spite of this heritage, as religious studies became established within the modern Western university, the relationship between religious studies scholars and theologians or missiologists became increasingly strained, with each group regarding the other with suspicion. Religious studies scholars were after a "scientific" approach to the subject, untainted by theological commitments, while theologians rejected the methodological naturalism and alleged "objectivity" of such endeavors.

Although religious studies have flourished in the academy since the 1960s[30] and there is no lack of scholarly books and journals dealing with

29. Eric J. Sharpe, *Comparative Religion: A History* (La Salle, IL: Open Court, 1986), 144–145.

30. See Donald Wiebe, "Religious Studies," in *The Routledge Companion to the Study of Religion*, edited by John R. Hinnells (New York: Routledge, 2005), 98–124.

religion, many today contend that the ways in which we typically think about and study religion are fundamentally flawed. Critics claim that our contemporary concept of religion—and of the religions as distinct, clearly definable entities—is a modern construction that emerged with the dissolution of Christendom in Europe, the growing secularization of European societies, and the repercussions from European colonialism and Christian missionary activity in Asia. The modern study of religion is said to treat religion (singular) as a clearly defined, essentially transhistorical and transcultural category, a genus, of which there are many species, such as Islam, Hinduism, Christianity, and Buddhism.[31] Thus, religion in general can be separated from other domains of collective human life, with the nonreligious identified as secular. All religions, as species of the genus religion, are said to share in a common essence that defines "the religious" and sets it apart from "the secular." It is precisely this understanding of a transhistorical and transcultural essence of religion, which then is manifest as the many religions, that is called into question by recent critics. Contrary to this popular way of thinking, the critics charge, there is no such thing as religion in this sense, nor should we think of Hinduism, Buddhism, or Islam as particular examples of this broader category.

There is an important truth in this criticism. Those attacking the essentialist notion of religion frequently point out that this concept is a modern one that would have seemed strange to people in the ancient world. Before the modern era, there was no single term that was used in the way that *religion* is used today. Ancient Greek and Latin, for example, did not have a single term that carried the same meanings as the English word *religion* does today.[32] The Latin word *religio* referred to fulfilling social and cultic obligations in ancient Rome. *Religio* plays a prominent role in Cicero's *De natura deorum* (The Nature of the Gods), where the term is linked to *pietas* (piety) and *sanctitas* (holiness). In Cicero's usage, "*religio* focuses on the appropriate human relationship to the gods. It belongs (*continetur*) to *deorum pius cultus* ('due worship of the gods') and is contrasted to *superstitio* in which *est timor inanis deorum* ('there is inane fear of the gods')."[33] Although himself a priest and a member of the

---

31. See, for example, Paul J. Griffiths, "The Very Idea of Religion," *First Things* 103 (May 2000): 30–35; William T. Cavanaugh, *The Myth of Religious Violence* (New York: Oxford University Press, 2009), chap. 2. The seminal work here is Wilfred Cantwell Smith, *The Meaning and End of Religion* (New York: Harper & Row, 1963).

32. On developments in meaning of *religio*, see Peter Henrici, "The Concept of Religion from Cicero to Schleiermacher," in *Catholic Engagement with World Religions: A Comprehensive Study*, edited by Karl J. Becker and Ilaria Morali (Maryknoll, NY: Orbis, 2010), 1–20.

33. Ibid., 2.

Board of Augurs of the Roman Republic, Cicero, like most intellectuals of the time, was a critic of the popular religious beliefs and practices of the masses, which were dismissed as superstitions.

Augustine was one of the few early Christian thinkers to give careful attention to *religio*, in his work *De vera religion* (On True Religion). For Augustine, however, *religio* did not refer to religion in general, in the modern sense of the term, or to specific religions such as Judaism, Christianity, Buddhism, or Hinduism. For Augustine, "*religio* meant worship, those patterns of action by which, in public, we self-consciously turn ourselves toward God in homage and praise. There could, he thought, be a right and proper ('true') way of worshipping God, just as there could be improper and damnable ('false') ways of doing so; and so there could be a true and many false 'religions.' "[34] While Augustine's focus was on the proper way of worshipping God and not on Christianity as an empirical, institutional religion as such, we must also remember that in contrasting the "true" way of worship with "false" ways, Augustine had in mind, among other things, the teachings and practices of Mani and Manichaeism. So the distinction between Christian belief and practice and the religious beliefs and practices of other groups was one that he was well aware of. Interestingly, with the Christianization of Europe after Constantine, *religio* or *religiones* was not used in reference to other, non-Christian ways of religious life.[35] In part, this was because of the lack of exposure to very different forms of religious life (even Islam was initially regarded as a Christian heresy). It was only with the fragmentation of Christendom and the voyages of discovery in the sixteenth century, bringing much greater awareness of different forms of religious life, that the terminology for the idea of religion in general and for religions as distinct entities developed.

Similarly, until the modern era, non-Western languages generally have not had single words that are equivalent to the English word *religion*. Eric Sharpe states: "In recent years, where non-western traditions have thought in 'religious' terms, they have done so through the medium of some European language. A Hindu writing in English may be happy enough to speak of 'religion': in Sanskrit, Hindi, or Tamil he must use words having a different connotation."[36] The Sanskrit term normally used in these contexts is *dharma*, which can be translated into English as "truth," "duty," "law," "order," and

---

34. Griffiths, "The Very Idea," 31.

35. Henrici, "The Concept of Religion," 6.

36. Eric J. Sharpe, *Understanding Religion* (New York: St. Martin's, 1983), 39.

"right." Similarly, the Japanese word for "religion" is *shukyo*, but this is a modern term that carries connotations somewhat foreign to traditional Japanese approaches to religious practices:

> [*Shukyo*] is a derived word that came into prominence in the nineteenth century as a result of Japanese encounters with the West and particularly with Christian missionaries, to denote a concept and view of religion commonplace in the realm of nineteenth-century Christian theology but at that time not found in Japan, of religion as a specific, belief-framed entity. The term *shukyo*, thus, in origin at least, implies a separation of that which is religious from other aspects of society and culture, and contains implications of belief and commitment to one order or movement—something that has not been traditionally a common factor in Japanese religious behaviour and something that tends to exclude many of the phenomena involved in the Japanese religious process.[37]

One reason premodern societies did not have a separate word for religion is that they did not make sharp distinctions between the religious and nonreligious dimensions of social life.[38] The tendency to differentiate the religious from other aspects of the social order and to regard religion as one part of a broader social and political system coincides with the growing secularization of European, American, and other societies worldwide.[39]

Not only is the concept of religion itself something of a modern innovation, but our views of particular religions are also often shaped by modern developments. This can be illustrated by a brief look at Hinduism. The idea of Hinduism as a distinct religion with defining beliefs is really a modern notion

---

37. Ian Reader, *Religion in Contemporary Japan* (London: Macmillan, 1991), 13–14. See also the extensive discussion in Jason Ananda Josephson, *The Invention of Religion in Japan* (Chicago: University of Chicago Press, 2012).

38. We should not assume, however, that everyone in the ancient world was devoutly religious or that the religious dimension permeated every aspect of communal life. Ancient Greece, the Roman Empire, ancient India, and China all have rich traditions of religious skepticism.

39. Secularization is itself a complex and controversial subject. Good discussions of the issues can be found in Judith Fox, "Secularization," *The Routledge Companion to the Study of Religion* edited by John R. Hinnells (New York: Routledge, 2005), 291–305; Peter Berger, "Reflections on the Sociology of Religion Today," *Sociology of Religion* 62, no. 4 (Winter 2001): 443–454. The most helpful interdisciplinary study of secularization in Europe and America is Charles Taylor, *A Secular Age* (Cambridge, MA: Harvard University Press, 2007).

that developed through the encounter between India and British colonialism, Western Christian missionary activity, and Indian nationalism during the eighteenth and nineteenth centuries. Geoffrey Oddie notes: "It is now well established that the terms 'Hindu' and 'Hinduism' were categories invented by outsiders in an attempt to interpret and explain the complexities they found in Indian religious and social life."[40] The word *Hindu* was originally the Persian variant of the Sanskrit term *sindhu*, referring to the Indus River. The early use of the term was primarily geographical, designating everything native to India, and carried no particular religious significance. Thus, in the early nineteenth century, long after the arrival of the British East India Company, "it was still not uncommon for references to be made to 'Hindoo Christians' and 'Hindoo Muslims' as distinct from those who were not native-born or culturally indigenous to the subcontinent."[41]

But the term *Hindu* increasingly took on religious meanings, and eventually, *Hinduism* was introduced as a word designating India's native religion (singular) in contrast to foreign religions such as Christianity. *Hinduism* was adopted in English publications by missionaries and Indians in the 1820s and 1830s, with the former using it as a negative contrast to Christianity, whereas the latter championed it as a positive alternative. *Hinduism* became a general category for the religious traditions of India that were not Islamic, Christian, Sikh, Zoroastrian, Jain, or Buddhist. Despite the bewildering variety of conflicting popular religious and philosophical traditions in this general category, it became common to use *Hinduism* to designate an indigenous, allegedly "coherent, comprehensive, and unified religious system that could be compared to other systems such as Christianity and Islam."[42] Hinduism became defined in terms of India's ancient Brahmanic traditions rooted in the Vedic scriptures, and, under the influence of modern Indian intellectuals such as Swami Vivekananda and Sarvepalli Radhakrishnan, it became especially identified with the esoteric mysticism and monism of the Advaita Vedanta tradition.[43]

---

40. See Geoffrey A. Oddie, "Constructing 'Hinduism': The Impact of the Protestant Missionary Movement on Hindu Self-Understanding," in *Christians and Missionaries in India: Cross-Cultural Communication Sinces*, edited by Robert Eric Frykenberg (Grand Rapids, MI: Eerdmans, 2003), 156.

41. Robert Eric Frykenberg, "Constructions of Hinduism at the Nexus of History and Religion," *Journal of Interdisciplinary History* 23, no. 3 (Winter 1993): 525.

42. Oddie, "Constructing 'Hinduism,'" 155.

43. See Brian K. Pennington, *Was Hinduism Invented? Britons, Indians, and the Colonial Construction of Religion* (New York: Oxford University Press, 2005); Torkel Brekke, *Makers of*

Some scholars, such as Wilfred Cantwell Smith, conclude on the basis of these historical and linguistic facts that the notion of religion as a distinct entity—and especially of the religions in the plural—is a modern confusion that ought to be abandoned.[44] Smith contends, for example, that "There are Hindus but there is no Hinduism."[45] Smith's provocative claim is intended to challenge us to look not at Hinduism as an abstract, reified system but rather at the actual commitments of Hindus. This is surely sound advice for any-one desiring to understand the lived realities of real Hindu communities. But the claim that the notion of religion in general or the concepts of particular religions such as Hinduism, Islam, and Buddhism ought to be abandoned is problematic.

On the one hand, there is no question that our contemporary understand-ing of religion, or even of particular religions such as Hinduism, is a mod-ern one that has been shaped by the fragmentation of Christendom and the growing secularization of European societies, the introduction of Europeans to the many diverse civilizations in Asia and Africa, and the complex dynam-ics resulting from European colonialist encounters with Asian peoples. Smith is also correct in warning us against essentializing or reifying the concept of religion. As we shall see, it is very difficult to define precisely what we mean by religion, and we must remember that religions, as empirical realities, are continually undergoing change as they adapt to fresh circumstances. But acknowledging all of this does not entail that *religion*, as the term is currently understood today, has no meaningful reference or that we cannot speak mean-ingfully about particular systems such as Hinduism or Buddhism or Islam.

The fact that our concept of religion today is a modern development does not necessarily mean that it is mistaken or unhelpful. Nor does the fact that *Hinduism* and *Buddhism* are to some extent modern constructs necessarily mean that such concepts are *merely* modern constructions. The academic landscape is full of concepts that were developed in modern times but help us to understand basic features of the world that were familiar to people in pre-modern times. The concept of H_2O, for example, was unknown in the ancient world, but that does not mean that people were unaware of water or could not make conceptual distinctions between water and oil. Similarly, although they did not have a word in their languages that means exactly what *religion* means

Modern Indian Religion in the Late Nineteenth Century (New York: Oxford University Press, 2002), 13–60.

44. See Smith, *The Meaning and End*, 53–79.

45. Ibid., 65.

today, people in ancient times were well aware of religious beliefs and rituals and were able to distinguish the beliefs and practices of various religious groups. Interestingly, before the introduction of Buddhism into Japan in the sixth century, the Japanese did not have a term for the traditional, indigenous religious tradition of Japan. But with the introduction of the (then) foreign religion, the term *Shinto* (way of the kami) was coined in order to distinguish the Japanese religious tradition from Butsudo (way of the buddhas).[46]

People who did not have special terms in their languages equivalent to the English word *religion* nevertheless were able to *be religious*, that is, to participate in activities and to hold beliefs and values that today we designate as religious. Moreover, people in ancient and medieval times were well aware of differences among religious communities. Those in twelfth-century India who worshipped Vishnu, for example, believed in reincarnation, and maintained strict caste distinctions were regarded as different from those who prayed to Allah, recited the Qur'an, and strove to emulate the prophet Muhammad. Making such distinctions among religious groups is not simply a matter of modern outsiders making (Western) judgments about religious communities that the Indians themselves would not acknowledge. Indian religious insiders regularly distinguished among groups, in some cases rejecting as heretical groups that were unacceptably different. Although India has long tolerated coexistence of diverse religious traditions, this does not mean that there were no divisions among religious traditions. Even in ancient times, the boundaries between those who today are known as Hindus and the early Buddhists and Jains were clear. The Brahmins rejected the followers of Gautama Buddha and Mahavira, the founder of Jainism, as sufficiently different that Buddhism and Jainism developed as religious traditions that were clearly distinct from what later came to be known as Hinduism. Since the followers of Gautama and Mahavira rejected the authority of the Vedas, they were rejected as heretics by the Brahmins.[47]

Acknowledging that "religion" and "the religions" are to some extent modern constructs does not necessarily mean that they are distortions that ought to be abandoned. Kim Knott states: "Scholars are generally in agreement

---

46. Joseph M. Kitagawa, *On Understanding Japanese Religion* (Princeton, NJ: Princeton University Press, 1987), 139. For a somewhat different understanding of the origin of Shinto, see Toshio Kuroda, "Shinto in the History of Japanese Religion," *Japanese Journal of Religious Studies* 7, no. 1 (1981): 1–21.

47. Wendy Doniger O'Flaherty, "The Origin of Heresy in Hindu Mythology," *History of Religions* 10, no. 4 (1971): 272.

that 'religion' is a historical and scholarly construct. This is not intended to belittle people's experience of the sacred or to judge the veracity of their religious claims. Rather, it recognizes that 'religion' is a concept used to identify, delimit and describe certain types of human behaviour, belief, organization and experience."[48] The issue is whether the notion of religion in general and particularized concepts of Hinduism, Buddhism, and Islam are useful categories for understanding and sorting out the lived realities of diverse religious communities. We think that, properly understood, they can be. If these terms are abandoned, then others would need to be introduced to depict the different religious communities, both in the ancient and medieval past and in the modern world.

Theological Understandings of Religion

A Christian theology of religions should offer a Christian theological understanding of the religions. Many theological perspectives on religions have been offered, but one of the most significant is that of the great Swiss theologian Karl Barth, in *Church Dogmatics* 1:2, paragraph 17, "The Revelation of God as the Abolition of Religion."[49] Based on a particular interpretation of this section, Barth has been largely regarded as harshly negative on the religions. Alan Race expresses the view of many when he states that Barth represents "the most extreme form of the exclusivist theory."[50] But recent studies have shown the inadequacy of such characterizations; Barth's views were more subtle and complex than initially presumed.[51]

Confusion over Barth's views is partly a result of problems of translation from the German into English. The standard English translation of Barth's *Dogmatics* has translated two key terms in ways that have been recently

---

48. Kim Knott, "How to Study Religion in the Modern World," in *Religions in the Modern World: Traditions and Transformations*, 2nd ed., edited by Linda Woodhead, Hiroko Kawanami, and Christopher Partridge (London: Routledge, 2009), 16.

49. See Karl Barth, *Church Dogmatics* 1:2, *The Doctrine of the Word of God*, edited by G. W. Bromiley and T. F. Torrance (New York: Scribner's, 1956), 280–361. The "paragraph" is more than eighty pages long.

50. Alan Race, *Christians and Religious Pluralism* (London: SCM, 1983), 11.

51. See Peter Harrison, "Karl Barth and the NonChristian Religions," *Journal of Ecumenical Studies* 23, no. 2 (Spring 1986): 207–224; Garrett Green, "Challenging the Religious Studies Canon: Karl Barth's Theory of Religion," *Journal of Religion* 75 (1995): 473–486; J. A. Di Noia, O.P., "Religion and the Religions," in *The Cambridge Companion to Karl Barth*, edited by John Webster (Cambridge, UK: Cambridge University Press, 2000), 243–257.

challenged. First, the translation of *Aufhebung der Religion* as "abolition of religion" has been criticized as missing the subtlety of Barth's position. Garrett Green has suggested "sublation" instead of "abolition."[52] Barth's discussion contains the tension between God's revelation as the dissolution and the elevation of religion, a dialectic captured better in "sublation" than in "abolition." Second, in this section, Barth also characterizes religion as *Unglaube*, a term translated as "unbelief." But Green argues that a better translation would be "faithlessness" or "unfaith."[53] For according to Barth, when judged by God's revelation, human religiosity is characterized by the lack of faith or "an unwillingness to yield to the saving power of divine grace and revelation, and to surrender all those purely human attempts to know and satisfy God which together comprise human religion and religiosity."[54]

Barth wrote before the theology of religions developed as a special focus of theology, and his interest was in the concept of religion itself, not the various religions as such. Di Noia points out that paragraph 17 falls within the broader context of Barth's discussion of the possibility of revelation in light of the work of the Holy Spirit.[55] Barth began this section with a critique of the manner in which liberal theology had placed the concept of religion, rather than God's revelation, at the center of theological inquiry. Theology thus brought about an unhealthy "reversal of revelation and religion": instead of interpreting human religiosity in light of God's self-revelation in Jesus Christ, theologians interpret revelation in terms of religion.[56] Barth was resolutely opposed to any attempt to identify God's revelation with even the best in human civilization, as he believed that nineteenth- and early-twentieth-century German theological liberalism had been guilty of doing. Only God can reveal God: "Revelation is God's self-offering and self-manifestation. Revelation encounters man on the presupposition and in confirmation of the fact that man's attempts to know God from his own standpoint are wholly and entirely futile; not because of any necessity in principle, but because of a practical necessity of fact. In revelation God tells man that He is God, and that as such He is his Lord. In telling him this, revelation tells him something utterly new, something which apart from revelation he does not know

---

52. See Green, "Challenging," 477. Peter Harrison proposes "superseding" as a better translation. See Harrison, "Karl Barth," 208, n. 3.

53. Green, "Challenging," 480.

54. Di Noia, "Religion and the Religions," 250.

55. Ibid., 246.

56. Barth, *Church Dogmatics* 1:2, 284.

and cannot tell either himself or others."[57] Di Noia observes: "It is this reversal of revelation and religion that Barth laments and, in paragraph 17, endeavors to correct."[58] And when religion is viewed in light of divine revelation, it is revealed as *Unglaube* or faithlessness. But this judgment is not one that flows simply from the comparison of Christianity as a religion with other religions. Barth claims that "it is only by the revelation of God in Jesus Christ that we can characterize religion as idolatry and self-righteousness, and in this way show it to be unbelief [*Unglaube*]."[59]

Divine revelation negates religion, but it also elevates or exalts religion. *Aufhebung* includes both poles of the dialectic. Revelation does not eliminate or destroy religion. Barth states: "[W]e do not need to delete or retract any-thing from the admission that in His revelation God is present in the world of human religion. But what we have to discern is that this means that *God* is present."[60] God's elevation of religion is seen where God's gracious activi-ty results in the Christian religion becoming the true religion. Barth was willing to speak of Christianity as the true religion but not because of any inherent virtue in the religion of Christianity itself. The empirical history of Christianity stands under God's judgment. The Christian religion, when seen in its flesh-and-blood history over the last two thousand years, "is not justi-fied because it is holy in itself—which it is not. It is made holy because it is justified. And it is not true because it is holy in itself—which it never was and never will be. But it is made holy in order to show that it is the true religion."[61] The only sense in which we can speak of Christianity as the true religion is one in which we speak of a "justified sinner."[62] Like a sinner justified by God's grace, Christianity can become the true religion insofar as it is taken up by divine grace.

In spite of Barth's strong Christocentrist understanding of revelation, he also acknowledges vestiges of divine revelation outside Scripture, as we noted in our discussion in chapter 3 of truth in the religions. In *Church Dogmatics* 4:3, Barth speaks of "other words" and "other lights": "We recognize that the fact that Jesus Christ is the one Word of God does not mean that in the Bible,

---

57. Ibid., 301.

58. Di Noia, "Religion and the Religions," 248.

59. Barth, *Church Dogmatics* 1:2, 314.

60. Ibid., 197.

61. Ibid., 359.

62. Ibid., 325.

the Church and the world there are not other words which are quite notable in their way, other lights which are quite clear and other revelations which are quite real... Nor does it follow from our statement that every word spoken outside the circle of the Bible and the Church is a word of false prophecy and therefore valueless, empty and corrupt, that all the lights which rise and shine in this outer sphere are misleading and all the revelations are necessarily untrue."[63] Joseph Di Noia concludes that according to Barth, "Christians can encounter the adherents of other religions in interreligious dialogue with the expectation that truth—what Barth calls Christ's 'free communication in parables of the kingdom' —will indeed be found there and that such truth is testable by reference to the criteria of agreement with Scripture and with church doctrine."[64]

Barth's approach forces an important methodological issue for a Christian theology of religions. Should our understanding of religion come from careful observation of religious phenomena in the world around us or from God's authoritative self-revelation in Jesus Christ and Scripture? The Indian theologian D. T. Niles tells the story of a conversation with Karl Barth that illustrates the issue. In light of Barth's characterization of religion as "unbelief," Niles once asked him how many Hindus he had actually met. Barth responded by saying, "None." "How then," asked Niles, "do you know that Hinduism is unbelief?" Barth replied, "A priori!"[65] While this is humorous, it illustrates well an approach to understanding religions that sees no need for phenomenological observation of actual religious traditions and relies entirely on biblical exegesis.

Although Barth's curt reply might suggest that he had no interest in the teachings and practices of actual religions, he was well aware of other religious traditions. In "The Revelation of God as the Abolition of Religion," discussed above, Barth actually offers a remarkably insightful discussion of the Pure Land tradition of Japanese Buddhism, noting clear parallels between aspects of Pure Land teachings and Protestant Christianity.[66] Structurally, Pure Land Buddhism, like Protestant Christianity, seems to be a religion of grace, since it teaches that there is nothing that wicked human beings can do

63. Ibid., 4:3, 97.

64. J. A. Di Noia, "Religion and the Religions," 255.

65. D. T. Niles, "Karl Barth—A Personal Memory," *South East Asia Journal of Theology* 11 (Autumn 1969): 10–11.

66. See Barth, *Church Dogmatics* 1:2, 340–344.

to earn or merit rebirth in the Pure Land, the soteriological goal. What, then, is distinctive about the Christian faith? Only one thing is decisive in setting the Christian faith apart, and this is "the name of Jesus Christ." After an examination of Pure Land Buddhism and some forms of *bhakti* Hinduism, Barth concludes: "It is not merely a matter of prudentially weighing the various possibilities of heathen development, which might eventually catch up with the differences we teach, but of a clear insight that the truth of the Christian religion is in fact enclosed in the one name of Jesus Christ, and nothing else. It is actually enclosed in all the formal simplicity of this name as the very heart of the divine reality of revelation, which alone constitutes the truth of our religion."[67]

One need not agree with Barth on all points to appreciate his vigorous insistence that we understand human religiosity in light of God's definitive self-revelation in Jesus Christ.[68] Barth reminds us of the sharp difference between a genuine *theology* of religions and comparative religions or the phenomenology of religions. But even as we insist on the priority of divine revelation, we must ask whether Scripture is all we need for formulating a theology of religions or whether we also need disciplines that help us to understand the religions we encounter in our world. We might approach this issue by examining the view of Paul Tillich, another theologian who late in his career tried to develop a Christian understanding of the religions.

In *Christianity and the Encounter of World Religions*, Tillich offers an influential definition of religion as "the state of being grasped by an ultimate concern, a concern which qualifies all other concerns as preliminary and which itself contains the answer to the question of the meaning of life."[69] Tillich's definition has been used both as a Christian theological account of human religiosity and as a phenomenological description of the religions we observe. But is religion, by Tillich's definition, something that applies to all human

---

67. Ibid., 343. For a helpful discussion of the relation of Pure Land Buddhist teachings to Protestant Christian understandings of salvation by grace alone, see Timothy C. Tennent, *Theology in the Context of World Christianity* (Grand Rapids, MI: Zondervan, 2007), chap. 6.

68. Most evangelicals will not accept what seems to be an implicit universalism in Barth's soteriology. With respect to the salvation of non-Christians, Barth maintains that ultimately, no "aversion, rebellion, or resistance on the part of non-Christians will be strong enough to resist the fulfillment of the promise of the Spirit which is pronounced over them too...or to hinder the overthrow of their ignorance in the knowledge of Jesus Christ and therefore of themselves as creatures reconciled in Him." Barth, *Church Dogmatics* 4:3, 355. On evangelicals and universalism, see chapter 4 above.

69. Paul Tillich, *Christianity and the Encounter of World Religions* (New York: Columbia University Press, 1963), 4.

beings or just to a subset of humankind? How inclusive is the concept of religion? Is everyone religious? Or does *religion* denote ways of thinking and behaving found among some people but not among others? While it certainly captures much of what is commonly associated with religious commitment, Tillich's definition is so broad that it excludes very little from the religious domain—virtually *everyone* is religious by his definition.

Such an understanding has certain theological advantages. Many theologians, for example, insist that all people, regardless of protestations to the contrary, are really inherently religious. Even those explicitly claiming to be nonreligious, even atheists, are religious in Tillich's sense, since there is something that for them serves as their ultimate commitment. This fits nicely with the Christian claim that no one is neutral with respect to God; each person stands in some relation to God the Creator, even if it is a relation of rebellion. As Johannes Blauw put it, "A man without 'religion' is a contradiction in itself.... Man is 'uncurably religious' because his relation to God belongs to the very essence of man himself. Man is only man as man-before-God."[70] As a theological judgment about human beings' response to God, this is undoubtedly correct. But here religion, or human religiosity, has become something that applies to all human beings, something that is an essential part of them as God's creatures. Religion, then, is something like a worldview. Everyone has one, and one's worldview reflects one's general orientation toward God, either worshipping God or resisting God.

But this raises the question of the purpose of a definition of *religion*. If the term *religion* is being used descriptively to pick out certain groups but not others or to refer to some ways of living as opposed to other ways, then Tillich's definition is not helpful, for it includes too much.[71] As we observe the ways in which people live, there is an important distinction to be made between those who, for example, believe in an eternal creator who has revealed himself to us, whether in the Bible or in the Qur'an, and who try to live in accordance with this conviction, and those who believe that this life is all there is and that there is nothing beyond the physical world to which we are accountable. These are two very different ways of living and understanding reality. We need some way to distinguish these groups, and the word *religious* is an appropriate category

---

70. Johannes Blauw, "The Biblical View of Man in His Religion," in *The Theology of the Christian Mission*, edited by Gerald H. Anderson (New York: McGraw-Hill, 1961), 32.

71. "Like any other word, 'religion' is subject to the semantic law that says that the more comprehensive a word's use is, the less it is filled with distinct meaning, until it ends up an empty shell." Henrici, "The Concept of Religion," 1.

for referring to the former group but not the latter. So, if we are looking for a definition that captures this distinction, we will need one that is more restrictive than that offered by Tillich.

Whether we should adopt a theological or a descriptive, phenomenological definition of *religion* will depend on the purposes the definition is intended to serve. If the intention is to provide an explanation of religious phenomena from an explicitly Christian perspective, then a theological understanding of religion is necessary. But it is important to see that even an explicitly theological explanation presupposes the logically more basic descriptive approach to religions. Since a theological definition provides a Christian understanding of what we observe in the religions, it is crucial that the theological account reflects accurately actual religious beliefs and practices. In other words, an adequate theological understanding of religion requires not only fidelity to the teachings of Scripture but also an accurate description of the institutions, beliefs, and practices of religious people. While a theological account must go beyond merely describing religious phenomena to offer a normative framework for understanding such realities, in doing so, it must build on an accurate depiction of the beliefs and behavior under consideration. So a theological definition of religion actually presupposes a descriptive, phenomenological understanding of religion. And this comes not simply from exegeting Scripture but from careful observation of the lived realities of actual religious communities.

A Phenomenological Understanding of Religion

It is important to begin with what can be considered paradigm cases of religion, noting significant features they share, and then proceeding to the more ambiguous cases. Surely, if the word *religion* has any meaning today, then Christianity, Islam, Buddhism, and Shinto are paradigm examples of religions. What features do they, and other religions, share?

Based on common characteristics of paradigm cases of religions, Roger Schmidt and his colleagues define religions as "systems of meaning embodied in a pattern of life, a community of faith, and a worldview that articulate a view of the sacred and of what ultimately matters."[72] We will adopt this definition as characterizing religions in a descriptive, phenomenological

---

72. Roger Schmidt et al., *Patterns of Religion* (Belmont, CA: Wadsworth, 1999), 10. See also Clifford Geertz's definition of religion in Geertz, "Religion as a Cultural System," in *The Interpretation of Cultures*, 90.

manner. Religions thus involve complex, integrative systems of meaning that
are rooted in particular understandings of what is ultimately real and significant (note echoes of Tillich's definition here). For theistic religions, what is
of ultimate significance is God, and everything else derives its significance
in relation to God. Nontheistic religions ascribe ultimate significance to a
particular state (*nirvana* or *sunyata*/emptiness in Buddhism) or cosmic principle or reality (the Dao in Daoism). Furthermore, religions find expression
in specific communities of people who try to live out the religious values and
ideals. A religion calls for a particular way of life, and adherents in good standing within the religion are expected to conform to the desired way of life.
Religions, in other words, include social institutions and practices. A religion
thus provides an all-encompassing interpretive framework within which people understand themselves and what they regard as truly ultimate and order
their lives accordingly.

The multifaceted nature of religion was emphasized by Ninian Smart, who
suggested seven dimensions for understanding a given religion.[73] The *ritual*
dimension involves ordered actions that carry significant meaning within
the religious community. Prayer, meditation, almsgiving, funerals, marriage
ceremonies, and sacrifices all can involve rituals. A second dimension is the
mythological or narrative dimension. Religions typically include rich narratives
about significant figures who model appropriate behavior or stories about the
origin of the cosmos or current state of affairs. Most religions also include
the *doctrinal* and/or *philosophical* dimensions. Doctrines can be thought of as
systematic attempts to clarify and integrate the central beliefs of a religious
tradition, and philosophies associated with religions are usually attempts to
understand reality using reason apart from but subordinated to religious and
doctrinal systems.

Religions characteristically have much to say about moral values and principles, resulting in the *ethical* dimension. The *social and institutional* dimension reflects patterns and mores dictating desirable relationships among the
believers in the religious community, in addition to the institutions that provide necessary structure to the tradition. The *experiential* dimension involves
the participation of the religious believer in the various rites and patterns of the
religious tradition (e.g., through worship, prayer, meditation, etc.). Finally, the
material dimension refers to the many visible or material objects—religious

---

73. See Ninian Smart, *The World's Religions*, 2nd ed. (Cambridge, UK: Cambridge University
Press, 1998), 11–22; and Smart, *Worldviews: Crosscultural Explorations of Human Beliefs*, 2nd
ed. (Englewood Cliffs, NJ: Prentice-Hall, 1995).

art, icons, buildings, gardens, instruments to help in worship, and so on—that express religious meanings or otherwise facilitate the practice of religion. Not all religions place the same significance on each of the dimensions. For some, religious teachings or doctrines are most important; others might minimize doctrine and emphasize the social dimension or ritual.

Finally, in thinking about religion, it is important to distinguish between what is often called formal or "high" religion and "folk" religion.[74] Formal religion refers to the official teachings and practices of a given religious tradition—the institutions, beliefs, and practices enjoined by the sacred scriptures and official authorities of the religion. Formal religions generally have carefully prescribed boundaries to protect the orthodoxy of the traditions, and considerable attention is given to interpreting implications of doctrine for proper living and for understanding the world around us.

Folk religion, by contrast, refers to the religious beliefs and practices of people not particularly interested in a systematic understanding of a religion's teachings. Folk religion often acknowledges a complex realm of spirits and demons and emphasizes the practical, existential concerns of everyday life (health, power, marriage, bountiful harvest, fear of death, the afterlife, the spirits, etc.). Folk practices often are at variance with the official teachings of high religion. But we should not assume that folk religion is "primitive" or premodern and that high religion is modern. Highly modernized societies such as Japan, Brazil, or the United States include folk religious traditions, and high religion flourished throughout Asia before the modern age.

Modernization, Globalization, and Religion

Religions change over time. This applies both to internal changes within religious traditions and to the public, social significance of religions. One way of tracking these changes is to observe the impact of modernization and globalization on religions. We might think of modernization roughly as the process of social and cultural transformation associated with the rise of industrialization, modern science, urbanization, free-market capitalism, and democratic forms of government. Premodern religions are clearly different from religious traditions that have been forced to come to grips with modernization.

Since the mid-twentieth century, we have entered a new phase in world history as geographically distant parts of the earth have become linked in

---

74. See Paul G. Hiebert, R. Daniel Shaw, and Tite Tiénou, *Understanding Folk Religion* (Grand Rapids, MI: Baker, 1999).

unprecedented ways. *Globalization* is the term used to refer to this new level of interconnectedness worldwide. Global connections are not necessarily new. Trade, war, and migrations of people linked people throughout the ancient world, and since the European voyages of discovery in the sixteenth century, cultures around the globe have been increasingly interconnected. But the late twentieth century introduced something new. As Nayan Chanda points out, "The big differences that mark the globalization of the early years with that of the present are in the *velocity* with which products and ideas are transferred, the ever-growing *volume* of consumers and products and their *variety*, and the resultant increase in the *visibility* of the process."[75]

At the heart of globalization is the reality that local patterns are shaped in significant ways by developments elsewhere. For Malcolm Waters, globalization is "a social process in which the constraints of geography on economic, political, social, and cultural arrangements recede, in which people become increasingly aware that they are receding, and in which people act accordingly."[76] Globalization is thus a process involving increased interrelatedness across traditional boundaries in multiple dimensions, including politics, economics, culture, and religion.

Globalization has affected religion in profound ways. Mark Juergensmeyer reminds us that religion has always been global, as "religious communities and traditions have always maintained permeable boundaries. They have moved, shifted, and interacted with one another around the globe. . . . Religion is global in that it is related to the global transportation of peoples, and of ideas."[77] Some religions in particular have moved intentionally across boundaries, becoming part of new cultural settings. Religions such as Christianity, Islam, and Buddhism are what Juergensmeyer calls transnational religions, or "religious traditions with universal pretensions and global ambitions." In these religions, "at the core of their faith is the notion that their religion is greater than any local group and cannot be confined to the cultural boundaries of any particular region."[78]

---

75. Nayan Chanda, *Bound Together: How Traders, Preachers, Adventurers, and Warriors Shaped Globalization* (New Haven, CT: Yale University Press, 2007), xiii; emphasis in original.

76. Malcolm Waters, *Globalization*, 2nd. ed. (New York: Routledge, 2001), 5.

77. Mark Juergensmeyer, "Thinking Globally about Religion," in *The Oxford Handbook of Global Religions*, edited by Mark Juergensmeyer (New York: Oxford University Press, 2006), 4–5.

78. Ibid., 7.

Buddhist Transformations

Buddhism is a good example of a transnational religion that has spread far beyond its point of origin to become a genuinely global religion. As it moved from the Indian subcontinent into northern and eastern Asia and then to North America and Europe, it changed in significant ways. The transformations were stimulated both by Buddhism's encounter with new local cultural and religious settings and the radical challenges posed by modernization, Western colonialism, and interactions with Christian missions. What we have in the highly modernized sectors of Asia and in the West are forms of Buddhism that have adapted to fresh circumstances and consequently sometimes bear little resemblance to forms of Buddhism in premodern Asia.

Siddhartha Gautama (traditionally, 563–483 B.C.), the founder of Buddhism, was born into a wealthy chieftain's family in northern India.[79] Determined to find the cause of suffering and pain, he rejected his luxurious lifestyle and became a wandering ascetic. After much meditation and ascetic discipline, Gautama experienced "enlightenment" and for the next forty years traveled throughout India preaching the dharma (truth) and attracting a large following.

The heart of the Buddha's (literally "awakened one") teaching is the Four Noble Truths. The First Truth states that all existence is characterized by *dukkha* ("suffering," "pain," or "discontent"). The Second Truth holds that the root cause of suffering is *tanha* (literally "thirst" but often translated as "desire"). It is not simply wrong desires but desire itself that results in suffering. The Third Truth says that when desire ceases, then suffering also ceases. The Fourth Truth introduces the Noble Eightfold Path, which sets out ideals in moral self-discipline, meditation, and wisdom that provide the way to eliminate desire and suffering.

The Buddha held that everything that exists is characterized by *anitya*, or impermanence, and is continually coming into being and passing out of being as a result of certain interrelated causal conditions. The Buddha rejected contemporary Hindu views about the reality of an enduring self (atman), an indestructible soul, which passes from one life to another. He claimed that belief in a substantial self is mistaken and results in the grasping or desire

---

79. Good introductions to Buddhism can be found in Donald S. Lopez Jr., *The Story of Buddhism: A Concise Guide to its History and Teachings* (New York: HarperCollins, 2001); Donald W. Mitchell, *Buddhism: Introducing the Buddhist Experience*, 2nd ed. (New York: Oxford University Press, 2008). For recent developments, see Terry C. Muck, "Missiological Issues in the Encounter with Emerging Buddhism," *Missiology* 28, no. 1 (January 2000): 35–46.

that produces suffering. What we normally think of as a person is merely the ever-changing combination of psychophysical forces—the "Five Aggregates" of matter, sensations, perceptions, mental formations, and consciousness. At death, what passes from this life to the next is not a soul but simply the cumulative karmic effects of actions that then produce in the next life the (mistaken) perception of an enduring person. Only nirvana is permanent, unconditioned, and ultimately real. But nirvana is not heaven or paradise in a Christian sense.[80] Rather, it is a state that is realized when the fires of desire and the conditions producing rebirth are eliminated. Since it is the absence of suffering in any form, it is a state of utter bliss. Yet because nirvana is said to be a realm without consciousness or beings, we would be mistaken to think that nirvana is a place where human souls will eventually feel bliss. There is no soul, hence nothing like Christian understandings of paradise.

Buddhism today is divided into two major groups, although with globalization, the distinctions between these families are breaking down. Theravada Buddhism, found in Sri Lanka, Burma, Thailand, Laos, and Kampuchea, accepts only the writings of the Pali canon as authoritative, emphasizes the Four Noble Truths in attaining nirvana, and generally avoids metaphysical speculation. Early Buddhists rejected Hindu belief in Brahman, and this atheism is retained in Theravada. Moreover, each person is said to be responsible for attaining his or her own enlightenment ("self-effort"), which is restricted to the few who can master the required disciplines.

Mahayana Buddhism is today found in China, Korea, Vietnam, Japan, and the West and includes a wide variety of schools. It has developed its own sacred texts and metaphysical doctrines. Whereas Theravada Buddhism emphasizes self-effort in attaining nirvana, Mahayana opened the way to the masses by acknowledging a vast multitude of spiritual beings, such as the bodhisattvas, who assist in the quest for enlightenment. Moreover, the Pure Land schools, the most popular form of Buddhism in Japan today, teach that rebirth in the Pure Land (a kind of Buddhist paradise) is possible, not by one's own efforts but solely by relying on the compassion, merit, and "other power" of the Amida Buddha. Although Theravada Buddhism regards Gautama largely as an extraordinary human being who attained enlightenment, Mahayana developed the metaphysically sophisticated doctrine of the Three Bodies of the Buddha (*Trikaya*).

---

80. On a popular level, however, lay Buddhists often do think of nirvana as a kind of paradise. In particular, in the later Pure Land traditions of Mahayana Buddhism in China and Japan, the Pure Land is often regarded as a paradise or heaven.

Buddhism has always been a missionary religion, moving intentionally beyond India, its land of origin, into southern and eastern Asia. As Buddhism spread, it encountered cultures and religious traditions very different from those of the Indian subcontinent. Mahayana Buddhism has been remarkably flexible in adapting to new environments. This is evident, for example, in Buddhism's encounter with indigenous Chinese culture and religion. When Buddhism entered China in the first century A.D., Confucianism and Daoism were already well established. The social and ethical framework of the Chinese, shaped by Confucianism, was based on the family, not the individual, and emphasized the virtue of filial piety (*hsiao*). Given the emphasis on filial piety and the ancestral cult, the individualism of Indian Buddhism, exemplified in the ideal of the celibate monk, made Buddhism seem suspect.[81] Thus Buddhism was attacked by Confucians for being socially subversive. One way Buddhists tried to show their support for Confucian values was by adopting the ancient practices of the ancestral cult and funeral rites.

Moreover, the notions of samsara (the repetitive cycle of rebirths) and karma, so central to Indian religious and philosophical thought, were lacking in the Chinese context. Release from samsara was not the burning issue for the Chinese that it had been for the Indians. Consequently, one finds in Buddhism in China, Korea, and Japan a decreasing emphasis on the notion of nirvana as release from samsara and greater stress on the much more positive notion of enlightenment in this life. The ideal became not so much release from samsara as harmony within the social and cosmic order, which is achieved through a penetrating and liberating insight into the true nature of reality.

As it spread throughout eastern Asia, Buddhism did not reject the popular indigenous religious cults and practices. It absorbed them. Buddhism adopted the ancient ancestor-veneration practices, common in China and Japan, and popular local deities were included in the Buddhist pantheon as buddhas or bodhisattvas. When it entered Japan in the sixth century, for example, Buddhism encountered the indigenous Japanese religion of Shinto, with its worship of the ubiquitous kami (deities). Early Shinto was largely hostile to the foreign religion, but eventually, Buddhism and Shinto achieved a kind of rapprochement, in which the original nature of the Shinto kami was said to be Buddha and the many kami were seen as the Buddha's manifestations

81. Kenneth K. S. Ch'en, *The Chinese Transformation of Buddhism* (Princeton, NJ: Princeton University Press, 1973), 15.

in Japan.[82] While relations between Buddhism and Shinto over the centuries have been uneasy at best, most Japanese today regard the two religions as complementary. Popular Buddhism in Japan thus includes worship of a vast pantheon of deities and higher beings, adapted from Shinto and folk religion.

Until recent times, Buddhism was found almost exclusively in Asia. But Buddhism has now come to the West and is establishing itself as a significant part of the religious tapestry of Europe and North America. The result has been the transformation, to some extent, of both Buddhism and the religious landscape of the West.[83] Recent scholars have demonstrated that what is known today as Buddhism—not only in the West but also in many modern Asian societies—is not simply a faithful transmission of the ancient teachings but rather a fresh kind of Buddhism shaped through encounters with Western colonialism, Christian missions, and modernization. In a seminal study, David McMahan refers to this as Buddhist modernism: "What many Americans and Europeans often understand by the term 'Buddhism,' however, is actually a modern hybrid tradition with roots in the European Enlightenment no less than the Buddha's enlightenment, in Romanticism and transcendentalism as much as the Pali canon, and in the clash of Asian cultures and colonial powers as much as in mindfulness and meditation."[84]

McMahan identifies three developments at the heart of Buddhist modernism: detraditionalization, demythologization, and psychologization.[85] Detraditionalization involves the modern tendencies to elevate reason, experience, and intuition over traditional practices and authority structures, so that Buddhist practice becomes individualized and privatized, a matter of personal choice. With demythologization, traditional Buddhist beliefs regarded as problematic for modern people—belief in the many levels of hell, meritorious actions, rebirth not only as humans but also as animals or hungry

---

82. See Ian Reader, *Religion in Contemporary Japan* (London: Macmillan, 1991), 38–40.

83. See Richard Hughes Seager, *Buddhism in America* (New York: Columbia University Press, 1999); Robert Wuthnow and Wendy Cadge, "Buddhists and Buddhism in the United States: The Scope and the Influence," *Journal for the Scientific Study of Religion* 43, no. 3 (2004): 361–378; James William Coleman, *The New Buddhism: The Western Transformation of an Ancient Tradition* (New York: Oxford University Press, 2001); *Westward Dharma: Buddhism Beyond Asia*, edited by Charles S. Prebish and Martin Baumann (Berkeley: University of California Press, 2002).

84. David L. McMahan, *The Making of Buddhist Modernism* (New York: Oxford University Press, 2008), 5. See also *Buddhism in the Modern World*, edited by David L. McMahan (London: Routledge, 2012).

85. McMahan, *The Making*, 42–59.

ghosts, and the existence of demons, spirits and gods—are ignored or reinterpreted in nonliteral terms. Similarly, during the past century, Buddhism has become especially linked to Western psychology, with Buddhist metaphysical claims being translated into psychoanalytic language and the interior life of the mind. Buddhism becomes a form of spiritual therapy that can be practiced quite apart from accepting the traditional doctrines it has advanced.[86]

Buddhist modernism is found not only in the West but also among well-educated Buddhists throughout Asia. Jay Garfield points out that "the effect of Western influence upon Buddhist Asia is not negligible: it is issuing in the dramatic, rapid transformation of those cultures. Asian Buddhist cultures are not only absorbing Western technologies and popular culture but also Western approaches to Buddhism itself, and this is often mediated by Western Buddhist texts and Western translations of Asian Buddhist texts."[87]

An especially interesting case is the transformation of Buddhism in nineteenth-century Ceylon, resulting in what has been called Protestant Buddhism.[88] Provoked by both British colonialist policies and Christian missionary practices and guided by the virulently anti-Christian pioneers of the Theosophical Society, Madame Blavatsky and Colonel Henry Steel Olcott, Buddhism in Ceylon enjoyed a resurgence of popularity and redefined itself as a tradition of ancient wisdom that is fully compatible with modern science and tolerant of all faiths. Yet even as Buddhism provided a protest movement against Western colonialism and Christian missions, it was itself heavily influenced by Protestant Christianity, especially in the increased significance given the laity and the greater emphasis placed on the written text in modern Buddhism. In 1881, the Theosophist Olcott published in English *A Buddhist Catechism*, an attempt to combine elements from various Buddhist traditions into one work that set out the basic tenets that all Buddhists should be able to accept. *A Buddhist Catechism* would eventually go through more than forty

---

86. For a good example of Buddhist modernism, see Stephen Batchelor, *Buddhism without Beliefs: A Contemporary Guide to Awakening* (New York: Riverhead, 1997).

87. Jay L. Garfield, "Translation as Transmission and Transformation," in *TransBuddhism: Transmission, Translation, Transformation*, edited by Nalini Bhushan, Jay L. Garfield, and Abraham Zablocki (Amherst: University of Massachusetts Press, 2009), 90.

88. See Richard Gombrich and Gananath Obeyesekere, *Buddhism Transformed: Religious Change in Sri Lanka* (Princeton, NJ: Princeton University Press, 1988); Richard Gombrich, *Theravada Buddhism: A Social History from Ancient Benares to Modern Colombo* (London: Routledge & Kegan Paul, 1988), chap. 7.

editions and be translated into more than twenty languages, and it was used in Sri Lankan schools into the late twentieth century.[89]

For many in the West, Buddhism has become identified with Zen Buddhism or, better, with a particular understanding of Zen. No one was more effective at shaping and propagating Zen to the West than the Japanese scholar and Buddhist missionary Daisetzu Taitaro Suzuki (1870–1966).[90] A disciple of Shaku Soen, a Buddhist participant in the 1893 World's Parliament of Religions in Chicago, Suzuki was introduced through Soen to Paul Carus (1852–1919), a prominent publisher. Carus, who had rejected the orthodox Christianity of his youth in favor of "a religion of science," was attracted to Buddhism.[91] In 1897, Suzuki moved to La Salle, Illinois, to work with Carus as a translator at Open Court Publishing. Thus began a long and prolific career for Suzuki as the major interpreter of Buddhism for the West. As a result of his many publications (more than a hundred books and articles on Buddhism), lectures, and extensive contacts with Western intellectuals, Suzuki became the most influential spokesman for Zen in the West.

Suzuki was an accomplished scholar and made important contributions to Buddhist studies. He was also highly effective in generating interest in Buddhism among Western audiences and in communicating paradoxical teachings in attractive ways. Suzuki is often regarded by Westerners as a dispassionate, rigorous scholar whose depiction of Zen is simply an objective restatement of ancient Buddhism for modern Western audiences. In fact, however, Suzuki's approach was highly controversial among Asian Buddhists: "Japanese Zen Buddhists were often astounded at the transformations Zen was undergoing in the West, and they differentiated between the

---

89. Stephen Prothero, *The White Buddhist: The Asian Odyssey of Henry Steel Olcott* (Bloomington: Indiana University Press, 1996), 101. Gombrich observes: "This document...deserves to rank as a Theosophical rather than a Buddhist creed. But this is not widely realized, notably in Britain, where the connections between Theosophy and organized Buddhism have been intimate." Gombrich, *Theravada Buddhism*, 186. Theosophists also exerted some influence on late-nineteenth-century Japanese Buddhism. See Yoshinaga Shin'ichi, "Theosophy and Buddhist Reformers in the Middle of the Meiji Period," *Japanese Religions* 34, no. 2 (July 2009): 119–131; Akai Toshio, "Theosophical Accounts in Japanese Buddhist Publications of the Late Nineteenth Century," *Japanese Religions* 34, no. 2 (July 2009): 187–208.

90. Suzuki provides two autobiographical accounts in his "Early Memories" and "An Autobiographical Account," both in *A Zen Life: D. T. Suzuki Remembered*, edited by Masao Abe (New York: Weatherhill, 1986), 3–26.

91. See Martin J. Verhoeven, "Americanizing the Buddha: Paul Carus and the Transformation of Asian Thought," in *The Faces of Buddhism in America*, edited by Charles S. Prebish and Kenneth K. Tanaka (Berkeley: University of California Press, 1998), 207–227.

traditional form of Japanese Zen and that which they called 'Suzuki Zen.'"[92] What Suzuki presented to the West was not simply the ancient dharma in English. It was a carefully crafted ideal of spirituality that essentialized "Eastern wisdom" in Japanese terms and offered it as an antidote to the crass materialism and rationalism of the West.

Suzuki's views were not simply the product of ancient Buddhist teachings but reflected various external influences. Between 1903 and 1924, for example, when his early writings on Zen were taking shape, Suzuki had strong interests in both Swedenborgianism and the Theosophical Society.[93] Suzuki translated four works of the mystic Emanuel Swedenborg (1688–1772) into Japanese and published a book-length study of Swedenborg in 1913. In the 1920s, Suzuki and his American wife, Beatrice, opened a Theosophical Lodge in Kyoto. Suzuki's approach to Zen reflected multiple influences, including the rising ethnic nationalism of Japan; Suzuki's encounters with Christianity, Swedenborgianism, and Theosophy; the views of philosopher and psychologist William James; and his reaction to modernity and the materialism of the West.

Suzuki emphasized the paradoxical and irrational elements in Japanese Zen, treating this as a central characteristic of Buddhism in general. For example, Suzuki spoke of the "irrationality" of satori (enlightenment), which was said to be a "pure," immediate experience of enlightenment that transcends concepts, doctrines, and rational reflection.[94] With Suzuki, the "nondual" experience of satori became central to Buddhism. But critics pointed out that this view was at odds with other traditional streams of Buddhism.[95] Buddhism has historically given careful attention to issues in logic and epistemology, and Theravada Buddhists in particular have emphasized the rationality of Buddhist principles.[96]

---

92. Heinrich Dumoulin, *Zen Enlightenment: Origins and Meaning*, translated by Joseph C. Maraldo (New York: Weatherhill, 1979), 7.

93. See Thomas Tweed, "American Occultism and Japanese Buddhism: Albert J. Edmunds, D. T. Suzuki, and Translocative History," *Japanese Journal of Religious Studies* 32, no. 2 (2005): 249–281.

94. Daisetz T. Suzuki, *The Essentials of Zen Buddhism: Selected from the Writings of Daisetz T. Suzuki*, edited by Bernard Phillips (Westport, CT: Greenwood, 1962), 163.

95. Dumoulin, *Zen Enlightenment*, 6.

96. See Hajime Nakamura, "Unity and Diversity in Buddhism," in *The Path of the Buddha*, edited by Kenneth W. Morgan (New York: Ronald Press, 1956), 372; K. N. Jayatilleke, *The Message of the Buddha*, edited by Ninian Smart (New York: Free Press, 1974), 43–44.

Suzuki also presented Japanese Zen as capturing the "essence" of not only Buddhism but "Eastern spirituality" in general. But critics charged that such essentializing of Buddhism ignores the historical roots of Zen and the great variety within Buddhism.[97] Suzuki did not hesitate to disparage the Theravada tradition as inadequately comprehending the core teachings of Gautama. The earlier Buddhists, we are told, were incapable of grasping the exalted teaching of the Buddha's enlightenment, which is captured in Zen.[98] For Suzuki, Zen expressed a uniquely Japanese spirituality, which itself exemplified the best of Asian thought and life. In a typical passage, Suzuki states that "in Zen are found systematized or rather crystallized, all the philosophy, religion, and life itself of the Far-Eastern people, especially the Japanese."[99] Robert Sharf observes that for Suzuki, "while Zen experience is the universal ground of religious truth, it is nonetheless an expression of a uniquely *Japanese* spirituality.... Zen is touted as the very heart of Asian spirituality, the essence of Japanese culture, and the key to the unique qualities of the Japanese race."[100] Needless to say, not only other Asian Buddhists but also Hindus, Sikhs, Jains, and Daoists would dispute the identification of "Eastern spirituality" with Japanese Zen.

As we have seen from this short look at Buddhism, religions are fluid and can change over time. There are several implications that follow for our understanding of religions. First, in trying to understand contemporary religious movements, it is not sufficient merely to study their historical roots and ancient doctrines. We must also examine how adherents of a religious tradition today understand their own tradition, especially when current perceptions are different from previous understandings within that tradition. While this is especially relevant for understanding Buddhist movements in the West, it is also relevant to the study of Asian Buddhist communities, since they are undergoing changes induced by modernization and globalization.

---

97. Dumoulin, *Zen Enlightenment*, 6.

98. See, for example, D. T. Suzuki, *Essays in Zen: First Series* (New York: Weidenfeld, 1961 [1949]), 164–166. For a contrasting Theravada perspective on Zen, see David Kalupahana, *Buddhist Philosophy: A Historical Analysis* (Honolulu: University of Hawaii Press, 1976), 163–177.

99. Suzuki, *The Essentials*, 8.

100. Robert Sharf, "The Zen of Japanese Nationalism," in *Curators of the Buddha: The Study of Buddhism under Colonialism*, edited by Donald S. Lopez Jr. (Chicago: University of Chicago Press, 1995), 128, 111; emphasis in the original.

Second, a religion can change so much as it moves from one context to another that it is no longer identifiable as the same religion. After fifteen hundred years of interaction with Japanese culture and indigenous religious traditions, Japanese Buddhism has become so different from what originally emerged in India twenty-five hundred years ago that some Japanese Buddhist scholars today question whether some of the more popular forms of Japanese Buddhism are really even Buddhist.[101] Similar questions arise with respect to new forms of Christianity and Islam as these religions become globalized.

This naturally raises the issue of how much change is acceptable within a religion before it loses its identity. Is Suzuki's Zen really Buddhism? Who decides what is authentically Buddhist? But while this question is a legitimate one for scholars of religion—and certainly for Buddhists themselves—there is a sense in which it is irrelevant for missiology. For in the missiological encounter with a given religious tradition, what is of most importance are the current self-understandings of adherents of that religious tradition. Thus, for example, in an encounter with Western Buddhists who have largely embraced Suzuki's depiction of Zen, what matters is not so much whether Suzuki's portrayal is consistent with ancient Buddhist traditions but rather the Western Zen Buddhists' current understanding and practice of Zen. For it is at that level that an encounter between their religious commitments and the gospel of Jesus Christ must occur. But whether the current manifestations of Buddhism in the West are authentically Buddhist or form a fresh religious innovation distinct from classical Buddhism is a matter for Buddhists themselves to resolve.

Third, the fact that religions change over time also has implications for missiological discussions of contextualization. The meanings of rituals, special terms, or institutions can change over time, so that we cannot settle debates over current issues simply by tracing the historical roots of particular terms or practices. In some cases, what once clearly had religious meanings can come to have meanings that are not obviously religious. A good example is the tea ceremony (*cha-no-yu*) in Japan, which originally was strongly influenced by the principles and values of Zen Buddhism and was initially conducted in Buddhist monasteries.[102] But the tea ceremony today is no longer thought

---

101. See Paul L. Swanson, "Why They Say Zen Is Not Buddhism: Recent Japanese Critiques of Buddha-Nature," in *Pruning the Bodhi Tree: The Storm over Critical Buddhism*, edited by Jamie Hubbard and Paul L. Swanson (Honolulu: University of Hawaii Press, 1997), 3–29.

102. See G. B. Sansom, *Japan: A Short Cultural History* (Stanford, CA: Stanford University Press, 1952), 345, 400; D. T. Suzuki, *Zen and Japanese Culture* (Princeton, NJ: Princeton University Press, 1959), starting at 272.

of as Buddhist so much as simply a Japanese cultural ceremony, and some Japanese Christian pastors have become masters of the ceremony, using it to establish ties between the Christian community and non-Christian Japanese. So in attempts to contextualize the gospel in local settings, it is not sufficient to trace the historical meanings of a particular term or practice. What must be determined are its current meaning and significance.

Religions and Cultures

From the preceding discussion, it is clear that religions and cultures are closely related. The categories of religion and culture overlap and share many things in common, yet they are distinct, and neither can simply be reduced to the other. Although the terms *culture* and *religion* can be used in English in the singular to refer to generic categories, thus suggesting that there is such a thing as culture or religion in the abstract, both concepts are rooted in the lived realities of particular cultures and particular religions. In thinking about religion, we are not concerned with the abstract, generic category of religion but rather with communities of people who "are religious" in identifiable ways—as Buddhists or Hindus or Muslims.

The similarities between religion and culture are evident when we think of religion in terms of the dimensions identified by Ninian Smart. The ritual, social, ethical, and material dimensions of religion overlap with what we normally speak of as societies or cultures. Since religions do not exist in abstraction but are the product of religious communities, it is not surprising to see this overlap with cultures. All religions, as rooted in communities of the faithful, include a social and cultural component. As we have seen in the example of Buddhism, the cultural expression of a given religion can change considerably as the religion adjusts to fresh cultural contexts.

But there clearly are differences between religion and culture. For example, although all religions include a cultural dimension, so long as we think of religion in terms of the definition offered by Schmidt above, it is not clear that all cultures include a religious dimension. There can be, and certainly seem to be today, societies or cultures that are nonreligious, or at least in which religious commitments have little social significance. So although we can conceive of cultures that have no obvious religious component, we cannot think of religions without some cultural manifestations.

Furthermore, the concepts of religion and culture are not coextensive, so that neither can be reduced to the other. For although religions are always culturally embedded, they also transcend particular cultures, so that *religion* and *culture* are not interchangeable terms. A religion such as Buddhism finds expression in many different societies and cultures, so that we have Thai Buddhism, Chinese Buddhism, Japanese Buddhism, and American Buddhism. Despite the many differences in the expression of Buddhism in these contexts, it is still Buddhism that we are talking about in these various cultures. Thai culture and American culture are quite different, and yet the same religion can find expression in both. Similarly, although there are various cultural expressions of Christianity—American Christianity, Kenyan Christianity, Korean Christianity—there is an important sense in which Christianity as a religion is distinct from any of these particular cultural expressions. Although the Christian gospel is always expressed in particular linguistic and cultural forms, it cannot be simply identified with any such cultural expression.

We noted earlier in this chapter that it is possible for a person or a group to be part of several distinct cultures simultaneously. A Pakistani American might, for example, simultaneously be part of American culture in general, second-generation Pakistani immigrant culture, Muslim culture, and the culture of doctoral students at the University of Chicago. Each of these cultural contexts is somewhat distinctive, but there is no reason the same person cannot participate in them simultaneously.

But can we say the same about religion? Can one have more than one religious identity at the same time? On the one hand, there are religious and social contexts in which an individual does identify with several religious traditions simultaneously. Studies of Japanese religions, for example, regularly record numbers of adherents of Shinto, Buddhism, and the various new religious movements that far exceed the total Japanese population, as many Japanese will self-identify with two or more religious traditions simultaneously.[103] Many Japanese do not think it strange to participate in more than one religious tradition. This raises obvious difficulties for Christians, who traditionally have not regarded such multiple religious belonging as an option.

But multiple religious belonging also is a growing phenomenon among Christians, especially in the West, who choose to identify with more than one religious tradition. Interfaith marriages are on the rise. And growing numbers of people say that they identify with more than one religious tradition.[104] Alan

---

103. See Reader, *Religion in Contemporary Japan*, 6; Jan Van Bragt, "Multiple Religious Belonging of the Japanese People," in *Many Mansions? Multiple Religious Belonging and Christian Identity*, edited by Catherine Cornille (Maryknoll, NY: Orbis, 2002), 7–19.

104. See Amy Frykhom, "Double Belonging: One Person, Two Faiths," *Christian Century* (January 25, 2011): 20–23.

Watts, for example, who became disillusioned with the Church of England, turned to the East and became a popular promoter of Zen in the West in the 1960s and '70s, characterized his own hybrid spirituality as "between Mahayana Buddhism and Taoism, with a certain leaning towards Vedanta and Catholicism, or rather the Orthodox Church of Eastern Europe."[105] Spiritual eclecticism is increasingly accepted in the West. The prominent Roman Catholic theologian Paul Knitter identifies himself as both a Christian and a Buddhist. Baptized as a Christian in 1939, Knitter publicly identified himself also as a Buddhist in 2008. But his new Buddhist identity is not meant to supersede his Christian identity. "For me," declares Knitter, "not only does double-belonging seem to work. It's necessary! The only way I can be religious is by being interreligious. I can be a Christian only by also being a Buddhist."[106]

Knitter's double-belonging stems from his commitments as a religious pluralist, and few evangelicals will follow him down that path. However, questions about double-belonging confront evangelicals in other ways. As we have seen, the debates among missiologists over C4 and C5 contextualization—whether a follower of Jesus can also self-identify as a Muslim and participate in Muslim rituals—concern questions about religious identity and whether a Christian should, in certain contexts, embrace language and practices that usually identify one as a Muslim. Is the term *Muslim* primarily a marker of religious identity, or does it also include social and cultural identity? Perhaps it is easiest to think of multiple religious identity in cases where the line between religion and culture is especially blurry, as with Confucianism. Thus, it does not seem as problematic to think in terms of a Confucian Christian as it does to think of a Buddhist Christian. And perhaps the C5 model is most plausible in cases in which the Islamic markers seem more cultural than religious.

The issue of multiple religious identities seems to indicate a difference in how we think of cultures and religions. It makes sense in some contexts to think of someone participating in several distinct cultural contexts simultaneously, because we do not normally think of cultures as being mutually incompatible. But one difficulty with multiple religious identification, at least in many cases, is the fact that religions, unlike cultures, include teachings or doctrines, and some of the central beliefs of the major religions are mutually incompatible. Can one be a genuine follower of Theravada Buddhism, which

105. As cited in *Asian Religions in America: A Documentary History*, edited by Thomas A. Tweed and Stephen Prothero (New York: Oxford University Press, 1999), 229.

106. Paul F. Knitter, *Without Buddha I Could Not Be a Christian* (Oxford, UK: Oneworld, 2009), 216.

denies the reality of both the soul and Brahman, while also fully embracing Vedanta Hinduism, which affirms the reality of both? Can one really be a traditional Christian, affirming the incarnation in Jesus of Nazareth and the Trinity, while also fully accepting the Islamic insistence that Jesus was merely a human prophet? And so on. Thus, one significant difference between religions and cultures is the doctrinal dimension of religion. While religions include much more than simply doctrines, they do involve fundamental claims about the nature of reality. Cultures, by contrast, do not usually involve such basic doctrines or claims about ultimate reality.[107]

This, in turn, leads to a further difference between religions and cultures. Whereas it does not make sense to speak of one culture being true or normative for all people at all times, there is an important sense in which we can speak of one religion being true and normative for all. A legitimate criticism of nineteenth-century Western missionaries is that they tended not to distinguish the gospel from European or American cultures and to assume that becoming a disciple of Jesus Christ also involved adopting Western culture. Few today would maintain that there is one culture that is somehow normative for all people in all places and times. We noted earlier the theme developed by Andrew Walls and Lamin Sanneh on the translatability of the gospel. The gospel can be translated into virtually any linguistic or cultural form, and in this sense, the gospel can become "at home" in any culture. But we cannot speak as easily of the translatability of the gospel into all religious frameworks. For some religions contain teachings and practices that are incompatible with orthodox Christian teachings, so that it makes no sense to think of translating the gospel into those religious frameworks—unless the problematic beliefs themselves were to be changed or abandoned.

Therefore, although one must qualify carefully what is meant, there is an important sense in which we can speak of one religion as being true or normative for all people. To say this is to claim that the central teachings of the religion are true and that the teachings apply to all humankind. Certainly, this is how Christians, Buddhists, and Muslims, for example, traditionally have thought about their own religion. Religions make claims about the nature of reality that are accepted by their adherents as true, and this puts religions in a category different from that of cultures.[108]

---

107. This is not to deny that basic assumptions and values are often implicit in a culture.

108. See Harold Netland, "Jesus Is the Only Way to God," in *Oxford Contemporary Dialogues*, edited by J. P. Moreland, Khaldoun Sweis, and Chad Meister (New York: Oxford University Press, 2013); *Can Only One Religion Be True? Paul Knitter and Harold Netland in Dialogue*, edited by Robert Stewart (Minneapolis, MN: Fortress, 2013).

Some Biblical Themes and the Religions

In developing an evangelical theology of religions, our understanding of religion must reflect the ambiguities in the concept and relationship between religion and culture. A helpful move in this direction was provided by the statement on religion in the Manila Declaration of the World Evangelical Fellowship, produced in 1992:

> The term "religion" refers to a complex phenomenon and it is important to distinguish between its various aspects. In many societies, religion forms an important part of their identity. As such, a diversity of religions—or, more accurately, a diversity of certain aspects of the religions—may be affirmed as part of the richness of God's good creation, although it must be immediately added that people have often sinfully used these religions, including Christianity, to create a false ultimacy and superiority for their own cultures and religious groups.
>
> Religions may also be understood as expressions of the longing for communion with God, which is an essential human characteristic since we are created in the image of God for the purpose of service to him, fellowship with him, and praise for him. Here also, while always corrupted by sin in practice, we may affirm in principle the goodness of a diversity of some aspects of the religions.
>
> We are not able, however, to affirm the diversity of religions without qualification because religions teach a path of salvation, or a concept of salvation, that is not consistent with God's saving action in Jesus Christ as recorded in the Bible. To the extent that a religion points away from Jesus Christ, we deny the validity of that religion. We would also deny the validity of the Christian religion should it fail to proclaim Jesus as the Christ, the Lord of all creation, the sole savior of the world.[109]

A viable theology of religions should capture the dialectical relationship between culture and religion and the tension between positive and negative elements in each.

In light of God's revelation in Scripture, how should we think about the phenomena we encounter in the various religions? We maintain that a biblically informed theology of religions should understand the religions in terms

---

109. "The WEF Manila Declaration," in *The Unique Christ in Our Pluralistic World*, edited by Bruce J. Nicholls (Grand Rapids, MI: Baker, 1994), 14–16.

of three interrelated biblical themes: creation and revelation, sin, and Satanic and demonic influence.

The possibility of religious expression is itself a gift of God in creation and revelation. We find among the peoples of the world the capacity to reflect on one's place within the cosmos, the awareness of a reality transcending the physical world, a yearning for the creator and life beyond physical death, the recognition that the world as we experience it is not the way it is supposed to be, and the search for ways to appease or propitiate God or the gods and to attain a better existence. All of this, which we identify with religion, is possible only because of the presence and activity of God the Father, Son, and Holy Spirit in creation and revelation, in enabling humankind to understand certain things about God and the cosmos.

Closely related to this is the notion of the *imago Dei*, that human beings are created in God's image. In particular, if we understand the image of God to include the capacities for reflection, communication, relationships with others, creative self-expression, and especially moral awareness, then it makes sense to think of the expression of these capacities in the religions as products of what God has given in creation. To be sure, with sin, these capacities are not expressed as they should be, resulting in idolatry. But the *possibility* of such expression in the first place, however misguided in actual fact, is a gift of God's grace in creation.

The doctrine of general revelation, considered in chapter 3, is also crucial for understanding religion. This is obviously closely related to the teaching on creation, as is evident in Calvin's notion of the *sensus divinitatis*. But what is especially emphasized here is God's self-revelation through the created order and human conscience, through which human beings are aware of some truths about God and our responsibility to him.

While Scripture affirms a general awareness of God and our accountability before him, it nowhere suggests that this rudimentary understanding is equally clear and complete for all persons or among cultures. It is consistent with the biblical witness to hold that the degree of precision and fullness of understanding can vary from person to person and from culture to culture. Indeed, we can expect diversity in such understanding within a society, from one generation to the next, so that there is a measure of fluidity in the specific content available through general revelation. This diversity in awareness of truth about God is reflected in cultures and religious traditions, with theistic traditions such as Islam and Judaism being much closer to Christianity than, say, Theravada Buddhism. What is emphasized in Scripture, however, is that such awareness is sufficient to hold people morally accountable to God for how they respond to it.

Thought of in these terms, the religious dimension of human life is an expression of humanity as God's creation and can be regarded, in part, as a response to God's self-revelation. As Christopher J. H. Wright puts it, "The whole human race, therefore, has the capacity of being addressed by God and of making response to him. Man is the creature who is aware of his account-ability to God."[110] Similarly, the Dutch missiologist J. H. Bavinck says, "Religion is the human answer to divine, or at least allegedly divine, revelation."[111]

The doctrines of creation and revelation have significant implications for how we think of religious others. For example, given God's general revelation and the fact that all people bear the divine image, we should not be surprised to find elements of truth and value in other religions. There is no reason to maintain that everything taught by non-Christians religions is false or that there is nothing of value in them. Not only is this not demanded by Scripture, but it is not consistent with what we see in other traditions. We can think of the religions as displaying, in varying degrees, a rudimentary awareness of God's reality through creation and general revelation.

This is not to suggest that God directly revealed himself to, say, the Buddha or Muhammad or that the sacred scriptures of the non-Christian religions are divinely inspired. But it is to acknowledge that the founding figures of other religious traditions, as human beings created in God's image and recipients of general revelation, had varying degrees of understanding of God's reality that can be reflected in their teachings and practices. Such understanding is partial and often distorted. For example, we have seen in chapter 5 that there are striking commonalities across religions in basic moral principles. One of these can be seen in the numerous expressions of the Golden Rule in the writings of the religions. But this should not be unexpected. After all, given that all people have access to God's general revelation and are created in his image, we should expect to see fundamental moral principles such as the Golden Rule reflected in the various religions. It would be surprising if this were not the case.

Furthermore, the teaching on creation in particular has implications for how we think about religious others. The unity of the human race as creatures bearing God's image means that the many differences among peoples are really secondary to what all human beings share in common. Commonalities

---

110. Christopher J. H. Wright, "The Christian and Other Religions: The Biblical Evidence," *Themelios* 9, no. 2 (1984): 4.

111. J. H. Bavinck, *The Church between Temple and Mosque* (Grand Rapids, MI: Eerdmans, 1966), 18.

across ethnic, cultural, and religious boundaries are ultimately more significant than the differences that distinguish them.

From the biblical teaching on creation and revelation, then, we can think of religions as expressions of a genuine, though misguided, search and longing for God. Persons are created in the image of God, with a capacity for being addressed by God and responding to him. In spite of sin, there remains a rudimentary awareness of God's reality and of our accountability to God. The religious dimension of humankind, then, can be seen in part as an expression of the creature reaching out for that intimacy with the creator for which we were made. This sense of longing for the divine was captured beautifully by the great North African theologian Augustine: "You [God] have made us for yourself, and our heart is restless until it rests in you."[112]

But of course, religions include more than simply expressions of humanity reaching out for God. Sin has corrupted all aspects of the human person and society, including the capacities giving expression to human religiosity. Religion, too, manifests the ravages of sin. Scripture teaches that although people have some awareness of God's reality and responsibility to him, they characteristically do not respond appropriately to this knowledge but rather suppress the truth and reject what they know to be right. This rebellion finds expression in the religious dimension of collective human life.

The paradox of humankind is that on the one hand, persons are created in the image of God and thus long for a proper relationship of the creature to the creator. But at the same time, they are rebels and sinners and thus try desperately to hide from God. While religion can be a way of reaching out to God, it can also be a means of hiding from him. Significantly, Jesus's harshest comments were directed against some of the Pharisees and some other leaders of Jewish religion, those who would have been regarded by their contemporaries as the most religious, the most pious, and the best that Judaism had to offer (Matt. 23:1–36).[113]

We must think here of sin on both the individual and the social or institutional level. To be sure, the Bible teaches that all persons are sinners. Thus,

---

112. Augustine, *Confessions*, translated by Henry Chadwick (Oxford, UK: Oxford University Press, 1991), 3.

113. Jesus criticized the hypocrisy of some Pharisees (not all, for Nicodemus and Joseph of Arimathea were Pharisees) but generally commended their teachings: "The scribes and the Pharisees sit on Moses' seat, so practice and observe *whatever* they tell you" (Matt. 23.2–3; emphasis added). Jesus' harshest criticisms were trained on the leaders of the Temple, not Jewish leaders and people generally. See Randall Buth and Brian Kvasnica, "Temple Authorities and Tithe-Evasion: The Linguistic Background and Impact of the Parable of the

there is individual sin, and each person is accountable to God for his or her sin. But sin and the effects of sin are also evident corporately, in society at large and in our social institutions. In this way, sin can become embedded structurally within cultures and religions.

Finally, a genuinely biblical perspective on other religions should also recognize that much religious activity and belief is influenced by the adversary, Satan. It would be too simplistic to hold that *all* non-Christian religious phenomena are merely Satanic in origin, but it would be equally naive to suggest that *none* of them is. The apostle Paul reminded his readers that the pagan sacrifices in Corinthian religion, which might have seemed quite innocent, were in fact offered to demons (1 Cor. 10:20). This is a sobering warning, which should caution us against undue optimism concerning non-Christian religious practices.

Both the Old and New Testaments consistently denounce as idolatry worship of other deities and participation in the rites of other religious traditions (Exod. 20:2–5; Deut 7:1–6, 7:25–26; Ps. 115; Isa. 41:21–24, 44:9–20; Acts 14:15, 17:16, 17:23–24, 17:29; 1 Cor. 8:4–6). Furthermore, Scripture speaks of those who are not yet saved as "spiritually blind" and under the power of the "god of this age" (2 Cor. 4:4; Eph. 4:17–18). We must recognize the reality of the spiritual realm, including Satan and demonic powers. There is a spiritual battle being waged between the kingdom of God and the god of this age, and demonic presence and activity are part of the religions. Too often, Western Christians have adopted a functional naturalism that while theoretically acknowledging the supernatural dimension in practice, ignores it. Thus, Paul Hiebert, for example, has called attention to the reality of what he terms the "excluded middle," a realm of "supernatural this-worldly beings and forces" that is widely acknowledged in non-Western societies.[114] In this realm, spiritual beings and forces distinct from the natural world are nevertheless understood to be present and active within it. While Western missionaries tend to ignore this dimension because of naturalistic biases, most non-Western societies assume it.

However, in calling for Western missionaries to take this reality more seriously, Hiebert also sounds an important warning: "We need to center our theology on God and his acts and not, as modern secularism and animism

Vineyard Tenants and the Son," in *Jesus's Last Week: Jerusalem Studies on the Synoptic Gospels*, Vol. 1, edited by R. S. Notley, B. Becker, and M. Turnage (Leiden: Brill, 2006), 53–80.

114. Paul Hiebert, *Anthropological Reflections on Missiological Issues* (Grand Rapids, MI: Baker, 1994), 189–201.

do, on human beings and their desires. We need to focus on worship and our relationship to God, and not on ways to control God for our own purposes through chants and formulas.... It is all too easy to make Christianity a new magic in which we as gods make God do our bidding."[115] In taking seriously the dimension of spiritual warfare, we must nevertheless avoid adopting an approach that amounts to little more than "Christian animism." Thus, in their important critique of this movement, Robert Priest, Thomas Campbell, and Bradford Mullen state: "Many missionaries and missiologists unwittingly have internalized and are propagating animistic and magical notions of spirit power which are at odds with biblical teaching, using such notions as the basis for missiological method."[116] A responsible theology of religions must avoid falling into a kind of Christian animism that regards the phenomena of other religions merely as manifestations of demonic activity and thinks of Christian response to other religions solely in terms of power encounters.

Conclusion

The concepts of culture and religion are heuristic tools that help us to sort out and understand aspects of collective human life. While they are necessary and helpful concepts, they are also ambiguous and raise some difficult questions. From the perspective of someone seeking to understand what it means to live as a disciple of Jesus Christ in today's world and to invite others to become disciples of Jesus, the most important issue is not how we draw the lines between culture and religion or whether a particular phenomenon is to be identified as religious or cultural. The important question is whether a particular teaching or pattern of behavior enables one to live as a disciple of Jesus Christ or hinders doing so. How we might conceptually categorize a belief or action is then a secondary issue.

The concern of Christians is with making disciples of Jesus Christ of all peoples, including sincere followers of other religions. Through God's guidance and power, Christians encourage those who are currently living in sinful rebellion against God to repent and become reconciled to God through Jesus Christ. To the extent that this requires rejecting belief and conduct normally identified as religious, we can speak of rejecting aspects of the religions.

---

115. Ibid., 200–201.

116. Robert J. Priest, Thomas Campbell, and Bradford A. Mullen, "Missiological Syncretism: The New Animistic Paradigm," in *Spiritual Power and Missions: Raising the Issues*, edited by Edward Rommen (Pasadena, CA: William Carey Library, 1995), 11–12.

Patterns associated with what we commonly call Hinduism, Buddhism, or Islam that inhibit a proper response to God must be rejected or modified. But where patterns of living and thinking identified as religious are either indifferent to the gospel or can be used in enabling a particular group to become disciples of Jesus Christ, making disciples would seem to involve appropriating such patterns into that group's Christian identity.

7

Christian Witness in a Multireligious World

THE CHRISTIAN FAITH is based on a message that is intended for all peoples, irrespective of geography, ethnicity, or culture. It is a message that not only conveys information but also calls for individual response. We cannot restrict the implications of the message simply to personal or individual concerns, for the Christian gospel has far-reaching social and communal implications. Nevertheless, at the heart of the New Testament gospel message is a call for a personal response of commitment to Jesus Christ as Lord.

Although this does not make the response of faith a strictly private matter, it marks a break with prevailing ancient religious views that linked religious expression to geography, ethnicity, or culture. Speaking of the early church, Lamin Sanneh observes: "The idea of faith as something personal made possible a mobile, nonterritorial response. The offer of salvation was premised on the honest and sincere conviction of persons as free agents, not on possessing a promised land. Territoriality ceased to be a requirement of faith."[1] Christians have as an integral component of their identity "the notion that their religion is greater than any local group and cannot be confined to the cultural boundaries of any particular region."[2] The Christian gospel is inherently missionary and pushes followers of Jesus to cross boundaries of geography, class, ethnicity, and religious affiliation in calling all peoples to commitment to Jesus and his kingdom. It is good news of redemption and reconciliation with God, which must be shared with a world ravaged by sin and evil.

---

1. Lamin Sanneh, *Disciples of All Nations: Pillars of World Christianity* (New York: Oxford University Press, 2008), 7.

2. Mark Juergensmeyer, "Thinking Globally about Religion," in *The Oxford Handbook of Global Religions*, edited by Mark Juergensmeyer (New York: Oxford University Press, 2006), 7.

The early Christian community—initially overwhelmingly Jewish—soon came to include both Jews and Gentiles and spread from Jerusalem to surrounding areas such as Rome, Antioch, and Alexandria. From there, the church spread throughout the Roman Empire and beyond, moving into what is now North Africa and all the way down the Nile to what is now Uganda, to South Asia, Europe, and, with the Nestorians, China. With the missionary movements of the eighteenth and nineteenth centuries and the remarkable growth of the church in the twentieth century, Christianity is today a genuinely global religion. The movement that began with Jesus and perhaps a few hundred disciples in a remote part of Palestine two thousand years ago is today "the largest and most widely disseminated religion in the world."[3] Sanneh states: "Christianity is the religion of over two thousand different language groups in the world. More people pray and worship in more languages in Christianity than in any other religion in the world."[4] It is the missionary impulse of the Christian community throughout the past twenty centuries that has resulted in a truly global church. This includes, of course, the modern missionary movements of the seventeenth through twentieth centuries, but at least as significant are the countless anonymous local Christians scattered about in the Middle East, North Africa, Europe, Asia, and Latin America who have quietly shared the gospel with their neighbors and, in ways often unknown to us, carried the gospel into new social and religious contexts.[5]

The missionary nature of the Christian gospel is something of an embarrassment to many in the West in current discussions on religious pluralism. Although most Christians today rejoice at the growth and globalization of the church, many are chagrined by the modern missions movements and the emphasis on evangelism and the need for conversion. As Lesslie Newbigin wryly observed, Western Christians are happy with the fact of the global church today, but "they are embarrassed about the thing that made it possible—namely the missions of the [nineteenth] century."[6] To be sure, there

---

3. Douglas Jacobsen, *The World's Christians: Who They Are and How They Got There* (Oxford, UK: Wiley-Blackwell, 2011), 1.

4. Lamin Sanneh, *Whose Religion Is Christianity? The Gospel beyond the West* (Grand Rapids, MI: Eerdmans, 2003), 69. See also Mark Hutchinson and John Wolffe, *A Short History of Global Evangelicalism* (Cambridge, UK: Cambridge University Press, 2012).

5. See Sanneh, *Disciples of All Nations*; Andrew F. Walls, *The Missionary Movement in Christian History: Studies in the Transmission of Faith* (Maryknoll, NY: Orbis, 1996).

6. Lesslie Newbigin, *A Word in Season: Perspectives on Christian World Missions* (Grand Rapids, MI: Eerdmans, 1994), 122.

is much in the history of modern missions that should cause us to pause and repent. Modern Western missionaries often were culturally insensitive, imposing on local peoples the social and cultural patterns of Europe or America and failing to relinquish power or control over ministries. Too often, missionaries were identified—whether intentionally or inadvertently—with political, military, and economic colonizers. Sadly, in many parts of the world, Christianity became identified with colonizing powers.

But although these mistakes and excesses must be candidly acknowledged, they should not be exaggerated. It is simplistic and misleading to dismiss modern missions as little more than the religious dimension of Western colonialism and imperialism. Individual missionaries and mission agencies often had an ambivalent relationship with colonialist institutions.[7] Although Western missionaries did benefit from the protection provided by colonialist powers, we must also remember that colonialist institutions such as the East India Company were often hostile to missionaries because they perceived missionaries as subversives who would undermine the colonizers' interests. The link between colonialism and missions was especially evident in India, yet even here the story is more complicated than often acknowledged. Consider the following observations by Vinoth Ramachandra:

Christian missions in India are routinely dismissed in contemporary Indian scholarship as simply an adjunct of colonialism. But, in fact, they were the soil from which both modern Hindu reform movements and Indian nationalism sprang. Most of the Indian intellectual and political leadership of the late nineteenth and early twentieth century emerged from Christian schools and colleges. Gandhi may have claimed to have been nurtured in the spiritual atmosphere of the *Bhavagad Gita*, but it was not from this text that he derived his philosophy of *ahimsa* (non-violence) and *satyagraha* ("truth-force"). The deepest influences on Gandhi came from the "renouncer" traditions of Jainism and the New Testament, particularly the Sermon on the Mount as mediated through the works of Tolstoy. Christians in India have long been in the forefront of movements for the emancipation of women, with missionary societies from Britain and the United States often giving the lead

7. See Brian Stanley, *The Bible and the Flag: Protestant Missions and British Imperialism in the Nineteenth and Twentieth Centuries* (Leicester, UK: InterVarsity, 1990); *Missions and Empire*, edited by Norman Etherington (New York: Oxford University Press, 2005).

where the colonial government was hesitant to tread for fear of upsetting local sensibilities.[8]

What is needed, then, is an honest assessment of the past that recognizes the ambiguous and sometimes confusing relationship between modern missions and colonialism, acknowledging both the good and the bad. Moreover, we should not assume that current mortification over modern missions is simply a matter of greater humility and cultural sensitivity today. As Newbigin observes, "The contemporary embarrassment about the missionary movement of the [nineteenth] century is not, as we like to think, evidence that we have become more humble. It is, I fear, much more clearly evidence of a shift in belief. It is evidence that we are less ready to affirm the uniqueness, the centrality, the decisiveness of Jesus Christ as universal Lord and Savior, the Way by following whom the world is to find its true goal, the Truth by which every other claim to truth is to be tested, the Life in whom alone life in its fullness is to be found."[9] Johannes Verkuyl concurs: "The subversion of the missionary mandate one encounters in various contemporary missiologies and models of theology of religions must simply be called what it is: betrayal of Jesus Christ."[10] What is needed, then, today is a model of Christian witness among religious others that is unashamedly faithful to the gospel of Jesus Christ and yet is contextually appropriate to the world of the twenty-first century.

Christian Mission

Evangelicals have been characterized by a concern for Christian mission. As we saw in chapter 1, David Bebbington identifies conversionism and activism as two of the four distinguishing marks of evangelicalism, and Alister McGrath lists the need for personal conversion and the priority of evangelism as two of the six fundamental convictions of evangelicals.[11] Not surprisingly,

---

8. Vinoth Ramachandra, *Faiths in Conflict? Christian Integrity in a Multicultural World* (Leicester, UK: InterVarsity, 1999), 78–79.

9. Newbigin, *A Word in Season*, 115.

10. Johannes Verkuyl, "The Biblical Notion of Kingdom: Test of Validity for Theology of Religion," in *The Good News of the Kingdom*, edited by Charles Van Engen, Dean S. Gilliland, and Paul Pierson (Maryknoll, NY: Orbis, 1993), 77.

11. See David Bebbington, *Evangelicalism in Modern Britain* (London: Unwin Hyman, 1989), 2–17; Alister McGrath, *Evangelicalism and the Future of Christianity* (Downers Grove, IL: InterVarsity, 1995), 55–56.

evangelicals have been strong supporters of Christian missions and have been actively involved in the modern missionary movements. Since the 1970s, there has been an ongoing discussion among evangelicals about the nature of Christian mission and how it should be conducted. Although a comprehensive treatment of the subject is impossible here, some salient themes in an evangelical understanding of mission and their implications for Christians in the twenty-first century should be noted.

Christian mission must be understood in light of the triune God and God's mission for the world. An understanding of God as Father, Son, and Holy Spirit and of God's purposes is thus crucial for an adequate understanding of the nature of Christian mission. Alan Roxburgh states: "Mission is the people of God giving witness to the reality of God through the church as the sign, foretaste, and presence of the kingdom. Mission must, therefore, be preoccupied with the nature of the One to whom it witnesses. We must speak of, announce, and witness to the God who is revealed as Father, Son, and Spirit. This revelation is only known in and through Jesus Christ. The mission of Jesus, the gospel of Jesus Christ, is the mission of the Trinitarian God who is at the heart of Jesus' revelation."[12] David Bosch also notes the centrality of the doctrine of the Trinity for a theology of mission: "Mission is, primarily and ultimately, the work of the Triune God, Creator, Redeemer, and Sanctifier, for the sake of the world, a ministry in which the Church is privileged to participate."[13] Mission is not something that the church launches on its own initiative or in its own power. Christians engage in mission only because God is a missionary God, working for the redemption of his creation. Timothy Tennent reminds us that Christian mission is more than simply a response to Christ's so-called Great Commission:

Mission, therefore, arises not simply as a response of obedience to a command given to the church (although it is never less than that) but as a joyful invitation *to participate with God* in His redemptive work in the world. God the Father is unfolding a grand narrative, of which his Son, Jesus Christ, is the central figure and we, as the church, are being called and empowered through God the Holy Spirit to participate in

---

12. Alan Roxburgh, "Rethinking Trinitarian Missiology," in *Global Missiology for the 21st Century: The Iguassu Dialogue*, edited by William D. Taylor (Grand Rapids, MI: Baker and World Evangelical Fellowship, 2000), 180.

13. David Bosch, *Transforming Mission: Paradigm Shifts in Theology of Mission* (Maryknoll, NY: Orbis, 1991), 392.

the unfolding of this grand narrative.... Therefore, mission is about simultaneously entering into the inner life of God as a missionary God, as well as entering into the world where the triune God is actively at work.[14]

God is not only holy, righteous, and morally pure but also loving, merciful, and compassionate. This character of God results in the sending of the Son by the Father and of the Spirit by the Father and the Son, for the sake of the redemption of a creation marred by sin. The sending of the church into the world is itself rooted in the prior sending of the triune God. Thus, in speaking of the mission of the Christian church in the world today, Christopher Wright observes: "Our mission (if it is biblically informed and validated) means our committed participation as God's people, at God's invitation and command, in God's own mission within the history of God's world for the redemption of God's creation."[15]

Just what is included within the scope of mission?[16] Does the term *mission* include everything that the church is called to be and to do, or is its scope more restricted? Evangelicals in the late twentieth century disagreed over what is included in mission and what, among various concerns, should have priority. But something of a consensus has emerged around the perspective of John Stott, who perhaps has had as great an influence on evangelical thinking and practice concerning Christian mission as anyone in the past half-century. According to Stott, while mission does not refer to everything that God is doing in the world or that the church is to do, it does describe "everything the church is sent into the world to do. 'Mission' embraces the church's double vocation of service to be 'the salt of the earth' and 'the light of the world.' "[17] Evangelical missiologists Donald McGavran and Arthur Glasser sound similar themes in their definition of mission as "carrying the gospel across cultural boundaries to those who owe no allegiance to Jesus Christ, and encouraging

---

14. Timothy C. Tennent, *Invitation to World Missions: A Trinitarian Missiology for the Twenty-First Century* (Grand Rapids, MI: Kregel, 2010), 61; emphasis in the original.

15. Christopher J. H. Wright, *The Mission of God: Unlocking the Bible's Grand Narrative* (Downers Grove, IL: InterVarsity, 2006), 23. See also Craig Ott and Stephen J. Strauss, *Encountering Theology of Mission: Biblical Foundations, Historical Developments, and Contemporary Issues* (Grand Rapids, MI: Baker, 2010), 61–74.

16. For a comprehensive discussion of what is included within the concept of mission, see David Bosch, *Transforming Mission*, 368–510.

17. John R. W. Stott, *Christian Mission in the Modern World* (Downers Grove, IL: InterVarsity, 1975), 30.

them to accept Him as Lord and Savior and to become responsible members of His church, working as the Holy Spirit leads, at both evangelism and justice, at making God's will done on earth as it is done in heaven."[18]

Our understanding of Christian mission must be shaped also by the biblical teaching on the kingdom of God. It is significant that the gospel of Matthew presents Jesus beginning his ministry by "preaching the good news [gospel] of the Kingdom" (Matt. 4:23); the gospel is directly linked to the kingdom of God. In Mark, Jesus begins his ministry by saying, "The time has come. The Kingdom of God is near. Repent and believe the good news" (Mark 1:14). The book of Acts ends with the apostle Paul in Rome, where he "preached the Kingdom of God and taught about the Lord Jesus Christ" (28:31).

The kingdom of God is a central, unifying theme in Scripture. Craig Ott and Stephen Strauss note: "The kingdom of God is the center of mission in the sense that it is the orientation point of mission.... The concept of the kingdom of God captures in a single phrase the divine intent to bring all things under [God's] rule, to reconcile all things to himself, to restore that which is fallen and corrupted, and to overthrow all powers in opposition to him and his reign of peace, joy, and righteousness."[19] Similarly, Johannes Verkuyl claims: "The heart of the message of the Old and New Testament is that God, the Creator of the universe and all earthly life, is actively engaged in the reestablishment of His liberating dominion over the cosmos and all of humankind."[20]

The notion of the kingdom of God is that of God's sovereign and dynamic reign. According to New Testament scholar George E. Ladd, "The Kingdom of God is the redemptive reign of God dynamically active to establish his rule among men, and...this Kingdom, which will appear as an apocalyptic act at the end of the age, has already come into human history in the person and mission of Jesus to overcome evil, to deliver men from its power, and to bring them into the blessings of God's reign."[21]

There is a tendency among some theologians of religions today to use the concept of the kingdom as a way to avoid what is perceived as excessive emphasis on the "uniqueness" of Jesus Christ. In his influential 1985 book

---

18. Donald McGavran and Arthur Glasser, *Contemporary Theologies of Mission* (Grand Rapids, MI: Baker, 1983), 26.

19. Ott and Strauss, *Encountering Theology*, 86.

20. Verkuyl, "The Biblical Notion," 72.

21. George Eldon Ladd, *A Theology of the New Testament* (Grand Rapids, MI: Eerdmans, 1974), 91. See also Ladd, *The Presence of the Future: The Eschatology of Biblical Realism* (Grand Rapids, MI: Eerdmans, 1974).

No Other Name? Paul Knitter, for example, claims that Jesus was "theocentric" and "kingdom-centric," and that Jesus's concern was simply to direct our focus to God's kingdom of righteousness and justice: "All his powers were to serve this God and this kingdom; all else took second place. 'Thy kingdom come; thy will be done' was the content of his prayer and his work."[22] Jesus did not regard himself as divine or the king. Knitter claims that "one of the essential characteristics of the Kingdom preached by Jesus was its this-worldly quality. For Jesus and for the church today, to seek the Kingdom of God is to seek the well-being of humankind in this finite world." According to Knitter, "The Kingdom of God therefore might be defined as the utopian vision of a society of love, justice, equality, based on the inner transformation or empowerment of human beings."[23] Given this understanding, it is hardly surprising that Knitter speaks of other religions as "agents of the Kingdom," "vehicles of grace," and "co-workers for the Kingdom."[24]

While we can agree with Knitter about the important "this-worldly" implications of the kingdom and rejoice whenever and wherever we find people promoting righteousness and justice, we reject reductionistic attempts to limit the kingdom to concerns in the present world. The biblical understanding of the kingdom cannot be reduced simply to moral agendas, however noble they might be. The kingdom is inherently about God's righteous reign and the transformation of sinful human beings through Christ's atoning work on the cross and the application of that work by the Spirit, so that the redeemed submit to God's reign and worship him in a restored creation. A biblically faithful understanding of the kingdom will be thoroughly Trinitarian, with a strong Christological focus on Jesus as king. As Verkuyl reminds us, "A truly Kingdom-centered theology is a thoroughly Trinitarian one: it is a theology which has God the Creator, the Redeemer, and the Comforter at its very heart."[25] One cannot speak of the kingdom of God in the New Testament without reference to the distinctive work of the Father, Son, and Holy Spirit.

In particular, in the New Testament, the coming of the kingdom is centered on the person and work of Jesus of Nazareth. Ladd states: "In Jesus the kingdom has come into history. God has done a new thing. He has visited his

22. Paul Knitter, *No Other Name? A Critical Survey of Christian Attitudes toward the World Religions* (Maryknoll, NY: Orbis, 1985), 173–175.

23. Paul Knitter, *Jesus and the Other Names* (Maryknoll, NY: Orbis, 1996), 116–117.

24. Ibid., 118–119.

25. J. Verkuyl, "The Biblical Notion," 72.

people in Jesus' mission, bringing to them the messianic salvation. The divine act requires a human response even though it remains a divine act."[26] Thus, Verkuyl rightly concludes, "A theocentric theology that is not simultaneously Christocentric simply cannot be termed Christian theology....There is no Kingdom without the King."[27] The Father has given the kingdom to the Son (Luke 22:29) so that it is in the person of the incarnate Son, Jesus of Nazareth, that the kingdom has invaded the present order and is a present reality. Jesus's ministry was empowered by the Holy Spirit (Luke 4:14), and it was through the Spirit that Jesus cast out demons, thereby demonstrating the presence of the kingdom (Matt. 12:28). And yet although it was inaugurated by Jesus's life and ministry, there also is a sense in which the kingdom is future. There is a future eschatological coming of the kingdom at the end of the age, culminating in the final judgment of the wicked and the renewal and transformation of the material order, the "new heaven and new earth" of Revelation 21. When the Son has accomplished the final defeat of "every rule and every authority and every power," including the final enemy, death, then "he delivers the kingdom to God the Father" (1 Cor. 15:24).

One objective of the divine rule—the kingdom—is the redemption of sinful human beings from the powers of sin and evil (Acts 26:16–18; 1 Cor. 15:23–28). The gospel of the kingdom is the announcement that "God is now acting among men to deliver them from bondage to Satan."[28] The connection between the kingdom of God and the mission of the church becomes clear when we consider that the church is called to participate in God's initiatives against the powers of evil. Bosch states: "Mission denotes the total task God has set the church for the salvation of the world, but always related to a specific context of evil, despair, and lostness."[29] Entrance into the kingdom means deliverance from the realm of darkness and Satan: "For he [God] has rescued us from the dominion of darkness and brought us into the kingdom of the Son he loves, in whom we have redemption, the forgiveness of sins" (Col. 1:13). Entrance into the kingdom is a supernatural event, the "new birth," which accompanies repentance. Jesus told the respected Jewish leader Nicodemus that one cannot see the kingdom of God unless he is "born again" (John 3:3). It is the special work of the Holy Spirit upon the repentant sinner that results in

---

26. Ladd, *The Presence of the Future*, 194.

27. Verkuyl, "The Biblical Notion," 77.

28. George Eldon Ladd, *The Gospel of the Kingdom* (Grand Rapids, MI: Eerdmans, 1959), 47.

29. Bosch, *Transforming Mission*, 412.

the new birth, or regeneration, and deliverance from the "dominion of dark-ness" to the kingdom of God (Jo–n 3:5-8; Titus 3:5). In light of the imminence of the kingdom, Jesus called people to repent and to align themselves with the gospel: "The time has come. The Kingdom of God is near. Repent and believe the good news" (Mark 1:15).

The proclamation of Christ's kingdom and the call to repentance are indis-pensable in Christian mission. According to Scripture, Jesus Christ is the only Lord and Savior for all humankind, including devout adherents of other reli-gions (see chapters 2 and 4 above). In obedience to the Lord and out of com-passion for the lost, we are to "make disciples" of all people (Matt. 28:18–20). Thus, a biblically faithful theology of religions must include a commitment to Christian mission—including evangelism. As Verkuyl observes, "To everyone of whatever religious persuasion the message must be repeated: 'The Kingdom of God is at hand; repent and believe in the Gospel.' In no circumstances may the Evangel be proclaimed in a neutral way. The Gospel always involves deci-sion....A theology and missiology informed by the biblical notion of the rule of Christ will never fail to identify personal conversion as one of the inclusive goals of God's Kingdom."[30] Thus, although it certainly involves much more than this, a biblical understanding of the kingdom must include the need for evangelism and conversion.

In a broad sense, the coming of the kingdom in Jesus is a direct challenge to all evil, wherever it might be and whatever form it might take. We see in Jesus' ministry the dual focus of the call to personal repentance resulting in conversion and meeting very tangible physical and social needs. Evil in both dimensions is addressed: "Jesus went throughout Galilee, teaching in their synagogues, preaching the good news of the kingdom, and healing every dis-ease and sickness among the people" (Matt. 4:23). Thus, Christian mission, too, should reflect both emphases: the call to repentance and acknowledg-ing Jesus as Lord and Savior as well as meeting the many tangible needs of people.

There are many implications from the notion of the kingdom of God as a theological foundation for our understanding of mission. Among the more significant is the truth that the triune God is already sovereignly at work throughout the world accomplishing his purposes and bringing about his rule. This has implications for how we approach our witness among religious others. Missiologist Paul Hiebert reminds us that God "is at work in the lives

---

30. Verkuyl, "The Biblical Notion," 72–73.

of the people to whom we minister, long before we come and long after we leave. It is he that saves, not we. It is he that builds the church, not we."[31]

Witness

Christ's followers are to be his witnesses, beginning locally and moving progressively "to the end of the earth" (Acts 1:8). Christians, as Christ's disciples, bear witness to the reality of God and God's redemptive love and transforming power through their lives and through verbal proclamation. The distinctively different manner of life to be found among Jesus' disciples speaks powerfully of the reality of God and brings glory to God. After speaking of his disciples as "salt and light" in the surrounding world, Jesus challenged them to "let your light shine before others, so that they may see your good works and give glory to your Father who is in heaven" (Matt. 5:16). The unity among Jesus's followers and the love they have for one another—and even for their enemies— bear witness to their identity with Christ and the fact that God's transforming power is at work in them (see Matt. 5:43–48; John 17:20–23; 1 John 3:11–24).

But it is also necessary to communicate verbally the gospel of Jesus Christ, explaining the message and urging others to accept Jesus as Lord. Thus, evangelicals have emphasized the importance of evangelism in Christian mission. The Lausanne Covenant (1974) sets out a view of evangelism that is widely adopted by evangelicals:

> To evangelize is to spread the good news that Jesus Christ died for our sins and was raised from the dead according to the Scriptures, and that as reigning Lord he now offers the forgiveness of sins and the liberating gift of the Spirit to all who repent and believe. Our Christian presence in the world is indispensable to evangelism, and so is that kind of dialogue whose purpose is to listen sensitively in order to understand. But evangelism itself is the proclamation of the historical biblical Christ as Savior and Lord, with a view to persuading people to come to him personally and so be reconciled to God.[32]

---

31. Paul Hiebert, "Evangelism, Church, and Kingdom," in *The Good News of the Kingdom*, edited by Charles Van Engen, Dean S. Gilliland, and Paul Pierson (Maryknoll, NY: Orbis, 1993), 160.

32. "The Lausanne Covenant," in *Let the Earth Hear His Voice*, edited by J. D. Douglas (Minneapolis: World Wide Pictures, 1975), 4.

Evangelism, from the Greek *euangelizomai*, means to bring or announce the good news, the *euangelion*, or the gospel. The New Testament speaks of the good news as an "eternal gospel" (Rev. 14:6), "the gospel of peace" (Eph. 6:15), "the gospel of Christ" (1 Cor. 9:12), "the gospel of the grace of God" (Acts 20:24), and "the gospel of the Kingdom" (Matt. 4:23, 24:14). Yet Scripture insists that there is only one gospel (Gal. 1:8). The apostle Paul identifies the gospel with the death of Jesus Christ for our sins, his burial, and his resurrection from the dead on the third day (1 Cor. 15:1–4). The gospel is "the power of God for salvation to everyone who believes, to the Jew first and also to the Greek" (Rom. 1:16).

For Christians today, the term *gospel* has become a shorthand way of referring to the total redemptive work of Jesus Christ. Thus, the Cape Town Commitment, from the Third Lausanne Congress in 2010, states: "The gospel announces as good news the historical events of the life, death and resurrection of Jesus of Nazareth. As the Son of David, the promised Messiah King, Jesus is the one through whom alone God established his kingdom and acted for the salvation of the world, enabling all nations on earth to be blessed, as he promised Abraham."[33] Similarly, John Stott observes: "The good news about Jesus that we announce is that he died for our sins and was raised from death, and that in consequence he reigns as Lord and Savior at God's right hand, and has authority both to command repentance and faith, and to bestow forgiveness of sins and the gift of the Spirit on all those who repent, believe and are baptized."[34]

The good news evangelizers proclaim, then, is that Jesus is Savior and Lord and that in his name we have forgiveness and redemption from sin, new life through the indwelling power of the Holy Spirit, and ultimately everlasting fellowship with God. But what is in view here is no "easy believe-ism" or cheap grace. For to confess Christ as Lord in the biblical sense is to acknowledge his sovereignty over all areas of life and to submit to his demands regardless of the cost. Nor is this simply a private affair between an individual and Jesus. Submission to the Lordship of Jesus Christ, with all that this entails, has revolutionary implications for our relations with others and how we treat the world around us (see chapter 5 above).

Evangelicals are well known for their emphasis on the Great Commission of Matthew 28, which is usually taken as giving the "marching orders" for

---

33. *The Cape Town Commitment: A Confession of Faith and a Call to Action* I.8.B (Peabody, MA: Didasko and Hendrickson, 2011), 23.

34. Stott, *Christian Mission*, 54–55.

Christian mission and evangelism. But evangelicals often treat Matthew 28:18–20 as a text that stands by itself, detached from the rest of Jesus's teaching in the gospel of Matthew. This often results in a misleading and superficial reading of the text as commanding Christians simply to go throughout the world and communicate some minimal information about Jesus Christ and the possibility of forgiveness of sins and eternal life with God. Once the "information transfer" has encompassed sufficient groups of people, they can declare that they have completed the Great Commission.

But Bosch reminds us: "It is inadmissible to lift these words out of Matthew's gospel, as it were, allow them a life of their own, and understand them without any reference to the context in which they first appeared."[35] The Great Commission must be understood in the broader context of the entire gospel of Matthew, and when we do so, we see how much richer and more challenging the text is than often assumed. The text itself states: "And Jesus came and said to them, 'All authority in heaven and on earth has been given to me. Go therefore and make disciples of all nations, baptizing them in the name of the Father and of the Son and of the Holy Spirit, teaching them to observe all that I have commanded you. And behold, I am with you always, to the end of the age'" (Matt. 28:18–20). The primary emphasis in the text is on "mak[ing] disciples" (*mathēteusate*).[36] So our first observation is that if we are to be faithful to our Lord, we must "make disciples" of all peoples—and this includes sincere adherents of other religions.

What does it mean to make disciples? What does a disciple of Jesus look like? Bosch notes that "disciple" (*mathetes*) occurs seventy-three times in Matthew: "The theme of discipleship is central to Matthew's gospel and to Matthew's understanding of the church and mission."[37] Clearly, making disciples involves much more than simply passing on some information about Jesus to others. Jesus' teachings in the gospel of Matthew—in the great discourses such as the Sermon on the Mount and the parables—provide a good picture of what a disciple is to look like. A disciple of Jesus is someone who lives his or her life in accordance with the teachings of Jesus, who follows what Jesus has commanded. In Matthew 22, we encounter a religious leader

---

35. Bosch, *Transforming Mission*, 57.

36. See D. A. Carson, "Matthew," in *The Expositor's Bible Commentary*, Vol. 8, edited by Frank E. Gabelein (Grand Rapids, MI: Zondervan, 1984), 595–596. R. T. France, *The Gospel of Matthew* (Grand Rapids, MI: Eerdmans, 2007) 1115,

37. Bosch, *Transforming Mission*, 73. For a helpful study of discipleship in Matthew, see Michael J. Wilkins, *Discipleship in the Ancient World and Matthew's Gospel*, 2nd ed. (Grand Rapids, MI: Baker, 1995).

who approached Jesus with a question about the greatest commandment. Jesus's answer to this question has implications for how we are to carry out the Great Commission: "And one of them, a lawyer, asked him a question to test him. 'Teacher, which is the great commandment in the Law?' And he said to him, 'You shall love the Lord your God with all your heart and with all your soul and with all your mind. This is the great and first commandment. And a second is like it: You shall love your neighbor as yourself. On these two commandments depend all the Law and the Prophets'" (Matt. 22:35–40; see also Deut. 6:4–5; Mark 12:28–34; Luke 10:25–37). Jesus' disciples are those who love God with their entire beings and who love their neighbors as they love themselves. Our neighbors today include followers of other religions; we are to love religious others.

Among the more significant of Jesus' many instructions to his disciples is the so-called Golden Rule in Matthew 7:12: "So whatever you wish that others would do to you, do also to them, for this is the Law and the Prophets." The ethical principle behind Jesus' statement has enormous ramifications for how Jesus' disciples are to treat others, including how Christians should engage in evangelism and witness among religious others. The Great Commission, the Great Commandment, and the Golden Rule are all at the heart of Jesus' teaching and help to define what a disciple of Jesus Christ is. Based on these texts, then, we have three obligations with respect to followers of other religions: (1) make disciples of religious others, (2) love religious others, and (3) treat religious others the way we would want to be treated by them.

Witness in a Multireligious World

But the world in which we are to make disciples of Jesus Christ is one marked by religious strife and deep suspicion. We live in a postcolonialist world that is acutely aware of the injustices of four centuries of Western imperialism and that believes—rightly or wrongly—that Christianity bears much of the blame for such injustice. All too often, ethnic, nationalistic, and religious tensions erupt into violence, causing many to despair of the possibility of diverse religious communities living together peacefully. Can Christians remain committed to Jesus Christ as the one Lord and Savior for all humankind and to the need for evangelism among adherents of other religions while also being appropriately accepting of religious diversity and working for harmonious relations among the religions? This is a watershed issue for evangelicals in the days ahead.

There are appropriate and inappropriate ways of engaging in evangelism. Given the realities in today's world, it is crucial that the church bear witness to the gospel of Jesus Christ in fresh and winsome ways that are not only faithful to the biblical message but also respectful and sensitive. The importance of the Great Commandment for making disciples was noted above. The message of the gospel, the motivation for mission, and the methods to be employed in mission all are rooted in God's love. As Bosch puts it, "Mission has its origin in the heart of God. God is a fountain of sending love. This is the deepest source of mission. It is impossible to penetrate deeper still; there is mission because God loves people."[38] Significantly, the Cape Town Commitment of 2010 gives eloquent expression to the importance of love in Christian mission and witness: "The mission of God flows from the love of God. The mission of God's people flows from our love for God and for all that God loves."[39] The Commitment acknowledges the centrality of the Great Commandment for mission: " 'Love your neighbour as yourself' includes persons of other faiths." The Commitment distinguishes evangelism from proselytizing and calls for humble, respectful witness that is "scrupulously ethical":

> We are called to share good news in evangelism, but not to engage in unworthy proselytizing. Evangelism, while it includes persuasive rational argument following the example of the Apostle Paul, is "to make an honest and open statement of the gospel which leaves the hearers entirely free to make up their own minds about it. We wish to be sensitive to those of other faiths, and we reject any approach that seeks to force conversion on them." Proselytizing, by contrast, is the attempt to compel others to become "one of us," to "accept our religion," or indeed to "join our denomination."[40]

For these reasons, the Commitment calls upon Christians to "reject any form of witness that is coercive, unethical, deceptive, or disrespectful."[41]

In addition to the importance of love, as expressed in the Great Commandment, the Cape Town Commitment also refers to another biblical theme that should inform our interactions with religious others: "[W]e respond to our high calling as disciples of Jesus Christ to see people of other faiths as neighbours in the biblical sense. They are human beings created in

---

38. Bosch, *Transforming Mission*, 392.

39. *The Cape Town Commitment*, I.1, 9.

40. Ibid., II.C.1, 47. The embedded citation is from the Manila Manifesto, section 12.

41. Ibid., II.C.1.A, 48.

God's image, whom God loved and for whose sins Christ died."[42] The fact that all people—including sincere adherents of other religions—are created in the image of God (Gen. 1:26–27, 5:1–3, 9:6; 1 Cor. 11:7; James 3:9) has significant implications for how we understand and relate to religious others. Despite our many differences, there is a basic unity as fellow creatures created by God between followers of Jesus and adherents of other religions. Consider the comments of Christopher Wright:

> As the image of God, man still reflects the Creator, responds to Him, recognizes His hand in creation and, along with the rest of the animal creation, looks to the hand of God for the very supports of life itself (Ps. 104:27f). God is involved in the whole life of man, for man is human only through his relationship to God. Man, therefore, cannot utterly remove God from himself without ceasing to be human.... Our fellow human being is first, foremost and essentially one in the image of God, and only secondarily a Hindu, Muslim, or secular pagan. So, inasmuch as his religion is part of his humanity, whenever we meet one whom we call "an adherent of another religion," we meet someone who, in his religion as in all else, has some relationship to the Creator God, a relationship within which he is addressable and accountable.[43]

Or, as Richard Mouw puts it, "Here is an important lesson for our present-day world, which is so torn apart by ethnic, racial, and religious antagonisms. God wants us to offer a fundamental respect to others purely on the basis of their humanness. Christians and Muslims, African Americans and Jewish Americans, heterosexuals and homosexuals, rich and poor—all are created in the divine likeness. In affirming the stranger, we are honoring the image of God."[44]

One of the many implications of this concerns the fundamental categories we use in thinking about religious others. If the primary category for identification that we use when encountering religious others is "Hindu" or "Buddhist" or "Muslim," then what is accentuated are the differences between us, what

---

42. Ibid., II.C.1, 47.

43. Christopher J. H.. Wright, "The Christian and Other Religions," *Themelios* 9 (January 1984): 5.

44. Richard J. Mouw, *Uncommon Decency: Christian Civility in an Uncivil World* (Downers Grove, IL: InterVarsity, 1992), 41.

sets us apart. Emphasis is given to what separates us and the barriers that need to be overcome if communication or relations are to be established.

On the other hand, if the primary category for the other is "fellow human being created by God and loved by God," then there is acknowledgment of a fundamental commonality that is more basic than any differences. The differences between Christians and Muslims or Hindus are real enough, but they are secondary. Commonalities across ethnic, class, cultural, and religious boundaries are ultimately more significant than any differences. When one recognizes what we have in common and gives this greater emphasis, then—although the differences remain—there is a basis for mutual respect and acceptance, from which bridges for communication and relationships can be established.

In 2011, a significant document concerning Christian witness in a religiously diverse world was produced by three groups that do not normally cooperate. After a five-year period of study, reflection, and dialogue, the Roman Catholic Pontifical Council for Interreligious Dialogue, the World Council of Churches, and the World Evangelical Alliance put forward a short document entitled *Christian Witness in a Multi-Religious World: Recommendations for Conduct*. The document provides a useful guide and echoes themes that are also found in evangelical documents such as the Cape Town Commitment.

Christian Witness in a Multi-Religious World begins by observing, "Mission belongs to the very heart of the church. Proclaiming the word of God and witnessing to the world is essential for every Christian. At the same time, it is necessary to do so according to gospel principles, with full respect and love for all human beings."[45] The document then offers twelve principles that should guide Christians in their witness to Jesus Christ in interreligious contexts. Several will be briefly noted, since they are especially significant.

The first principle echoes a theme we have already emphasized, namely, that Christians are to act in accordance with God's love: "Christians believe that God is the source of all love and, accordingly, in their witness they are called to live lives of love and to love their neighbors as themselves (cf Matthew 22:34–40; John 14:15)." As we have seen, this theme is also prominent in the Cape Town Commitment.

The third principle calls for moral integrity and humility in the lives of Christians: "Christians are called to conduct themselves with integrity, charity,

45. *Christian Witness in a Multi-Religious World*, http://www.oikoumene.org/en/resources/documents/wcc-programmes/interreligious-dialogue-and-cooperation/christian-identity-in-pluralistic-societies/christian-witness-in-a-multi-religious-world (accessed November 15, 2013).

compassion and humility, and to overcome all arrogance, condescension and disparagement (cf Galatians 5:22)." Christ's witnesses are to be men and women of moral integrity, truthful and honest in speech, compassionate and generous with those in need, and humble and gracious in demeanor.

The sixth guiding principle is especially significant in a world torn apart by religious tension and violence. Christians are to reject violence or the abuse of power in witness: "Christians are called to reject all forms of violence, even psychological or social, including the abuse of power in their witness. They also reject violence, unjust discrimination or repression by any religious or secular authority, including the violation or destruction of places of worship, sacred symbols or texts."[46] In setting out the qualities that are to be found in his disciples, Jesus said, "Blessed are the peacemakers, for they shall be called sons of God" (Matt. 5:9). When Jesus' disciples respond to violence and persecution not with further violence but rather by working for peaceful relations, it can be a powerful witness to the transformative power of God's grace.[47]

The seventh principle speaks to the importance of freedom of religion and belief: "Religious freedom including the right to publicly profess, practice, propagate and change one's religion flows from the very dignity of the human person which is grounded in the creation of all human beings in the image and likeness of God (cf Genesis 1:26). Thus, all human beings have equal rights and responsibilities. Where any religion is instrumentalized for political ends, or where religious persecution occurs, Christians are called to engage in prophetic witness denouncing such actions." This is also affirmed in the Cape Town Commitment, which urges Christ's followers to "strive for the goal of religious freedom for all people." Even as it calls for upholding human rights by defending freedom of religious conscience, however, the Commitment also encourages believers to be good citizens and "to seek the welfare of the nation where we live," promoting the common good.[48]

---

46. In calling for the rejection of all forms of violence, this principle could be interpreted as an endorsement of strict pacifism, which rejects even the legitimate use of violence by the state to protect its citizens. But since the context here is Christian witness, it is better to understand this as rejection of oppression, unwarranted pressure, or coercion in Christian witness and not necessarily a commitment to pacifism as such.

47. See David W. Shenk, "The Gospel of Reconciliation within the Wrath of Nations," *International Bulletin of Missionary Research* 32, no. 1 (January 2008), 3–9; Miroslav Volf, *Exclusion and Embrace: A Theological Exploration of Identity, Otherness, and Reconciliation* (Nashville, TN: Abingdon, 1996).

48. *The Cape Town Commitment*, II.C.6, 52.

The promotion of human rights, and especially the right of freedom of religious conscience, including conversion, is especially significant today. Since the choice for conversion can be an expression of one's religious conscience, societies around the world should be encouraged to promote and protect the freedom of religious choice. The twentieth century witnessed the rise of some of the most totalitarian and despotic regimes in human history, but ironically, it also produced an unprecedented emphasis on the dignity of the human person and the importance of preserving human rights.[49] Many nations today claim to support the United Nations Universal Declaration of Human Rights in its affirmation of the right of all people to freedom of conscience, including the right to change one's religion or belief.[50] But there are many places today where, despite such professions, there is no tolerance of religious conversion. In many cases the dominant religious tradition persecutes those with different views and practices. In some Islamic societies those who decide to follow Jesus as Lord and Savior face severe persecution. Christians must work to promote religious liberty and freedom of conscience globally, but as they do so they must also protect the rights of religious minorities within their own societies. Moreover, Christians should remind others that the notion of human dignity, upon which the principles of human rights are based, only makes sense within a framework that sees human beings as created by God and bearing God's image.

Finally, the tenth principle notes the importance of honesty and respect in witness: "Christians are to speak sincerely and respectfully; they are to listen in order to learn about and understand others' beliefs and practices, and are encouraged to acknowledge and appreciate what is true and good in them. Any comment or critical approach should be made in a spirit of mutual respect, making sure not to bear false witness concerning other religions." Among other things, this means that in their depictions of religious others, Christians are to be fair and honest, refusing to promote misleading characterizations or caricatures and resisting language that incites fear or hatred. The command in the Decalogue not to bear false witness against one's neighbor also applies to religious others (Exod. 20:16).

---

49. See Lynn Hunt, *Inventing Human Rights: A History* (New York: Norton, 2007); *Religion and Human Rights: An Introduction*, edited by John Witte Jr. and M. Christian Green (New York: Oxford University Press, 2012).

50. "Universal Declaration of Human Rights," Article 18, in ibid., 226. See Perez Zagorin, *How the Idea of Religious Toleration Came to the West* (Princeton, NJ: Princeton University Press, 2003).

Each of these principles is important and has rich implications for Christian witness in our multireligious world. But if we were to reduce things to just one general principle, it would be difficult to improve upon Jesus' teaching in the so-called Golden Rule: "So whatever you wish that others would do to you, do also to them, for this is the law and the prophets" (Matt. 7:12). This principle has many applications, including how Christians should live in a multireligious world and bear witness to Jesus Christ among religious others. How, for example, should Christians engage in evangelism among religious others? In answering this, it helps to reflect on how we would like to be treated by someone from another religion eager to convert us to his or her faith. Evangelizers should treat religious others the way they would wish to be treated by them. This basic ethical principle has profound implications not only for evangelism but also for how Christians should engage in public discourse or pursue public policy in societies that are religiously diverse.

Bearing witness to Jesus Christ in appropriate ways in our multireligious world also involves civic virtue, or being good and responsible citizens both in our own countries and in the broader global community. Circumstances vary enormously from country to country, but we will make a few brief remarks about what this might mean for Christians living in the United States.

What does it mean to live as disciples of Jesus in the United States in the early twenty-first century? Responding appropriately to this question will require proper navigation of two sets of obligations upon American Christians: first, their responsibilities as disciples of Jesus Christ, and second, their obligations as good citizens, both locally and globally. Politically, the United States is a republic with a constitution that explicitly rules out the establishment of a state religion and guarantees the free exercise of religion. American society is also becoming remarkably diverse, with an astonishing variety of religious traditions found there. Historically, America is a nation that has been influenced by Christian values and principles, with a dominant Christian population. But American society today includes many different religious traditions, and it is expected to become even more diverse in the decades ahead. While most Americans still identify as Christian in some sense, there are growing numbers of Buddhists, Hindus, Sikhs, Jains, and Baha'is, along with Jews and Mormons. There is also a growing percentage of Americans who claim to be nonreligious, either atheist or simply agnostic.

Being a disciple of Jesus Christ will mean being a good and responsible citizen of the United States, honoring the legal and social expectations of the land unless it becomes clear that doing so is incompatible with one's responsibilities as Christ's disciple. Dual obligations as Christ's disciples and citizens can be considered on at least three distinct levels. First, there is the dimension of one's interpersonal relationships with religious others. Second, there is the domain involving Christian presence and conduct in the broader society or what is often referred to as the public sector. Finally, given our globalizing world, we must also consider the implications of Christian presence and conduct in a world of religious tensions. The principles noted above are relevant on all three dimensions.

Jesus' teaching in the so-called Golden Rule, for example, not only should shape individual Christian behavior with others, but it can also serve as a guiding principle for a social ethic in religiously diverse societies. It applies both to cases in which Christians make up the majority and to those in which they are the minority, but it has special relevance to the former. Should the religious majority—Christians in most parts of the United States—determine public policy based *simply* on their own religious commitments? What if the situation were different, and evangelical or Catholic Christians were the minority in a society dominated by atheists or Hindus or Muslims or, as in Provo, Utah, by Mormons? At the heart of the Golden Rule is a thought experiment: If conditions were reversed, and I were to find myself in the position of the other, would I want to be treated in the manner in which I am considering treating the other? If not, then I should not treat the other in this manner. This has significant implications for how Christians conduct evangelism and witness, for personal relationships with religious others, and for public-policy disputes in highly diverse societies.[51]

Interreligious Dialogue

As we conclude this chapter, we will give attention to two issues that are especially significant for Christian witness in religiously diverse contexts. The first is the issue of interreligious dialogue and its relation to Christian witness and mission. The second issue receives less attention but is nevertheless significant: the role of apologetics or the defense of the Christian faith in Christian mission in a pluralistic world.

If we think of interreligious dialogue as a two-way conversation between Christians and religious others, then it seems that this is something that

---

51. A helpful document addressing religious liberty and the place of religious commitments in the public domain is the Williamsburg Charter, drafted principally by the evangelical Os Guinness. The Charter is reprinted in Guinness, *The Case for Civility: And Why Our Future Depends on It* (New York: HarperCollins, 2008), 177–198. See also Ramachandra, *Faiths in Conflict?* 141–165.

goes back to the time of Jesus and the apostles. Jesus' conversation with the Samaritan woman in John 4 was with someone who was not only ethnically but also religiously different. Paul's encounters with the polytheists in Acts 14 or with the Stoics and Epicureans in Acts 17 presumably involved a two-way conversation or dialogue. Interestingly, the verb *dialegomai*, from which the English word *dialogue* is derived, is often used in the New Testament to describe Paul's activity. The term is frequently translated into English as "reasoned" and is used of Paul's activity in the Jewish synagogues (Acts 17:2, 17:17, 18:4), in the marketplace in Athens (17:17), in the school of Tyrannus (19:9), and in the church at Troas (20:7, 20:9). A careful study of Paul's encounters with Jews and Gentiles alike indicates that he often engaged in what we might call informal dialogue—conversations with religious others involving clarifying misunderstandings, responding to questions and challenges, raising questions, arguing for a position, and trying to persuade others to change their commitments. Yet, as John Stott observes, "the subject of [Paul's] dialogue with the world was one which he always chose himself, namely Jesus Christ, and its object was always conversion to Jesus Christ."[52] Understood in this sense, interreligious dialogue has been a part of Christian witness throughout the centuries, including the modern missionary movements of the eighteenth and nineteenth centuries. Indeed, it is difficult to see how Christian witness might occur among followers of other religions without such informal dialogue.

But the term *interreligious dialogue* has taken on distinctive meanings in the twentieth century, becoming associated with assumptions and practices that evangelicals find problematic. What is particularly significant here is formal dialogue between religions or organized gatherings of representatives from two or more religious traditions in which well-defined procedures are followed in pursuit of agreed-upon objectives. Interreligious dialogue in this sense has become increasingly prominent since the 1970s in the agenda of the World Council of Churches. Many evangelicals, by contrast, have been suspicious of dialogue because of the perception that the ways in which it is typically practiced in these circles undermine evangelical theological and missiological commitments. Thus the 1974 Lausanne Covenant, for example, states: "We also reject as derogatory to Christ and the gospel every kind of syncretism and dialogue which implies that Christ speaks equally through all religions and ideologies." But the Covenant does not reject dialogue entirely, as it recognizes that "[o]ur Christian presence in the world is indispensable to

52. Stott, *Christian Mission*, 63.

evangelism, and so is that kind of dialogue whose purpose is to listen sensitively in order to understand."[53]

Forms of interreligious dialogue that presume that God's revelation in the incarnation and the written Scriptures is not definitive or that Jesus Christ in principle is not superior to other religious leaders or that followers of other religions do not need to be reconciled to God through Christ will be rejected by evangelicals. A problematic assumption of many involved in interreligious dialogue is the idea that genuine dialogue cannot take place if either party is convinced about the definitive truth of its own tradition. Paul Knitter, for example, maintains that

> Dialogue must be based on the recognition of the possible truth in all religions; the ability to recognize this truth must be grounded in the hypothesis of a common ground and goal for all religions.... Authentic listening is therefore not possible if one partner presumes that the others have only an "incomplete" truth or that they possess truth only insofar as it conforms with the norm of "my truth."... The deepest level of dialogue cannot be a matter of "apples and oranges." To try to formulate what this means, we can say that there must be the same ultimate reality, the same divine presence, the same fullness and emptiness—in Christian terms, the same God—animating all religions and providing the ultimate ground and goal of dialogue.[54]

For Knitter, "dialogue is not possible if any partner enters it with the claim that they possess the final, irreformable truth."[55] Elsewhere, he speaks of interreligious dialogue as "a conversation where no religion has 'the fullness of truth' and is a final winner."[56] Similarly, Donald Swearer says: "If we believe that our particular perception of religious truth is the *only* correct one, then genuine dialogue does not take place at all."[57]

---

53. "Lausanne Covenant," sections 3 and 4, in *New Directions in Mission and Evangelization 1: Basic Statements 1974–1991*, edited by James A. Scherer and Stephen B. Evans (Maryknoll, NY: Orbis, 1992), 254–255.

54. Knitter, *No Other Name?* 208–209.

55. Ibid., 211.

56. Paul Knitter, "Paul Knitter Responds to Gavin D'Costa and Daniel Strange," in Gavin D'Costa, Paul Knitter, and Daniel Strange, *Only One Way? Three Christian Responses on the Uniqueness of Christ in a Religiously Plural World*, (London: SCM, 2011), 157.

57. Donald K. Swearer, *Dialogue: The Key to Understanding Other Religions* (Philadelphia: Westminster, 1977), 41; emphasis in original.

Paul Ingram, who has long been active in Buddhist-Christian dialogue, also claims that those involved in interreligious dialogue should regard it as a quest for truth: "Dialogue is a quest for truth where 'truth' is understood as relational in structure. Truth can have no confessional boundaries in a universe governed by general and special relativity. Interreligious dialogue is meaningful as it grows out of our common humanity as persons whose sense of what it means to be human expresses itself through different, yet valid and real, encounters with the Sacred, however the Sacred is named."[58] Moreover, Ingram holds that in genuine dialogue, there cannot be any ulterior motive, including the desire for the conversion of the other: "Engaging in dialogue with a Buddhist merely for the purpose of comparing Buddhist doctrine and practice with Christian doctrine and practice in order to evangelize Buddhists undermines the integrity of Christian and Buddhist tradition. Engaging in dialogue in order to convert persons to one's own particular faith tradition is a monologue, not a dialogue."[59]

Much could be said by way of response to this understanding of dialogue, but a few brief comments will have to suffice. It is, of course, important to approach dialogue with followers of other religious traditions with sincerity, humility, and a genuine willingness to listen and learn. We have already noted that evangelicals can learn from other religious traditions,[60] and in their encounters with religious others, they must listen carefully to them, seek to understand their perspectives, and be open to being challenged and even changed in some respects as a result of the dialogues. But evangelicals cannot accept the assumptions underlying the comments of Knitter, Swearer, and Ingram quoted above. Notice that on Knitter's understanding of dialogue, only pluralists (those who acknowledge that there is "the same ultimate reality, the same divine presence, the same fullness and emptiness—in Christian terms, the same God—animating all religions") can participate in real interreligious dialogue. But why should we accept that stipulation? That is not likely to be any more acceptable to traditional Muslims or Buddhists than it is to orthodox Christians. Furthermore, why should we accept Ingram's claim that genuine dialogue is incompatible with the desire for the conversion of the other?

Terry Muck is an evangelical who has been actively involved in Buddhist-Christian dialogue for more than thirty years, serving for ten years

---

58. Paul O. Ingram, *The Process of Buddhist-Christian Dialogue* (Eugene, OR: Wipf & Stock, Cascade, 2009), x.

59. Ibid., ix.

60. See chapter 3 above.

as editor of the journal *Buddhist-Christian Studies*. Responding specifically to Ingram's claims, Muck says: "As an evangelical Christian, I must admit that I have what Paul Ingram calls this missionary ulterior motive. I think most Christians have it. To be honest, I think most Buddhists also have this as an ulterior motive. And I would turn Paul's second comment on its head and say that what undermines the integrity of both the Christian and Buddhist traditions is the failure to see that they are both essentially missionary in nature; to try to minimize this feature is to misunderstand both traditions badly."[61] Commenting on Ingram's contention that participants in interreligious dialogue should do so in a common search for truth, Muck observes: "[Ingram's requirement] that persons involved in interreligious dialogue see it as a quest for truth, enlarges the scope of dialogue to a width and breadth that it simply cannot bear. No matter how one defines truth, dialogue—especially with the requirements set forth [by Ingram]—is ill equipped to discover it. If one cannot bring firm commitments to the dialogue table, then out the window go rational authorities, warrants, appeals to logic (whatever logical system one might choose), or anything resembling cognitive thought."[62] On the one hand, we agree that interfaith dialogue can be a search for truth as we are always learning more about other traditions and our own. But we also agree with Muck here in rejecting the notion that truth must be confined to pluralist assumptions. If dialogue is based on these assumptions, then it will hardly be surprising that evangelicals reject dialogue.

But there is no reason to regard such assumptions as essential to interreligious dialogue, and evangelicals are increasingly acknowledging that appropriate forms of interreligious dialogue are an important component of Christian mission. As early as 1978, evangelical missiologist David Hesselgrave challenged evangelicals to become involved in appropriate forms of interreligious dialogue.[63] The Manila Manifesto (1989), from the Second International Congress on World Evangelization, explicitly links interreligious dialogue with evangelism as part of Christian witness: "In the past we have sometimes been guilty of adopting towards adherents of other faiths attitudes of ignorance, arrogance, disrespect and even hostility. We repent of this. We

---

61. Terry C. Muck, "Interreligious Dialogue: Conversations That Enable Christian Witness," *International Bulletin of Missionary Research* 35, no. 4 (October 2011): 188.

62. Ibid.

63. David Hesselgrave "Interreligious Dialogue—Biblical and Contemporary Perspectives," in *Theology and Mission: Papers Given at Trinity Consultation No. 1*, edited by David J. Hesselgrave (Grand Rapids, MI: Baker, 1978), 227–240.

nevertheless are determined to bear a positive and uncompromising witness
(1 Tim. 2:5–7) to the uniqueness of our Lord, in his life, death and resurrection, in all aspects of our evangelistic work including interfaith dialogue."[64]
The importance of dialogue is reaffirmed in the Cape Town Commitment of
2010: "We affirm the proper place for dialogue with people of other faiths,
just as Paul engaged in debate with Jews and Gentiles in the synagogue and
public arenas. As a legitimate part of our Christian mission, such dialogue
combines confidence in the uniqueness of Christ and the truth of the gospel
with respectful listening to others."[65]

Evangelicals recognize that interreligious dialogue can serve many
positive purposes, including deepening understanding of other religions,
enhancing mutual respect, reducing tensions, and fostering cooperation in
appropriate ways for the common good.[66] Terry Muck suggests that evangelicals should look upon interreligious dialogue as "one of a large number of
interactive modes we have with people of other religious traditions—a very
important mode, to be sure, but not the only mode." He contends that we
should "define dialogue in such a way that it can be seen as an activity that
does accomplish something indispensable in furthering good relationships
with people of religious traditions not their own."[67] Thus dialogue can include
modes such as proclamation, discussion, argumentation, and even apologetics. Muck emphasizes that a "missional theology of dialogue" will be "based
on an orthodox recognition of God's revelation to all" and "must fully embrace
Christian humility." Furthermore, it "must be grounded in a love of neighbor"
and "makes known to all involved commitment to Christian witness."[68] These
are important and helpful guidelines for constructing an evangelical approach
to interreligious dialogue.[69]

64. "Manila Manifesto," A.3, in *New Directions in Mission and Evangelization 1: Basic Statements 1974–1991*, edited by James A. Scherer and Stephen B. Evans (Maryknoll, NY: Orbis, 1992), 297.

65. *The Cape Town Commitment*, II.C.1.E, 48.

66. For a perceptive analysis of Hindu-Christian dialogue in India by an evangelical, see Bob Robinson, *Christians Meeting Hindus: An Analysis and Theological Critique of the Hindu-Christian Encounter in India* (Carlisle, UK: Regnum, 2004).

67. Muck, "Interreligious Dialogue," 188.

68. Ibid., 191–192.

69. See also Douglas McConnell, "Missional Principles and Guidelines for Interfaith Dialogue," *Evangelical Interfaith Dialogue* 1 (Winter 2010): 3–6.

A significant example of evangelical involvement in interreligious dialogue was provided by the faculty of Fuller Theological Seminary in Pasadena, California. In 2005, Fuller joined with the Salam Institute of Peace and Justice and the Islamic Society of North America in participating in the Conflict Transformation Program of Dialogue with Muslims and Evangelical Christians. The purpose of the three-year project sponsored by the U.S. Department of Justice was "to seek common practices, patterns, and pathways for conflict reduction, resolution, and transformation between faiths as well as to learn how to better resolve differences within our individual faiths."[70] Increasingly, evangelicals, on both nonformal and formal or institutional levels, are building bridges to other faith communities in an effort to defuse religious tensions and establish mutual understanding and respect.

The desire for better mutual understanding, finding common ground, and reduction of tensions can also coexist with an interest in clarifying differences between evangelical Christianity and other religious traditions. Evangelicals have been involved on various levels in dialogue with Mormons.[71] Since both Mormons and evangelical Christians claim to be faithful to the teachings of Jesus Christ, one might expect to find considerable common ground between these traditions. But upon closer examination, it becomes apparent that despite some commonalities, there are deep and significant differences between them. In the case of evangelical–Mormon dialogues, evangelicals' concerns for understanding Mormons and reducing tensions between evangelicals and Mormons are accompanied by the desire to show how Mormon teachings depart from the historic orthodox Christian tradition and why such departures are significant. Interreligious dialogue here involves interreligious apologetics.

Interreligious Apologetics

We noted above that Terry Muck includes apologetics as a possible mode of interreligious dialogue. In doing so, Muck runs against the prevailing consensus not only of many involved in dialogue but also of many in missions in

---

70. *Peace-Building By, Between, and Beyond Muslims and Evangelical Christians*, edited by Mohammed Abu-Nimer and David Augsberger (Lanham, MD: Lexington, 2009), xii.

71. See Richard J. Mouw, *Talking with Mormons: An Invitation to Evangelicals* (Grand Rapids, MI: Eerdmans, 2012); Craig Blomberg and Stephen E. Robinson, *How Wide the Divide? A Mormon and Evangelical in Conversation* (Downers Grove, IL: InterVarsity, 1997); Gerald R. McDermott and Robert L. Millett, *Evangelicals and Mormons: Exploring the Boundaries* (Vancouver, BC: Regent College, 2011).

general, who regard apologetics as irrelevant or even detrimental to Christian witness in multireligious settings. Christian apologetics is often perceived as a modern Western response to the various challenges posed by the European Enlightenment. According to this perception, there may be a place for apologetics in the modern West, but there is no place for it in encounters with other religions. Interreligious apologetics is at best a Western, theistic concern that is not shared by Asian religious traditions, and it is inappropriate, or even counterproductive, in Christian witness among religious others. But this common assumption is seriously misleading, and we agree with Muck that when properly understood and practiced, apologetics can be an indispensable component in Christian witness.

The term *apologetics*, derived from the Greek *apologia*, refers to the activity of defending the claims of the Christian faith against criticisms that arise. In ordinary use today outside of theological circles, the term is generally pejorative. To call someone an apologist for the tobacco industry or the insurance industry is to suggest that he or she cannot be relied on to give an objective assessment; that person has an agenda that distorts his or her perspective. Similarly, an apologist for the Christian faith is often dismissed as someone who is hopelessly biased and thus cannot offer an objective case for Christian theism. It could well be that a different term would be more appropriate today, but given its established use in theological circles, we will continue to use it here. Regardless of the term used, the activity is more important than the word, and that is what we will be considering. Mark Hanna has helpfully defined Christian apologetics as "a systematic response of the reflective and culturally informed Christian to attacks that inevitably come upon the truth claims of the Christian faith."[72]

It is important to see that apologetics, understood as providing reasons for one's own commitments and raising questions about the beliefs of others, is not a modern, post-Enlightenment innovation but can be traced back to the early church fathers. During the second and third centuries, Christian apologists such as Justin Martyr, Claudius Apollinaris, Athenagoras, Tatian, Theophilus of Antioch, Clement of Alexandria, Tertullian, and Origen responded to critics with important defenses of Christian belief and practice.[73]

---

72. Mark Hanna, *Crucial Questions in Apologetics* (Grand Rapids, MI: Baker, 1978), 63.

73. See Robert M. Grant, *Greek Apologists of the Second Century* (Philadelphia: Westminster, 1988); *Apologetics in the Roman Empire*, edited by Mark Edwards, Martin Goodman, and Simon Price (Oxford, UK: Oxford University Press, 1999); Avery Dulles, *A History of Apologetics* (Philadelphia: Westminster, 1971), chap. 2.

Whereas during the first four centuries, Christian apologists addressed issues arising from Judaism or the surrounding Greco-Roman world, by the eighth century, attention turned to a new challenge: Islam. With the rapid rise of Islam in the eighth and ninth centuries, Christians in places such as Damascus and Baghdad came to grips with Islamic religious and intellectual currents by producing works in apologetics and theology. John of Damascus (d. 749), for example, wrote the *Fount of Knowledge*, which not only was a systematic compendium of orthodox Christian teachings but also provided a "response to the commanding intellectual challenge of Islam" and was intended "to discredit the religious and intellectual claims of Islam in the eyes of inquiring Christians."[74] Theodore Abu Qurrah (d. 830), a disciple of John of Damascus, wrote *God and the True Religion*, a work that confronts the problem of choosing among Zoroastrian religion, Samaritan religion, Judaism, Christianity, Manichaeism, and Islam—all of which claim divine revelation. He attempted to demonstrate that "Christianity presents the most plausible idea of God, exhibits the fullest understanding of man's actual religious needs, and prescribes what appear to be the most appropriate remedies."[75]

One of the earliest accounts of a Christian engagement with Buddhism is found in the diaries of William of Rubruck, a Franciscan friar who reached the Mongol court in 1253. William gives a fascinating account of a debate between a Buddhist and himself in 1254 before Mongke Khan, the grandson of the notorious Mongol ruler Genghis Khan. It is clear from William's account (which is our only source for the debate) that William and the Buddhist engaged in a vigorous exchange as each probed perceived weaknesses in the other's worldview. The Buddhist pressed hard on the problem of evil, an issue that Buddhists regard as devastating for monotheism: "If your God is as you say, why does he make the half of things evil?" When William insisted that all that proceeds from God is good, the Buddhist demanded, "Whence then comes evil?"[76]

The remarkable work of the sixteenth-century Jesuit missionary scholar Matteo Ricci in China was noted in chapter 6. In 1603, Ricci published *On the True Meaning of the Lord of Heaven*, an impressive work in Christian

---

74. Sidney H. Griffith, *The Church in the Shadow of the Mosque: Christians and Muslims in the World of Islam* (Princeton, NJ: Princeton University Press, 2008), 42.

75. Dulles, *A History of Apologetics*, 74.

76. Richard Fox Young, *"Deus Unus or Dei Plures Sunt?* The Function of Inclusivism in the Buddhist Defense of Mongol Folk Religion against William of Rubruck (1254)," *Journal of Ecumenical Studies* 26, no. 1 (1989): 115. See also Samuel Hugh Moffett, *A History of Christianity in Asia*, Vol. 1 (New York: HarperCollins, 1992), 409–414.

apologetics that attempts to establish the existence of a personal creator God and thus show the inadequacy of Daoist and Buddhist conceptions of religious ultimacy.[77] Ricci had a significant impact on the Chinese cultured elite, and a number of Confucian literati became Christians through his ministry. Thus there is a long history of Christian apologetics with respect to other religions before the modern era.

Furthermore, contrary to popular assumptions, the attempt to defend the truth of one's own religious beliefs through appeal to reason and argument and to persuade others to accept them is not unknown among traditional Asian religious traditions. While it is true that some traditions within Hinduism, Buddhism, and Daoism minimize the role of reason, many other traditions within these religions historically have made use of rigorous rational analysis in supporting religious claims. Hindus, Buddhists, and Jains debated whether there are enduring substantial souls (Hindus and Jains said yes; Buddhists denied this) or whether a creator God exists (some Hindus said yes; Jains and Buddhists denied this).[78] The introduction of Christianity to Asian cultures was often regarded by Hindus, Muslims, and Buddhists as a direct threat to their teachings and ways of life. Christian witness often was met with hard-hitting intellectual responses by Hindus, Muslims, and Buddhists, who attempted to show the falsity or irrationality of Christian claims.[79] It is clear, then, that even before the modern era, there was a long tradition of interreligious apologetics, with Christians and adherents of other religions engaging in vigorous debate, each community trying to show the

---

77. See Matteo Ricci, *The True Meaning of the Lord of Heaven*, translated by Douglas Lancashire and Peter Hu Kuo-chen (St. Louis, MO: Institute of Jesuit Sources, 1985).

78. For Buddhist critiques of the existence of God, see Parimal G. Patil, *Against a Hindu God: Buddhist Philosophy of Religion in India* (New York: Columbia University Press, 2009); Arvind Sharma, *The Philosophy of Religion: A Buddhist Perspective* (Delhi: Oxford University Press, 1995). For analysis of such critiques, see Paul Williams, "Aquinas Meets the Buddhists: Prolegomena to an Authentically Thomas-ist Basis for Dialogue," in *Aquinas in Dialogue: Thomas for the Twenty-First Century*, edited by Jim Fodor and Christian Bauerschmidt (Oxford, UK: Blackwell, 2004), 87–117; Keith Yandell and Harold Netland, *Buddhism: A Christian Exploration and Appraisal* (Downers Grove, IL: InterVarsity, 2009), 180–192.

79. See Richard Fox Young, *Resistant Hinduism: Sanskrit Sources on Anti-Christian Apologetics in Early Nineteenth Century India* (Vienna: Institut für Indologie der Universität Wien, 1981); R. F. Young and S. Jebanesan, *The Bible Trembled: The Hindu-Christian Controversies of Nineteenth Century Ceylon* (Vienna: Institut für Indologie der Universität Wien, 1995); *Religious Controversy in British India*, edited by Kenneth W. Jones (Albany: SUNY Press, 1992); *Hindu-Christian Dialogue: Perspectives and Encounters*, edited by Harold Coward (Maryknoll, NY: Orbis, 1989); *Christianity through Non-Christian Eyes*, edited by Paul J. Griffiths (Maryknoll, NY: Orbis, 1990).

intellectual superiority of its own position. This is hardly surprising, for religious leaders have characteristically understood their religious claims to be of great significance, and those within a particular tradition have been expected to accept these teachings as true and to live accordingly. It is accepted across the religions that counterassertions from other traditions, which implicitly call into question one's own commitments, must be addressed and challenged if they are unwarranted.

But interreligious apologetics strikes many today as distasteful and inappropriate in a multireligious world. As noted above, many maintain that interreligious encounters should be marked by the search for mutual understanding and common ground and that arguing for the truth of one's own position is incompatible with this. Thus, Paul Griffiths speaks of "an underlying scholarly orthodoxy on the goals and functions of interreligious dialogue" that maintains that "understanding is the only legitimate goal; that judgment and criticism of religious beliefs and practices other than those of one's own community [are] always inappropriate; and that an active defense of the truth of those beliefs and practices to which one's community appears committed is always to be shunned."[80] In *An Apology for Apologetics*, Griffiths provides a trenchant critique of this view, arguing that in certain circumstances, religious communities actually have an obligation to engage in interreligious apologetics. He argues that if representative intellectuals of a specific religious community come to believe that some or all of their own core doctrines are incompatible with some claims made by representatives of another religious community, then they have an obligation to respond to the alien religious claims by attempting to show that the alien claims are unjustified or at least that one's own beliefs are not threatened by such claims.[81]

Griffiths holds that there is both an epistemic and a moral component to this obligation.[82] Since religious communities hold their own religious beliefs to be true, when a particular community is confronted by other claims challenging these beliefs, it has an epistemic duty to consider whether the challenge makes it epistemically unacceptable for the community to continue with its beliefs. Furthermore, most religions maintain not only that their claims are true but also that there is salvific value in accepting and acting on these beliefs as true. Griffiths argues that if a religious community believes that

---

80. Paul Griffiths, *An Apology for Apologetics: A Study in the Logic of Interreligious Dialogue* (Maryknoll, NY: Orbis, 1991), xi.

81. Ibid., 3.

82. Ibid., 15–16.

humankind suffers from a general malady (sin, ignorance), that its central religious claims are true, and that accepting and acting appropriately upon these beliefs can bring about deliverance from the malady, then the community has an ethical obligation to share this good news with those outside the tradition, trying, in appropriate ways, to persuade them to accept these beliefs.

We contend that appropriate forms of apologetics are necessary as part of a comprehensive Christian witness today. In many contexts today, evangelism naturally leads to questions and critiques of Christian claims. It is crucial that these questions be addressed in a responsible and sensitive manner. William Abraham recognizes the importance of appropriate forms of apologetics in Christian witness today. Abraham's concern is not with witness in interreligious contexts but rather witness in the secular societies of post-Christendom Europe and North America. But his insights also apply to challenges from religious diversity and pluralism. Abraham contends that the evangelist today needs to be prepared to respond to a range of intellectual questions prompted by modernity:

> There will be no advance against the acids of modernity if Christians simply proclaim the good news of the kingdom, or invite people to a personal decision, and leave it at that.... All sorts of intellectual issues need to be addressed. Misunderstandings and confusion need to be cleared up; points of contact should be established; the intellectual content of the gospel must be expressed clearly and concisely; past errors have to be acknowledged and due repentance performed; and nothing should be spared in the effort to give a reason for the hope that is within one.[83]

Not surprisingly, there is a recognition among some evangelicals that Christian witness in our pluralistic, relativistic world demands a fresh approach to Christian apologetics. When John Stott, who was instrumental in founding the Lausanne Movement, reflected back on the twenty years since the first Congress on World Evangelization at Lausanne in 1974, he made a clear link between a responsible apologetic and effective evangelism:

---

83. William J. Abraham, *The Logic of Evangelism* (Grand Rapids, MI: Eerdmans, 1989), 207. See also Abraham, "A Theology of Evangelism: The Heart of the Matter," in *The Study of Evangelism: Exploring a Missional Practice of the Church*, edited by Paul W. Chilcote and Laceye C. Warner (Grand Rapids, MI: Eerdmans, 2008), 23–27.

We evangelical people need to repent of every occasion on which we have divorced evangelism from apologetics, as the apostles never did. We have to argue the Gospel we proclaim. We need to be able to say confidently to our hearers what Paul said to Festus: "What I am saying is true and reasonable" (Acts 26:25). We cannot possibly surrender to the current understanding of "pluralism" as an ideology that affirms the independent validity of every religion. Our task, rather, is to establish the criteria by which truth claims can be evaluated and then to demonstrate the uniqueness and finality of Jesus Christ.[84]

The Christian faith competes today with a bewildering variety of religious and nonreligious perspectives. Religious diversity and disagreement raise perplexing questions, both for followers of Jesus Christ and for those still considering the gospel message. With the many alternatives available today, why should one become or remain a Christian? Given the widespread disagreement among religions, can one reasonably suppose that his or her own particular religious tradition is true and all others are false? Does not the fact of widespread disagreement undermine the plausibility of any particular claim to distinctive truth? The challenges to Christian faith today come not only from secularists and atheists but also from those who are deeply religious. Given globalization, people today are aware of religious diversity and disagreement as never before. Moreover, many today—including many Christian theologians—question whether it is possible to assess the truth or rationality of alternative religious worldviews in a nonarbitrary manner. There are, we are told, no nonarbitrary criteria on the basis of which we might conclude that one religious perspective is more likely to be true than others.[85] Thus, Christian apologetics in the days ahead must contend with some fresh issues, including sophisticated challenges from intellectuals in other religions and a pluralistic and relativistic ethos that rejects any particular religion as distinctively true.

---

84. John Stott, "Twenty Years after Lausanne: Some Personal Reflections," *International Bulletin of Missionary Research* 19, no. 2 (April 1995): 54.

85. Religious relativism and skepticism are widespread today. For more on principles that might be used in assessing various worldviews, see Harold Netland, *Encountering Religious Pluralism* (Downers Grove, IL: InterVarsity, 2001), 284–307; Michael Peterson, William Hasker, Bruce Reichenbach, and David Basinger, *Reason and Religious Belief,* 5th ed. (New York: Oxford University Press, 2013), 337–340; *Interpreting across Boundaries: New Essays in Comparative Philosophy,* edited by Gerald James Larson and Eliot Deutsch (Princeton, NJ: Princeton University Press, 1988).

The kind of issues dealt with in interreligious apologetics will differ somewhat from the issues addressed in apologetics in contexts of post-Christendom agnosticism or atheism. Some questions, of course, will be similar. The question of God's existence and the problem of evil will be central for Buddhists and Jains and also for secular agnostics and atheists. Questions about the deity of Jesus Christ are relevant for both atheists and Muslims, Hindus, and Buddhists. But other issues are especially significant in an interreligious context. How is one to know which, if any, sacred scriptures are indeed divinely inspired? Why accept the Bible as God's Word but not the Qur'an? Many religions include miracle claims.[86] Are they all to be accepted as true? If not, why should we accept the miracle claims in the Bible but not those in other religious texts? Do certain mystical states provide direct access to ultimate reality? If not, why not? How should we assess reports of religious experiences in the many religions? Are they all veridical? How do we distinguish those that are veridical from those that are not? And so on.

Those engaging in interreligious apologetics must take the necessary time to study other religious traditions carefully, making sure that they understand other religious worldviews accurately and are not simply dealing with simplistic caricatures. This will demand rigorous and extensive study, mastering the languages necessary for study of their authoritative texts and supplementing literature-based research with ethnographic studies of religious communities. Furthermore, responsible interreligious apologetics will be fair in its treatment of other religious worldviews, willingly acknowledging what is true and good in them even as it points out what is false or otherwise problematic. The objective is not to score easy points at the expense of the other but rather to understand the other's position adequately so that one can provide compelling reasons for considering what the Scriptures say about the gospel of Jesus Christ.

Given the deep ethnic, cultural, and religious tensions in our world, those engaging in interreligious apologetics must be especially careful not to inflame such tensions unnecessarily. They should be sensitive to potential misunderstandings and the importance of culturally appropriate means

---

86. See Kenneth L. Woodward, *The Book of Miracles: The Meaning of the Miracle Stories in Christianity, Judaism, Buddhism, Hinduism, and Islam* (New York: Touchstone, 2000); David K. Clark, "Miracles in the World Religions," in *In Defense of Miracles*, edited by R. Douglas Geivett and Gary Habermas (Downers Grove, IL: InterVarsity, 1997), 199–213; Craig S. Keener, *Miracles: The Credibility of the New Testament Accounts*, 2 vols. (Grand Rapids, MI: Baker, 2011). See also *The Cambridge Companion to Miracles*, edited by Graham H. Twelftree (New York: Cambridge University Press, 2011), especially the essays in parts 3 and 4.

of persuasion. Interreligious encounters do not occur in a historical or cultural vacuum; both sides of the encounter bring with them the accumulated heritage of the past and the potential for misunderstandings in the present. Effective use of morally acceptable and culturally appropriate means of persuasion requires appreciation of the past and present realities within which the interreligious encounter takes place.

Christian apologists should also be sensitive to perceptions of symbolic power within interreligious encounters. The attempt to persuade religious others that they should change their fundamental beliefs and accept core Christian claims as true can easily be perceived as an inappropriate assertion of power, especially if the Christian is associated with significant cultural, economic, political, or military frameworks of power. Moreover, any activity that is manipulative or coercive or otherwise infringes upon the dignity of the other must be rejected. Historical factors make interreligious apologetics in certain contexts especially difficult. Contexts in which Christianity has been closely associated with cultural superiority, racism, or economic exploitation make interreligious apologetics particularly problematic. Christians should be especially careful about apologetic encounters with religious communities, such as Jewish and Muslim communities, that have suffered greatly in the past at the hands of Christendom. Christian apologists in interreligious contexts must not only be skilled at defending the truth of the Christian message, but they must also be winsome and gracious, serving as peacemakers and instruments of reconciliation as appropriate. But when conducted properly, Christian apologetics with respect to other religious worldviews is an essential and significant part of Christian witness and discipleship.

As we conclude this chapter, we return to the centrality of the gospel for Christian mission and witness. The heart of the gospel of Jesus Christ is the message of the cross, for, in the words of Christopher Wright, "The cross and resurrection of Jesus bring us to the central point of the whole line of redemption in history. Here is God's answer to every dimension of sin and evil in the cosmos and all their destructive effects."[87] Yet, as Ramachandra reminds us, this is a scandalous message:

> The message of the cross is scandalous, for it tells us that it is not the "good Christian" or the "sincere Hindu" or the "devout Muslim" or the "men and women of good will" who are recipients of the vision of God.

87. Christopher J. H. Wright, *The Mission of God's People: A Biblical Theology of the Church's Mission* (Grand Rapids, MI: Zondervan, 2010), 43.

Rather, that it is the bad Christian, the bad Hindu, the bad Buddhist—those who know themselves to be moral failures—who may well be closer to the kingdom of God. This can be so simply because salvation is through grace, mediated in the cross of Christ, received in faith. I know of no statement more subversive of the "world religions" than Paul's description in Romans 4:5 of the Father of the Lord Jesus Christ as "him who justifies the ungodly."[88]

It is not human religiosity at its best that makes us acceptable to God; the cross speaks to us of our spiritual bankruptcy and the need for mercy and grace among even the most pious of us. The cross is God's gracious answer to our spiritual helplessness. It is this message of God's action in Christ on our behalf that is at the very heart of our Christian witness and an evangelical theology of religions.

A skeptical world is watching the church to see how evangelical Christians respond to the growing presence of religious others in our midst. In the days ahead, evangelicals must demonstrate that they can both be faithful to Jesus Christ as the one Lord and Savior for all peoples and work for peace, harmony, and mutual respect among adherents of different religions. Yes, they must engage in responsible evangelism among followers of other faiths. But they must also be active in promoting justice and protecting the rights of minority religious communities. So even as they embrace Buddhists, Hindus, and Muslims as fellow human beings created in God's image and as fellow citizens, they must also humbly urge them to be reconciled to God through Jesus Christ. For this is what it means to live as Christ's disciples in light of the gospel in a world with many religious paths.

88. Ramachandra, *Faiths in Conflict?* 116.

PART TWO

Responses

Response 1

Lamin Sanneh

IF I WERE to give this response a title, it would be "Truth and Divergence." Let me explain.

The truth of the case for salvation may be self-evident to believers in terms of their own tradition even where there is much divergence about how that case applies to other religious traditions and their adherents. Taking an evangelical perspective, this book returns to that familiar issue by examining how Christians should regard other religious traditions and their adherents without contradiction or compromise. It squares up to the challenge of how one may defend the truth claims of the gospel while at the same time responding positively and candidly to other religions. It is the specifically evangelical understanding of this question that is the concern of the authors, and that focus is the background of this response.

Debate and argument belong with the self-understanding of Christians, and a vast array of sources and experiences have been introduced into the growing religious core of the faith. That process did not produce just a mottled and diverse religious tradition; it also bequeathed a rich heritage of intellectual and cultural influences to the religion. The same may be said of other religions, with Islam, for instance, exhibiting another striking example of it. We would not recognize these religions from their relatively simple origins when we view them from the standpoint of later developments. As Carl Becker rightly noted, "The religion now known as Islam is as near to the preaching of Muhammed [sic] or as remote from it, as modern Catholicism or Protestant Christianity is at variance or in harmony with the teaching of Jesus. The simple beliefs of the prophet and his contemporaries are separated by a long course of development from the complicated religious system in its unity and diversity which Islam now presents to us."[1]

The charge with which thinking Christians have had to contend is one that bedevils them with intolerance of other religions and cultures, and as they scurry for cover, Christians have been inclined to speak from both sides of their mouths by, on the one hand, being willing to forgo their own exclusive

---

1. C. H. Becker, *Christianity and Islam* (London and New York: Harper, 1909), 9.

religious claims while, on the other, being eager to appear tolerant by defending the right of others to hold on to the truth claims of their religion by which
Christians must be judged. But is this a plausible position? Can Christians
demand that interfaith dialogue be undertaken on the basis that no one religion has the fullness of truth and no one is the final winner without requiring
other religions to abandon their claims of particularity and, in that way, strip
religions of their raison d'être? Can we put those words into the mouth of a
Muslim and still claim that we are promoting respect and understanding of
Islam? Furthermore, what is the point of dialogue when disagreement has
been rendered moot by the disavowal of particular truth claims? Can we know
ourselves as religious persons without the religious sources of our identity
and without the capacity to discriminate and to evaluate? Must interreligious
encounter involve making a hostage of each of our particular traditions before
we can undertake it? The objection of critics of religious uniqueness that if we
privilege one particular perception of religious truth as the only correct one,
we make true dialogue impossible and open ourselves to the charge of intolerance sounds like an implicit attack on what makes the religious traditions of
others also distinctive. The individual truth claims that religions privilege in
terms of what they consider primary and characteristic of them is now given
up to make way for dialogue. The corollary of the attack on religious uniqueness is that strife and intolerance are the price we will pay for our refusal to
surrender claims of religious uniqueness: our guilt rises from our faith commitment in its specific nature.

The response of the book to this charge seems to me sound as it stands;
there is no need to rehearse it at this stage. The important argument that the
Christian encounter with the Jesus of Scripture and tradition compels reflection on the truth claims made by and for Jesus properly begets the question
about where such claims leave other truth claims. Christian truth claims turn
out to be pertinent to the inquiry that other religions undertake on grounds of
their own. A central piece of that inquiry is that problems of human rebellion
and sin are facets of the freedom and choice that define our moral nature.
Christian teaching looks to the divine initiative in love and grace for remedy
without making divine intervention coercive or mechanistic. The human will,
implicated in rebellion and sin, is to the same extent implicated in consent
and trust: the Church affirms that no one is saved against his or her will.
The element of self-incrimination that aids and abets personal moral decep-
tion such as that involved in sin supplies the fuel of rebellion when we fail to
respond to what God offers us in spirit and truth.

In this respect, I am persuaded by the argument that if there is any truth
to the claim that salvation is the reward of faith and of trust in the salvific

merits of Christ as God has made that known to us, it cannot be acceptable to conclude that the existence of other ways of being religious gives the lie to the Christian way, or vice versa. If we concede the right of other religions to veto the Christian teaching that conflicts with their claims, we would allow them to reject us by values based on their equally partial claims, precisely the charge critics have leveled at Christians. The world of interreligious encounter would have the illusion of generous inclusion and diversity while being riddled with unspoken intolerance and exclusion. This is a case not of "the rooster being out of tune with the choir" but, as C. S. Lewis put it, of the day when a dog in the manger has become the tyrant of the universe. According to this way of thinking, the fact that some people may be excluded from salvation means that no one can be granted salvation unless we have the assurance that no one can be excluded. It sounds like a generous and open-minded position, but it is really another version of hard-line exclusivist thinking.

Does this mean that we are imprisoned behind walls of permanent exclusion and separation? The book argues that we are not, and I concur. There are shafts of truth occurring in other religions, just as there is evidence among their adherents of genuine moral striving about whose precise nature and ultimate outcome we must be modestly open-minded. Salvation is not something we do to or for others, however generously we may esteem them. However admirable it may be, a vague religious goodwill is unworthy of the truth to which we must give ourselves in the first instance without presuming on our worthiness or on that of others.

The central question to which all this discussion points concerns truth as God's exclusive prerogative and testimony rather than as a cultural trophy that we possess to dispose of as we deem fit. This is the book's greatest strength, in the sense that such a view of truth is consistent with itself and with the demands of mutual responsibility in interreligious encounter. The fundamental challenge of religions includes that of accounting for the world we share with others with respect to belief in God, the Way, or Ultimate Truth. The Christian account as set forth in this book seeks to relate that challenge to the world as we know and experience it—that is, the world as God has made it and given to us, and us to it. God is in us as God is also in the world, and it is in the nature of faith commitment that in certain crucial situations, the Church must resist the temptation to speak when it should act.

Three stages are involved in the Christian understanding of God's self-witness and of salvation. The first is that God as the ultimate truth is beyond our comprehension though not unconnected to our affinity and capacity for encounter with truth. The second is that so far as only truth is worthy of itself—so far as truth cannot contradict itself—God's self-witness is the definitive and final divine measure. That self-witness is how Scripture and tradition have presented Christ to us (John 1:18, 10:30, 10:38; Matt. 11:27; Col. 1:19, 2:9). The work of the Holy Spirit belongs in this sphere of God's self-witness and has the function of confirming and safeguarding apostolic teaching. The Spirit vindicates the person and ministry of Christ as God's self-disclosure and to that extent is authoritative for faith and conduct without prevarication. The third stage has to do with salvation as the act of God so understood and our place in the divine economy by virtue of our response.

The challenge for Christian faith is whether and how a response to the salvific power of God can or may occur in other religions without that requiring membership in the Church. It is an unavoidable question yet one that does not require multilateral streamlining to be resolved. The historical evidence of variety and diversity of faith commitment should not become the target of attack that stipulates uniformity or conformity as the basis of sound belief. Truth and difference are not a contradiction. That paradox occurs widely in culture and is recognized as such, as the British philosopher Mary Midgley noted: "It is because there is no pre-set single priority system available that cultures [and religions] differ so much, and because their basic problems [of moral freedom] are the same, they are, none the less, so similar."[2] Similarity is not at the expense of difference here, and so the search for a Holy Grail of religious equality is a false one. While there is no single aim for human life, as Midgley rightly points out, there is an intrinsic coherence that manifests itself in meaning and purpose. This does not mean that the mission of the Church exists to make conquest of other religions a prerequisite and a goal; it means, to amend Bonhoeffer, that the Church is but the diverse and growing members of humanity in which Christ has taken complete and compelling form.[3] The evangelical witness is about how the truth-bearing power of the triune God's self-witness affects the perennial multifaceted moral quest for meaning and purpose and how its perspective-altering consequences bring us into harmony with God's self-declared purpose and its vindication in Christ. This book makes it clear that the presence of other religions is not in conflict

2. Mary Midgley, "On Being Terrestrial," in *Objectivity and Cultural Divergence*, Royal Institute of Philosophy Lecture Series 17, edited by S. C. Brown (Cambridge: Cambridge University Press, 1984), 79–91, 89. As cited by Midgley, Darwin observed that "the social instincts—the prime principle of man's moral constitution—with the aid of active intellectual powers and effect of habit, naturally lead to the golden rule—'As ye would that men should do to you, do ye to them likewise,' and this lies at the foundation of morality." Charles Darwin, *The Descent of Man* (Princeton, NJ: Princeton University Press, 1981 [1871]), 105.

3. Dietrich Bonhoeffer, *Ethics* (London: SCM, 1971), 64.

with the values of tolerance and diversity but is the occasion for commitment to those values.

In Albert Camus's novel *L'Étranger*, we have a description of a priest confronting an unbeliever. The priest pulls out a drawer, brings out a silver crucifix, and brandishes it in the face of his recalcitrant friend to try to break him down. Commenting on this episode, the English writer Geoffrey Ainger says that Jesus did not call us to wave the cross; he called us to carry it.[4] This is not just a rhetorical point, because "every time Christ is made more real to someone else through my presence or my words, he is made more real to me."[5] The witness to the gospel is his or her own first convert.

There are strains of evangelical theology that are not consistent with this stringent understanding of mission and witness, and the book discusses some of these. The "insider movement" is one case in point. It concerns Muslim followers of 'Isa, the Muslim name for Christ, who are resolved to remain within the Muslim community. Evangelical attitudes toward such "insiders" run the gamut from full rejection of any association with Islam to embrace of Muslim and culture though retaining an admiration for 'Isa. What seems to be the driving force of the insider movement is a centuries-long Muslim resistance to Christianity and the desire to break the logjam. The numbers involved are statistically insignificant, and the citadel of resistance remains largely unassailable. Meanwhile, the price being paid to breach it may be too high, with the insiders themselves being open to reprisals from their neighbors and their overseas evangelical supporters tying themselves up in fruitless theological wrangles about truth and contextualization. A splintering Christian witness, full and sufficient salvation in Christ in one direction and an abridged and sequestered faith in the other, merely plays into the Muslim view of Christianity as a construct devised purely by human hands, thus falling well short of the sovereign criterion that only truth is worthy of itself. We cannot see the sun except in its own light. The muezzin's *allahu akbar*, "God than whom is nothing greater," towers with context-defying authority to constitute a rebuke to Christian faintheartedness. The insider movement concedes the primacy of that Muslim claim and is a long way from the definitive divine self-witness offered without ambiguity or reservation that this book so lucidly sets forth.

---

4. Cited in John V. Taylor, *The Go-Between God: The Holy Spirit and the Christian Mission* (London: SCM, 1972), 139.

5. Ibid.

In broad terms, I take this book as a cautionary lesson against conceding that religions exist only to maximize their own advantage at the expense of others, that they are infected by an insidious crypto-Darwinism that leaves them invested in their survival as the crown of all their striving. There are many inscrutable questions about the ultimate fate of human beings concerning their status before the God who reveals and redeems, who saves and judges, and who warns and guides, but in the face of the light in which we see all light, the world of other religions is not incomprehensible, nor are the demands of faith and witness irrelevant:

> Many a man who rejects the formulae of theological Christology because he understands them amiss may yet existentially have a perfectly genuine Christian faith in the Incarnation of the Word of God. Anyone who contemplating Jesus, his cross and death, really believes that here the living God has spoken to him the final, decisive, irrevocable word that delivers him from all bondage to the existential categories of his sinful, death-doomed existence, believes in the reality of the Jesus of Christian faith, believes in the Incarnation of God's Word, whether or not he realizes the fact.[6]

---

6. Karl Rahner and Herbert Vorgrimler, "Jesus Christ," in *Concise Theological Dictionary*, edited by Cornelius Ernst and translated by Richard Strachan (London: Burns and Oates, 1965), 241.

Response 2

Veli-Matti Kärkkäinen

I WHOLEHEARTEDLY WELCOME the publication of this new work by two leading evangelical scholars of religions. In many respects, the project advances
the continuing quest for a more proper response to religions by Christian
theologians in general and evangelical ones in particular. Let me first briefly
mention the main benefits of this monograph and then elaborate on a few.
First of all, rather than continuing the standard abstract and formal theology
of religions—an approach that usually ends up being just that, abstract and
formal, without much in specific to say to any particular issue—McDermott
and Netland adopt the doctrine of the Trinity as the main control and lens. This
is a significant move and is in keeping with the increasing scholarship in the
field of theology of religions.[1] A second important merit of the present work
is the move toward what is nowadays called comparative theology. Whereas
theology-of-religions discourse stays at the more generic level, comparative
theology—gleaning from but also going beyond the alleged "neutral" standpoint of the religious-studies paradigm—seeks to engage other faith traditions
by looking at specific topics such as revelation and community. Comparative
theology provides a challenging interdisciplinary platform as it calls for basic
knowledge of not only Christian theology but also other faith traditions.[2] The

---

1. Raimundo Panikkar, *The Trinity and the Religious Experience of Man* (Maryknoll, NY: Orbis,
1973); Jacques Dupuis, *Toward a Christian Theology of Religious Pluralism* (Maryknoll,
NY: Orbis, 1998); Gavin D'Costa, *The Meeting of Religions and the Trinity* (Maryknoll,
NY: Orbis, 2000); S. Mark Heim, *The Depths of the Riches: A Trinitarian Theology of Religious
Ends* (Grand Rapids, MI: Eerdmans, 2001); Keith E. Johnson, *Rethinking the Trinity and
Religious Pluralism: An Augustinian Assessment* (Downers Grove, IL: InterVarsity, 2011);
Veli-Matti Kärkkäinen, *Trinity and Religious Pluralism: The Doctrine of the Trinity in Christian
Theology of Religions* (Aldershot, UK: Ashgate, 2004). For a sympathetic and critical assess-
ment of these (and some other) proposals, see Veli-Matti Kärkkäinen, "'How to Speak of the
Spirit among Religions': Trinitarian 'Rules' for a Pneumatological Theology of Religions,"
International Bulletin of Missionary Research 30, no. 3 (July 2006): 121–127. For my own con-
structive proposal in critical dialogue with these theologies and engaging the teachings of
four living faiths (Jewish, Muslim, Buddhist, and Hindu), see Veli-Matti Kärkkäinen, *Trinity
and Revelation*, Vol. 1 of *Constructive Christian Theology for the Pluralistic World* (Grand Rapids,
MI: Eerdmans, 2014), especially chaps. 14 and 15.

2. Understandably, comparative-theology scholars come from two main backgrounds: some
are trained primarily in religions (Francis X. Clooney), others in theology (Keith Ward).

authors of this book ably carry on this task. Whereas the (former) Oxford theologian-philosopher Keith Ward attempted a comparative theology project by first looking at the other faith traditions and only then constructed a Christian proposal,[3] the current work delves first into Christian resources and then subsequently into comparative work. Both approaches are fine and legitimate. Third, it is significant that the religious and theological conversation also includes the topic of religious life (chapter 5), in other words, the ethical and "practical" aspects. For some curious reason, that part of the dialogue between religions is often missed, although in practice, the lifestyle-related questions, including their ethical/moral implications, often arise at the forefront of the encounter between people of living faiths. Anyone who has lived in a multireligious environment, particularly in a minority, knows experientially how dominant these issues loom in everyday life. Related to this issue is the careful consideration of the relation of religion to culture (chapter 6), which succeeds in going beyond the rather limited "contextualization" conversation that evangelicals have had now for several decades.

Engaging this project, I was asking again and again: What is pluralism? How do these authors conceive it? Sure, the book includes a brief discussion of pluralism in chapter 1 and usefully engages various types of Christian pluralisms from what I have come to call John Hick's "first-generation pluralism" with its assumption of the common core of all religions, to Raimundo Panikkar's Hindu-Christian cosmotheandrism with its insistence on real differences among religions (although with a hope for "convergence" in the future), to Mark Heim's distinctively Trinitarian approach to religions. Clearly, the authors are well versed in the plurality of religious pluralisms. Therefore, for the sake of the clarity of the book and its argumentation, it would have been highly useful to begin to develop an elusive typology of pluralisms. Indeed, currently, we should speak of "pluralisms" (plural) on the analogy of "postmodernisms." As the paradigm of pluralism, Hick's naive and philosophically/theologically problematic "rough-parity" approach perhaps looms too large in the conversation. With this in mind, I wonder if the introductory chapter 1 could have been planned quite differently. Rather than delving into the now-well-known history of the theology of religions (on which there are useful guides available, short and long), a more detailed scrutiny of the

3. Keith Ward, *Religion and Revelation: A Theology of Revelation in the World's Religions* (Oxford, UK: Clarendon, 1994); Ward, *Religion and Creation* (Oxford, UK: Clarendon, 1996); Ward, *Religion and Human Nature* (Oxford, UK: Clarendon, 1998); Ward, *Religion and Community* (Oxford, UK: Clarendon, 2000). Curiously, the invaluable contribution of Ward's writings is ignored in this project (and, strangely, in one passing comment, Ward is made a pluralist).

phenomenon of religious pluralisms would have been in order. Let me also add (knowing well that books are always better written in hindsight) that the fairly detailed discussion of evangelicalism in the same chapter repeats the standard material and approaches among evangelical scholars. I wonder if those fairly sterile and abstract definitions of evangelicalism stand in need of some refining, redefinition, and perhaps "opening up" in light of the drastically changed situation in the world and the church at the beginning of the twenty-first century. The two authors, both on the forefront of evangelical engagement with the "world," would have been ideal candidates for such an enterprise (I hope their future writings will take this up).

On the engagement of revelation (chapter 3), I wonder if a more focused look at the understanding of the nature and role of Scripture in other faiths would yield more specific results for the dialogue. It is a curious fact that all living faiths have produced huge amounts of sacred literature, some of it "canonical," some "secondary." In the future, the way to go might be to work "from below," as it were: rather than relying on generic statements about what, say, various types of Buddhists teach about salvation, begin instead with the self-understanding of Buddhists, Hindus, Muslims, and others as expressed in their writings. (For all types of Christian pluralists, it is "bad news" that virtually without exception, all living faiths hold their Scriptures as divinely inspired, in some sense or another, and hence as ultimate authority—even Theravadins do so in practice, because their Scriptures are the only way to access the means to the way of enlightenment as experienced by Shakyamuni.)

Back on the positive side, the authors' viewing the topic of salvation through the lenses of the vision of His Holiness the Dalai Lama and John Hick makes a great entry point, in that it goes beyond the abstract categories and instead considers some specifics. That same chapter helpfully begins by observing that it is particularly the question of salvation that has contributed to the conflicts and even violence among religions. With regard to the topic of violence, however, I think something more and something deeper should be said, because it is such an urgent issue not only between Christians and other faiths but also among non-Christian faith traditions, as evident, for example, in the continuing conflicts on the Indian subcontinent. Perhaps a whole chapter could have been devoted to this important topic. If not that, then, at least have a solid discussion of the role of violence in the Christian understanding of salvation, most prominently in the events of the cross. The harsh critique of the presence and alleged advocacy of violence in atonement theories comes not only from various corners of Christian theology but also from religious scholars and some writers of other faith traditions. This chapter would have offered a marvelous opportunity to respond.

One of the topics that is conspicuously missing in this comparative-theology discourse has to do with the theology of creation and humanity. Is this lack because evangelicals by and large have not typically focused on those inter-related topics? On the other hand, we know that all living faiths possess a rich reservoir of creation cosmologies, including humanity's place therein. Talk about human beings—us!—would offer a great platform of dialogue (as Ward's *Religion and Human Nature* testifies). Furthermore, yet another theo-logical topic has been missed, namely, eschatology. That is even stranger in light of the fact that of all topics, the end times have occupied (and continue to occupy) evangelical minds. Again, religions provide us with a matrix of eschatological visions, hopes, and myths. By registering these two main areas of dogmatic theology missing in the conversation, I am not necessarily sug-gesting that they should have been there; I am just wondering why they are missing.

Regarding the comparative-theology conversation in this book, let me make an observation that probably reflects my own discipline (systematic and ecumenical theology) as much as anything else. While the biblical materi-als and some useful historical theological considerations are present in the discussion, oddly enough, the rich reservoir of contemporary systematic/con-structive/doctrinal theologies is ignored. However, that is where many of the responses to the kinds of challenges tackled in this book have been offered in recent decades.

Back to the lens of the Trinity through which the challenge and oppor-tunity of interfaith dialogue is approached in this study, let me make this observation: after chapter 2, which richly and usefully develops a Trinitarian account of the Christian doctrine of God, Trinity is not visible much in the rest of the book. What I mean is simply this: while Trinitarian grammar cer-tainly is assumed and there are occasional brief references to the Trinity, one wonders what would have happened if throughout the book, an intentionally Trinitarian approach had been applied. What might have been the shape of the Christian doctrine of revelation fashioned in a Trinitarian grammar? Or the doctrine of salvation? And so forth. It seems to me that Christological (and to a lesser extent, patrological) criteria and resources are brought to bear on the discussion quite extensively. However, the pneumatological resources are strangely missing, and the role of the Holy Spirit in the world, among the religions, and even in Christian faith is fairly thin. True, some "turns" to the Spirit in the contemporary theology-of-religions discourse are in need of careful critique, and the book does that well. Yet a constructive pneumatologi-cal orientation in a healthy Trinitarian framework would have made the book stronger and more dynamic.

Response 3

Vinoth Ramachandra

IN PLURALIST SOCIETIES, Christians bring to the public arena not only the liberal political virtues of tolerance and social inclusion but also a gracious liberality—in biblical idiom, a "love for the stranger." This entails an eagerness to understand, appreciate, and learn from others who are different even as we profoundly disagree with them.

To what extent does such a generous sensibility depend on getting our theological models of the Trinity "correct"? One has only to glance at the politics of societies shaped by Eastern Orthodoxy to wonder what impact Trinitarian theology has on the lives of professional theologians and church leaders, let alone "ordinary" church members. Should one conclude that too much has been claimed for theology and too little attention paid to the canonical narrative and social practices on which all good theology rests and which is constitutive of the Church's identity?

McDermott and Netland rightly argue that the language of Trinity is not the coupling of an abstract principle of unity with an abstract principle of difference in order to explain the nature of reality. That language seeks, rather, to make sense not of a philosophical puzzle but of a particular set of historical events centered in Jesus of Nazareth. The God disclosed in these events has a narrative identity, so the Trinitarian identification of God presupposes the truth and epistemic centrality of that narrative in the Church's engagement with the world, including the world of "religions." Forgetfulness of the historical origins of that language, our authors point out, lies behind the misguided attempts by some theologians in recent years (both in the West and in Asia) to ground religious plurality in the Trinitarian being of God. Bland endorsements of difference skate over those differences that need to be confronted as idolatrous.

So far, so good. The propensity to idolatry is pervasive in human thought and behavior, and Trinitarian theology is not immune to it. Do McDermott and Netland sufficiently heed this caution in their own account?

Imagine a young Hindu student of comparative religion in a typical secular university in the United States. She observes that there are well over fifty Christian groups on her campus, many calling themselves "evangelical" and divided on ethnic, denominational, and organizational lines. They compete with one another for her conversion. The churches in the city are no less fragmented, and she learns of rivalries and backbiting among the pastors. There is no coming together for any act of worship, no sharing of material or training resources. These "evangelical" churches, she discovers, export their divisions and rivalries overseas in the name of "missions."

All of this leaves her thoroughly perplexed. She is aware of how Jesus himself spoke of the credibility of his message as depending on the visible unity of his disciple community: "As you, Father, are in me and I am in you, may they also be one in us, so that the world may know that you have sent me" (John 17:21); "I in them and you in me, that they may become completely one, so that the world may know that you have sent me and have loved them even as you have loved me" (John 17:23). She has read the Pauline epistles. The Church is the body of Christ, and its unity is not an impossible distant ideal but a present reality, in the Spirit, that has to be maintained (Eph. 4:3).

Thus, our Hindu student would vehemently disagree with McDermott and Netland's conclusion to their book: "A skeptical world is watching the Church to see how evangelical Christians respond to the growing presence of religious others in our midst." She would reply that a skeptical world is unimpressed, because the gulf between the Church's rhetoric of reconciliation and her practice—and particularly the failure of evangelical Christians to love one another, let alone other Christians—makes Christian truth claims quite incredible. And note that in rejecting the truth of the gospel, she is invoking an epistemological criterion drawn from the biblical tradition itself.

I would add that the problem here is not the fact of disunity and division, for this is evident in the apostolic Church itself. Sin will mar our relationships until the *eschaton*. Rather, it is the lack of any anguish, any agonizing of spirit, among "evangelical" leaders over their disobedience to Christ that distinguishes them from the apostles and postapostolic fathers. Christians in the ancient world sensed that failure of love among Christians threatened the very existence of the church. The suggestion that Christ is divided fills Paul with horror (e.g., in 1 Cor. 1:12–13). Clement of Rome writes to the same church at Corinth around the end of the first century:

> Why must there be all this quarrelling and bad blood, these feuds and dissensions among you? Have we not all the same God, and the same Christ? Is not the same Spirit of grace shed upon us all? Have we not all the same calling in Christ? Then why are we rending and tearing asunder the limbs of Christ, and fomenting discord among our own

body? Why are we so lost to all sense and reason that we have forgotten our membership of one another? Your disunity has led many astray; and, yet, in spite of the discouragement and doubt it has sown in many minds and the distress it has brought upon us all, you still persist in your disaffection.[1]

Deconstructing Belief/Practice

Our Hindu student's insight into the blind spots of evangelicalism may stem partly from the fact that the Hindu identity is defined by practice rather than belief. As Frits Staal says, a Hindu "may be a theist, pantheist, atheist, communist and believe whatever he likes, but what makes him into a Hindu are the ritual practices he performs and the rules to which he adheres, in short, what he *does*."[2] However, even in Christian tradition, the relationship between belief and practice has never been one-way. The Mennonite historian Alan Kreider reminds us that before Christendom, conversion involved a comprehensive change in a person's behavior, belonging, and beliefs—and in that order. It might be (and often was) accompanied by a powerful experience, although this was not considered as significant as the baptismal candidate's proven change of behavior and willingness to identify with a community in which he associated with people drawn from all walks of life, including his personal, tribal, and "national" enemies.

"The early Christian catechists," writes Kreider, "were attempting not so much to impart concepts as to nurture communities whose values would be different from those of conventional society. Christian leaders assumed that people did not think their way into a new kind of life; they lived their way into a new kind of thinking. The candidates' socialization and their professions and life commitments would determine whether they could receive what the Christian community considered to be good news."[3] If so, might this be the reason, as Kreider suggests, that early Christian conversions produced a truly

1. Clement of Rome, First Epistle to the Corinthians, 46 (ca. A.D. 96 AD), in *Early Christian Writings: The Apostolic Fathers*, translated by Maxwell Staniforth (Harmondsworth, UK: Penguin, 1968), 47. Note how Trinitarian language slips in, so naturally, to undergird appeals for unity.

2. Quoted in Gavin Flood, *An Introduction to Hinduism* (Cambridge, UK: Cambridge University Press, 1996), 53.

3. Alan Kreider, *The Change of Conversion and the Origin of Christendom* (Harrisburg, PA: Trinity Press International, 1999), 23; emphasis added.

countercultural movement, whereas evangelistic programs in our time make people "Christians" but unconverted?

Stanley Jones was an American Methodist missionary-scholar of the mid-twentieth century who spent most of his life in India and was a personal friend of Mahatma Gandhi. This was his assessment of the tragedy and the challenge of Gandhi's relationship with Christians:

> Mahatma Gandhi did not see in the Cross what the convinced Christian sees, namely, God was in Christ reconciling the world unto Himself and that He was bearing our sins in His body on the Tree. Gandhi did not see that. But what he did see, namely, that you can take on yourself suffering, and not give it, and thus conquer the heart of another—that he did see in the Cross and that he put into practice and put into practice on a national scale. The difference, then, is this: we as Christians saw more in the Cross than Gandhi and put it into operation less; Gandhi saw less in the Cross than we and put it into practice more. We left the Cross a doctrine, Gandhi left it a deed.[4]

Jones also noted that Gandhi refused to preach anything that he had not tried: "When I urged him to go to Europe before the war, hoping that his very presence there would be a call to peace instead of war, his reply was simple: 'I have not demonstrated peace in my country, how can I preach it in Europe?' "[5]

This is the kind of challenge that interfaith relationships bring. As Christians work alongside others on issues of common public concern, opportunities arise for all to ask probing questions of one another that disclose the assumptions and values on which they conduct their lives. Outside of some Western contexts, people for the most part are not embarrassed to talk freely about their religious beliefs and even engage in vigorous argument. And, as McDermott and Netland rightly state, criticism—provided it does not descend to caricature and invective—is a form of respect for another's views. We do not know what we really believe, let alone how far our lives conform to what we claim to believe, until we engage in such dialogue with others who are radically different. And such dialogue includes exposure to the best exponents of another faith, whether religious or secular, through personal engagement or by way of their writings.

4. E. Stanley Jones, *Mahatma Gandhi: An Interpretation* (London: Hodder & Stoughton, 1948), 105.

5. Ibid., 106.

Formal interfaith dialogue events, involving leaders or scholars from different religious communities, address the wider social and political contexts of their communities. Thus, Christian-Muslim dialogue in the United States cannot sidestep the politics of the Middle East and the co-optation of large sections of the evangelical church by right-wing political and corporate interests.[6] Similarly, Buddhist-Christian dialogue in Sri Lanka cannot avoid confronting the way Sinhala-Buddhism has become a chauvinist ideology that has promoted militarism and violence against other communities.

Apart from showing unconditional grace toward the ungodly and godforsaken, the triune God challenges the world of religions in the following ways:

(a) This God expresses outrage at the injustice in his world. The anger of the biblical God against injustice and the oppression of the poor has no parallel in any of the major Asian religious traditions. Indeed, it subverts them at a basic level. Anger and protest, not quiescence and complacency, are therefore intrinsic to the witness of the Church of the triune God.

(b) This God shares in the pain and groaning of his world. John Calvin spoke boldly of the "wounds of God," not only with reference to the cross but also in terms of human beings as icons of God. For Calvin, notes Nicholas Wolterstorff, to injure a human being is to injure God; to commit injustice is to inflict suffering on God: "Behind and beneath the social misery of our world is the suffering of God. If we truly believed that, suggests Calvin, we would be much more reluctant than we are to participate in the victimizing of the poor and the oppressed and the assaulted of the world. To pursue justice is to relieve God's suffering."[7]

Wolterstorff observes that Calvin went further. In his Commentary on Habakkuk 2:6, Calvin claims that the cries of the victims are the *very cry of God*. The lament "How long?" is God giving voice to his own lament.[8] One rarely finds such thoughts expressed in Calvinist circles today. Expressing solidarity with the downtrodden by staying with them in situations of suffering and hopelessness and sharing their lament should be a distinctive mark of a witnessing Church.

---

6. In particular, Christian Zionism and the silence of so many evangelical leaders vis-à-vis assaults on the civil liberties of Arab-Americans since September 11, 2001, atrocities committed by the Israeli state (including war crimes), and the use of drones by U.S. forces in northwest Pakistan and elsewhere.

7. Nicholas Wolterstorff, "The Wounds of God: Calvin on Social Injustice," *Reformed Journal* (June 1987): 16.

8. Ibid., 17.

(c) This God saves his world. This is a radically this-worldly understanding of salvation—the redemption of the earth and of human work, the healing of relationships, and the transformation of God's creation to reflect his indwelling reign of justice and peace.

This vision presents a profound challenge to all theologies of religions. As I have written elsewhere, "Why is it assumed, throughout the huge glut of theological literature on religious pluralism, that it is in the realm of 'the religions of the world' that the human-divine encounter is primarily to be located, and that among all the activities of the human spirit (scientific exploration, musical performance, the pursuit of justice, caring for the elderly, and so on) it is in the realm of 'religious experience' that the saving activity of the divine Spirit is to be discerned? Surely the Good News of Jesus Christ radically calls into question these assumptions."[9]

It is surprising, then, that these distinctive and subversive features of the gospel do not receive prominence in McDermott and Netland's otherwise comprehensive exposition.

Deconstructing Labels

Was Calvin an "evangelical"? Surely our response should be "Does it matter?" I confess to being disconcerted by frequent references to "evangelicals think that" and "what evangelicals believe" in the authors' text. Ironically, many of the writers they quote extensively (e.g., Newbigin, Bosch, Sanneh, myself) would not recognize themselves among the definitions of "evangelicals" in the opening chapter.[10] For instance, I have never understood what phrases such as "the primacy of evangelism" mean and would like to see how this is embodied in the lives of those to whom such phrases seem important. It is also possible to accept penal substitution as a central Pauline metaphor and still deny that it encapsulates the heart of the gospel or that it is the most relevant way to communicate the significance of the cross in many (if not most) contexts.

It is not surprising that all these definitions are from authors (e.g., Bebbington, Noll, McGrath) who, to the best of my knowledge, have never lived

---

9. Vinoth Ramachandra, "Truth and Pluralism," in *Mission in Context: Explorations Inspired by J. Andrew Kirk*, edited by John Corrie and Cathy Ross (Farnham, UK, and Burlington, VT: Ashgate, 2012), 137.

10. I work for an organization that has "evangelical" in its title, but there are many of us who understand this in an adjectival sense (as in "evangelical ethics" or "evangelical lifestyle") and not as a noun. We are committed to living out the *evangel* in all areas of life but not to the theological and cultural "baggage" associated with "evangelicalism."

outside the West and whose writings reveal little awareness of non-Western church histories and theologies. "Historic evangelicalism," notes Andrew Walls, "is a religion of protest against a Christian society that is not Christian enough.... The tension between the principle of Christendom and its realization in practice is the history of Western Christianity."[11] Evangelicalism is a reaction against nominal and deist Christianities. Asian and African Christians, however, wrestle with different theological histories and challenges.[12] Is not the attempt to make a thin, albeit important, slice from Anglo-American history normative for the world Church (which is what hard-line evangelicals do) simply an act of cultural imperialism?

McDermott and Netland, of course, do not do this. They acknowledge their debt to a wide range of authors who do not share their own convictions, and their critiques are not only thoughtful and penetrating but always nuanced and gracious.

But I am still left wondering what is gained by prefixing Trinitarian to their theology and, more fundamentally, whether a "theology of religions" is possible. Insofar as theology is a rational enterprise, a "theology of religions" seeks to encompass the enormous range of phenomena that are counted as "religious" and bring them under some overarching framework of understanding and evaluation. I suggest that the enterprise is bound to fail.

First, this is because such theologies invariably narrow the range of "religions" with which they engage. Primal religions are routinely neglected, as are "secular religions" such as nationalism, consumerism, humanism, or Marxism (all of which have a global reach). Indeed, secular humanism fulfills all the descriptions of religion given by McDermott and Netland in chapter 6 and is a far bigger cultural force in North America and western Europe than Christianity or Islam.[13] Moreover, the shopping mall, the health club, the football stadium, the stock exchange, and Independence Day celebrations are great places for studying religious behavior. They are the new temples and sacred icons of the late-modern world, all surrounded by elaborate liturgies,

---

11. Andrew F. Walls, "The Evangelical Revival, the Missionary Movement, and Africa," chap. 7 of *The Missionary Movement in Christian History: Studies in the Transmission of Faith* (New York: Orbis, 1996), 81.

12. Not only "evangelical" but also "liberal," "fundamentalist," and "charismatic" reflect Western theological battles. Those in the U.S. South who identify themselves as "evangelicals" belong to churches or parachurch organizations that were founded by conservative North American or British missionaries in the mid-twentieth century; or they were themselves trained in conservative American or British seminaries.

13. The British Humanist Association seeks recognition as a religious organization.

rituals, the aura of the mysterious; they place a high premium on community and communal loyalty. By treating religion as a separate academic discipline, we may be blinding ourselves to the ways in which religion is flourishing among so-called secular peoples.

Second, these theologies tend toward reductionism, diluting the sheer "otherness" of the other's practices and beliefs. They risk sacrificing the complexity and distinctiveness of each particular faith tradition. Is it not better to acknowledge that our human condition is such that we are faced with incompatible, perhaps even incommensurable, ultimate ends among which we have to choose?

Response 4

Christine Schirrmacher

THERE ARE FEW subjects more important to Christian theology of religions than interreligious dialogue. And the sort of interreligious dialogue that is of particular importance today, in the current geopolitical environment, is dialogue between Christians and Muslims. It might be helpful for readers of this book to touch on important moments of dialogue and encounter in the shared history of these two communities and then to reflect briefly on what this might mean for dialogue today.

When Christians and Muslims encounter each other and begin a conversation today, this is not their first encounter but the latest in their fourteen hundred years of shared history—a history that began in the lifetime of Muhammad, the founder and creator of Islam. In the seventh century A.D., he conducted the first dialogues, and had the first controversies, with Jews and Christians on the Arabian Peninsula on the question of the true revelation of God.

After this period of theological conversation in the seventh century, there followed periods of power-political encounter between Islam and Christianity, territorial conquest, and armed confrontation, but also the translation of the Greek works of antiquity by Arab scholars in the Middle Ages. On the whole, Muslims over the centuries had as little authentic knowledge about the content of the Bible and of the Christian faith as Christians had about Islam and the Qur'an. The first Latin translation of the Qur'an was made, to be sure, as early as 1142, when the abbot of the cloister at Cluny, Petrus Venerabilis, commissioned the two scholars Robert of Ketton and Hermann of Dalmatia, but centuries were still to pass before the Western world dealt more intensively with the teachings of Islam and with the Qur'an. Even the reformer Martin Luther had difficulties in 1542 finding an exact translation of the Qur'an in Latin. He was not able to do so and was able to find only rough translations of the Qur'an that were more summaries than translations. This was thoroughly symptomatic, for nine hundred years after the origin of Islam it was above all apologetic texts that still molded the image of Islam—and these texts frequently included false claims about "the others."

Translation: Dennis L. Slabaugh

In the first centuries after its emergence, then, Islam was largely ignored and underestimated by Western scholars and theologians. In the Middle Ages, it was insulted and slandered, and in the transition to the modern age—especially in the "century of mission"—it was considered conquered and thought to be vastly inferior to Christianity. All of these attitudes and approaches kept Europe's theologians from dealing more intensively with Islam and its claim. Today Islam has become the second-largest world religion and, at the same time, not only a religion but also a social order and a power not to be underestimated.

Today, in the twenty-first century, we have more information available to us than perhaps ever before in history. We know more about Islam and the other religions than we ever have known previously. Today we ought not to be satisfied with dealing superficially with the religion of other human beings but rather ought to attempt to understand their faith and their thought in the way that they themselves understand their religion, without preconceived opinions and without prejudices. This does not mean renouncing one's own point of view but rather quite the opposite. Only the person who knows what he or she believes, and can argue for it, is capable of fruitful dialogue with someone who believes something else. Of course, at the same time, he or she must listen respectfully to the other. In the case of Islam, an engagement with its faith and thought, as presented in this book, is essential.

Islam and Christianity in History

We know only little from the first forty years of Muhammad's life. He was born around the year 570 in Mecca. His father died probably before his birth, and his mother died in about 576, when he was about six years old, which left Muhammad an orphan. He was a merchant by trade and in all probability did not come from an influential family. The Qur'an suggests his lack of means and noble descent (11:91, 93:6–8) when it poses the question, "Why is not this Qur'an sent down to some leading man?" (43:31).

Islam originated in about A.D. 610 on the Arabian Peninsula. Muhammad had the impression, presumably through visions—so, at least, does the Islamic tradition (the hadith) tell us—that God had commissioned him to proclaim a message to the Arabs (who venerated a multitude of gods and spirits): There is only one omnipotent God, before whom all human beings must answer in the Last Judgment.

In Mecca, where Muhammad proclaimed Islam approximately from 610 to 622, he encountered bitter resistance. To be sure, some Arabs in Muhammad's home city accepted Islam, but on the whole, Muhammad found little approval. Because the Meccans finally threatened him, Muhammad emigrated in 615 together with several supporters to neighboring Abyssinia (present-day Ethiopia). Eighty-three adult men, women, and children are said to have belonged to this first emigrant group. But the pressure of persecution from Mecca did not abate, so a second emigration took place in 622. Muhammad and his remaining loyal followers turned to the neighboring city of Medina, together with his loyal companion Abu Bakr, who later was to become Muhammad's first successor (caliph).

In Medina, the history of Islam took two decisive turns. Muhammad was no longer merely a religious leader of his supporters but swiftly became the arbitrator between hostile groups. Soon afterward, he also became a military leader who conducted several wars. He became a lawgiver and, closely following Arab common law, created a marital and family law for the first community of Muslims and also a criminal law. Thus, Islam had become a religion, a social order, and, in the person of Muhammad, also a system of political rule.

In Medina at the time of Muhammad's arrival in 622, there lived two Arab tribes, three Jewish tribes, and also some Christians. In Medina between 622 and 632, Muhammad gradually defeated those who did not recognize him as the prophet of God and military leader—not only Arab tribes but also the Jews of Medina who had opposed him.

Muhammad and the Jews and Christians

In all probability, Muhammad was made acquainted with some fundamentals of the Christian and Jewish faiths through oral accounts rather than independent study of the Old and New Testaments. While in Muhammad's lifetime only individual parts of the Old and New Testaments had been translated into Arabic, several apocryphal texts—Jewish and Christian—also existed, such as a childhood gospel of Jesus in Arabic. Traces of these apocryphal texts are found in the Qur'an and the Islamic tradition. This is why the Qur'an contains traces not only of biblical narrative material but also of apocryphal texts and special doctrines.

Muhammad seems to have begun conducting "religious conversations" with Jews and Christians about God and his activity soon after 622 in Medina, and he apparently was acquainted with basic biblical content and traditions. For the Qur'an makes numerous references to aspects of the content of the Old and New Testaments but supplies its own interpretation of them. Among these, the stories about the prophets in the Qur'an are of particular significance. Muhammad derives the justification for his own mission as God's messenger from the reports about the prophets: Just as God called Adam, Abraham, and Moses as heralds of the one creator and judge, so did he commission Muhammad as the last in the series of prophets, as the "Seal of the Prophets" (33:40).

Hence Muhammad at first acknowledged the revelatory character of the Jewish and Christian writings that preceded the Qur'an and characterized Jews and Christians as "People of the Book" (Arabic *ahl al-kitab*) or "possessors of the writings." Among these earlier texts, the Qur'an mentions the "Torah" (Arabic *taurah*), which was given to Moses; the "Psalms" (Arabic *zabur*) of David; and the "Gospel" (Arabic *injil*) of Jesus. For this reason, the Qur'an, strictly speaking, understands itself not as a new revelation (41:43) but rather as a renewal of an eternal message from God, the creator and judge.

When the Qur'an speaks about Jews and, above all, about Christians, it paints a multifaceted picture. At first, it speaks laudably above all about the Christians. In the first years of the growing familiarity between Muslims and Christians, the piety, love, humility, and faith of the Christians are praised especially. The Qur'an remarks: "You will find those who stand nearest the believers in love among those who say, 'We are Nasara [Christians],' because among these are men devoted to learning and men who have renounced the world, and they are not arrogant" (5:82). Christians possess knowledge of God because they believe in God and the Last Day and for this reason need to have no fear before the Judgment (2:62).

In Muhammad's relationship to the Jews, though, negative developments began to emerge rather soon. They reject his divine mission. The Qur'an threatens the Jews now with "wrath upon wrath" (2:90). Muhammad increasingly condemned the Jewish faith, and also the way of life of the Jews in Medina, as false and deceitful (2:88, 5:13, 2:61, and others). Muhammad's belligerent confrontations with the Jews began in 624. From 624 to 627, he defeated the three large Jewish tribes in Medina, besieged them, and expelled them from the city.

The Christians residing in Arabia were, with great probability, members of the Syrian Monophysite church of Melkite, Jacobite, and Nestorian character who had split off from the Byzantine imperial church. The much smaller number of Christians residing in Medina—not organized in firm tribal units or religious groups—were apparently merchants, hermits, and monks above all. Muhammad had theological conversations with them, the initial phase of which was part of his campaign to win their support and following.

But when support for Muhammad was not forthcoming, not only from the Jews but also from the Christians, his relationship to the Christians became more distant. Muhammad began to reject individual Christian convictions as false, because they were not in agreement with his message. The end point was the condemnation of the Christians as unbelievers (5:72) who adhered to grave errors, such as the status of the Son of God and the Trinity, and thereby committed the unforgiveable sin of polytheism. But this must be qualified by pointing out that the Qur'an always portrays the Trinity as a triad composed of God the Father, Mary his wife, and Jesus, the son in common from their marriage (5:116). In the end, it remains unclear whether Muhammad, in apologetic defense against Christian positions, himself undertook this interpretation or if it had been presented in this way by Christian groups in his environs. Another possibility is that he found it so formulated in apocryphal writings or even in Syrian or Abyssinian church practice. This misunderstanding on the part of the Qur'an is virtually an appeal to Christians today to remove it through conversation, in order to give Muslims the chance to understand the Christian faith in the way it understands itself. But there is no other way to accomplish this than conversation together. And through this conversation, there is much to be learned about "the other."

Christians and Muslims: Encounter and Conversation

The fact that today, for the first time in history, so many Muslims and Christians live together as neighbors means not only a great social and political challenge but also a tremendous chance to break down prejudices, to hear from each other instead of about each other, and to get to know each other "at first hand." The Islamic and Western worlds today have moved more closely together than ever before.

On the one hand, Islam in many of its basic statements (the belief in the creator and judge, for example) is closer to the Christian faith than to other religions—Buddhism or Hinduism, for example. On the other hand, what is also important in the Muslim view is not just a general belief in the creator and judge but its belief in Muhammad's mission and thereby the truth of the Qur'an. This is expressed already in the Islamic confession of faith: "There is no God except Allah, and Muhammad is his prophet." Muhammad's status as prophet stands on the same level as the confession of the one God. Thus many Muslims, to be sure, will consider Christianity to be wrong, but they still will be interested in finding out more, especially about the person Jesus Christ, who is described in the Qur'an very positively and assumes a special position in it. This history of commonalities and differences is virtually an appeal to Christians and Muslims to get to know the other's religion better and to view it not just through one's own "lens" but for once through the lens of the other.

The encounter does not begin at rock bottom, either for Christians or for Muslims. The Qur'an, just as does Islamic tradition and theology, speaks about Christians and their faith. Many Muslims consider all the people in the West to be Christians and attribute their political or moral conduct to their faith. We ourselves are called on to remove misunderstandings and to break down prejudices by means of our lives and our conduct. There is only one way to do this. We must talk with each other! We ought to do this frequently and in detail. The present book gives us valuable guidance in doing so.

Continuing the Conversation: A Few Last Words

WE ARE GRATEFUL to Lamin Sanneh, Veli-Matti Kärkkäinen, Vinoth Ramachandra, and Christine Schirrmacher for their thoughtful responses to what we have written. Their essays make some incisive observations and raise important issues, not all of which can be addressed here. We find ourselves in hearty agreement with much that is in the responses (perhaps desiring to nuance some statements a bit) and, on occasion, simply in disagreement with some points that are made. This is what makes for healthy and fruitful dialogue. Our understanding has been enriched through these reflections. Although we cannot provide the thorough treatment that the issues deserve, we draw this book to a close with a few brief observations.

Lamin Sanneh grew up as a Muslim in the Gambia in West Africa, and so he has a unique perspective on interreligious relations. We appreciate the eloquent way in which he explains that tolerance and truth are not mutually exclusive. We can hold to what we think is definitive truth but still be tolerant and accepting of those who differ with us. The situation of religious pluralism in which most of us live, he suggests, should not compel us to keep our faith under a bushel basket or to change our beliefs to accommodate a universalism or pluralism that is in its own way exclusivist. Sanneh wisely advises that the Christian tradition does not tell us everything we want to know about the final destinies of non-Christians and that we must recognize that some of this is hidden in God's inscrutable purposes.

Vinoth Ramachandra appropriately laments the scandalous gap between what Jesus Christ calls the church to be and do in the world and what people actually see when they look at the lives of Christians. He quite rightly calls attention to the disunity, divisiveness, and competition among evangelicals, rebuking them for their lack of anguish and sorrow over such sin. According to the biblical tradition itself, Christian love for others and outrage against injustice provide ways for others to recognize the truth of the gospel. But all too often, evangelicals fail to model the unity that Christ prayed for or to love others in the way Jesus instructed us or to stand clearly against injustice. Evangelicals need to listen carefully to the words of Jesus: "Why do you call me, 'Lord, Lord,' and not do what I tell you?" (Luke 6:46); and "Not everyone who says to me, 'Lord, Lord' will enter the kingdom of heaven, but the one who does the will of my Father who is in heaven" (Matt. 7:21). Ramachandra has forcefully reminded us of the radical and subversive nature of the church as it lives as a transformed community and of the centrality of such living in Christian witness.

In emphasizing the need for radical behavior that is genuinely Christlike, however, Ramachandra seems to pit belief or doctrine against behavior in what appears to be an unnecessary dichotomy. To be sure, too many Christians—perhaps especially evangelicals—focus excessively on belief and ignore the hard ideals that Christ sets for his followers. But surely, the answer to such reductionism is not to minimize belief (including the church's teaching on the Trinity) but to give greater attention to living as Christ commands us. Ramachandra also rightly draws attention to the complexity of interreligious encounters when they occur in the contexts of bitter political disputes, and he highlights the importance of evangelicals speaking out for justice in such disputes. While his evaluation of Israel is highly contested, it reminds us that all Christians should strive for the just and fair treatment of all parties and protection of the rights of the innocent.

Both Veli-Matti Kärkkäinen and Ramachandra express dissatisfaction with our use of some categories or terms. Kärkkäinen, for example, points out the ambiguity of the term *pluralism* and suggests that it would have been helpful to have a typology of pluralisms, delineating various meanings of the term today. He also questions our use of the term *pluralist* in describing Keith Ward. He is right, of course, in noting the diverse ways in which the word *pluralism* is used today and the diversity of perspectives that can, in some sense, be called pluralist. We defined our use of the term in this book, but we are wary of general taxonomies that attempt to categorize meanings of disputed terms such as *exclusivism, inclusivism, pluralism,* or *particularism.* Labels are slippery, and we must be careful in using them to describe the views of others. With respect to Ward, much depends on which of Ward's many writings one cites, since his views vary. For example, in an important article, Ward defends what he calls "soft pluralism" and distinguishes it from what he calls the "hard pluralism" of John Hick.[1]

---

1. Keith Ward, "Truth and the Diversity of Religions," *Religious Studies* 26, no. 1 (March 1990): 1–18.

Kärkkäinen and Ramachandra register discomfort with the category of evangelicalism, or at least the way we describe it in chapter 1. We acknowledge that the term *evangelical* has different meanings in diverse settings and that trying to set the boundaries of evangelicalism is an almost impossible task.[2] But this is true of many concepts that nevertheless serve useful purposes. The crucial question is whether there is an identifiable movement or group of Christians who, despite their own denominational or theological associations and their differences on many other issues, share the beliefs and commitments outlined in chapter 1. It seems clear to us that there is, that such Christians are found throughout the world and not only in Europe and North America, and that international associations such as the Lausanne Movement and the World Evangelical Alliance provide institutional identity markers for these believers. Many Christians in Asia, Latin America, and Africa, with proper qualifications, do identify themselves as evangelicals. So it is a bit disingenuous to suggest that language about global evangelicalism is simply Anglo-American cultural imperialism. We do not mean to suggest that only evangelicals are "real" Christians or even that all those we refer to approvingly in the text are evangelicals (as we pointed out in the first chapter). And it is true that our understanding and definition of evangelicals will change somewhat as we take into account the emerging realities of Christians around the world. But our concern is to address issues and themes especially relevant to the many Christians who find themselves described in chapter 1.

Both Kärkkäinen and Ramachandra raise questions about the nature of the enterprise attempted in this book. Ramachandra questions whether a theology of religions is even possible. Much, of course depends on what one means by a theology of religions. We have spelled out our views, and the reader will need to judge whether it is a plausible or even possible enterprise. One reason given for Ramachandra's doubts is his apparent belief that the category "religion" or "the religious" is used too narrowly and that a theology of religions would need to provide a theological framework for understanding primal religions and "secular religions" such as nationalism, secular humanism, and Marxism, along with cultural institutions such as the shopping mall, health club, or football stadium. Our position is that if the category of religion includes everything, then a theology of religions is no more promising than

---

2. Even among American Christians who identify themselves as evangelicals, there is disagreement over just what the term means. See *Four Views on the Spectrum of Evangelicalism*, edited by Andrew David Naselli and Collin Hansen (Grand Rapids, MI: Zondervan, 2011).

a theory of everything. This is why in chapter 6, we develop a model with a more restrictive meaning of religion.

Another reason Ramachandra doubts the possibility of a theology of religions is that he thinks the enterprise is reductionist in diluting the otherness of the religions. We would agree that such reductionism occurs whenever observers caricature another religion and make no serious attempt to go below the surface and acknowledge deeper complexities. But this book does not attempt to catalog other religions or to describe them in any sort of systematic way. Instead, it looks at the significance of *Christian* concepts for understanding and evaluating other religions: Trinity, revelation, salvation, conversion, Christian practice, witness, and the relation between faith and culture.

Kärkkäinen correctly notes a number of important subjects that are not treated in this book, and his helpful suggestions for ways in which these issues might have been treated here would move the current work more in the direction of a systematic theology, with special reference to questions about other religions, or what is sometimes called comparative theology. Strictly speaking, this is neither an exercise in systematic theology nor a work of comparative theology. It is an attempt to explore select issues in the theology of religions that are of special significance for evangelicals (while profiting from and critically analyzing the work of many nonevangelicals) and to do so by highlighting the distinctively Trinitarian nature of Christian theology.

Christine Schirrmacher reminds us that interreligious encounters—especially dialogues between Muslims and Christians today—do not occur in a social or historical vacuum. She is right. Even as we listen carefully to the other and seek to remove obstacles to peaceful coexistence in our globalizing world, we must acknowledge the historical realities of the past fourteen hundred years. Knowing that history will help us not to repeat past mistakes and to bear witness with more sensitivity and effectiveness. Today more than ever, we must, as she puts it, "talk to one another," making sure we "hear from" one another, and not simply talk *at* one another. We think she would agree that the best interreligious dialogue must not be content with agreeing on least-common-denominator platitudes but should be willing to explore our deepest differences in a spirit of respect and friendship. Without this determination to converse respectfully about real differences, these dialogues accomplish little.

Our respondents have honored us with their essays, raising issues that demand further thought and exploration. Others will no doubt pick up where we leave off and pursue these important questions. May the conversation continue.

Name Index

Picart, Bernard, 18,

Pierard, Richard, 4,

Pinnock, Clark, 38–39, 41n, 46n, 75–76, 150, 151, 153, 158–159,

Piper, John, 148n, 149,

Plantinga, Cornelius, 133–135,

Plato, 14, 21, 116, 117–119,

Pocock, Michael, 11n,

Pope Benedict XIV, 213

Pope Benedict XVI, 34, 191–192,

Pope Clement XI, 214

Pope Gregory VII, 16,

Pope Innocent X, 213

Pope John XXIII, 30,

Pope John Paul II, 33, 170,

Pope Paul III, 17,

Pope Paul VI, 33,

Pope Pius XII, 214

Popkin, Richard, 18n,

Priest, Robert J., 216n, 217n, 255,

Prothero, Stephen, 48, 130, 242n,

Quinn, Philip, 37,

Race, Alan, 12, 227,

Rahbar, Daud, 65–66, 68,

Rahner, Karl, 30, 46, 156, 170, 172, 300

Ramachandra, Vinoth, x, xi, 84, 259–260, 291–292, 305–312, 319–322

Ratzinger, Cardinal Joseph, 34,

Read, Cynthia, x,

Reader, Ian, 223, 240n, 247n,

Reitan, Eric, 173–176,

Ricci, Matteo, 211–213, 285–286,

Richard, Ramesh, 148–149,

Robinson, John A.T., 170, 171, 173,

Rockefeller, John D., 26,

Romero, Oscar, 192,

Rommen, Edward, 11n,

Ross, Andrew, 211n, 212,

Roxburgh, Alan, 261,

Runzo, Joseph, 37,

Russell, Bertrand, 169,

Saint Francis, 16,

Saladin, 17,

Samartha, Stanley, 55, 122–123,

Samuel, Vinay, 10n

Sanders, John, 39, 41n, 150- 151, 153,

Sanneh, Lamin   x, xi, 5n, 64, 71, 72, 165n, 219, 249, 257, 258, 295–300, 310, 319,

Schirrmacher, Christine, x, xi, 313–318, 319, 322

Schleiermacher, Friedrich, 169, 171, 172,

Schmidt, Roger, 233,

Schmidt, Wilhelm, 113–114,

Schreiter, Robert, 41, 42,

Schroder, Roger, 33,

Sharf, Robert, 244,

Sharpe, Eric, 22n, 24n, 25n, 220n, 222,

Shankara, 131

Shenk, Wilbert R., 22n,

Shinran, 108, 110,

Smart, Ninian, 234, 246,

Smith, Gordon, 161, 164,

Smith, Judson, 23,

Smith, Wilfred Cantwell, 28–29, 37, 87n, 97, 129n, 221n, 225,

Socrates, 14, 15, 21, 118–119,

Speer, Robert E., 23n, 27,

Staal, Frits, 307

Stonehouse, N.B., 107–108,

Stott, John, 5, 137n, 151–152, 153, 262, 268, 278, 288–289,

Strange, Daniel, 41n, 105n, 147,

Strauss, Stephen, 263

Stuart, Moses, 179,

Sugden, Chris, 10n,

Sumner, George, 77,

Suzuki, Daisetz Taitaro, 242–245,

Swearer, Donald, 279,

Swinburne, Richard, 175n,

Subject Index